SHONEN JUMP MANGA EDITION

1

[PLANET CAMP]

KENTA SHINOHARA

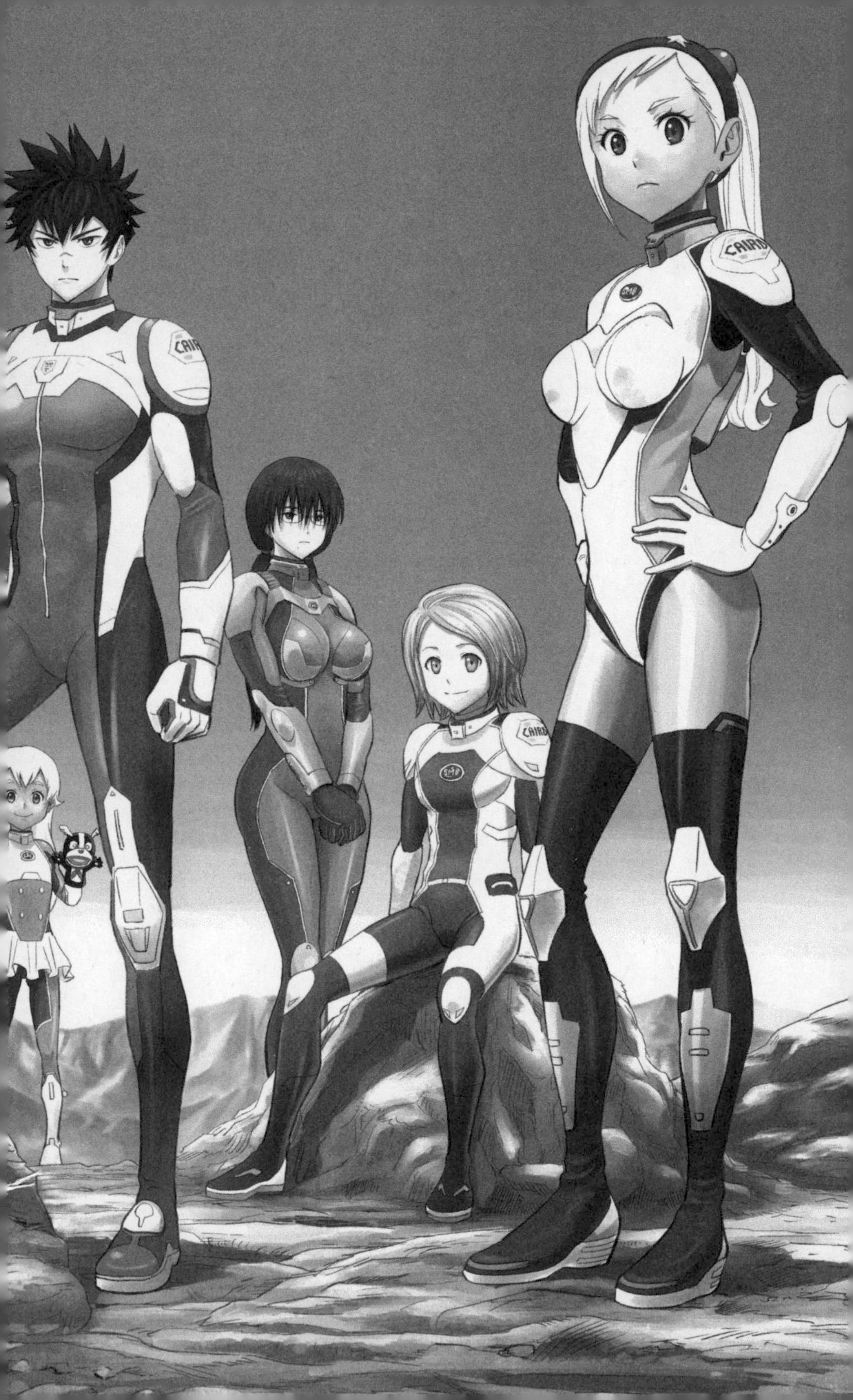
CAIRD

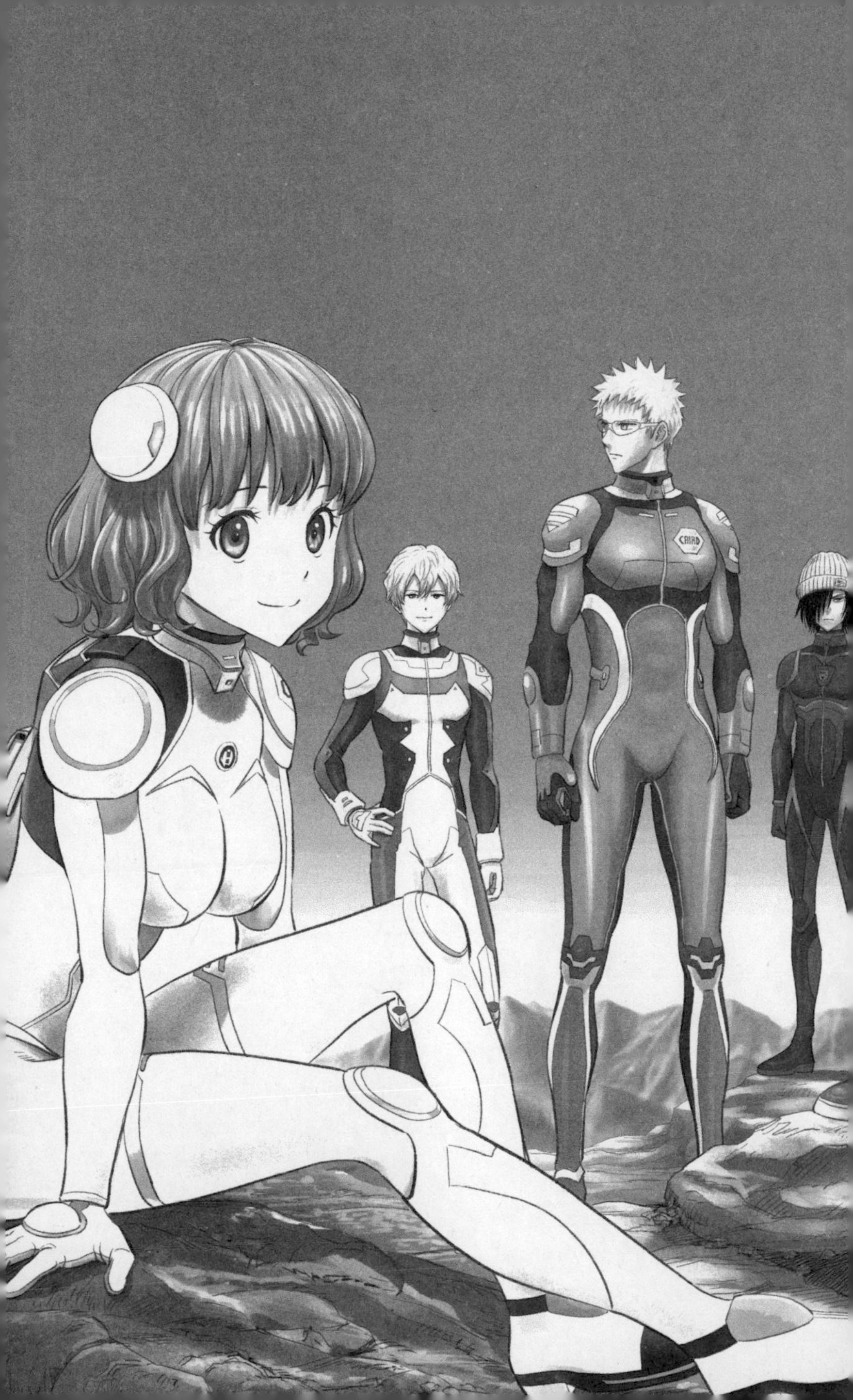
CAIRD

ASTRA
LOST IN SPACE
CONTENTS

1

[PLANET CAMP]

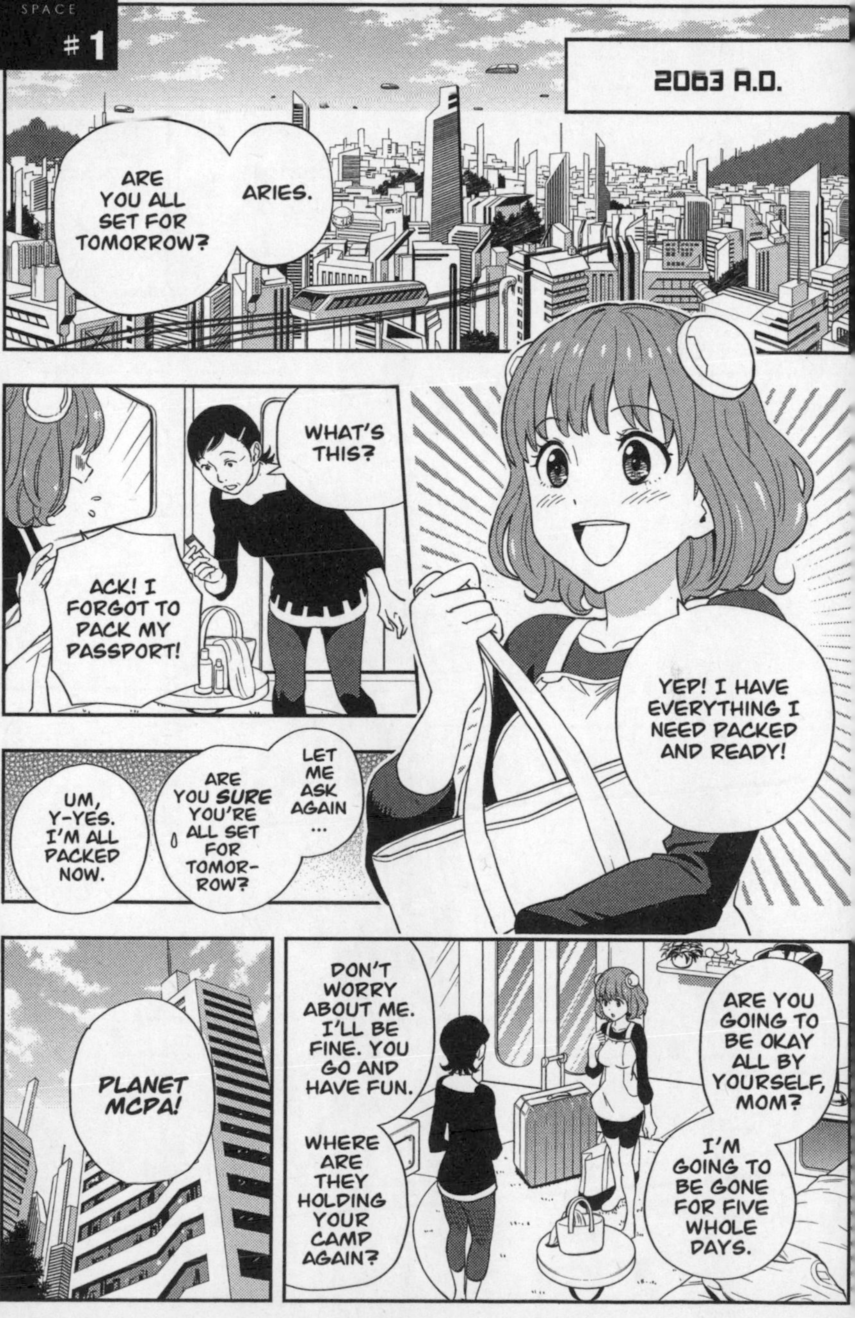
2063 A.D.
ARIES.
ARE YOU ALL SET FOR TOMORROW?
YEP! I HAVE EVERYTHING I NEED PACKED AND READY!
WHAT'S THIS?
ACK! I FORGOT TO PACK MY PASSPORT!
LET ME ASK AGAIN...
ARE YOU SURE YOU'RE ALL SET FOR TOMOR-ROW?
UM, Y-YES. I'M ALL PACKED NOW.
ARE YOU GOING TO BE OKAY ALL BY YOURSELF, MOM?
I'M GOING TO BE GONE FOR FIVE WHOLE DAYS.
DON'T WORRY ABOUT ME. I'LL BE FINE. YOU GO AND HAVE FUN.
WHERE ARE THEY HOLDING YOUR CAMP AGAIN?
PLANET MCPA!

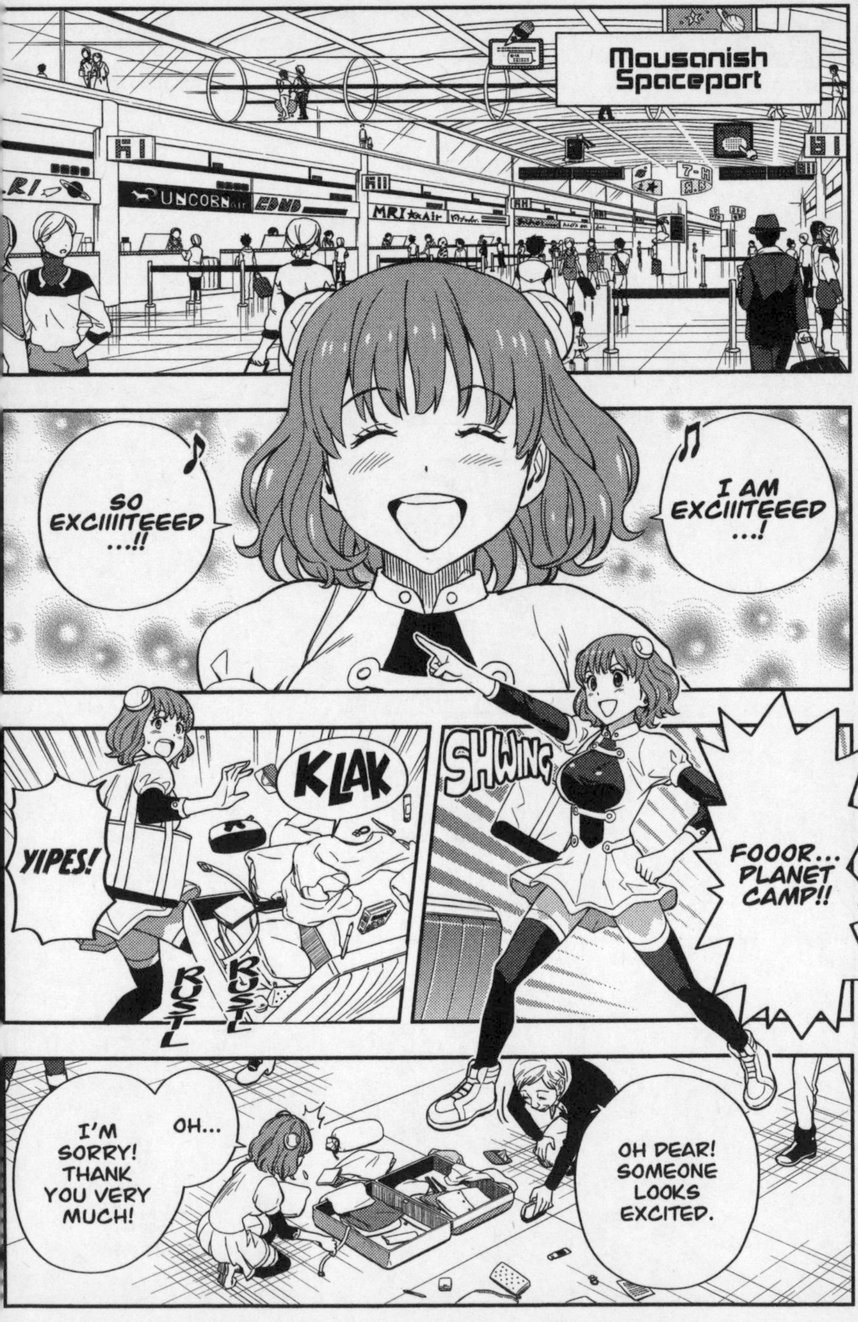
Mousanish Spaceport
I AM EXCIIIITEEED ...!
SO EXCIIIITEEED ...!!
SHWING
FOOOR... PLANET CAMP!!
KLAK
YIPES!
RUSTL
RUSTL
OH DEAR! SOMEONE LOOKS EXCITED.
OH...
I'M SORRY! THANK YOU VERY MUCH!

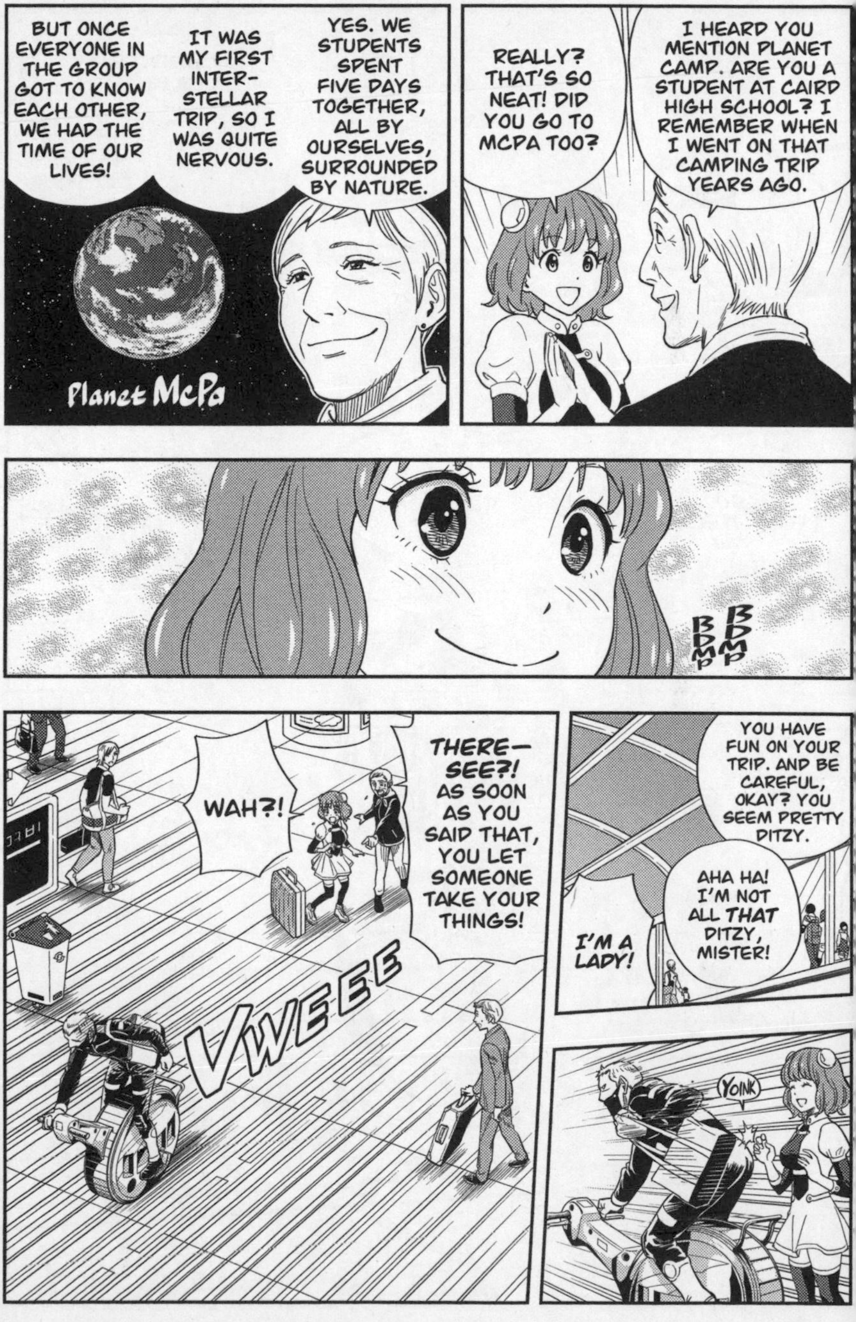
I HEARD YOU MENTION PLANET CAMP. ARE YOU A STUDENT AT CAIRD HIGH SCHOOL? I REMEMBER WHEN I WENT ON THAT CAMPING TRIP YEARS AGO.
REALLY? THAT'S SO NEAT! DID YOU GO TO MCPA TOO?
YES. WE STUDENTS SPENT FIVE DAYS TOGETHER, ALL BY OURSELVES, SURROUNDED BY NATURE.
IT WAS MY FIRST INTER-STELLAR TRIP, SO I WAS QUITE NERVOUS.
BUT ONCE EVERYONE IN THE GROUP GOT TO KNOW EACH OTHER, WE HAD THE TIME OF OUR LIVES!
Planet McPa
BDMP
BDMP
YOU HAVE FUN ON YOUR TRIP. AND BE CAREFUL, OKAY? YOU SEEM PRETTY DITZY.
AHA HA! I'M NOT ALL THAT DITZY, MISTER!
I'M A LADY!
YOINK
THERE—SEE?! AS SOON AS YOU SAID THAT, YOU LET SOMEONE TAKE YOUR THINGS!
WAH?!
VWEEE

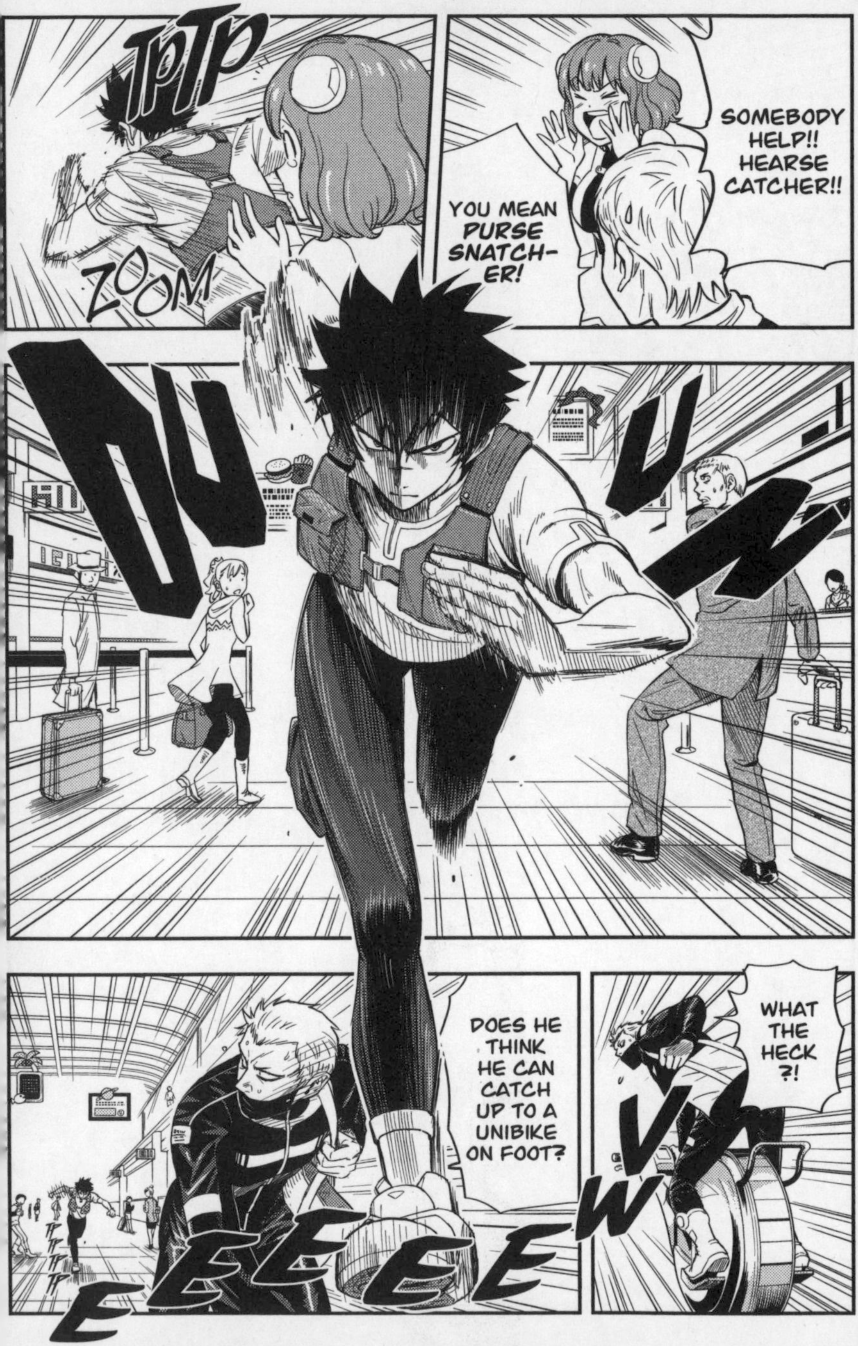
SOMEBODY HELP!! HEARSE CATCHER!!
YOU MEAN PURSE SNATCHER!
TPTP
ZOOM
WHAT THE HECK?!
DOES HE THINK HE CAN CATCH UP TO A UNIBIKE ON FOOT?
TP TP TP TP
EEEEEW

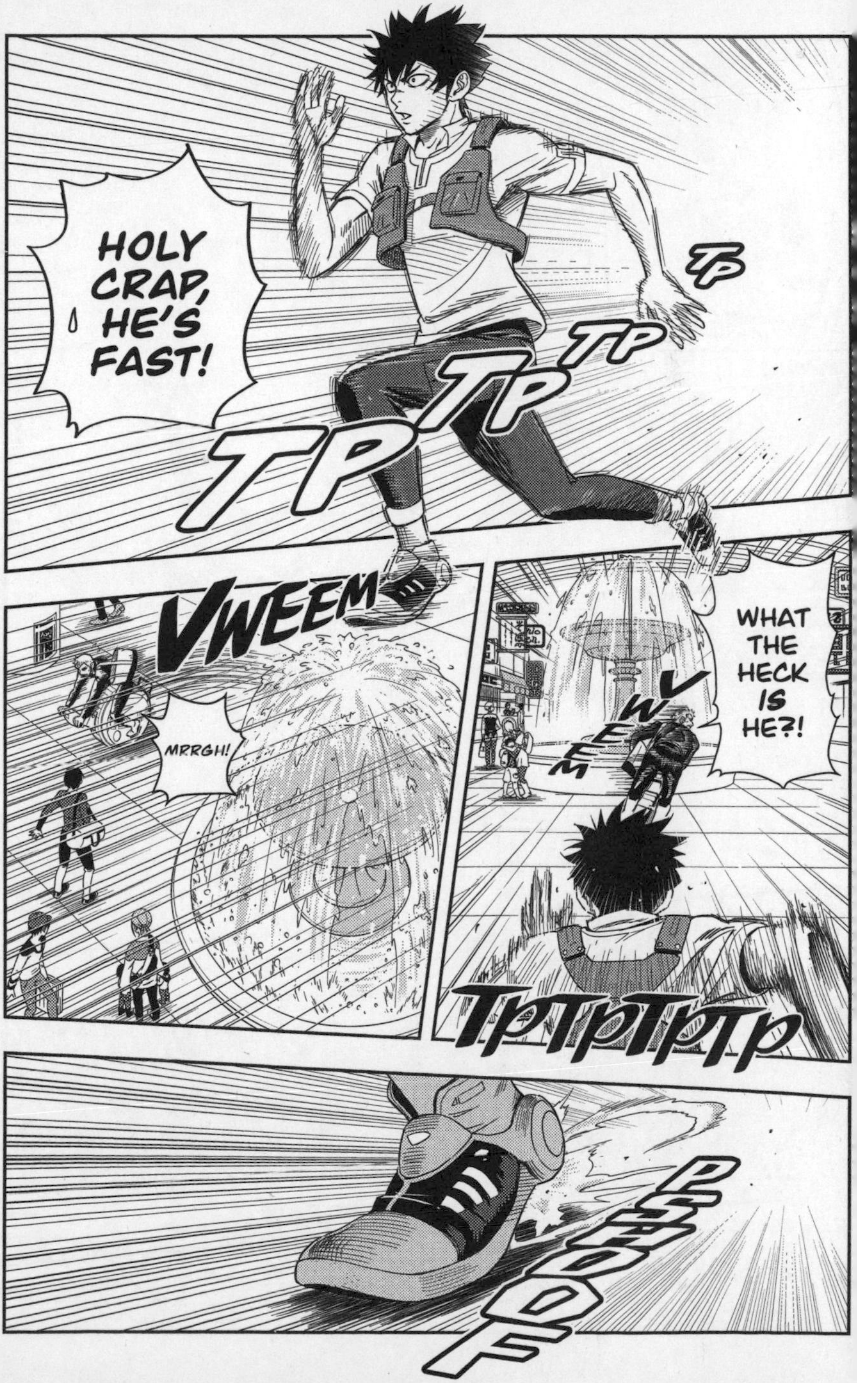

TP
TP
TP
TP
HOLY CRAP, HE'S FAST!
WHAT THE HECK IS HE?!
VWEEM
TPTPTPTPTP
VWEEM
MRRGH!
PSHOOF

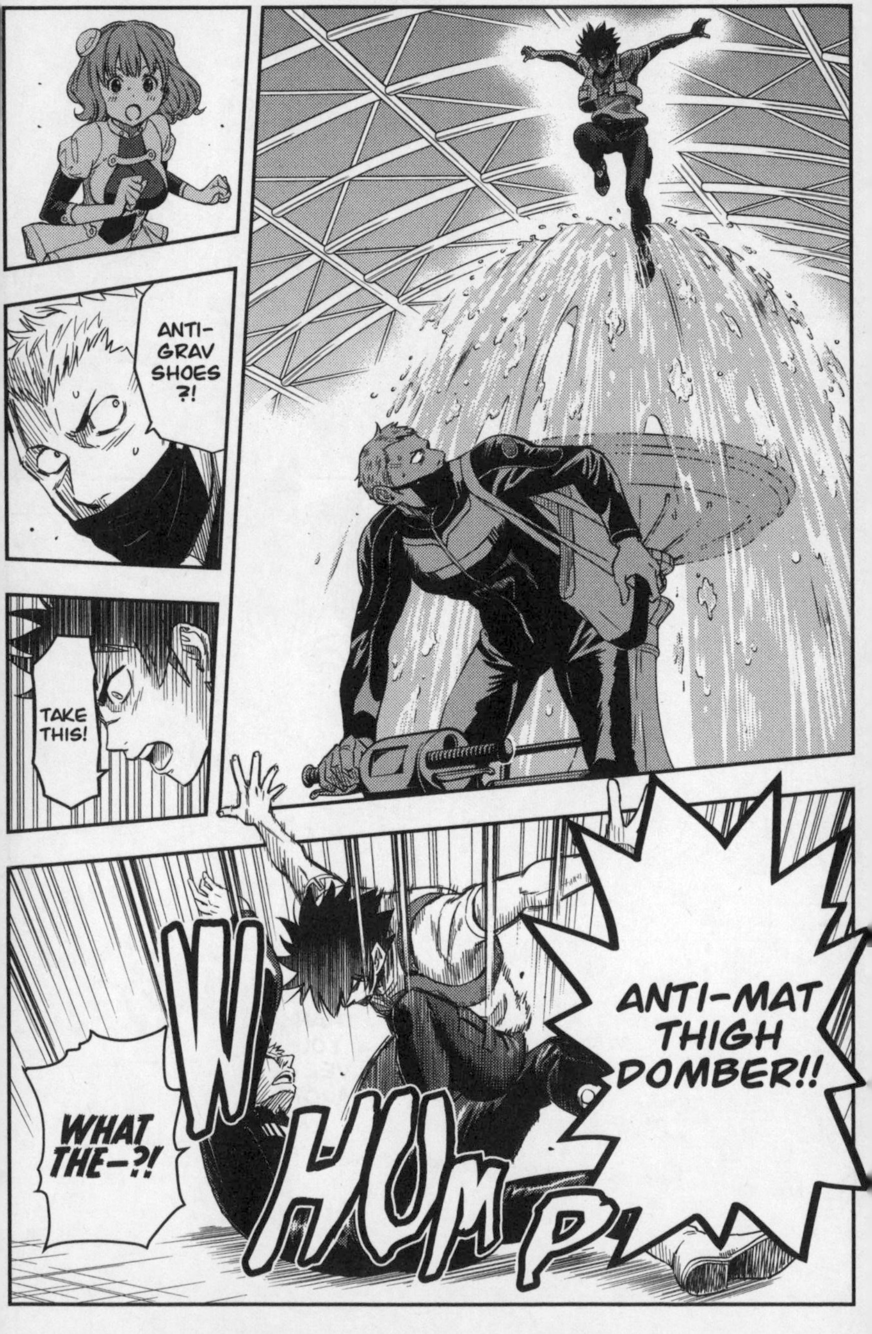
ANTI-GRAV SHOES?!
TAKE THIS!
ANTI-MAT THIGH DOMBER!!
WHUMP
WHAT THE-?!

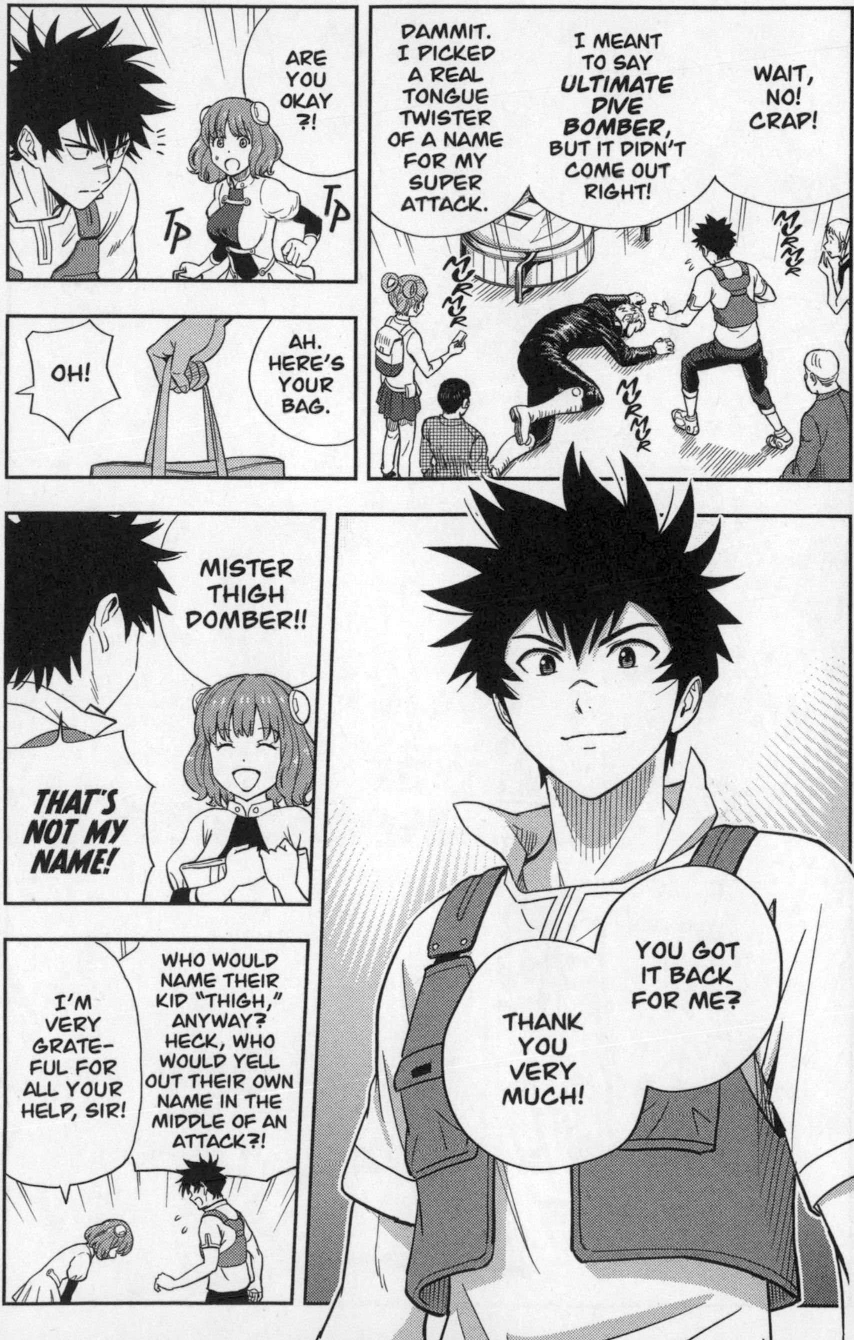
WAIT, NO! CRAP!
I MEANT TO SAY ULTIMATE DIVE BOMBER, BUT IT DIDN'T COME OUT RIGHT!
DAMMIT. I PICKED A REAL TONGUE TWISTER OF A NAME FOR MY SUPER ATTACK.
MURMUR
MURMUR
MURMUR
ARE YOU OKAY?!
TP
TP
AH. HERE'S YOUR BAG.
OH!
YOU GOT IT BACK FOR ME?
THANK YOU VERY MUCH!
MISTER THIGH DOMBER!!
THAT'S NOT MY NAME!
WHO WOULD NAME THEIR KID "THIGH," ANYWAY? HECK, WHO WOULD YELL OUT THEIR OWN NAME IN THE MIDDLE OF AN ATTACK?!
I'M VERY GRATE-FUL FOR ALL YOUR HELP, SIR!

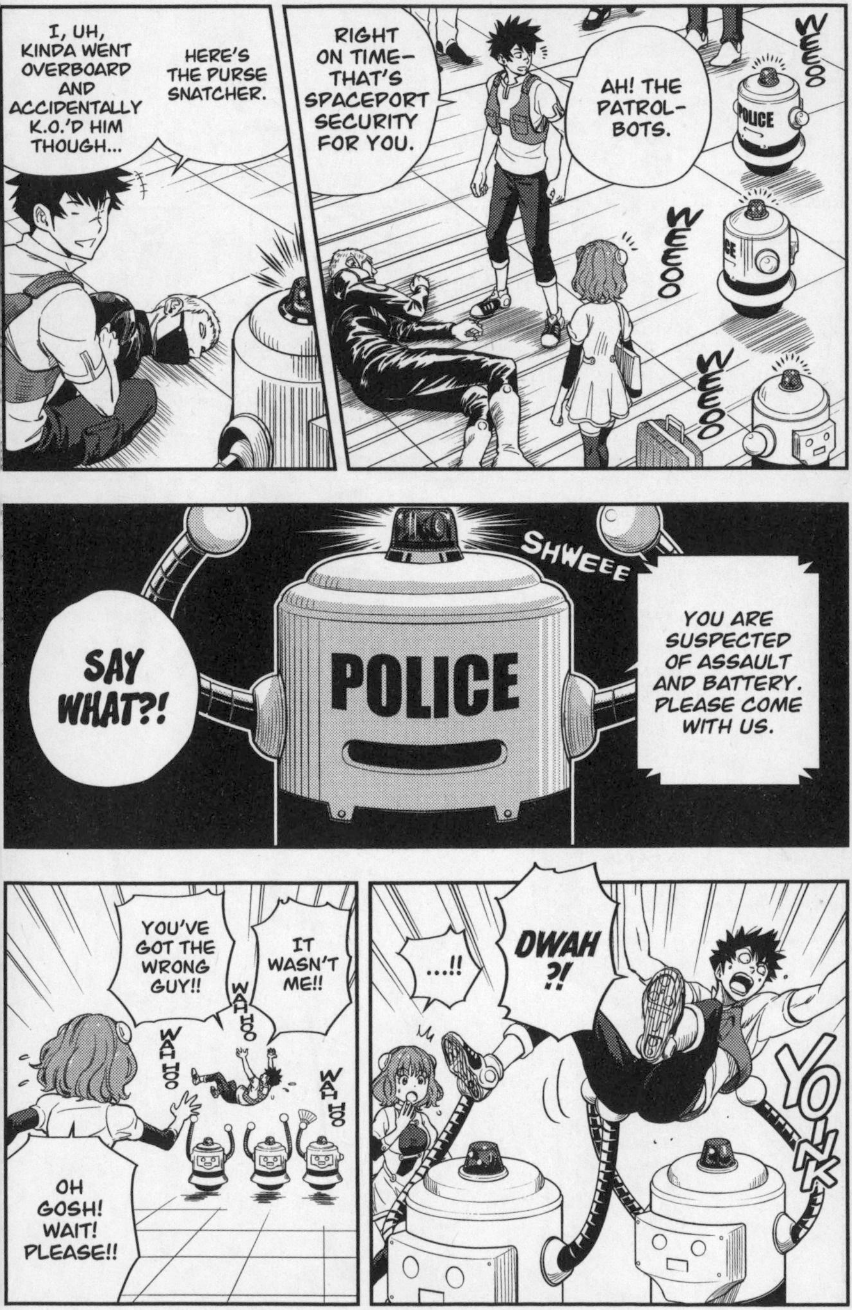
WEEOO
AH! THE PATROL-BOTS.
RIGHT ON TIME—THAT'S SPACEPORT SECURITY FOR YOU.
WEEOO
WEEOO
HERE'S THE PURSE SNATCHER.
I, UH, KINDA WENT OVERBOARD AND ACCIDENTALLY K.O.'D HIM THOUGH...
SHWEEE
YOU ARE SUSPECTED OF ASSAULT AND BATTERY. PLEASE COME WITH US.
POLICE
SAY WHAT?!
YOINK
DWAH?!
...!!
IT WASN'T ME!!
YOU'VE GOT THE WRONG GUY!!
WAH HOO
WAH HOO
WAH HOO
OH GOSH! WAIT! PLEASE!!

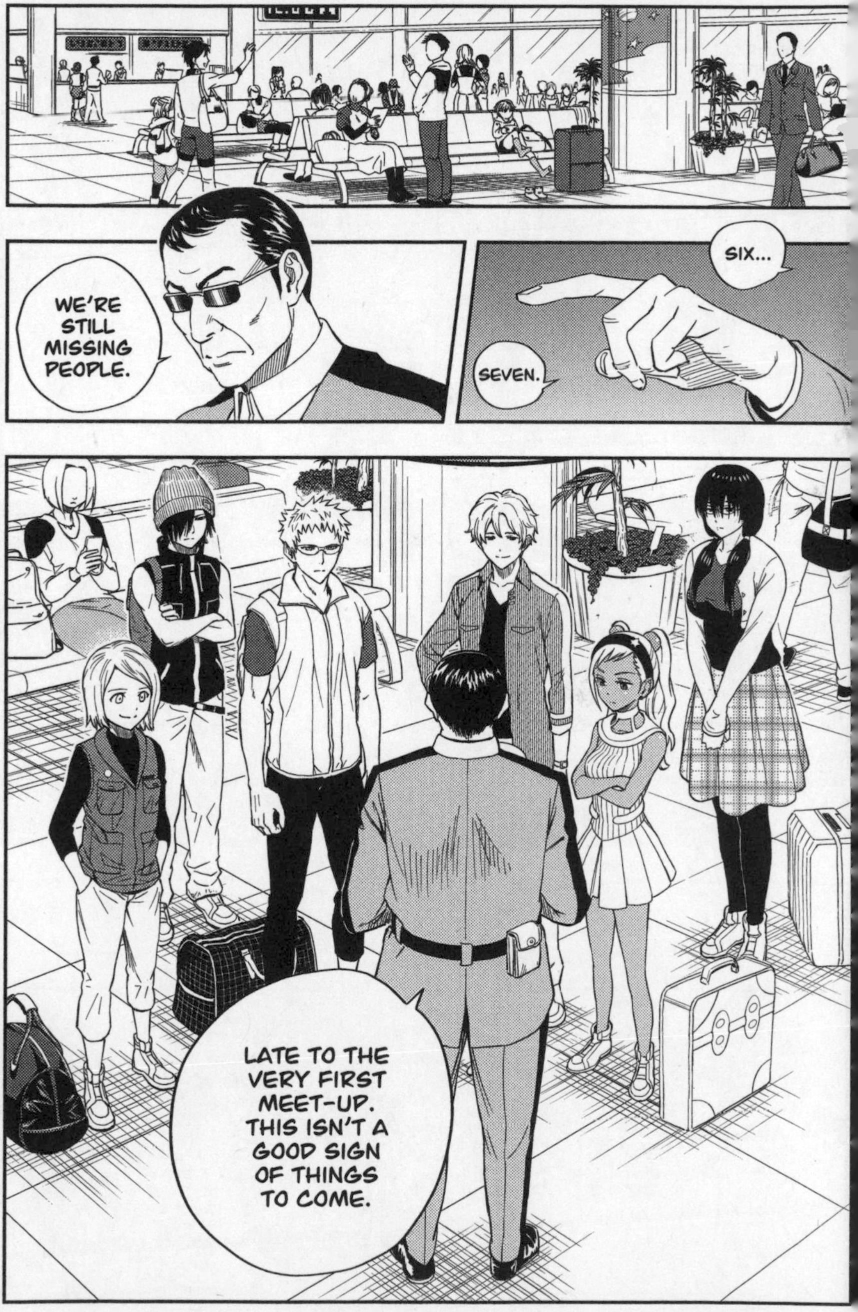
SIX...
SEVEN.
WE'RE STILL MISSING PEOPLE.
LATE TO THE VERY FIRST MEET-UP. THIS ISN'T A GOOD SIGN OF THINGS TO COME.

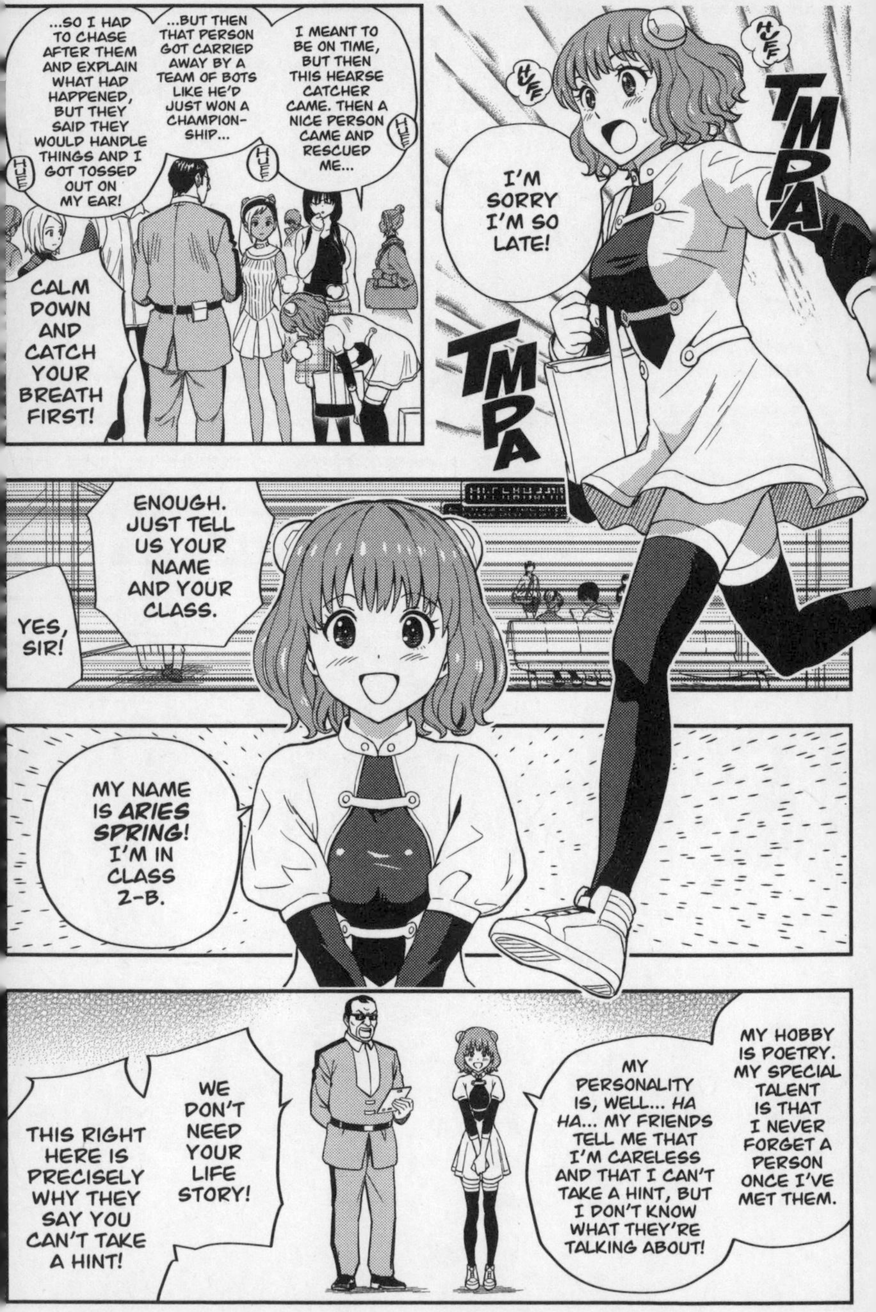
HUFF
HUFF
TMPA
TMPA
I'M SORRY I'M SO LATE!
I MEANT TO BE ON TIME, BUT THEN THIS HEARSE CATCHER CAME. THEN A NICE PERSON CAME AND RESCUED ME...
HUFF
...BUT THEN THAT PERSON GOT CARRIED AWAY BY A TEAM OF BOTS LIKE HE'D JUST WON A CHAMPION-SHIP...
HUFF
...SO I HAD TO CHASE AFTER THEM AND EXPLAIN WHAT HAD HAPPENED, BUT THEY SAID THEY WOULD HANDLE THINGS AND I GOT TOSSED OUT ON MY EAR!
HUFF
CALM DOWN AND CATCH YOUR BREATH FIRST!
ENOUGH. JUST TELL US YOUR NAME AND YOUR CLASS.
YES, SIR!
MY NAME IS ARIES SPRING! I'M IN CLASS 2-B.
MY HOBBY IS POETRY. MY SPECIAL TALENT IS THAT I NEVER FORGET A PERSON ONCE I'VE MET THEM.
MY PERSONALITY IS, WELL... HA HA... MY FRIENDS TELL ME THAT I'M CARELESS AND THAT I CAN'T TAKE A HINT, BUT I DON'T KNOW WHAT THEY'RE TALKING ABOUT!
WE DON'T NEED YOUR LIFE STORY!
THIS RIGHT HERE IS PRECISELY WHY THEY SAY YOU CAN'T TAKE A HINT!

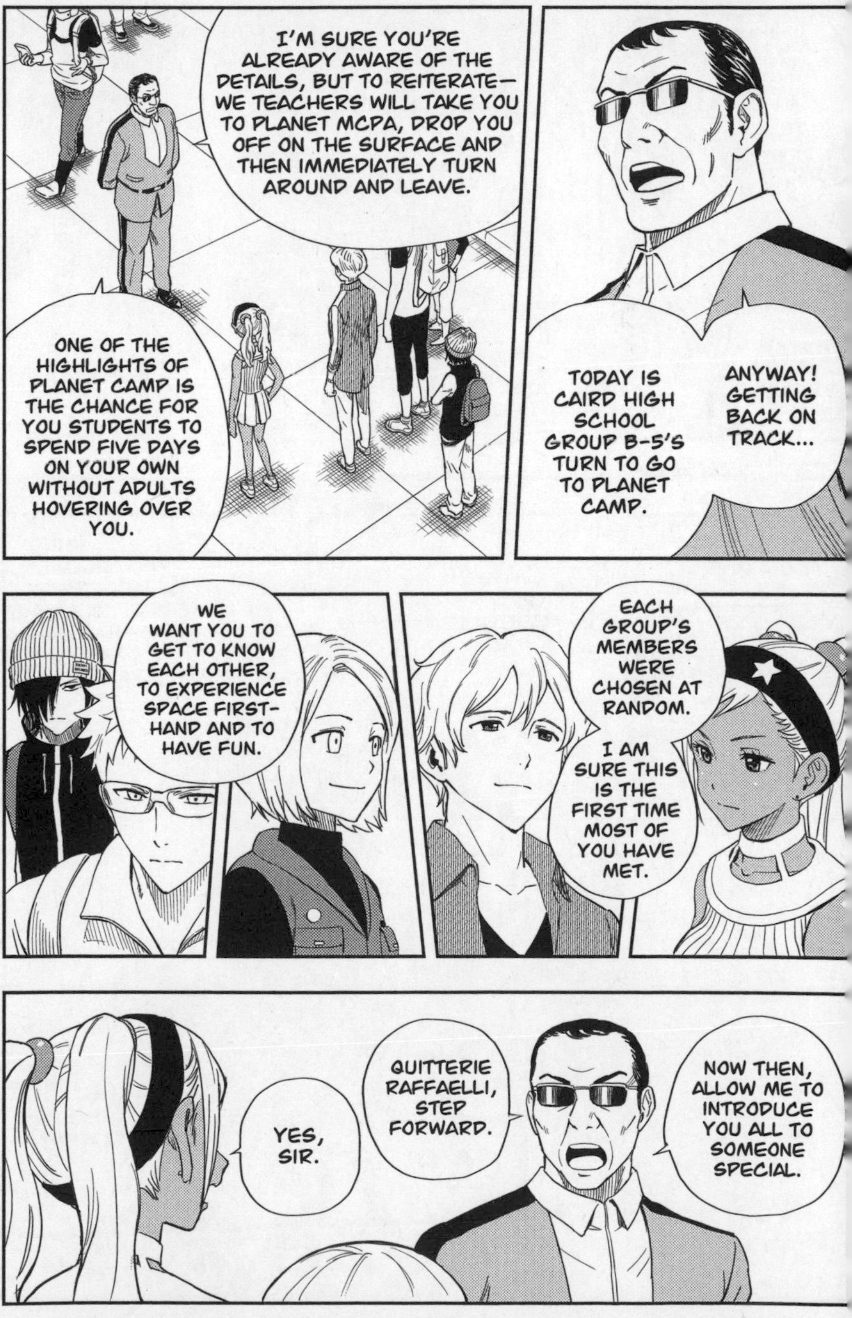
ANYWAY! GETTING BACK ON TRACK...
TODAY IS CAIRD HIGH SCHOOL GROUP B-5'S TURN TO GO TO PLANET CAMP.
I'M SURE YOU'RE ALREADY AWARE OF THE DETAILS, BUT TO REITERATE—WE TEACHERS WILL TAKE YOU TO PLANET MCPA, DROP YOU OFF ON THE SURFACE AND THEN IMMEDIATELY TURN AROUND AND LEAVE.
ONE OF THE HIGHLIGHTS OF PLANET CAMP IS THE CHANCE FOR YOU STUDENTS TO SPEND FIVE DAYS ON YOUR OWN WITHOUT ADULTS HOVERING OVER YOU.
EACH GROUP'S MEMBERS WERE CHOSEN AT RANDOM.
I AM SURE THIS IS THE FIRST TIME MOST OF YOU HAVE MET.
WE WANT YOU TO GET TO KNOW EACH OTHER, TO EXPERIENCE SPACE FIRST-HAND AND TO HAVE FUN.
NOW THEN, ALLOW ME TO INTRODUCE YOU ALL TO SOMEONE SPECIAL.
QUITTERIE RAFFAELLI, STEP FORWARD.
YES, SIR.

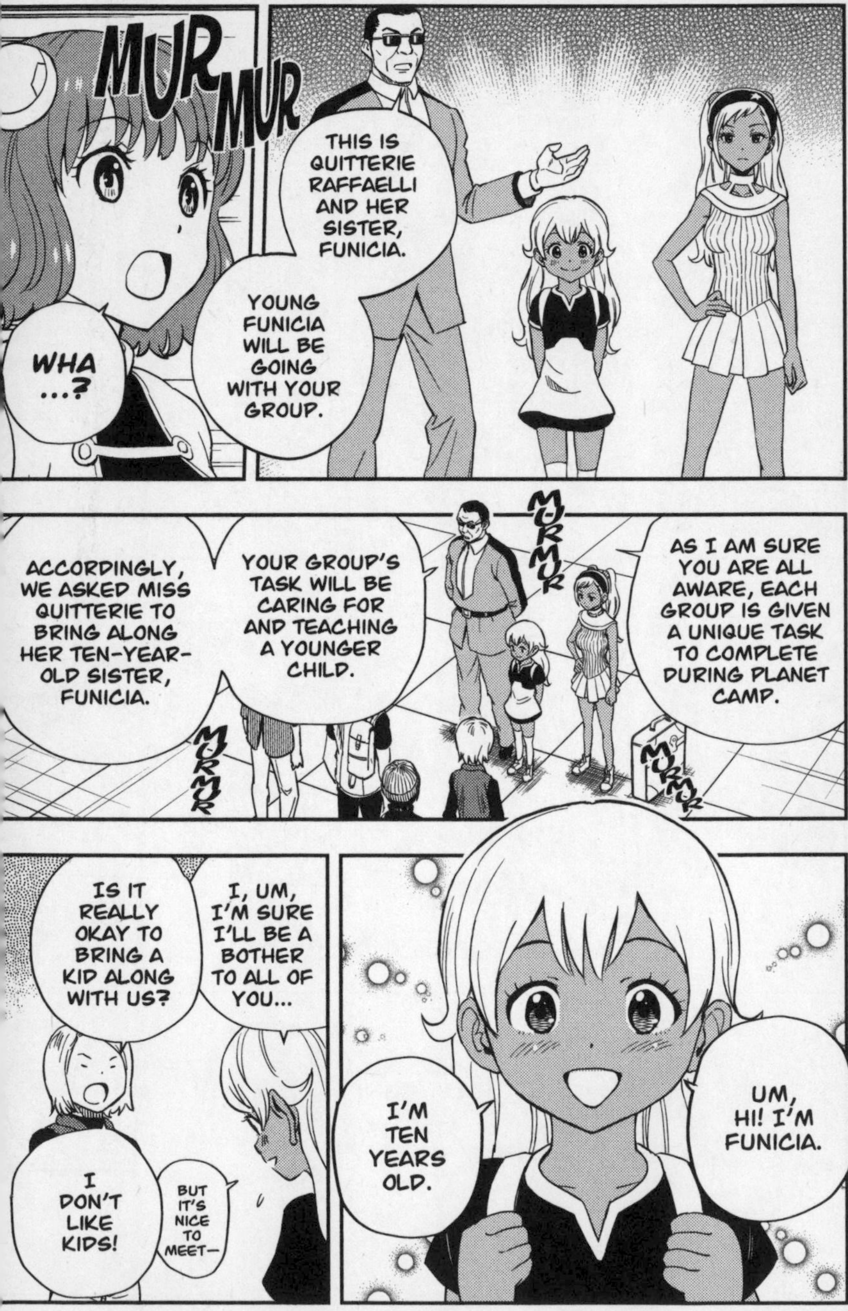
THIS IS QUITTERIE RAFFAELLI AND HER SISTER, FUNICIA.
YOUNG FUNICIA WILL BE GOING WITH YOUR GROUP.
MUR MUR
WHA...?
MURMUR
AS I AM SURE YOU ARE ALL AWARE, EACH GROUP IS GIVEN A UNIQUE TASK TO COMPLETE DURING PLANET CAMP.
YOUR GROUP'S TASK WILL BE CARING FOR AND TEACHING A YOUNGER CHILD.
ACCORDINGLY, WE ASKED MISS QUITTERIE TO BRING ALONG HER TEN-YEAR-OLD SISTER, FUNICIA.
MURMUR
MURMUR
UM, HI! I'M FUNICIA.
I'M TEN YEARS OLD.
I, UM, I'M SURE I'LL BE A BOTHER TO ALL OF YOU...
IS IT REALLY OKAY TO BRING A KID ALONG WITH US?
BUT IT'S NICE TO MEET—
I DON'T LIKE KIDS!

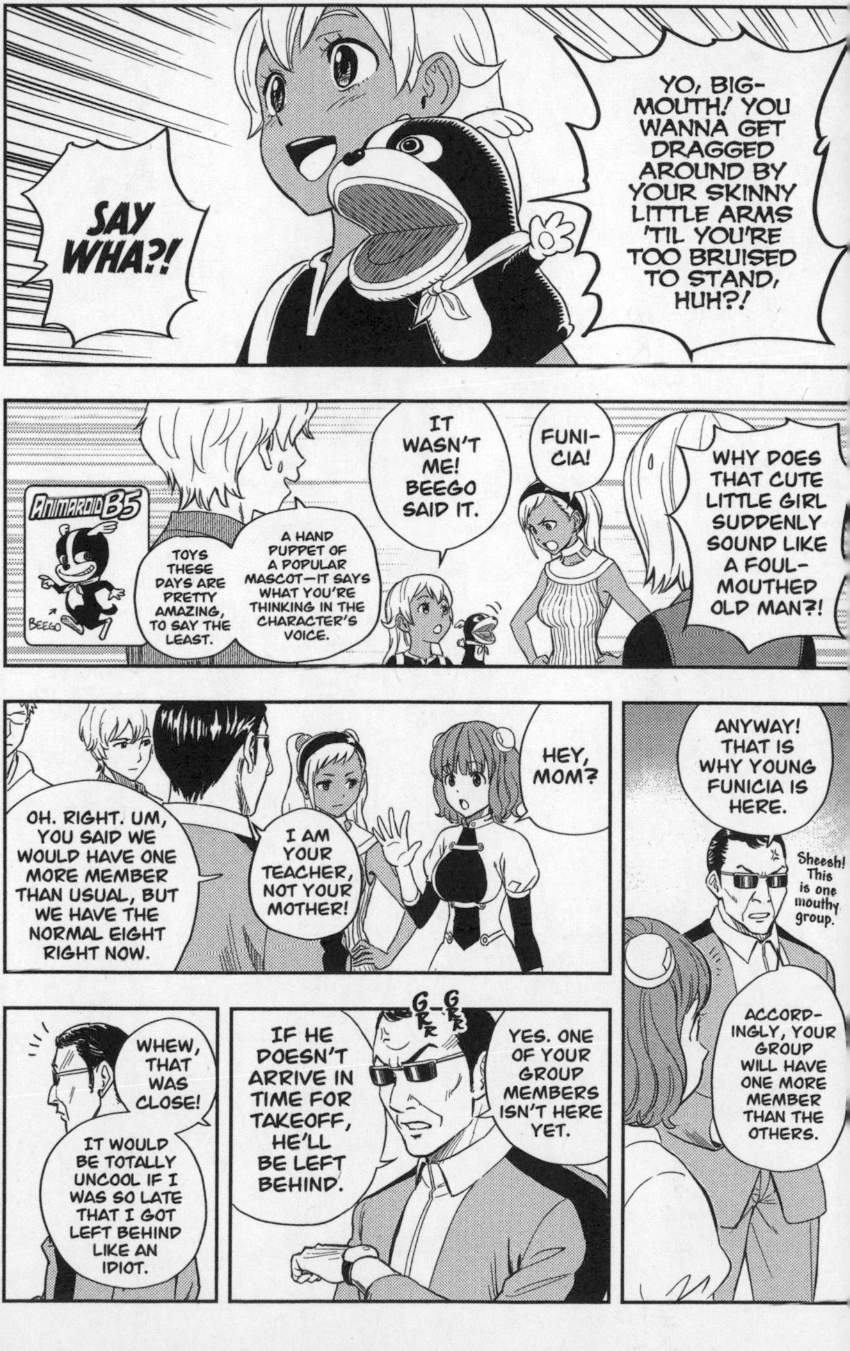
YO, BIG-MOUTH! YOU WANNA GET DRAGGED AROUND BY YOUR SKINNY LITTLE ARMS 'TIL YOU'RE TOO BRUISED TO STAND, HUH?!
SAY WHA?!
WHY DOES THAT CUTE LITTLE GIRL SUDDENLY SOUND LIKE A FOUL-MOUTHED OLD MAN?!
FUNI-CIA!
IT WASN'T ME! BEEGO SAID IT.
A HAND PUPPET OF A POPULAR MASCOT—IT SAYS WHAT YOU'RE THINKING IN THE CHARACTER'S VOICE.
TOYS THESE DAYS ARE PRETTY AMAZING, TO SAY THE LEAST.
ANIMAROID B5
BEEGO
ANYWAY! THAT IS WHY YOUNG FUNICIA IS HERE.
Sheesh! This is one mouthy group.
ACCORD-INGLY, YOUR GROUP WILL HAVE ONE MORE MEMBER THAN THE OTHERS.
HEY, MOM?
I AM YOUR TEACHER, NOT YOUR MOTHER!
OH. RIGHT. UM, YOU SAID WE WOULD HAVE ONE MORE MEMBER THAN USUAL, BUT WE HAVE THE NORMAL EIGHT RIGHT NOW.
YES. ONE OF YOUR GROUP MEMBERS ISN'T HERE YET.
G-GRR
IF HE DOESN'T ARRIVE IN TIME FOR TAKEOFF, HE'LL BE LEFT BEHIND.
WHEW, THAT WAS CLOSE!
IT WOULD BE TOTALLY UNCOOL IF I WAS SO LATE THAT I GOT LEFT BEHIND LIKE AN IDIOT.

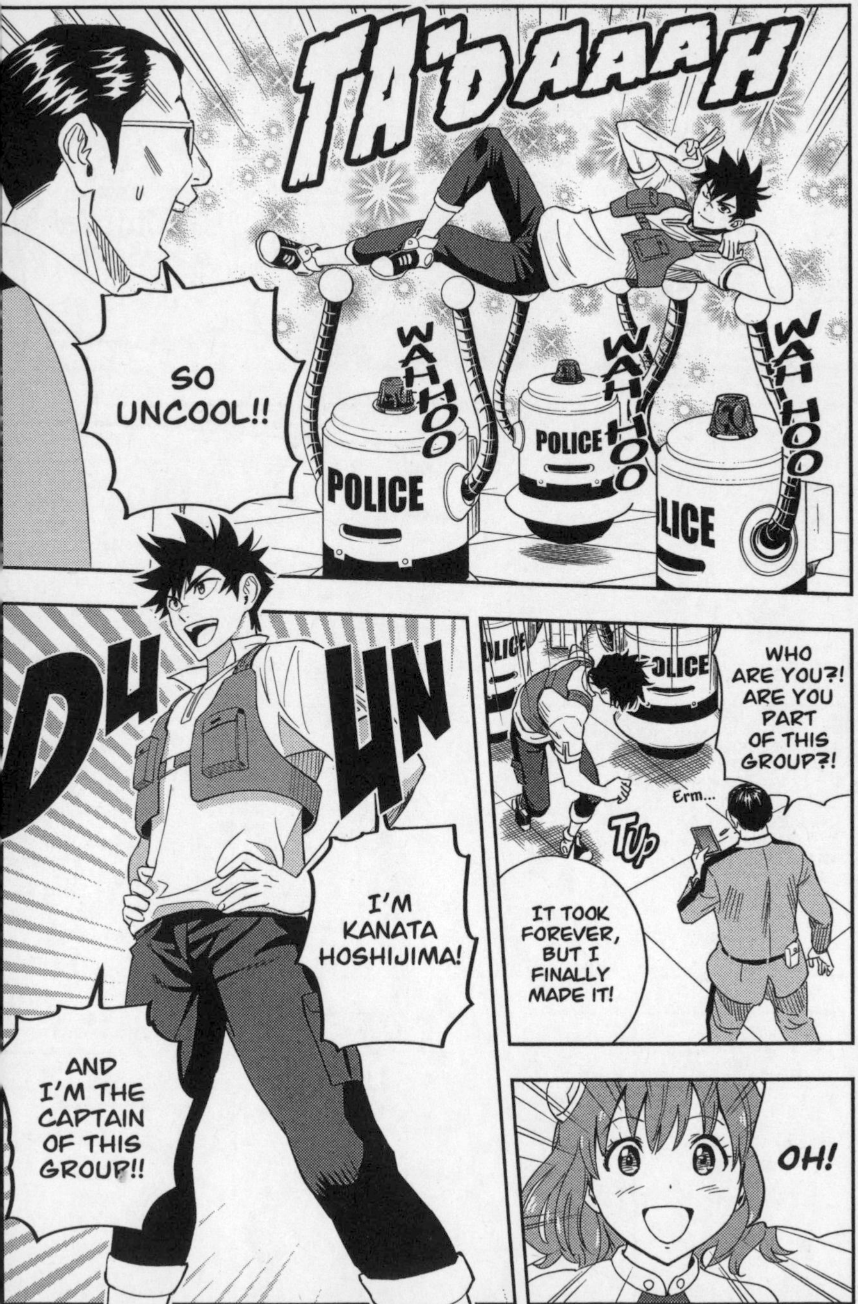
TA'DAAAH
WAHHOO
WAHHOO
WAHHOO
POLICE
POLICE
LICE
SO UNCOOL!!
WHO ARE YOU?! ARE YOU PART OF THIS GROUP?!
Erm...
Tup
IT TOOK FOREVER, BUT I FINALLY MADE IT!
OH!
DUHUN
I'M KANATA HOSHIJIMA!
AND I'M THE CAPTAIN OF THIS GROUP!!

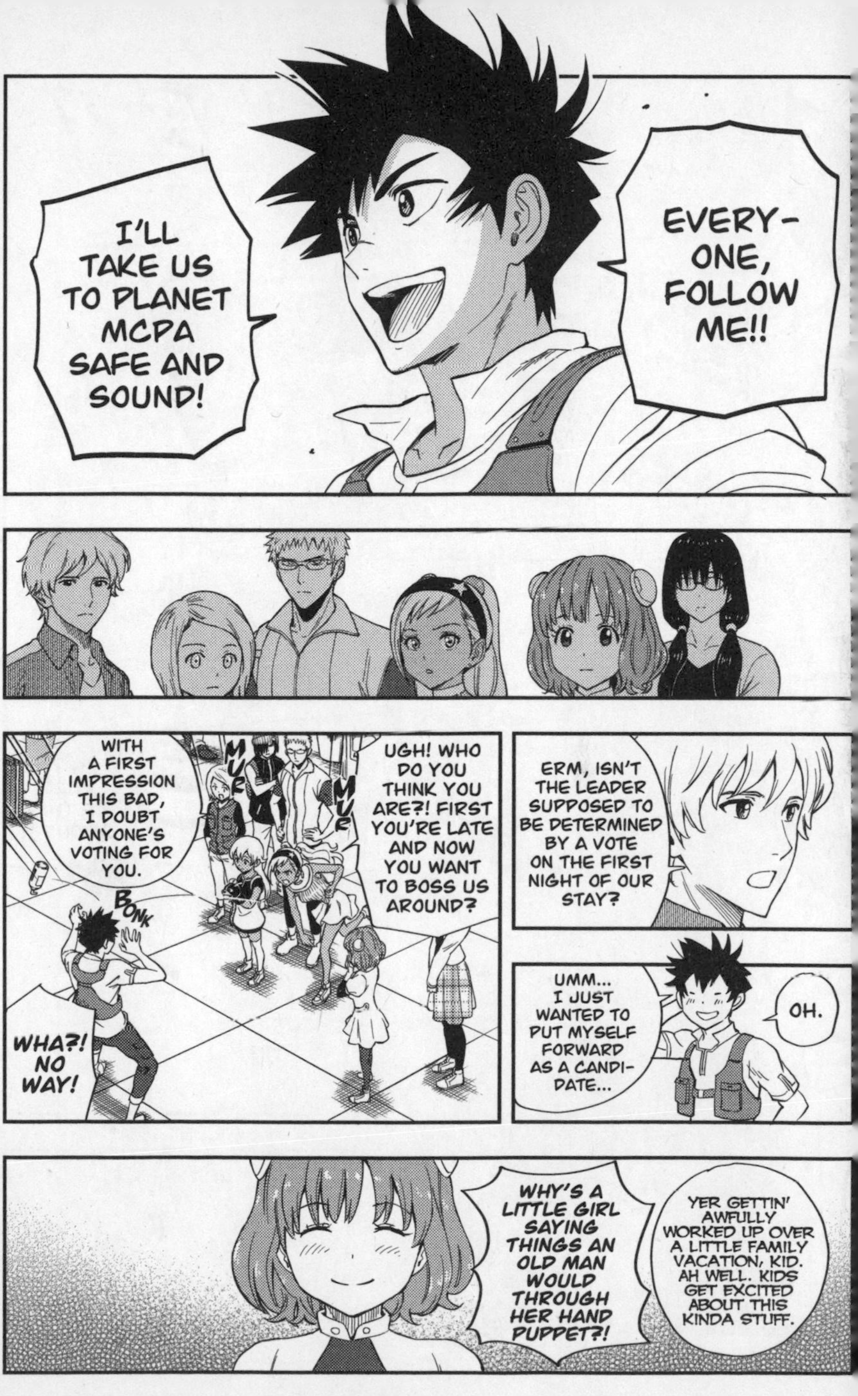
EVERY-ONE, FOLLOW ME!!
I'LL TAKE US TO PLANET MCPA SAFE AND SOUND!
ERM, ISN'T THE LEADER SUPPOSED TO BE DETERMINED BY A VOTE ON THE FIRST NIGHT OF OUR STAY?
OH.
UMM... I JUST WANTED TO PUT MYSELF FORWARD AS A CANDI-DATE...
UGH! WHO DO YOU THINK YOU ARE?! FIRST YOU'RE LATE AND NOW YOU WANT TO BOSS US AROUND?
MUR
MUR
WITH A FIRST IMPRESSION THIS BAD, I DOUBT ANYONE'S VOTING FOR YOU.
BONK
WHA?! NO WAY!
YER GETTIN' AWFULLY WORKED UP OVER A LITTLE FAMILY VACATION, KID. AH WELL. KIDS GET EXCITED ABOUT THIS KINDA STUFF.
WHY'S A LITTLE GIRL SAYING THINGS AN OLD MAN WOULD THROUGH HER HAND PUPPET?!

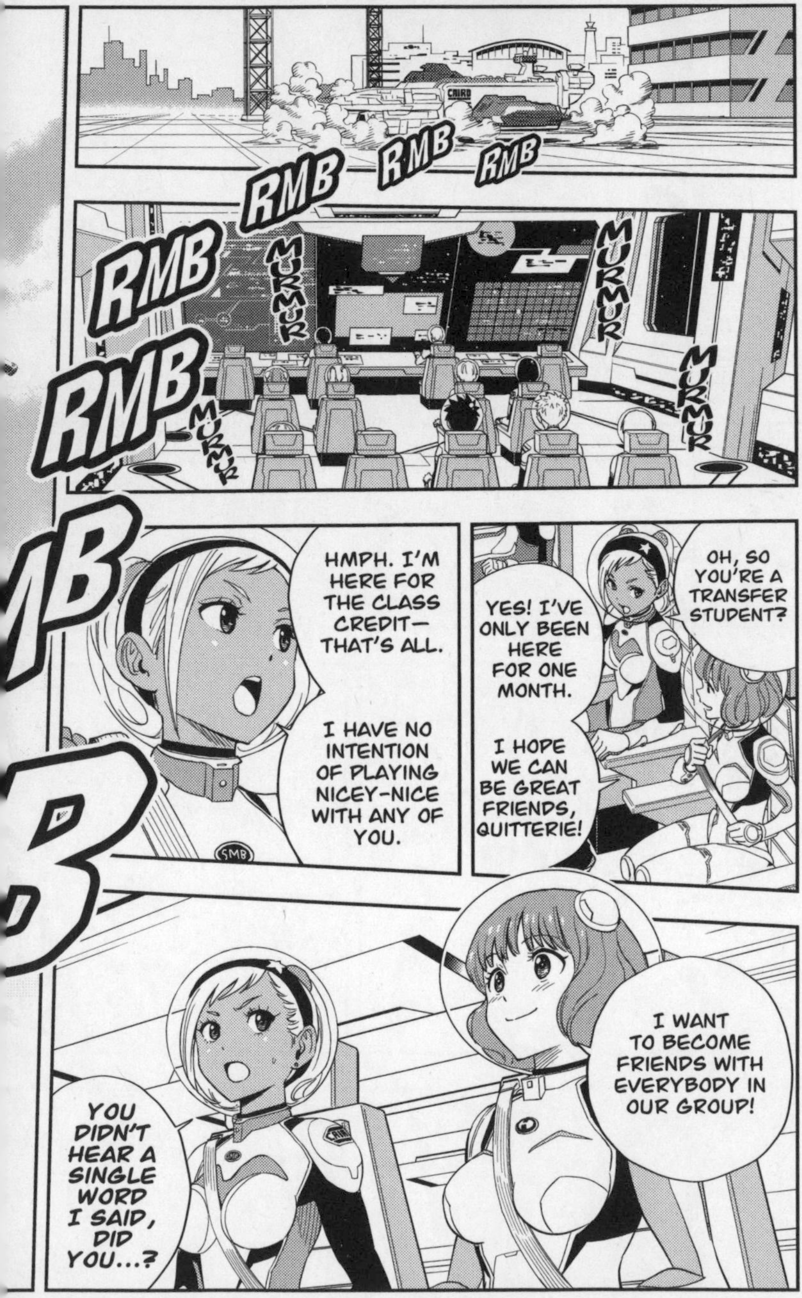
RMB
RMB
RMB
RMB
RMB
MURMUR
MURMUR
MURMUR
MURMUR
OH, SO YOU'RE A TRANSFER STUDENT?
YES! I'VE ONLY BEEN HERE FOR ONE MONTH.
I HOPE WE CAN BE GREAT FRIENDS, QUITTERIE!
HMPH. I'M HERE FOR THE CLASS CREDIT— THAT'S ALL.
I HAVE NO INTENTION OF PLAYING NICEY-NICE WITH ANY OF YOU.
I WANT TO BECOME FRIENDS WITH EVERYBODY IN OUR GROUP!
YOU DIDN'T HEAR A SINGLE WORD I SAID, DID YOU...?

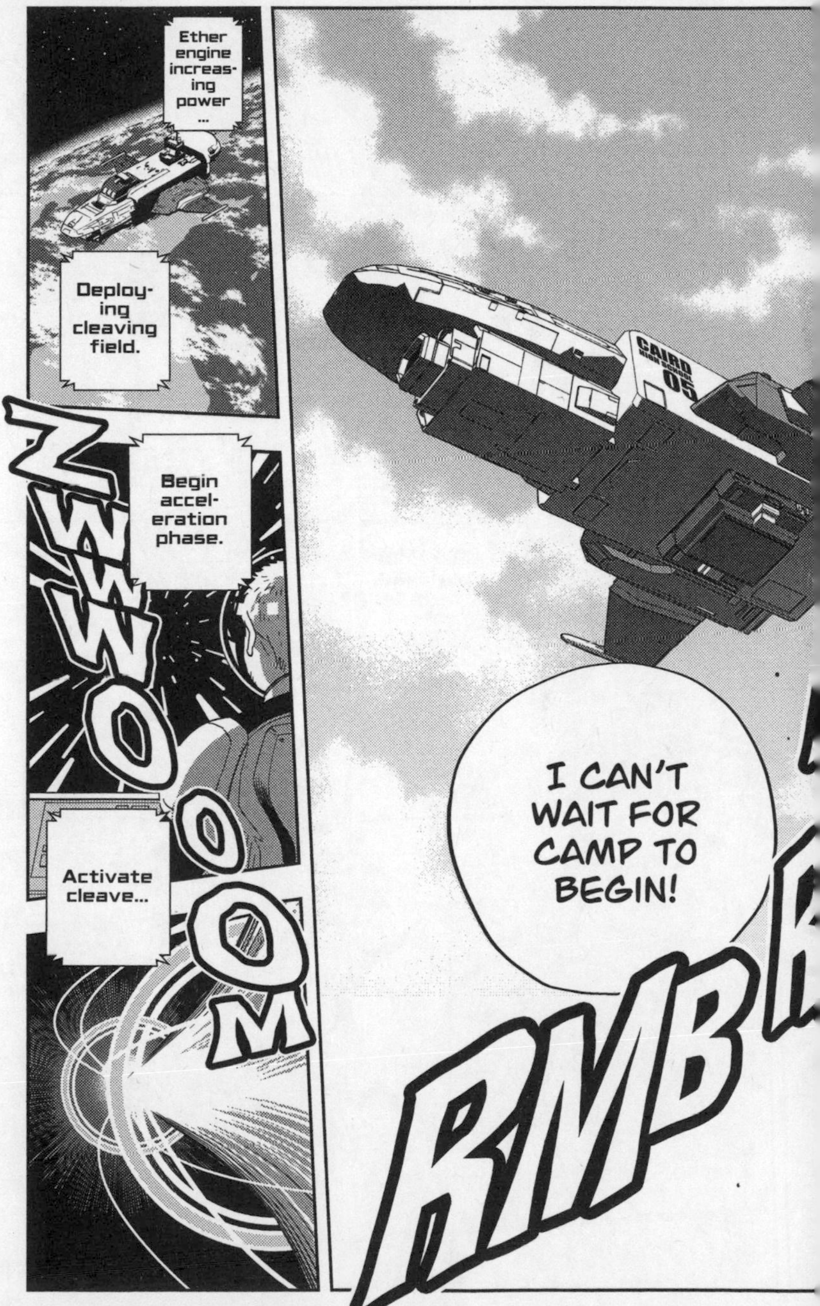
I CAN'T WAIT FOR CAMP TO BEGIN!
RMB
Ether engine increas-ing power ...
Deploy-ing cleaving field.
ZWWWOOOOM
Begin accel-eration phase.
Activate cleave...

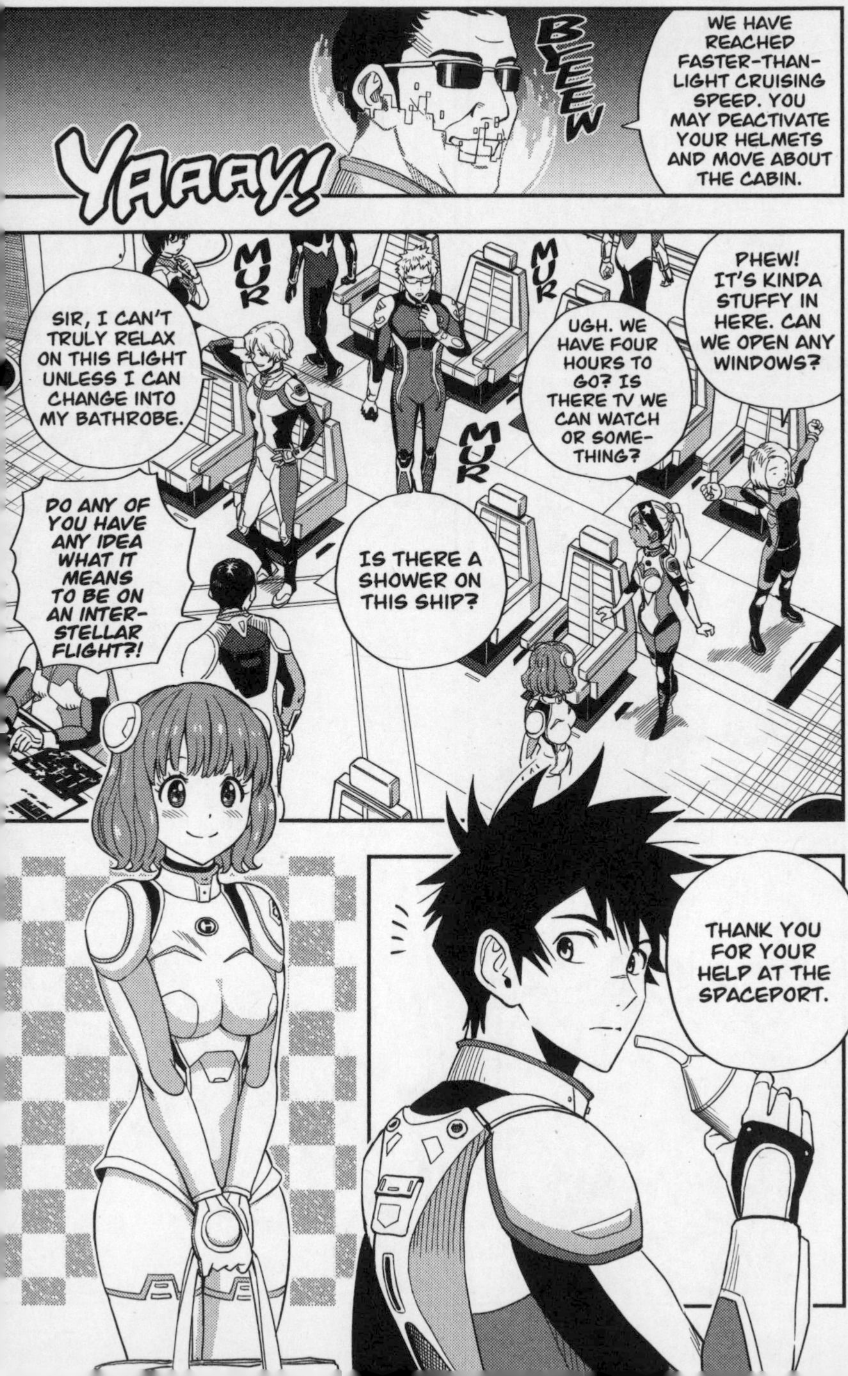
WE HAVE REACHED FASTER-THAN-LIGHT CRUISING SPEED. YOU MAY DEACTIVATE YOUR HELMETS AND MOVE ABOUT THE CABIN.
BYEEW
YAAAAY!
PHEW! IT'S KINDA STUFFY IN HERE. CAN WE OPEN ANY WINDOWS?
MUR
UGH. WE HAVE FOUR HOURS TO GO? IS THERE TV WE CAN WATCH OR SOME-THING?
MUR
SIR, I CAN'T TRULY RELAX ON THIS FLIGHT UNLESS I CAN CHANGE INTO MY BATHROBE.
MUR
IS THERE A SHOWER ON THIS SHIP?
DO ANY OF YOU HAVE ANY IDEA WHAT IT MEANS TO BE ON AN INTER-STELLAR FLIGHT?!
THANK YOU FOR YOUR HELP AT THE SPACEPORT.

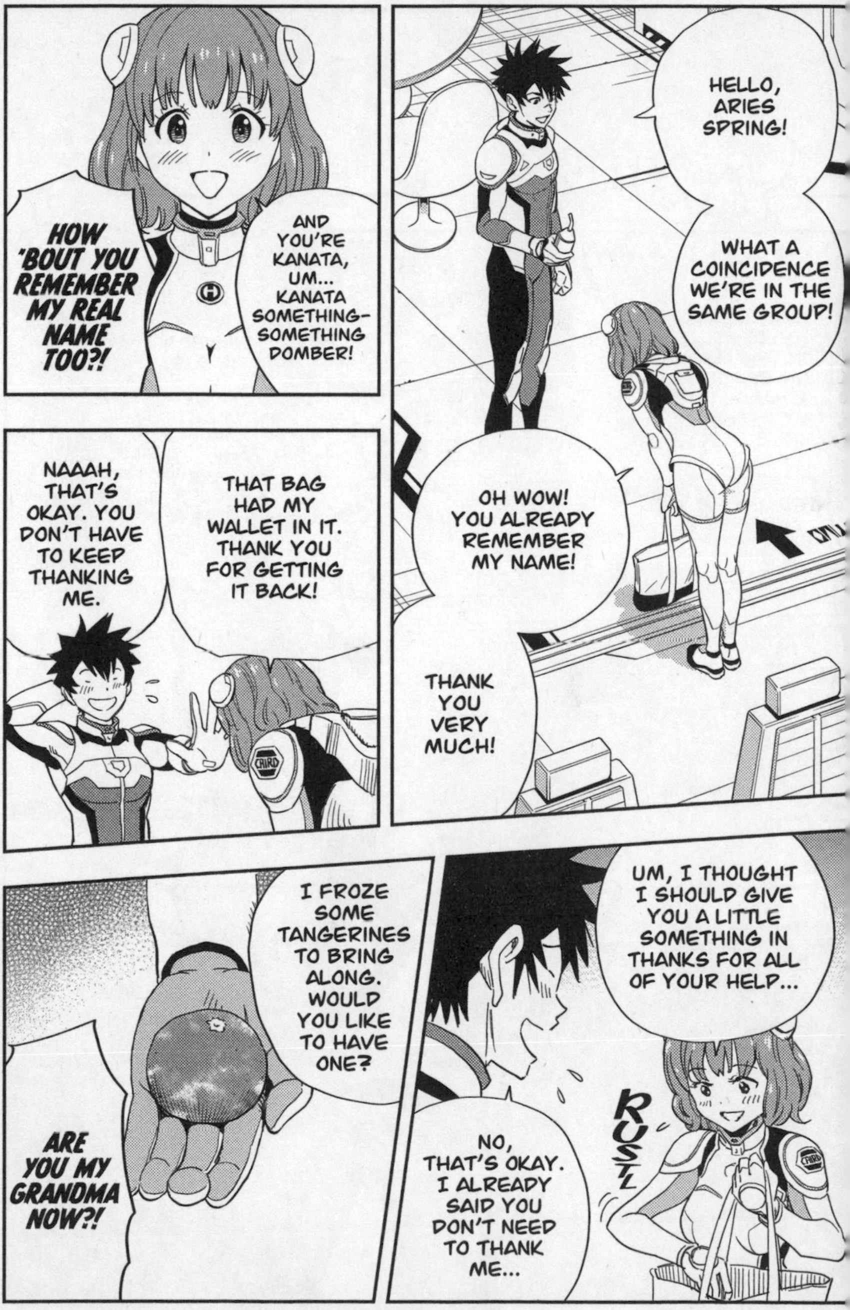
HELLO, ARIES SPRING!
WHAT A COINCIDENCE WE'RE IN THE SAME GROUP!
OH WOW! YOU ALREADY REMEMBER MY NAME!
THANK YOU VERY MUCH!
AND YOU'RE KANATA, UM... KANATA SOMETHING-SOMETHING DOMBER!
HOW 'BOUT YOU REMEMBER MY REAL NAME TOO?!
THAT BAG HAD MY WALLET IN IT. THANK YOU FOR GETTING IT BACK!
NAAAH, THAT'S OKAY. YOU DON'T HAVE TO KEEP THANKING ME.
UM, I THOUGHT I SHOULD GIVE YOU A LITTLE SOMETHING IN THANKS FOR ALL OF YOUR HELP...
RUSTL
NO, THAT'S OKAY. I ALREADY SAID YOU DON'T NEED TO THANK ME...
I FROZE SOME TANGERINES TO BRING ALONG. WOULD YOU LIKE TO HAVE ONE?
ARE YOU MY GRANDMA NOW?!

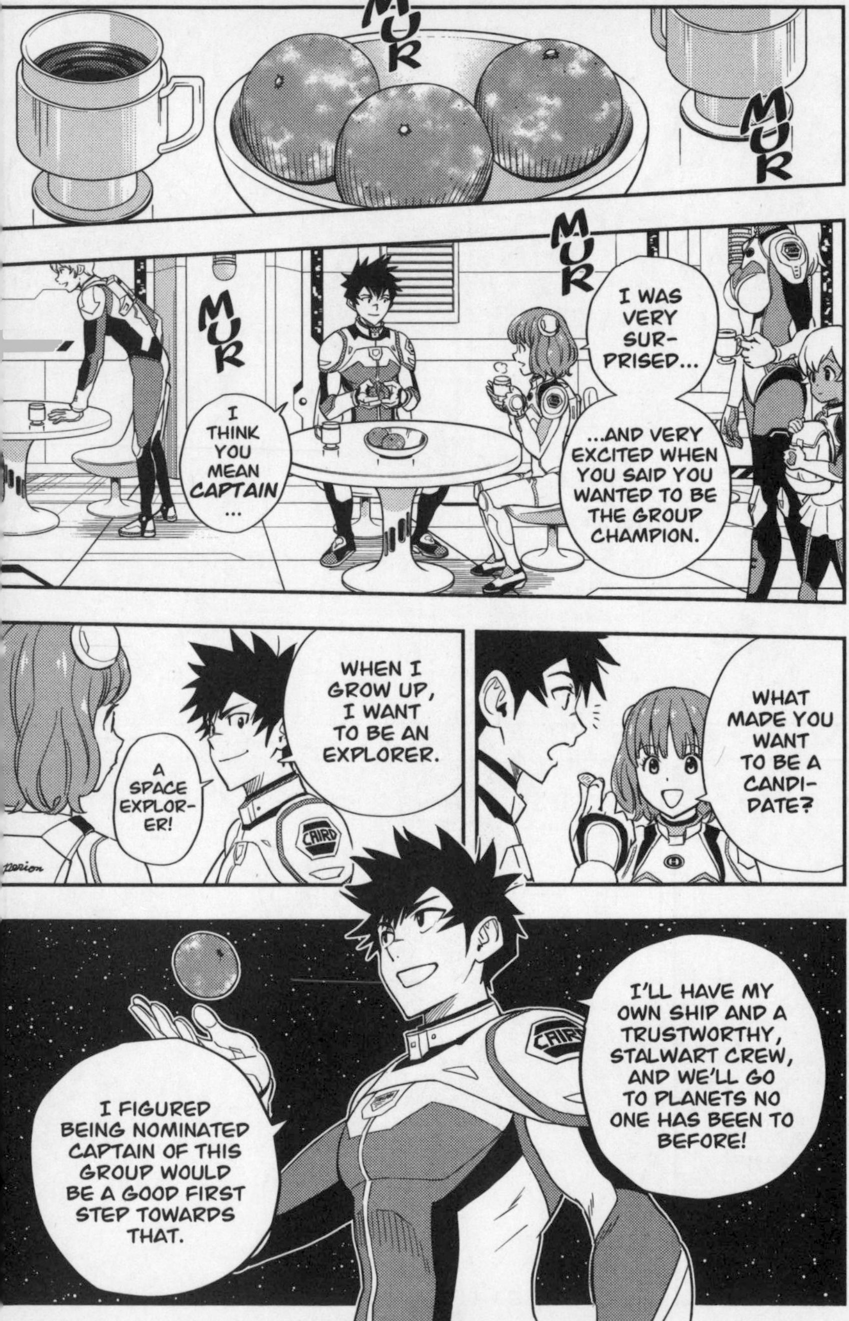
MUR MUR
MUR MUR
MUR MUR
MUR MUR
I WAS VERY SURPRISED...
...AND VERY EXCITED WHEN YOU SAID YOU WANTED TO BE THE GROUP CHAMPION.
I THINK YOU MEAN CAPTAIN...
WHAT MADE YOU WANT TO BE A CANDIDATE?
WHEN I GROW UP, I WANT TO BE AN EXPLORER.
A SPACE EXPLORER!
I'LL HAVE MY OWN SHIP AND A TRUSTWORTHY, STALWART CREW, AND WE'LL GO TO PLANETS NO ONE HAS BEEN TO BEFORE!
I FIGURED BEING NOMINATED CAPTAIN OF THIS GROUP WOULD BE A GOOD FIRST STEP TOWARDS THAT.

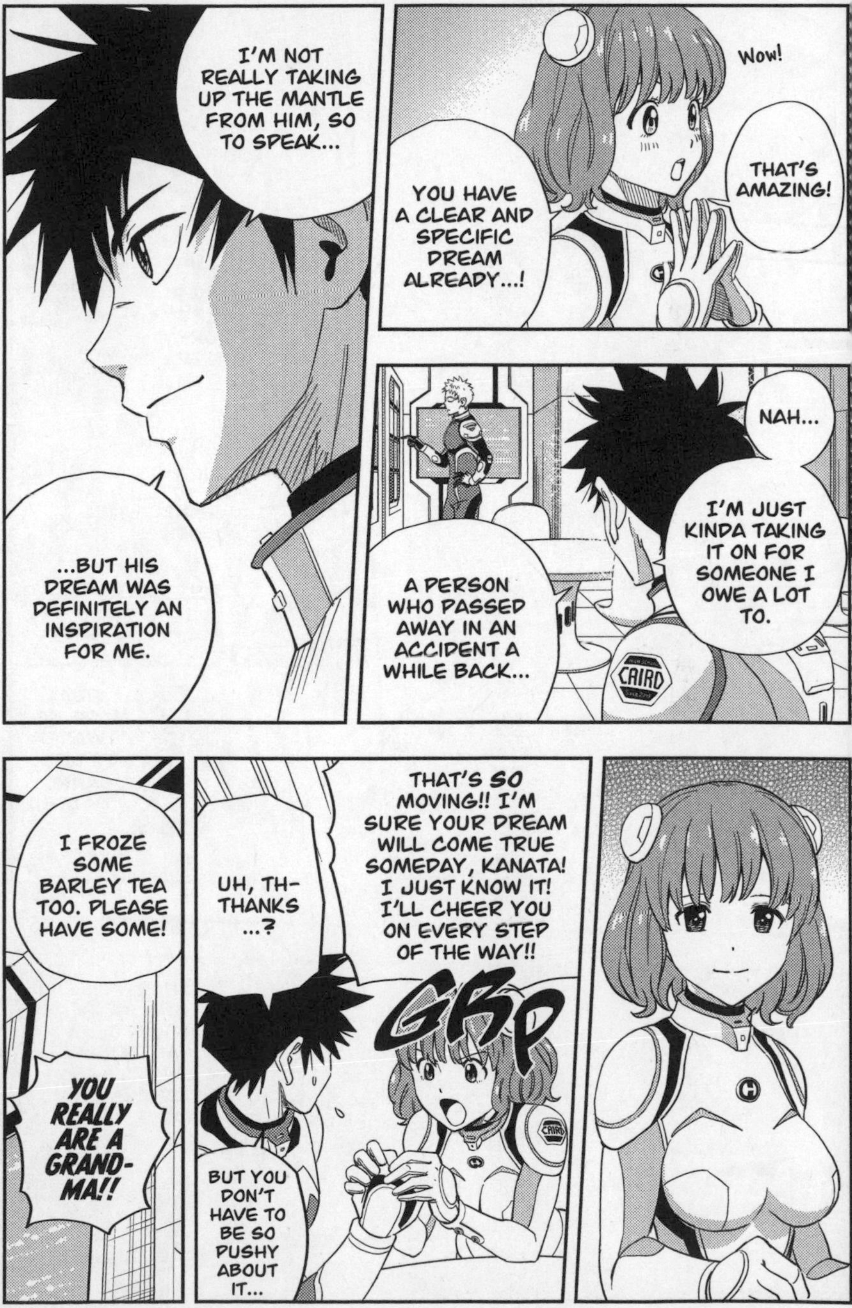
Wow!
THAT'S AMAZING!
YOU HAVE A CLEAR AND SPECIFIC DREAM ALREADY...!
NAH...
I'M JUST KINDA TAKING IT ON FOR SOMEONE I OWE A LOT TO.
A PERSON WHO PASSED AWAY IN AN ACCIDENT A WHILE BACK...
I'M NOT REALLY TAKING UP THE MANTLE FROM HIM, SO TO SPEAK...
...BUT HIS DREAM WAS DEFINITELY AN INSPIRATION FOR ME.
THAT'S SO MOVING!! I'M SURE YOUR DREAM WILL COME TRUE SOMEDAY, KANATA! I JUST KNOW IT! I'LL CHEER YOU ON EVERY STEP OF THE WAY!!
GBP
UH, TH-THANKS ...?
BUT YOU DON'T HAVE TO BE SO PUSHY ABOUT IT...
I FROZE SOME BARLEY TEA TOO. PLEASE HAVE SOME!
YOU REALLY ARE A GRAND-MA!!

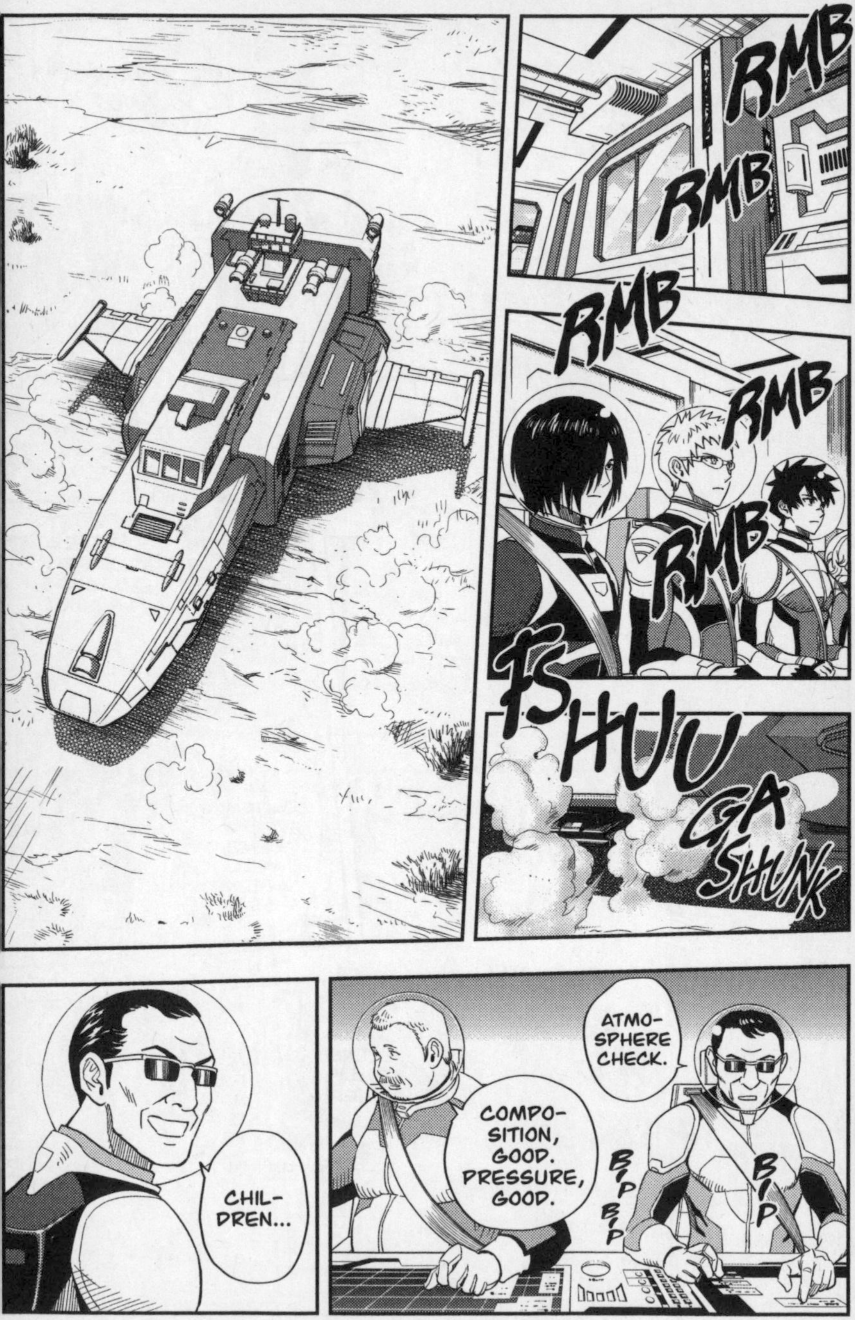
RMB
RMB
RMB
RMB
RMB
FS
HUU
GA
SHUNK
ATMO-SPHERE CHECK.
BIP
BIP
COMPO-SITION, GOOD. PRESSURE, GOOD.
BIP BIP BIP
CHIL-DREN...

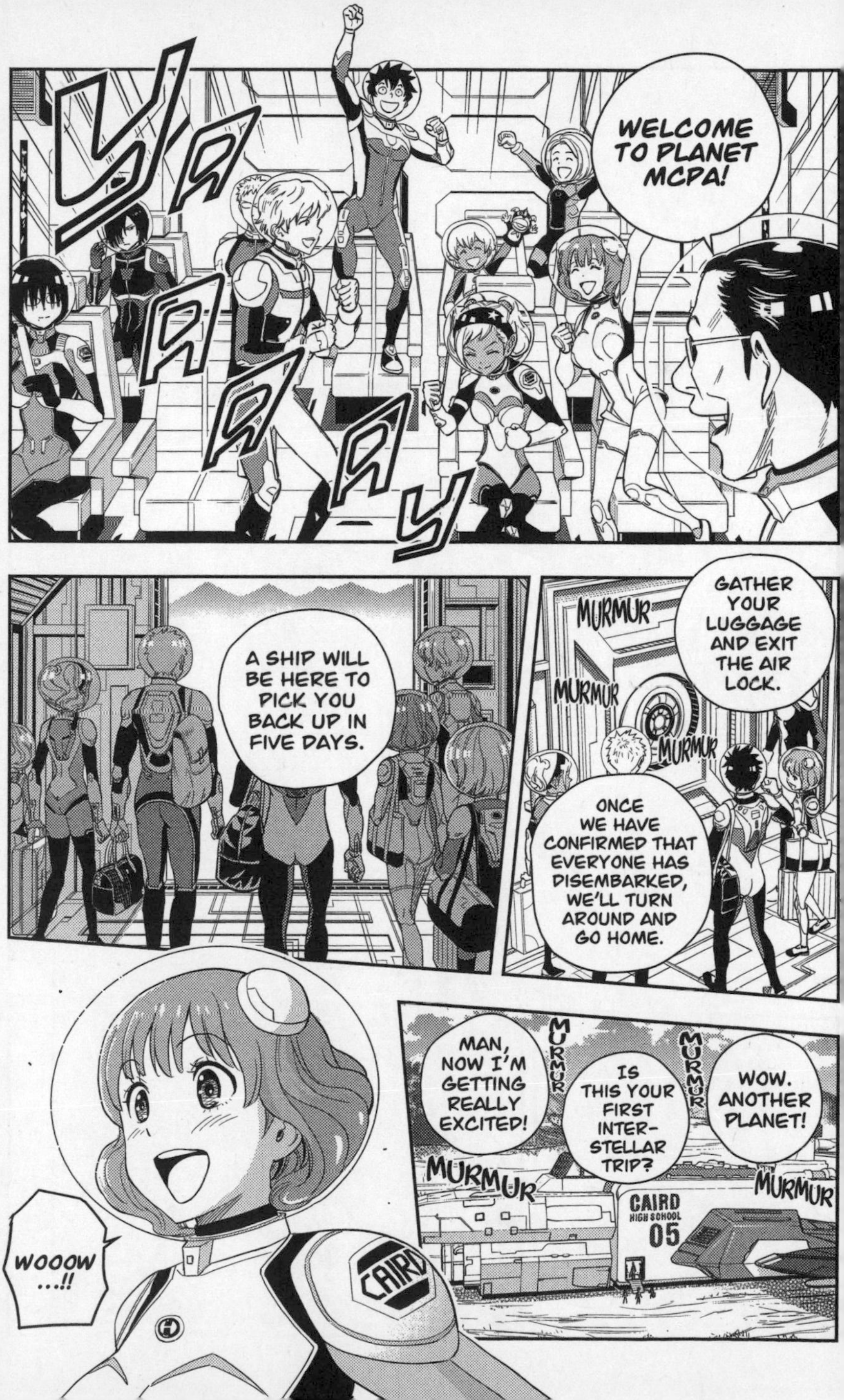
WELCOME TO PLANET MCPA!
YAAAAAY
GATHER YOUR LUGGAGE AND EXIT THE AIR LOCK.
MURMUR
MURMUR
MURMUR
ONCE WE HAVE CONFIRMED THAT EVERYONE HAS DISEMBARKED, WE'LL TURN AROUND AND GO HOME.
A SHIP WILL BE HERE TO PICK YOU BACK UP IN FIVE DAYS.
WOW. ANOTHER PLANET!
MURMUR
MURMUR
IS THIS YOUR FIRST INTER-STELLAR TRIP?
MURMUR
MAN, NOW I'M GETTING REALLY EXCITED!
MURMUR
CAIRD HIGH SCHOOL 05
WOOOW ...!!
CAIRD

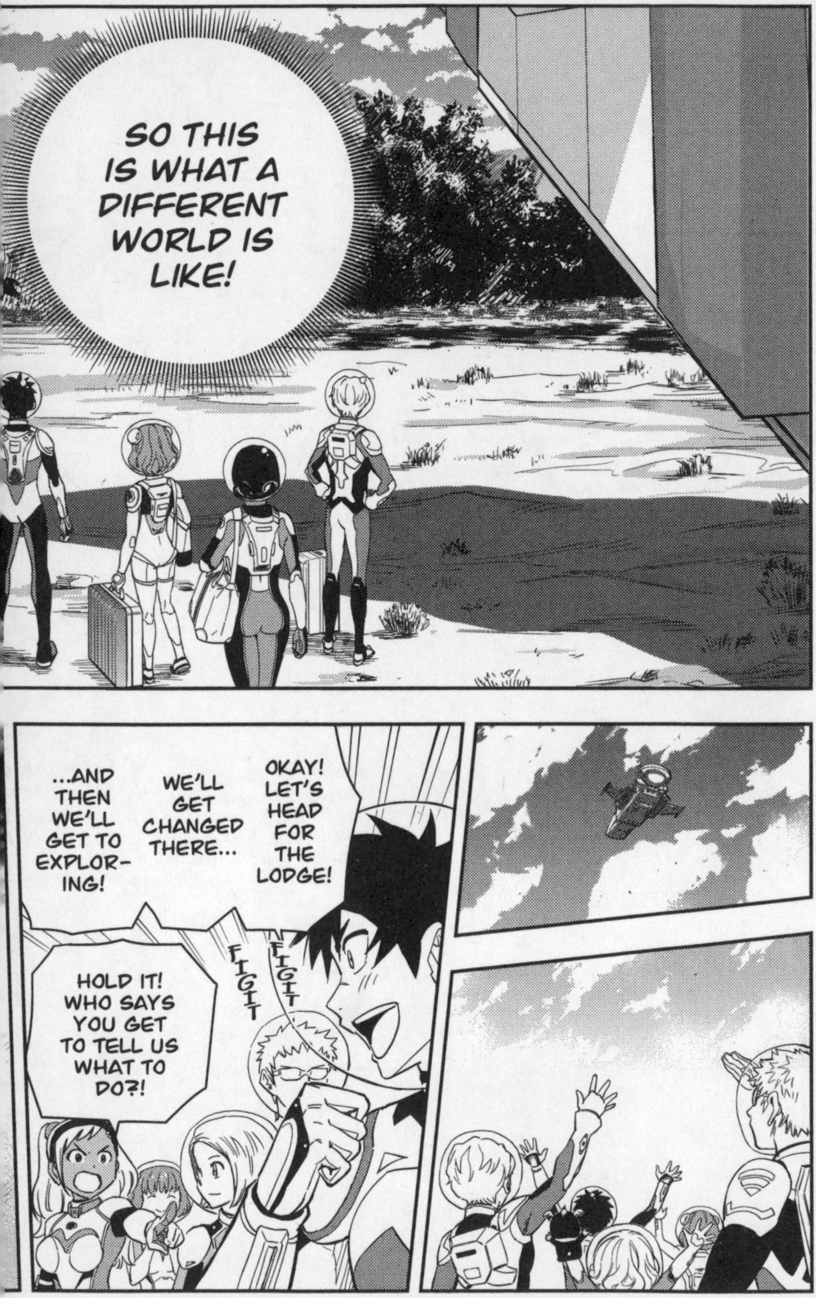
SO THIS IS WHAT A DIFFERENT WORLD IS LIKE!
OKAY! LET'S HEAD FOR THE LODGE!
WE'LL GET CHANGED THERE...
...AND THEN WE'LL GET TO EXPLOR-ING!
FIGIT
FIGIT
HOLD IT! WHO SAYS YOU GET TO TELL US WHAT TO DO?!

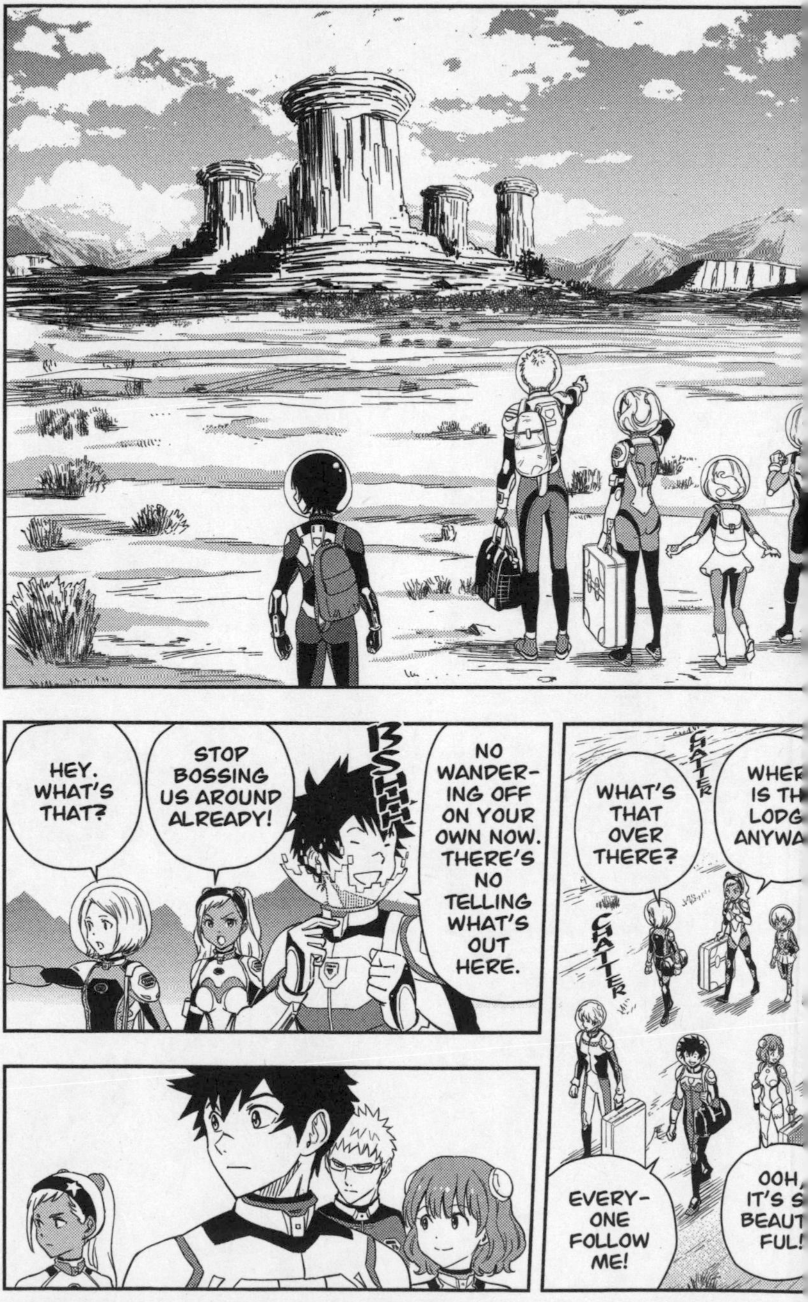
WHER IS TH LODG ANYWA
CHATTER
WHAT'S THAT OVER THERE?
CHATTER
OOH, IT'S S BEAUT FUL!
EVERY-ONE FOLLOW ME!
NO WANDER-ING OFF ON YOUR OWN NOW. THERE'S NO TELLING WHAT'S OUT HERE.
BSHHH
STOP BOSSING US AROUND ALREADY!
HEY. WHAT'S THAT?

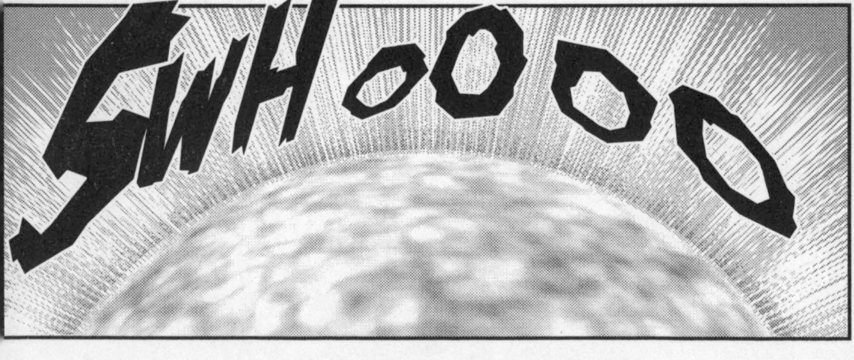

SWHOOOO

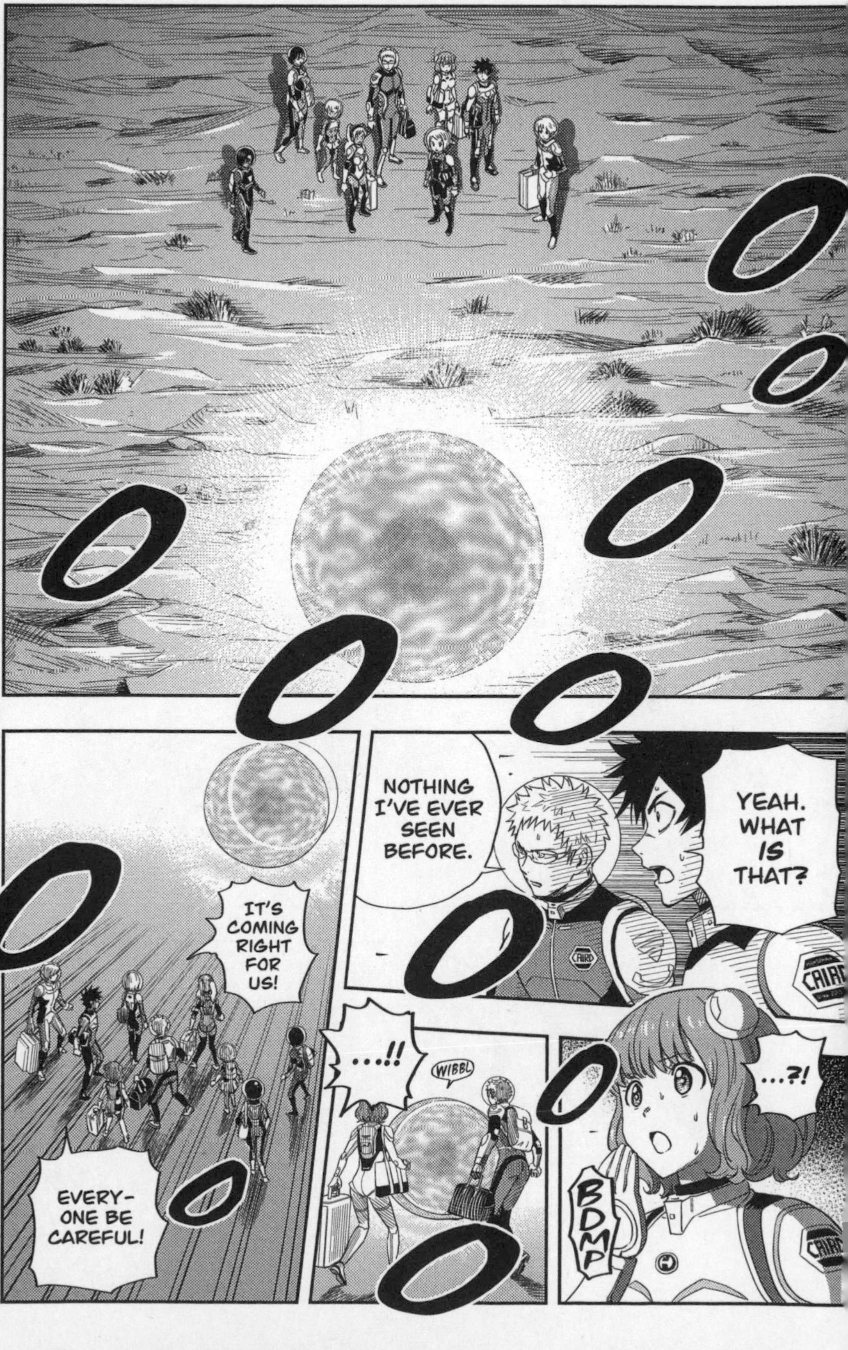
YEAH. WHAT IS THAT?
NOTHING I'VE EVER SEEN BEFORE.
...?!
BDMP
...!!
WIBBL
IT'S COMING RIGHT FOR US!
EVERY-ONE BE CAREFUL!

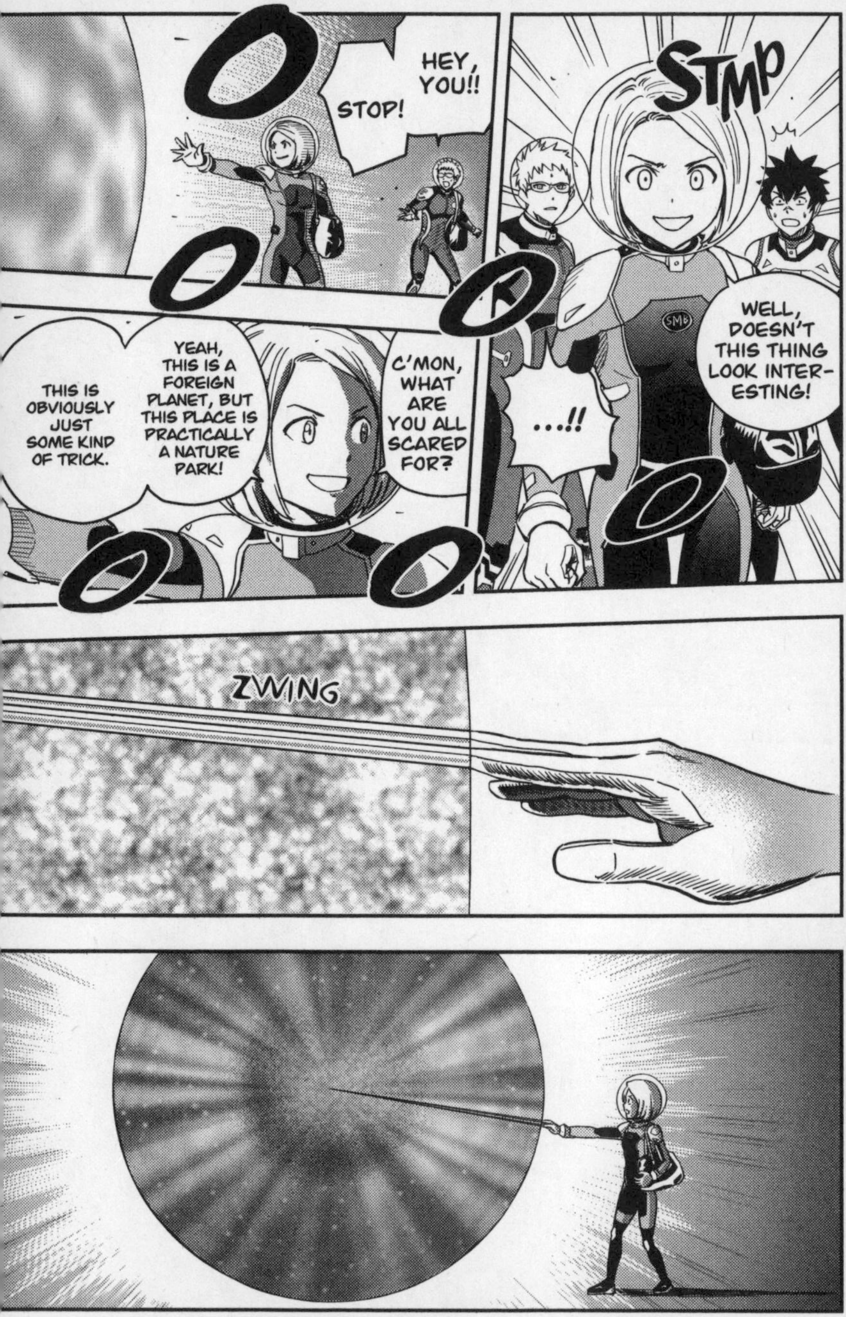
STMP
WELL, DOESN'T THIS THING LOOK INTER-ESTING!
...!!
HEY, YOU!!
STOP!
C'MON, WHAT ARE YOU ALL SCARED FOR?
YEAH, THIS IS A FOREIGN PLANET, BUT THIS PLACE IS PRACTICALLY A NATURE PARK!
THIS IS OBVIOUSLY JUST SOME KIND OF TRICK.
ZWING

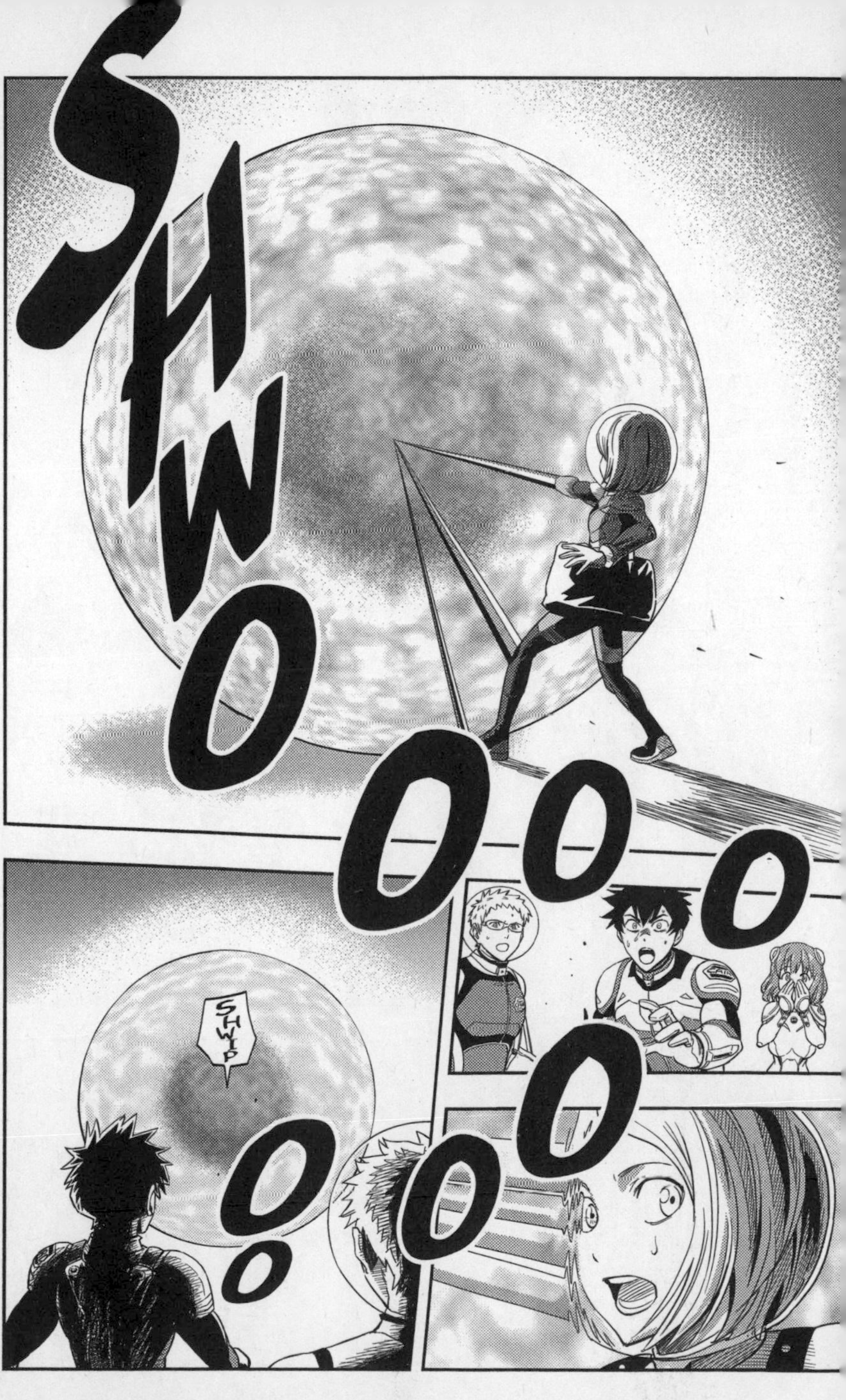
SHWOOOOOOOOO
SHWIP

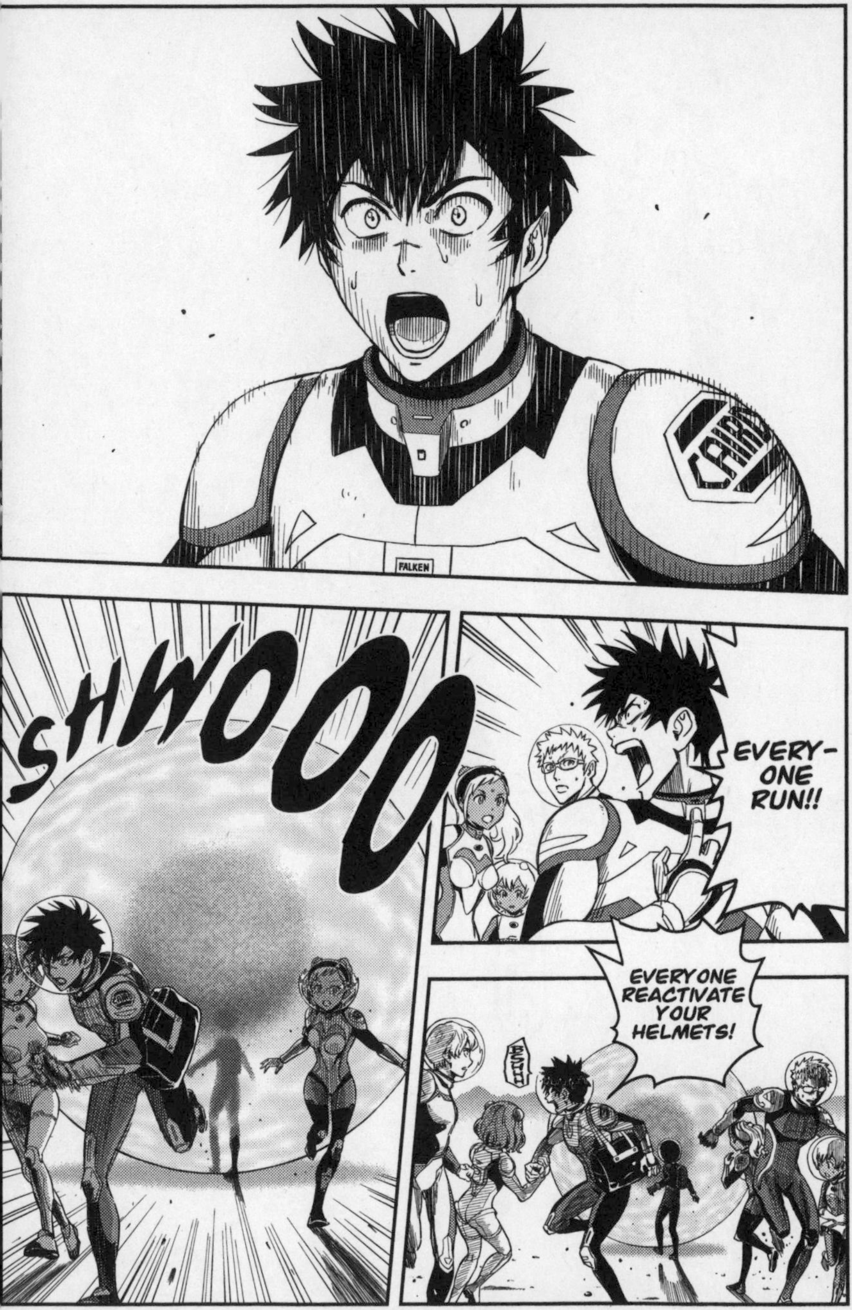
FALKEN
EVERY-
ONE
RUN!!
EVERYONE
REACTIVATE
YOUR
HELMETS!
SHWOOO

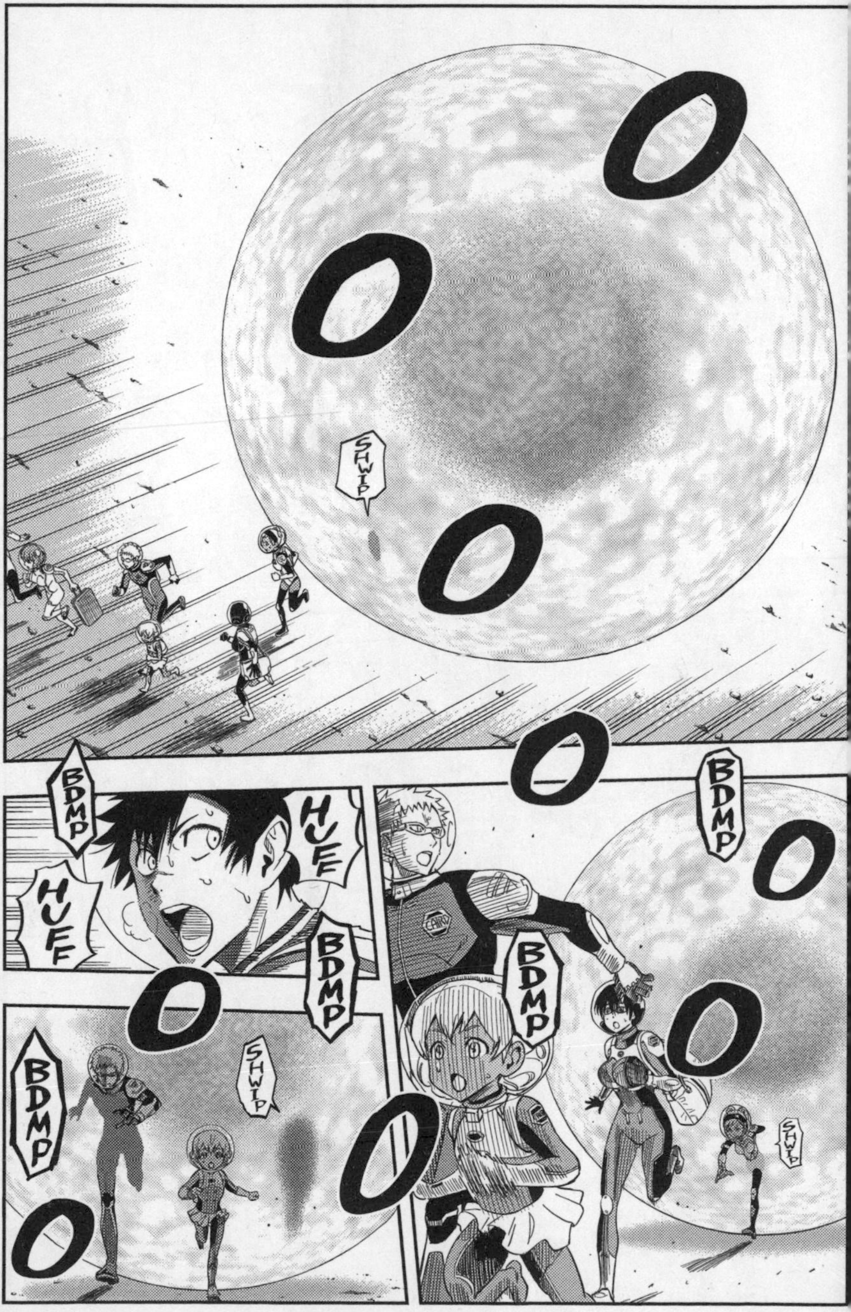

OOO
SHWIP
BDMP
BDMP
SHWIP
HUFF
BDMP
HUFF
BDMP
SHWIP
BDMP

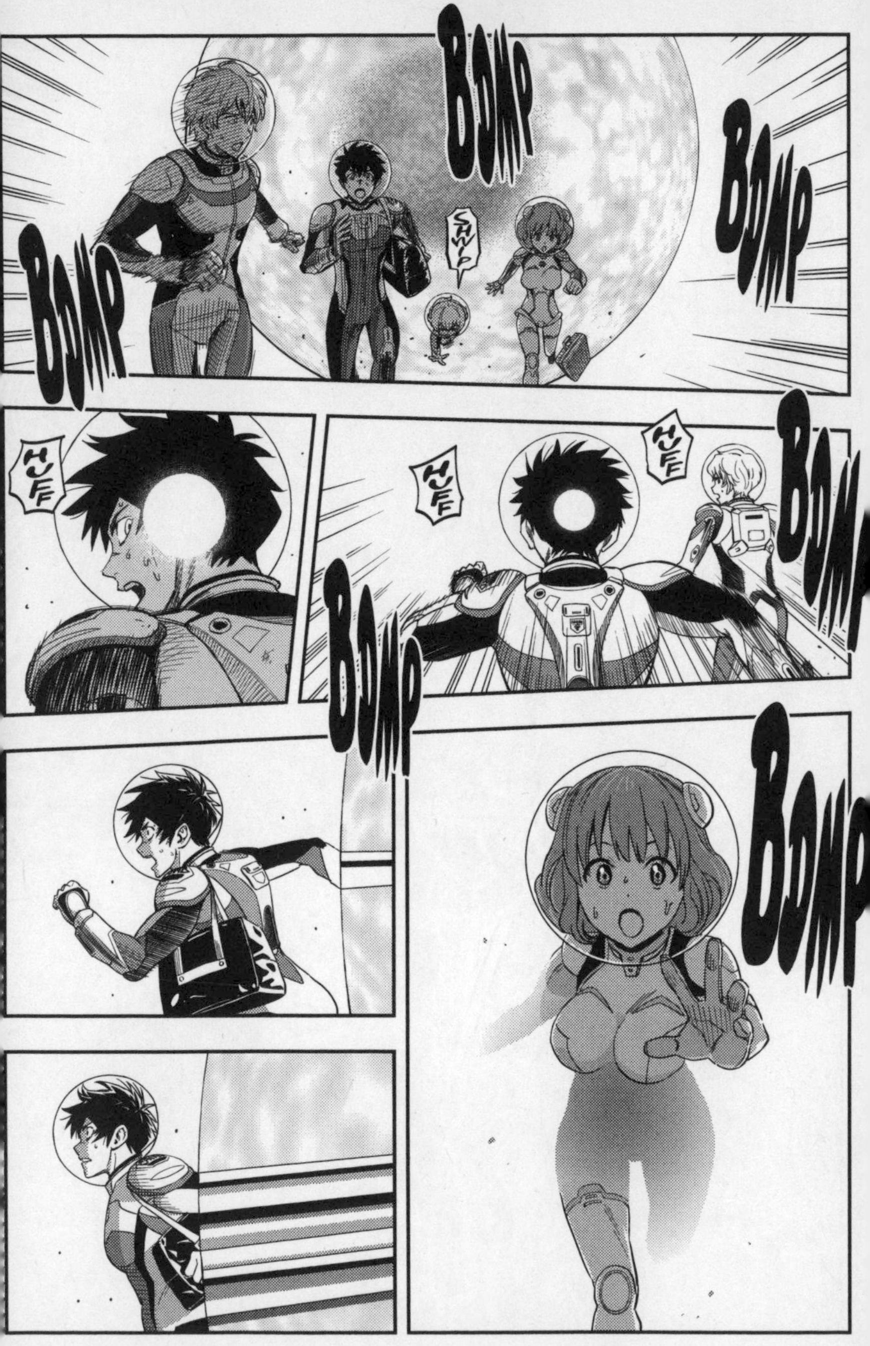
BDMP
BDMP
SHWIP
BDMP
BDMP
HUFF
HUFF
BDMP
HUFF
BDMP

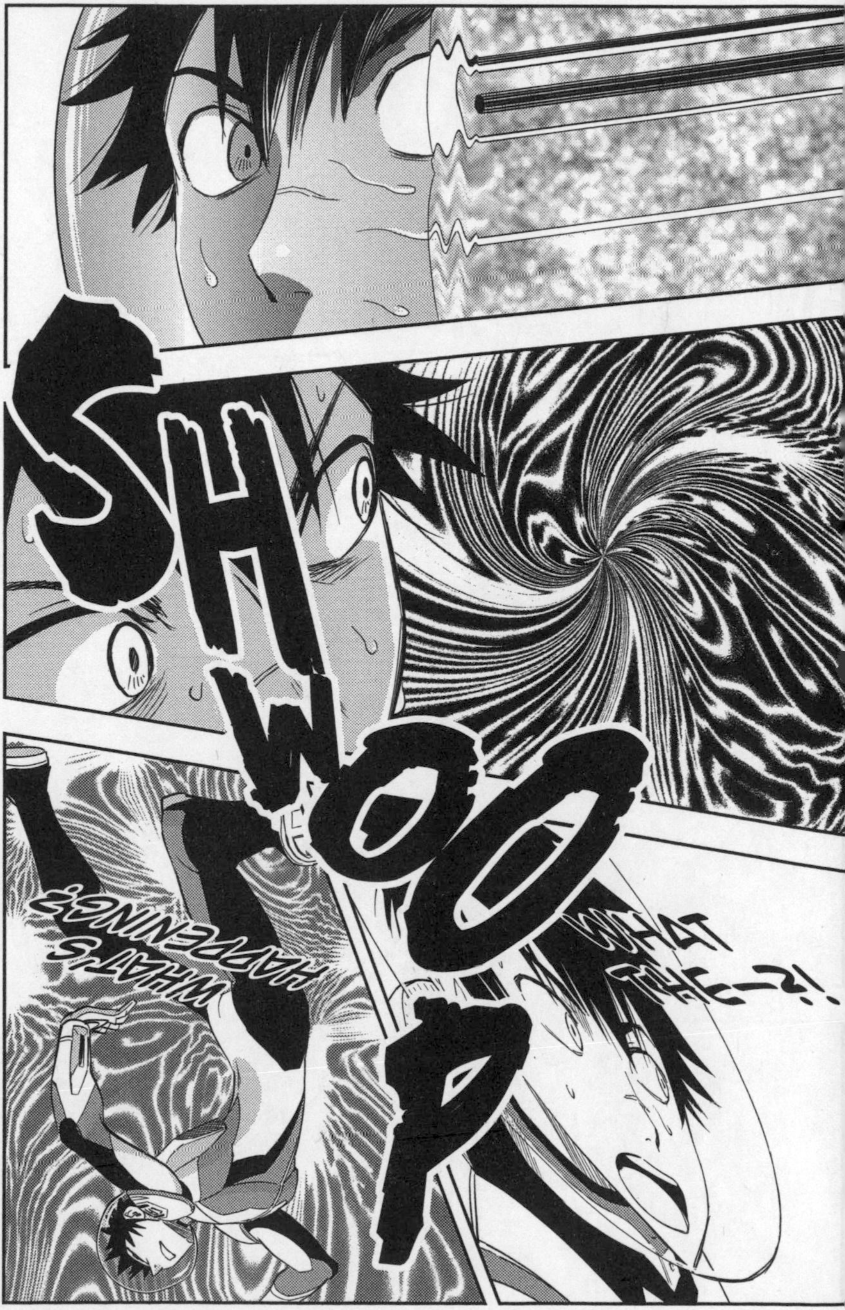
SHWOOP
WHAT THE--?!
WHAT'S HAPPENING?

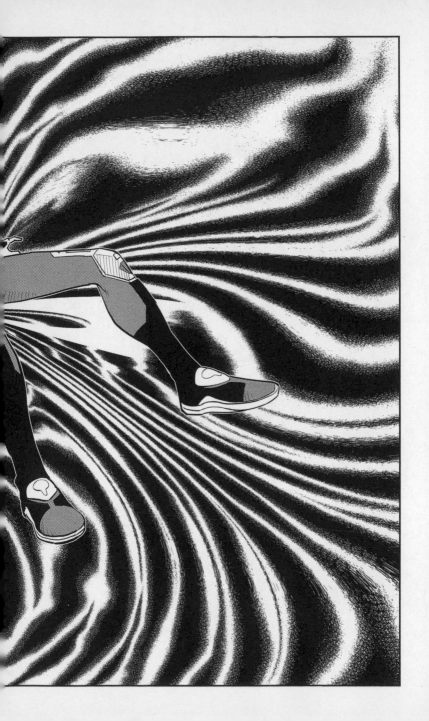

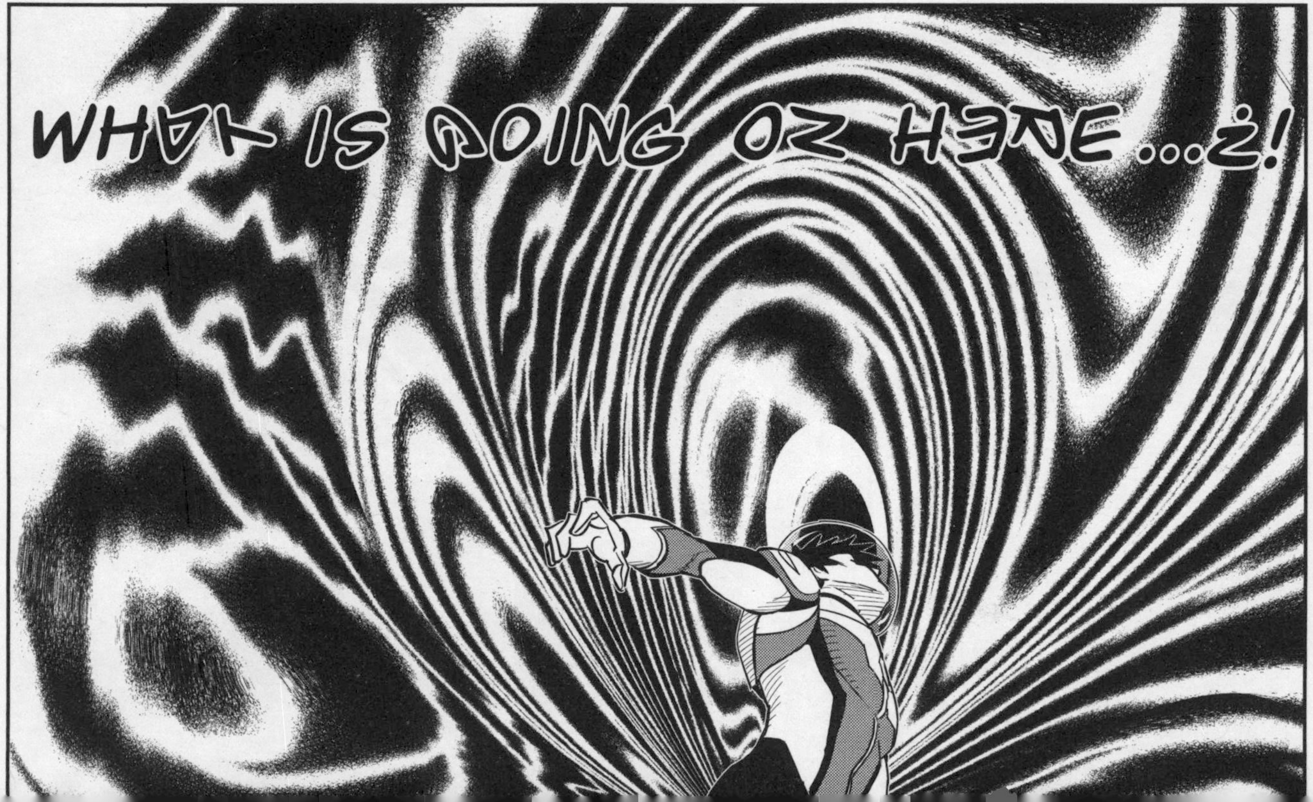
WHAT IS GOING ON HERE...?!

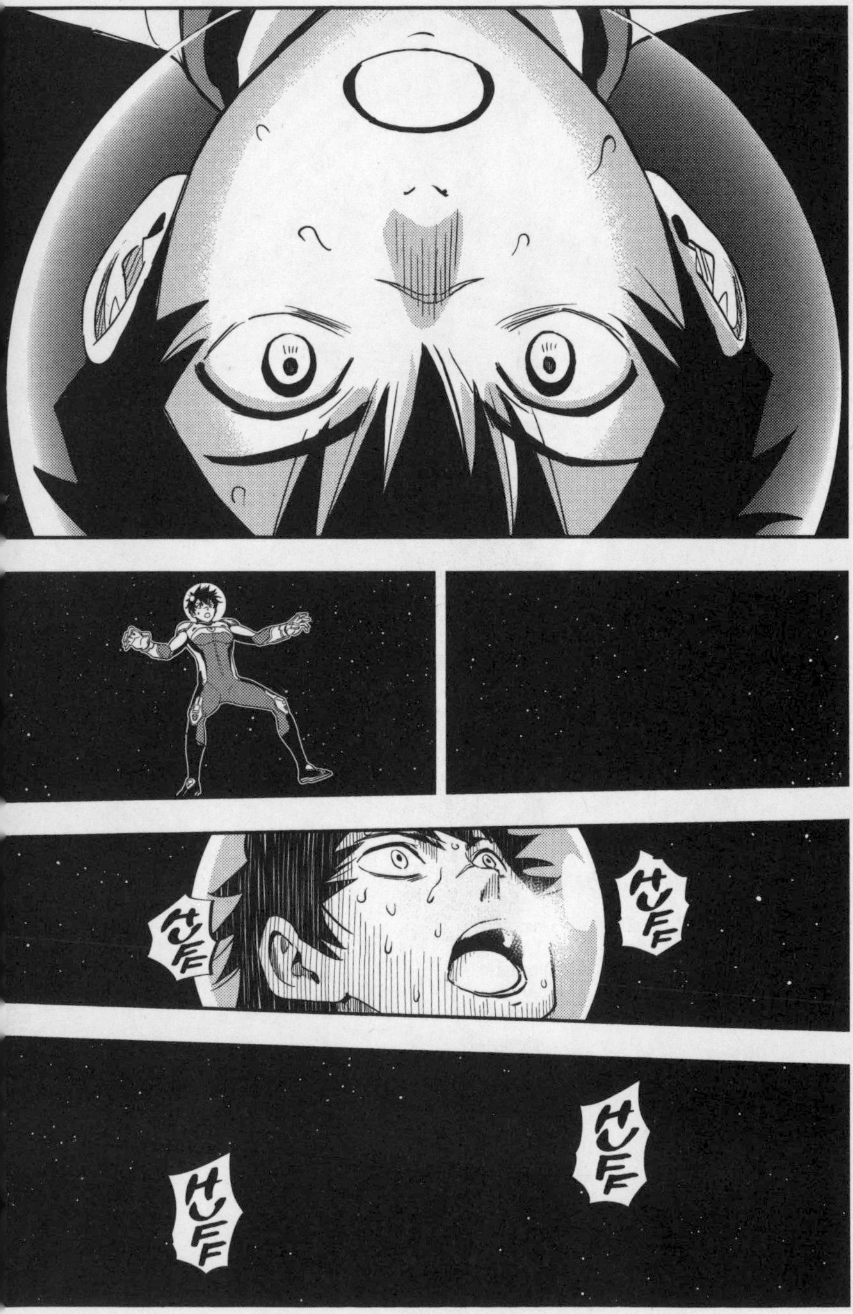
HUFF
HUFF
HUFF
HUFF

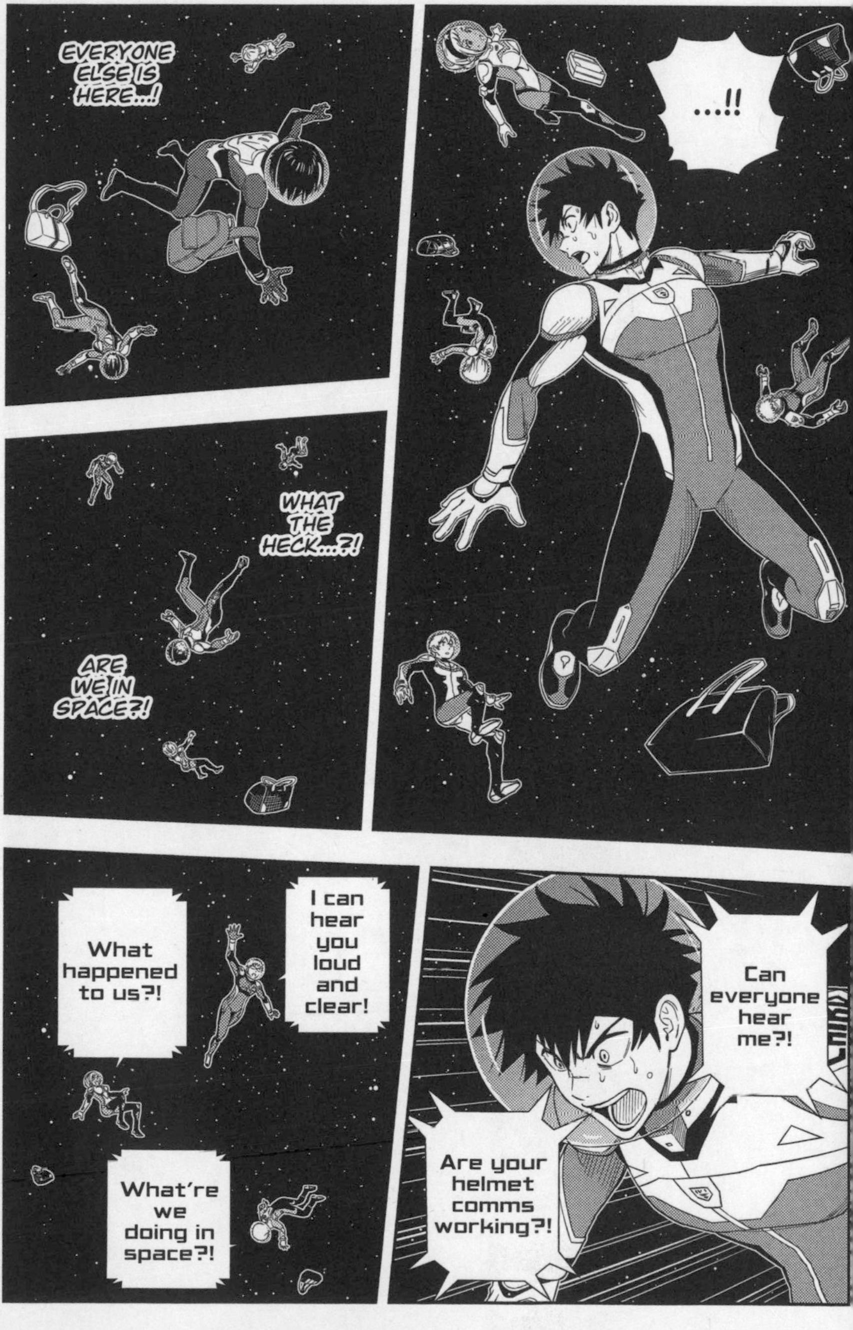
...!!
EVERYONE ELSE IS HERE...!
WHAT THE HECK...?!
ARE WE IN SPACE?!
Can everyone hear me?!
Are your helmet comms working?!
I can hear you loud and clear!
What happened to us?!
What're we doing in space?!

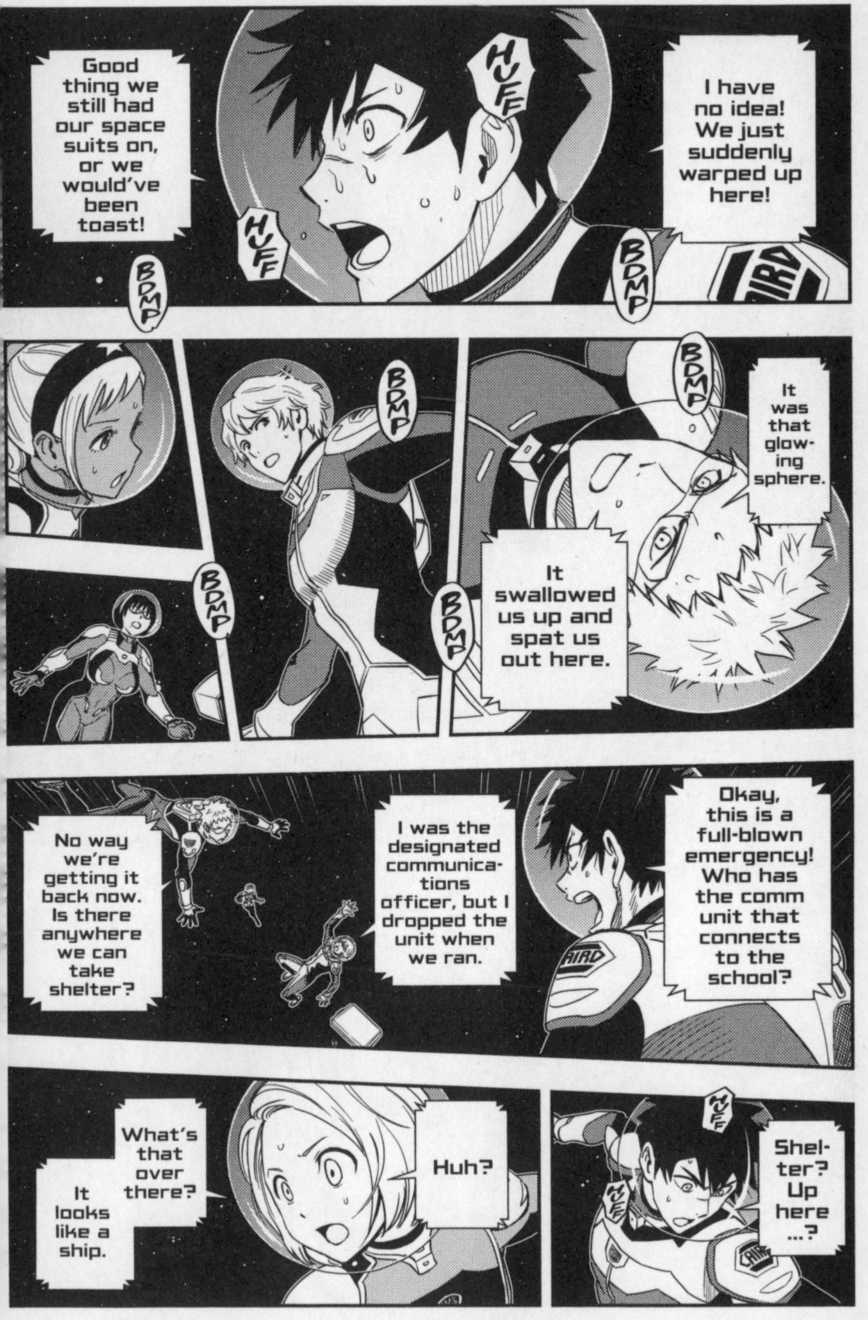
I have no idea! We just suddenly warped up here!
HUFF
Good thing we still had our space suits on, or we would've been toast!
HUFF
BDMP
BDMP
BDMP
It was that glowing sphere.
It swallowed us up and spat us out here.
BDMP
BDMP
BDMP
Okay, this is a full-blown emergency! Who has the comm unit that connects to the school?
I was the designated communications officer, but I dropped the unit when we ran.
No way we're getting it back now. Is there anywhere we can take shelter?
HUFF
Shel-ter? Up here ...?
HUFF
Huh?
What's that over there?
It looks like a ship.

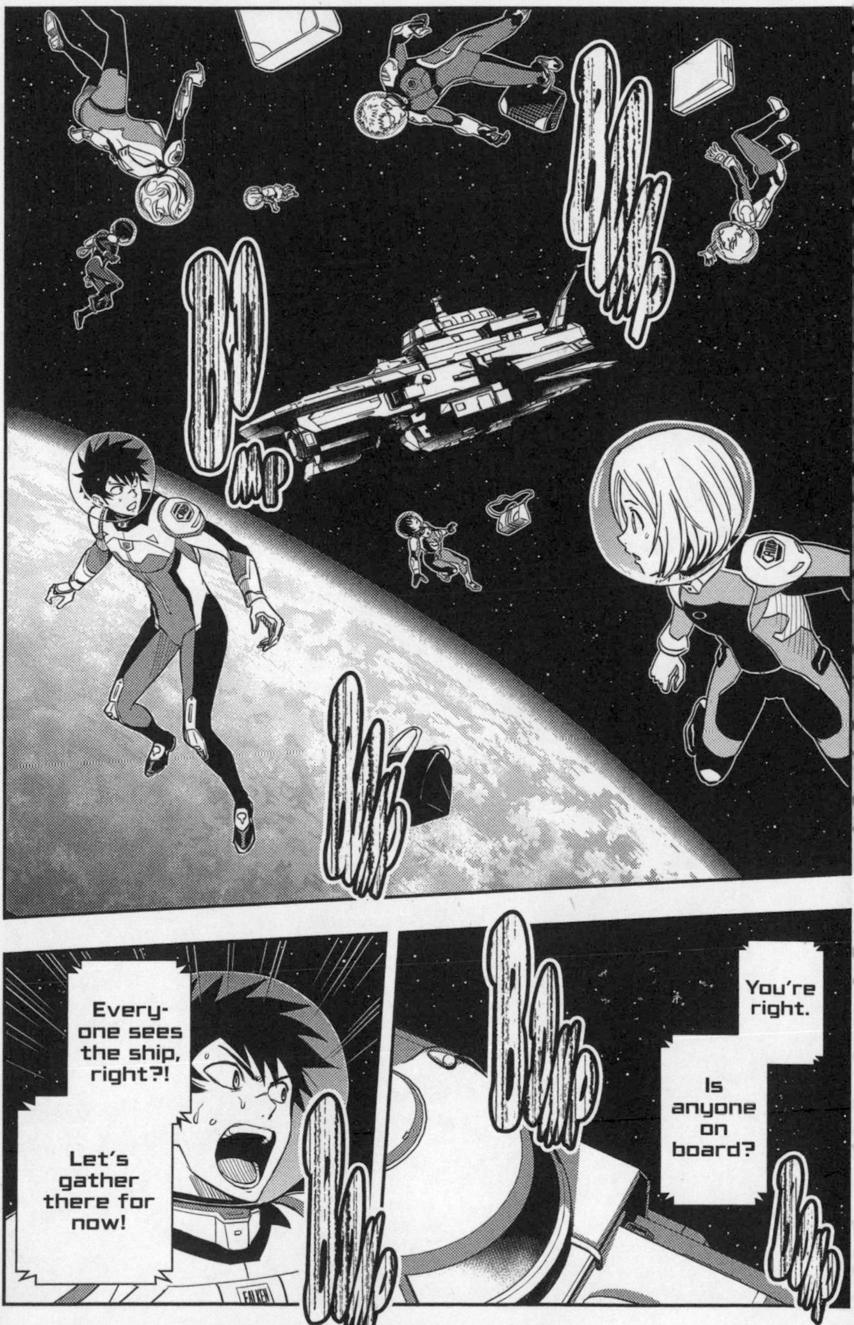
You're right.
Is anyone on board?
Every-one sees the ship, right?!
Let's gather there for now!

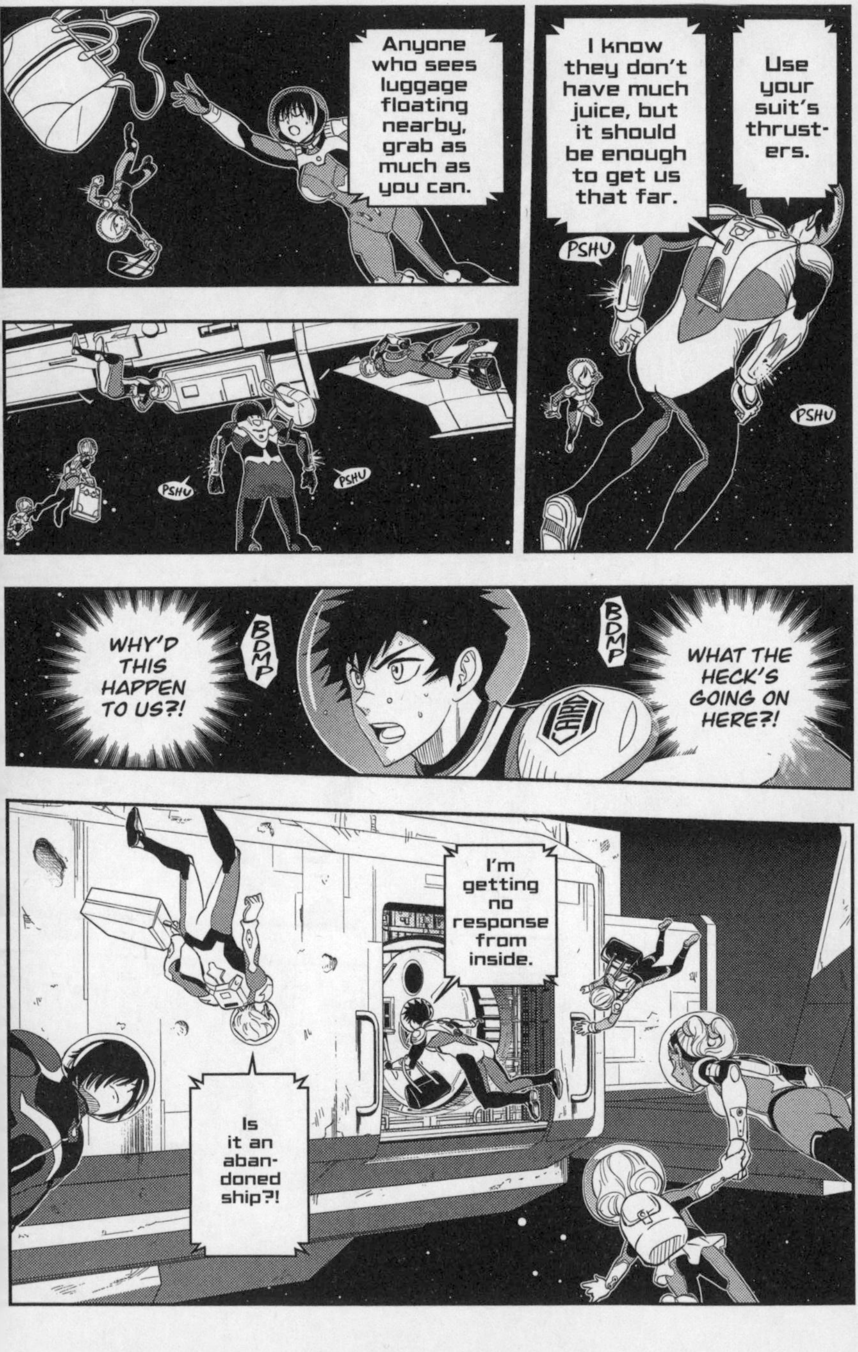
Use your suit's thrust-ers.
I know they don't have much juice, but it should be enough to get us that far.
PSHU
PSHU
Anyone who sees luggage floating nearby, grab as much as you can.
PSHU
PSHU
BDMP
WHAT THE HECK'S GOING ON HERE?!
BDMP
WHY'D THIS HAPPEN TO US?!
I'm getting no response from inside.
Is it an aban-doned ship?!

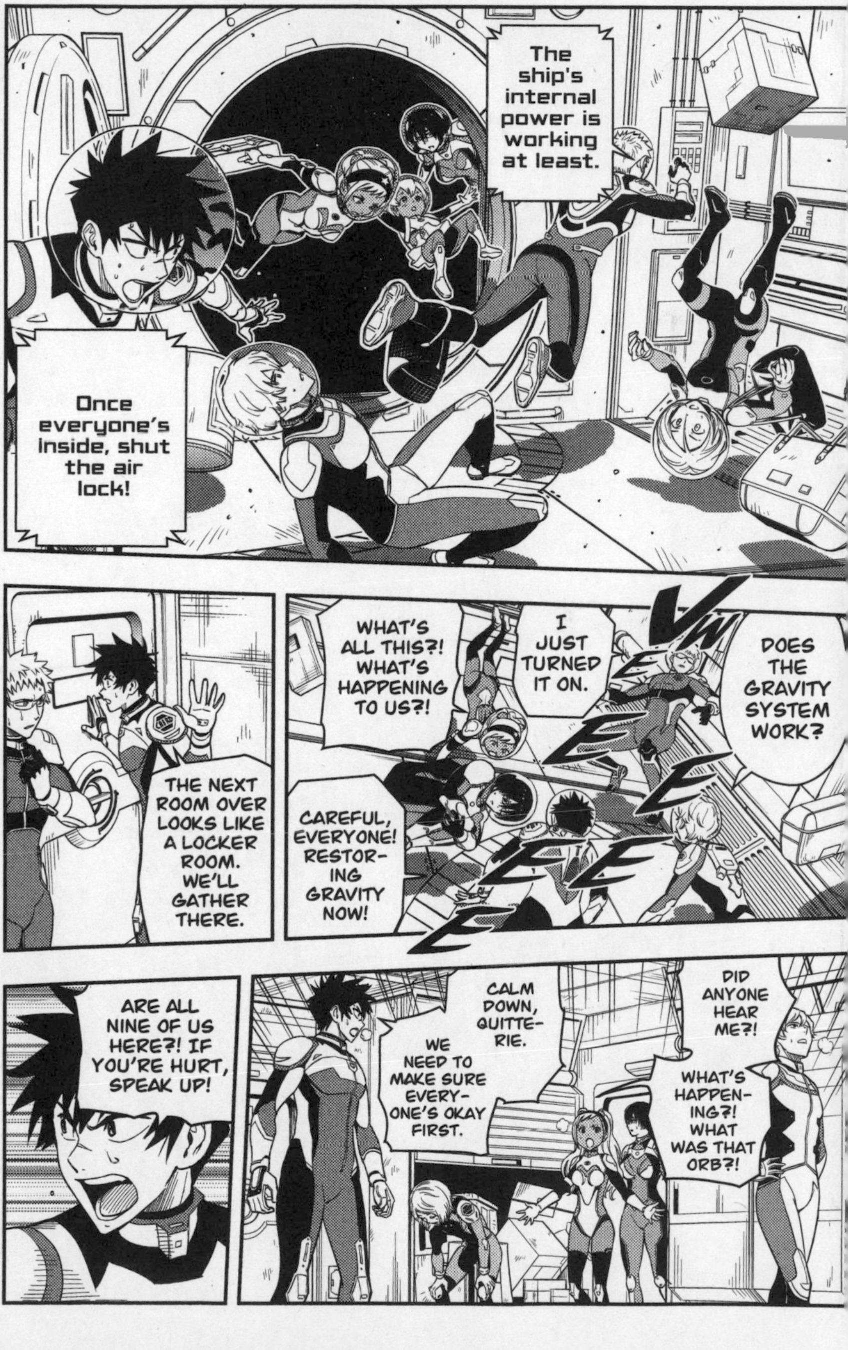

The ship's internal power is working at least.
Once everyone's inside, shut the air lock!
DOES THE GRAVITY SYSTEM WORK?
I JUST TURNED IT ON.
WHAT'S ALL THIS?! WHAT'S HAPPENING TO US?!
CAREFUL, EVERYONE! RESTORING GRAVITY NOW!
THE NEXT ROOM OVER LOOKS LIKE A LOCKER ROOM. WE'LL GATHER THERE.
DID ANYONE HEAR ME?!
WHAT'S HAPPENING?! WHAT WAS THAT ORB?!
CALM DOWN, QUITTERIE.
WE NEED TO MAKE SURE EVERYONE'S OKAY FIRST.
ARE ALL NINE OF US HERE?! IF YOU'RE HURT, SPEAK UP!

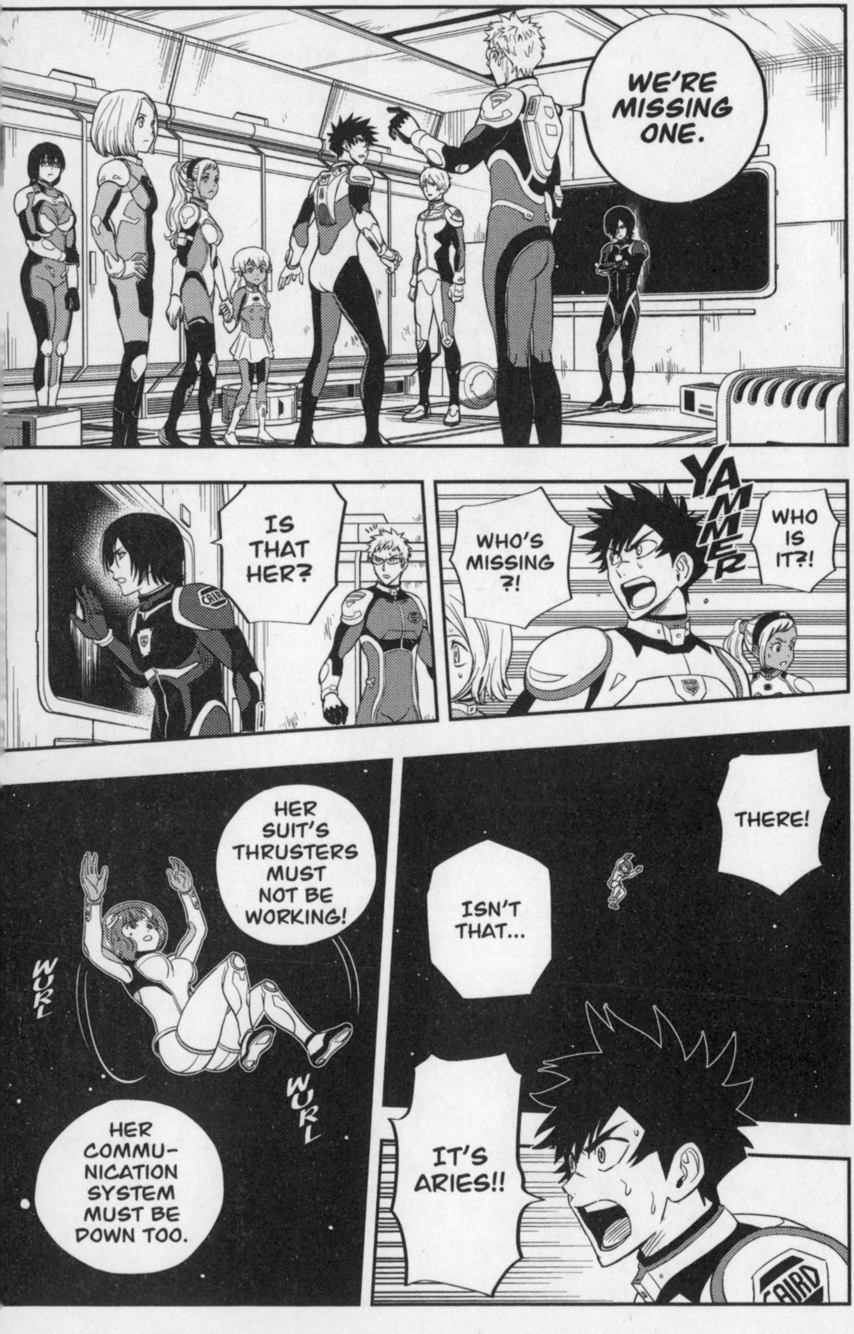
WE'RE MISSING ONE.
YAMMER
WHO IS IT?!
WHO'S MISSING ?!
IS THAT HER?
THERE!
ISN'T THAT...
IT'S ARIES!!
HER SUIT'S THRUSTERS MUST NOT BE WORKING!
WURL
WURL
HER COMMU-NICATION SYSTEM MUST BE DOWN TOO.

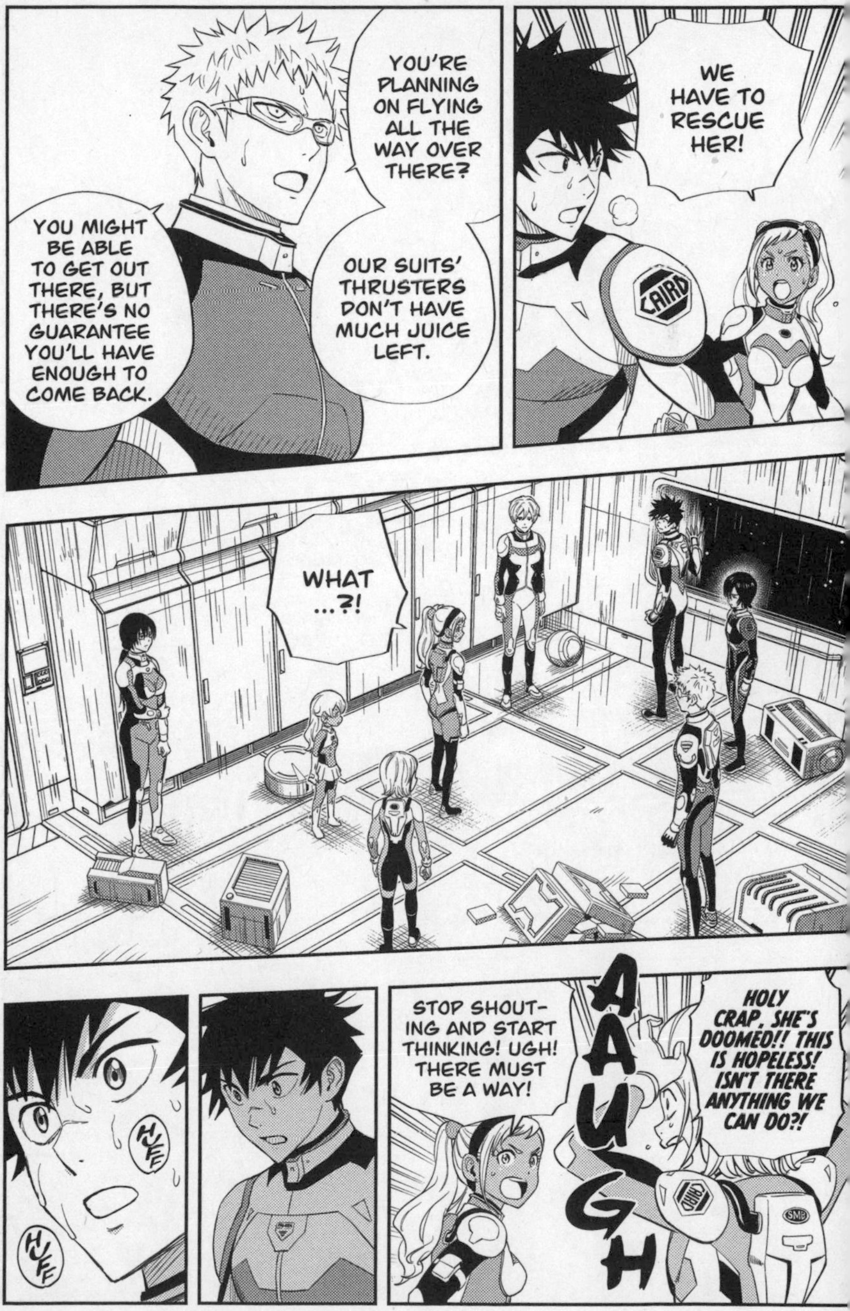
WE HAVE TO RESCUE HER!
YOU'RE PLANNING ON FLYING ALL THE WAY OVER THERE?
OUR SUITS' THRUSTERS DON'T HAVE MUCH JUICE LEFT.
YOU MIGHT BE ABLE TO GET OUT THERE, BUT THERE'S NO GUARANTEE YOU'LL HAVE ENOUGH TO COME BACK.
WHAT ...?!
HOLY CRAP, SHE'S DOOMED!! THIS IS HOPELESS! ISN'T THERE ANYTHING WE CAN DO?!
AAUGH
STOP SHOUT-ING AND START THINKING! UGH! THERE MUST BE A WAY!
HUFF
HUFF

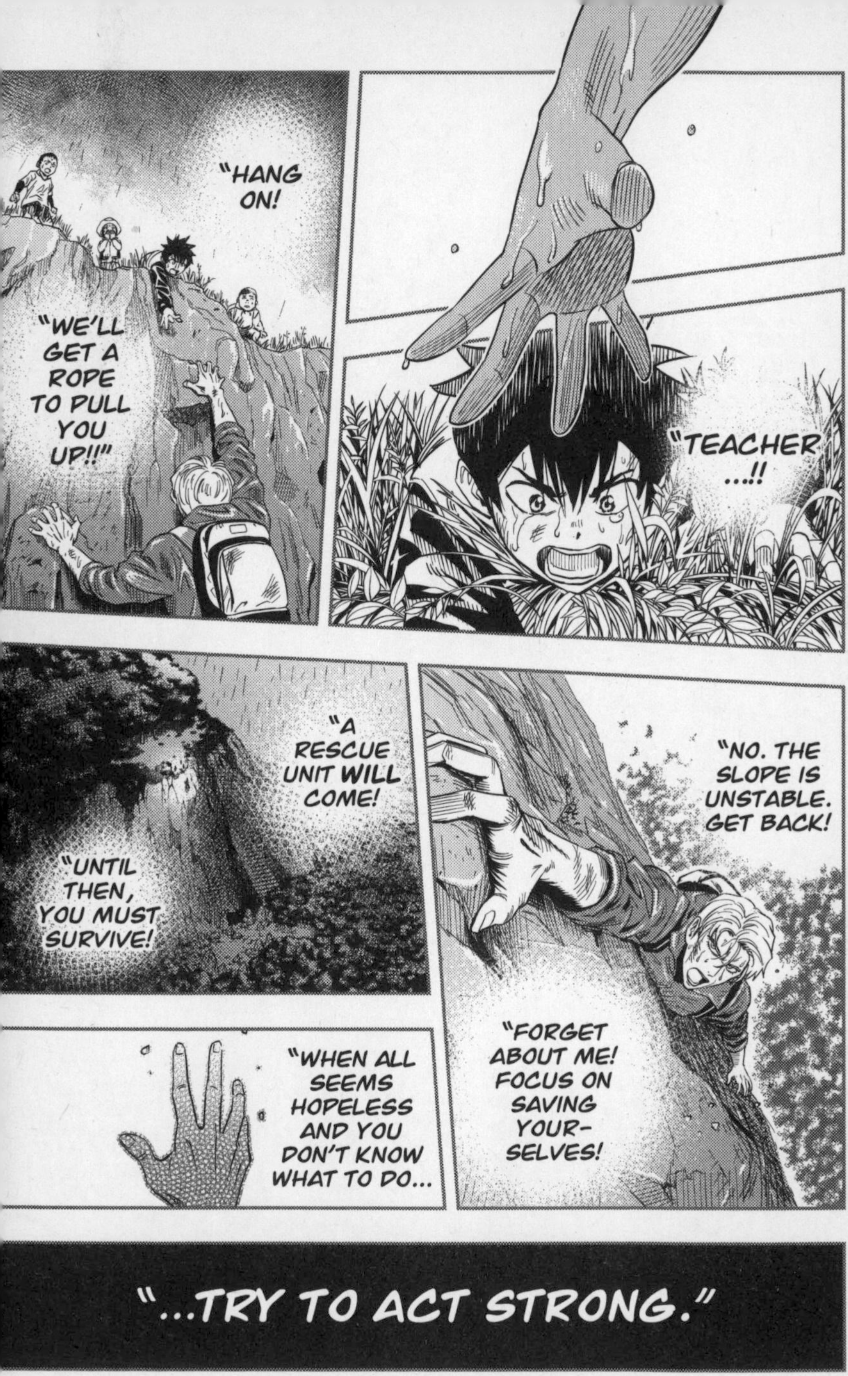
"TEACHER ...!!
"HANG ON!
"WE'LL GET A ROPE TO PULL YOU UP!!"
"NO. THE SLOPE IS UNSTABLE. GET BACK!
"FORGET ABOUT ME! FOCUS ON SAVING YOUR-SELVES!
"A RESCUE UNIT WILL COME!
"UNTIL THEN, YOU MUST SURVIVE!
"WHEN ALL SEEMS HOPELESS AND YOU DON'T KNOW WHAT TO DO...
"...TRY TO ACT STRONG."

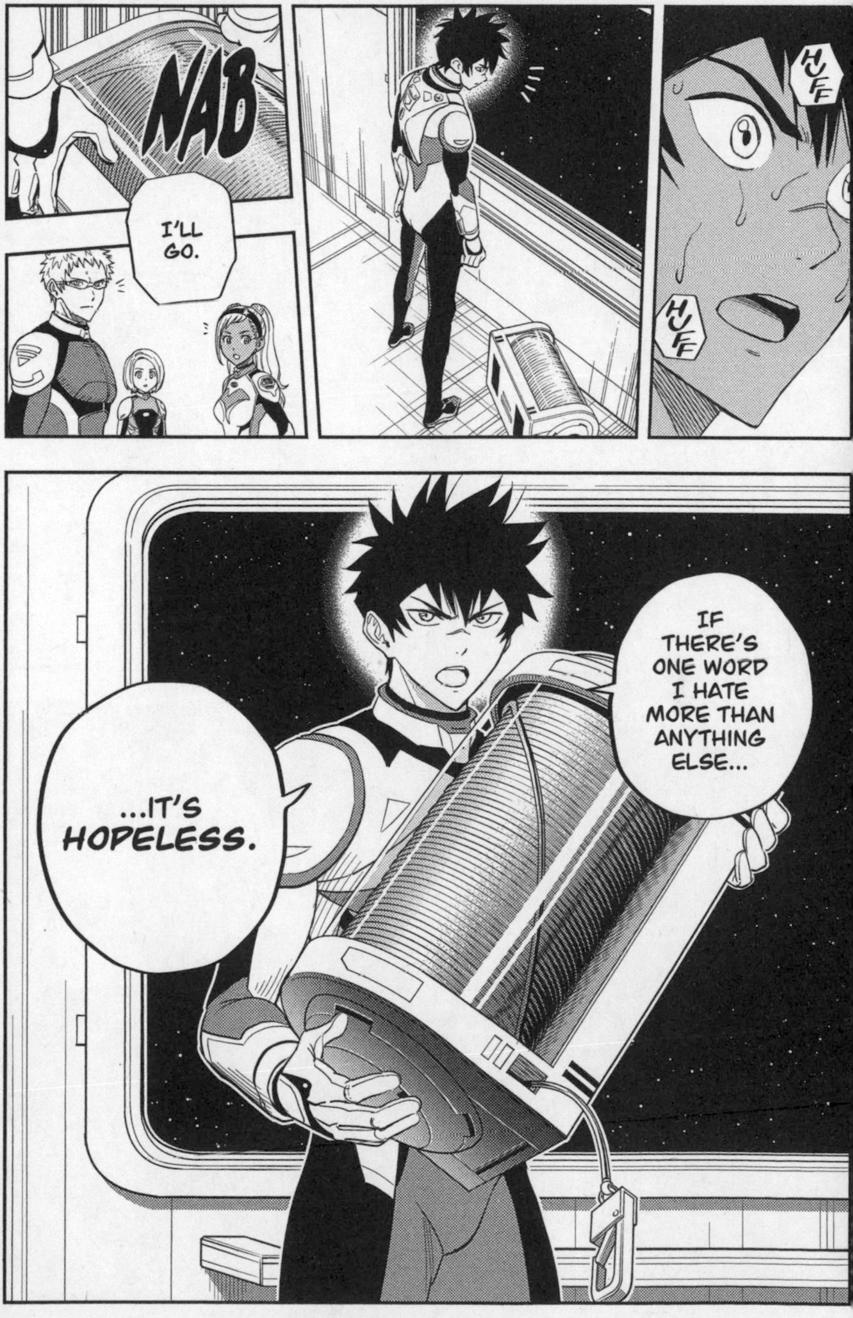
HUFF
HUFF
NAB
I'LL GO.
IF THERE'S ONE WORD I HATE MORE THAN ANYTHING ELSE...
...IT'S HOPELESS.

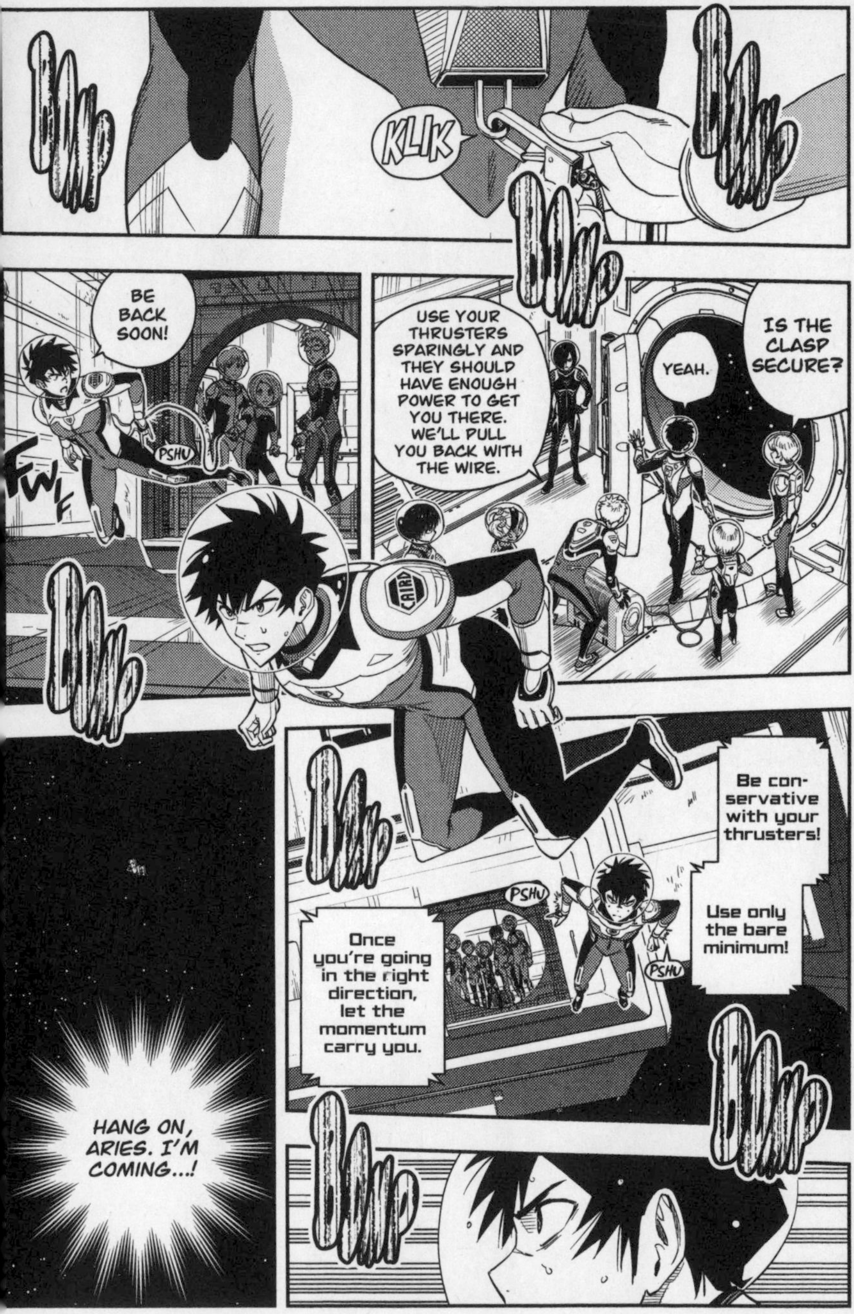
KLIK
IS THE CLASP SECURE?
YEAH.
USE YOUR THRUSTERS SPARINGLY AND THEY SHOULD HAVE ENOUGH POWER TO GET YOU THERE. WE'LL PULL YOU BACK WITH THE WIRE.
BE BACK SOON!
PSHU
FWIF
Be conservative with your thrusters!
Use only the bare minimum!
PSHU
PSHU
Once you're going in the right direction, let the momentum carry you.
HANG ON, ARIES. I'M COMING...!

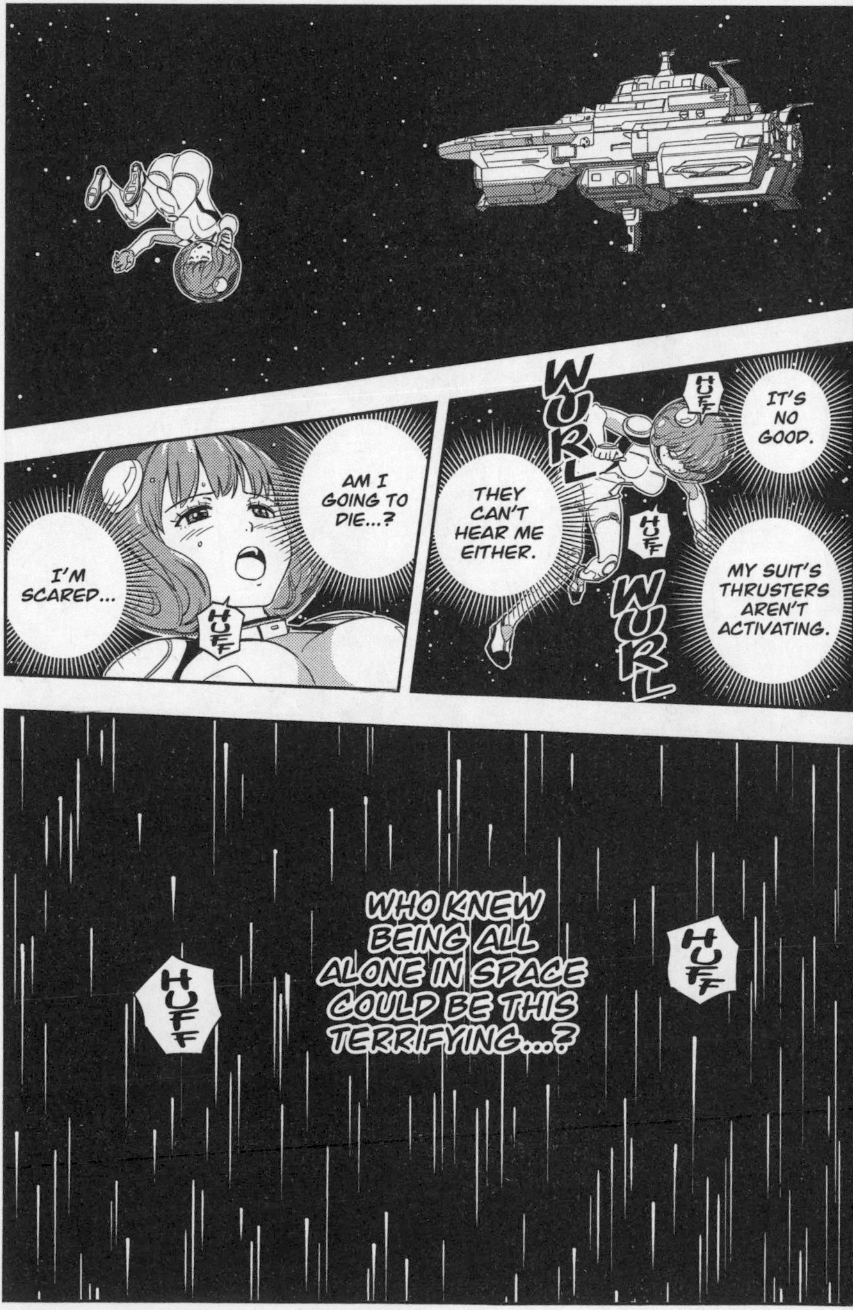
IT'S NO GOOD.
HUFF
WURL
THEY CAN'T HEAR ME EITHER.
HUFF
MY SUIT'S THRUSTERS AREN'T ACTIVATING.
WURL
AM I GOING TO DIE...?
I'M SCARED...
HUFF
HUFF
WHO KNEW BEING ALL ALONE IN SPACE COULD BE THIS TERRIFYING...?
HUFF

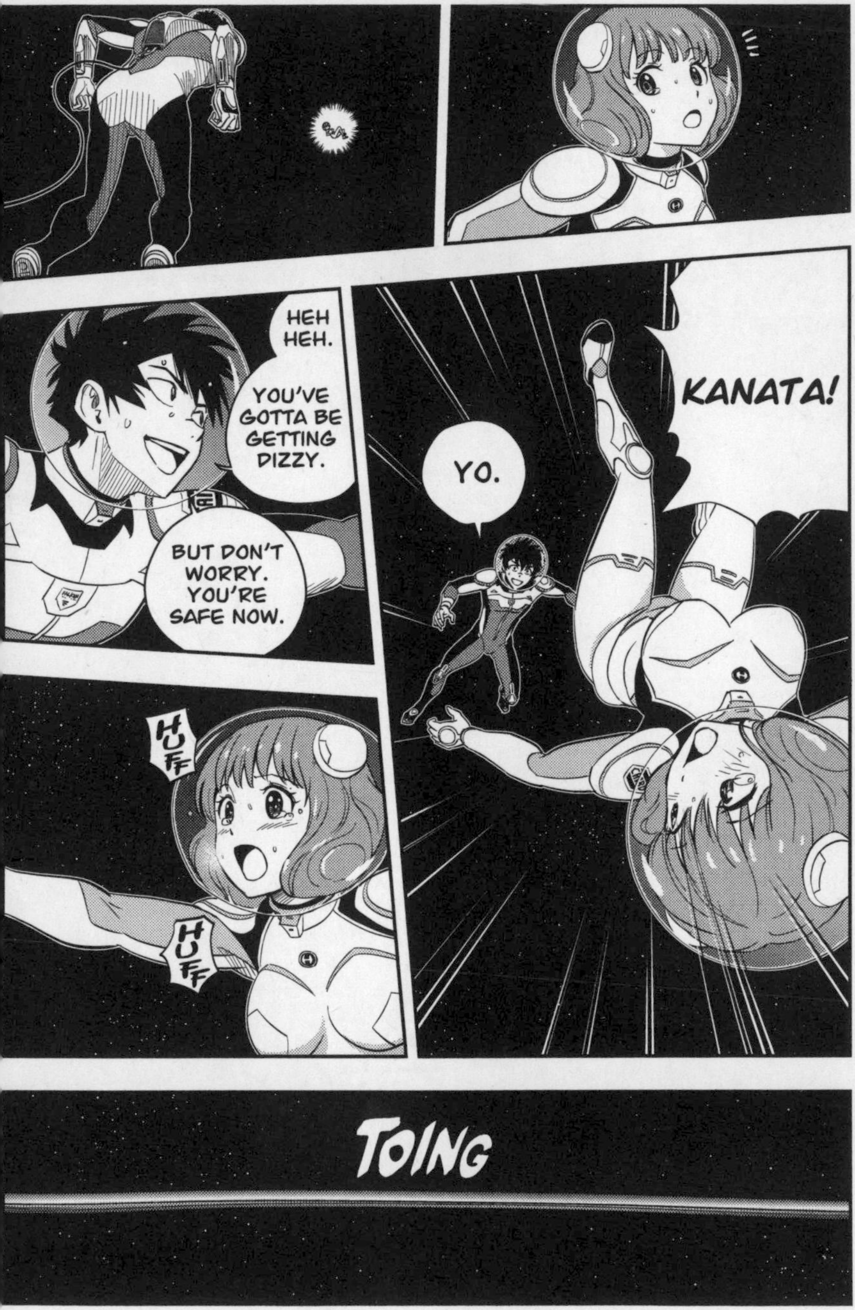
KANATA!
YO.
HEH HEH.
YOU'VE GOTTA BE GETTING DIZZY.
BUT DON'T WORRY. YOU'RE SAFE NOW.
HUFF
HUFF
TOING

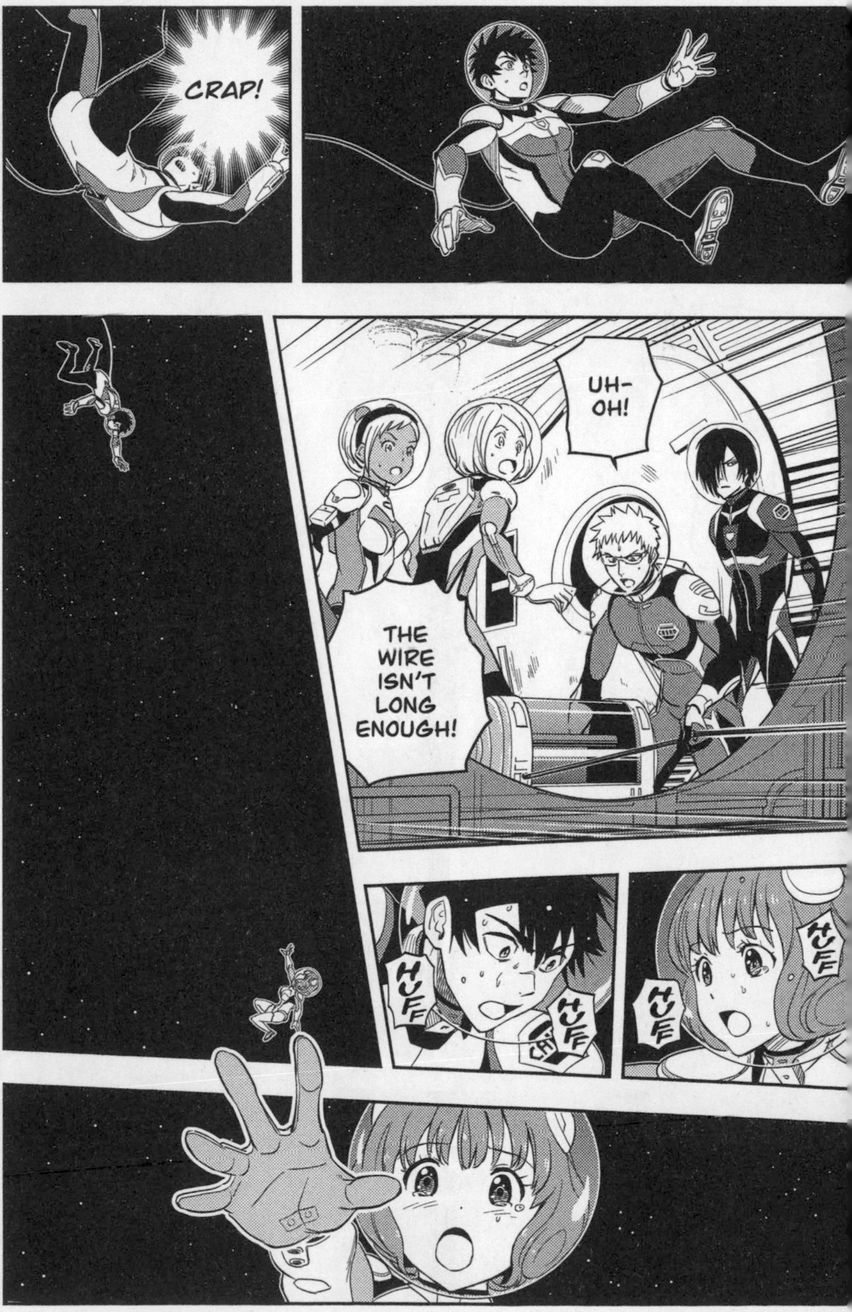
CRAP!
UH-OH!
THE WIRE ISN'T LONG ENOUGH!
HUFF
HUFF
HUFF
HUFF

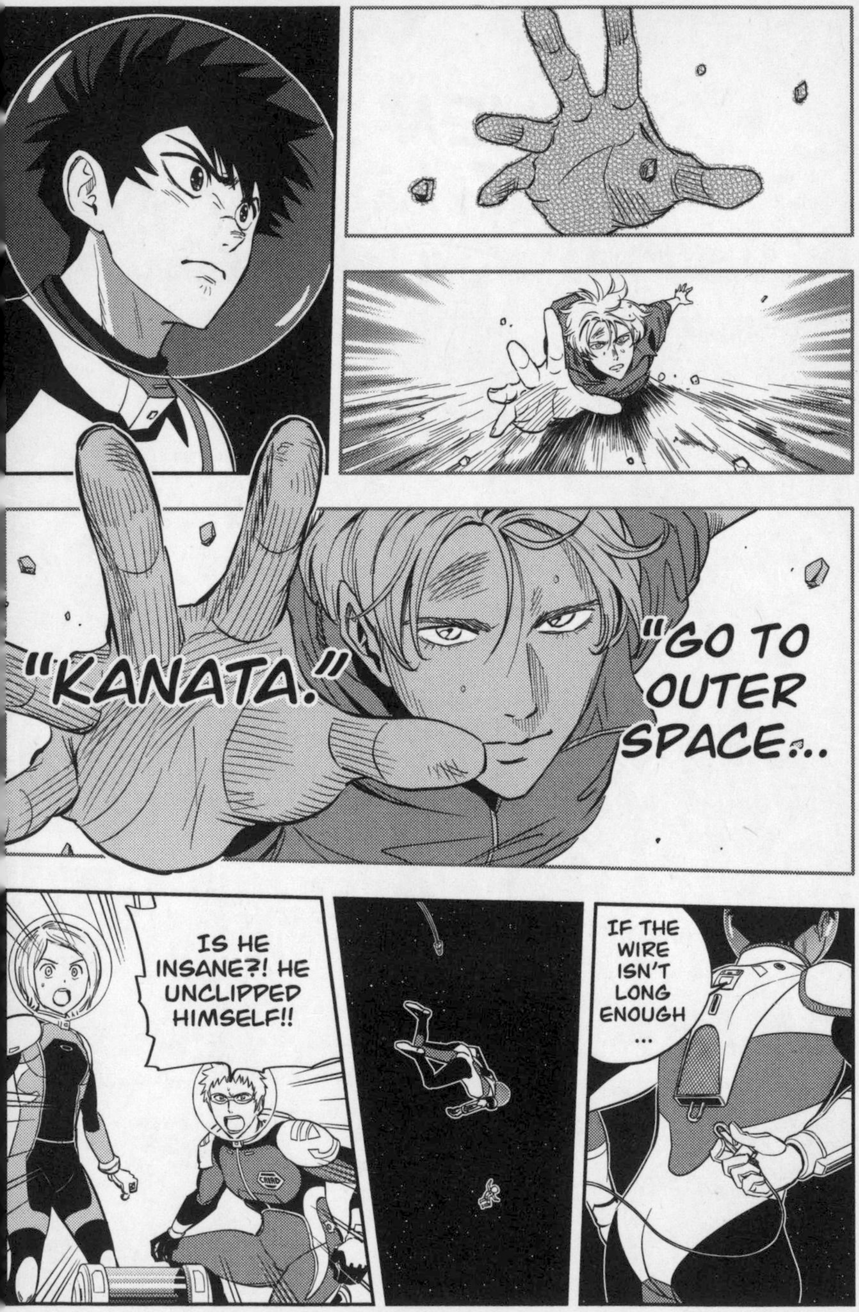
"GO TO OUTER SPACE...
"KANATA."
IF THE WIRE ISN'T LONG ENOUGH ...
IS HE INSANE?! HE UNCLIPPED HIMSELF!!

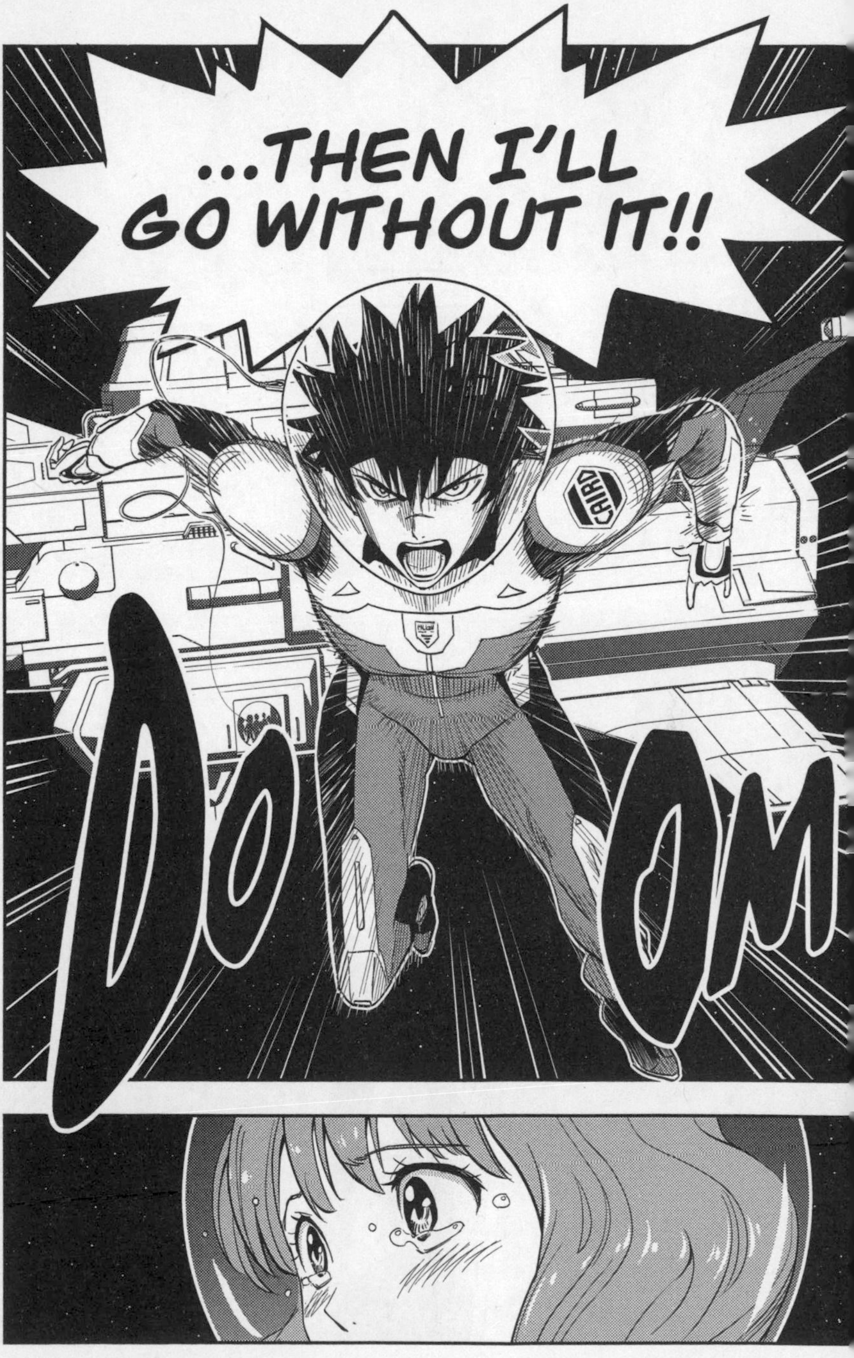
...THEN I'LL GO WITHOUT IT!!
CAIRD
DOOM

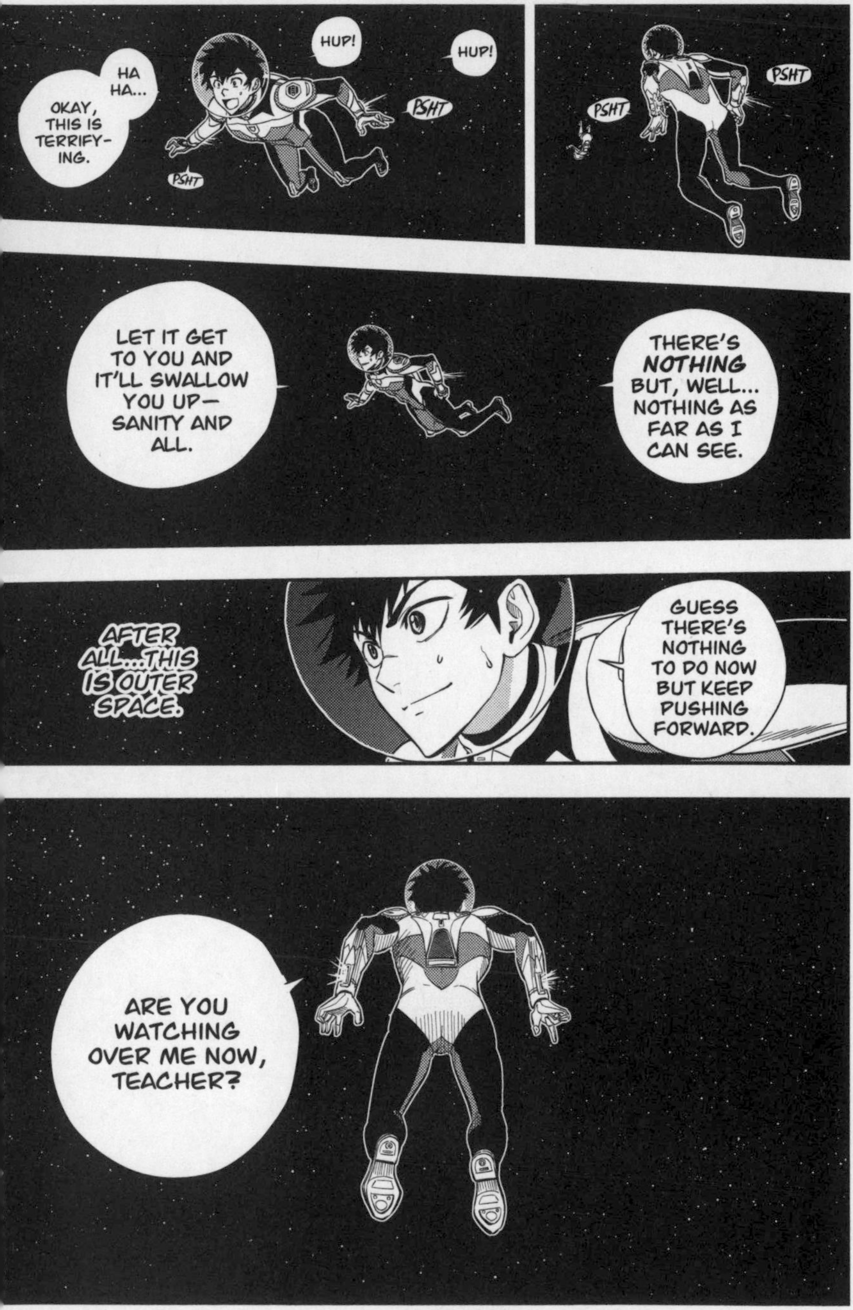
PSHT
PSHT
HUP!
HUP!
PSHT
HA HA... OKAY, THIS IS TERRIFYING.
PSHT
THERE'S NOTHING BUT, WELL... NOTHING AS FAR AS I CAN SEE.
LET IT GET TO YOU AND IT'LL SWALLOW YOU UP—SANITY AND ALL.
GUESS THERE'S NOTHING TO DO NOW BUT KEEP PUSHING FORWARD.
AFTER ALL...THIS IS OUTER SPACE.
ARE YOU WATCHING OVER ME NOW, TEACHER?

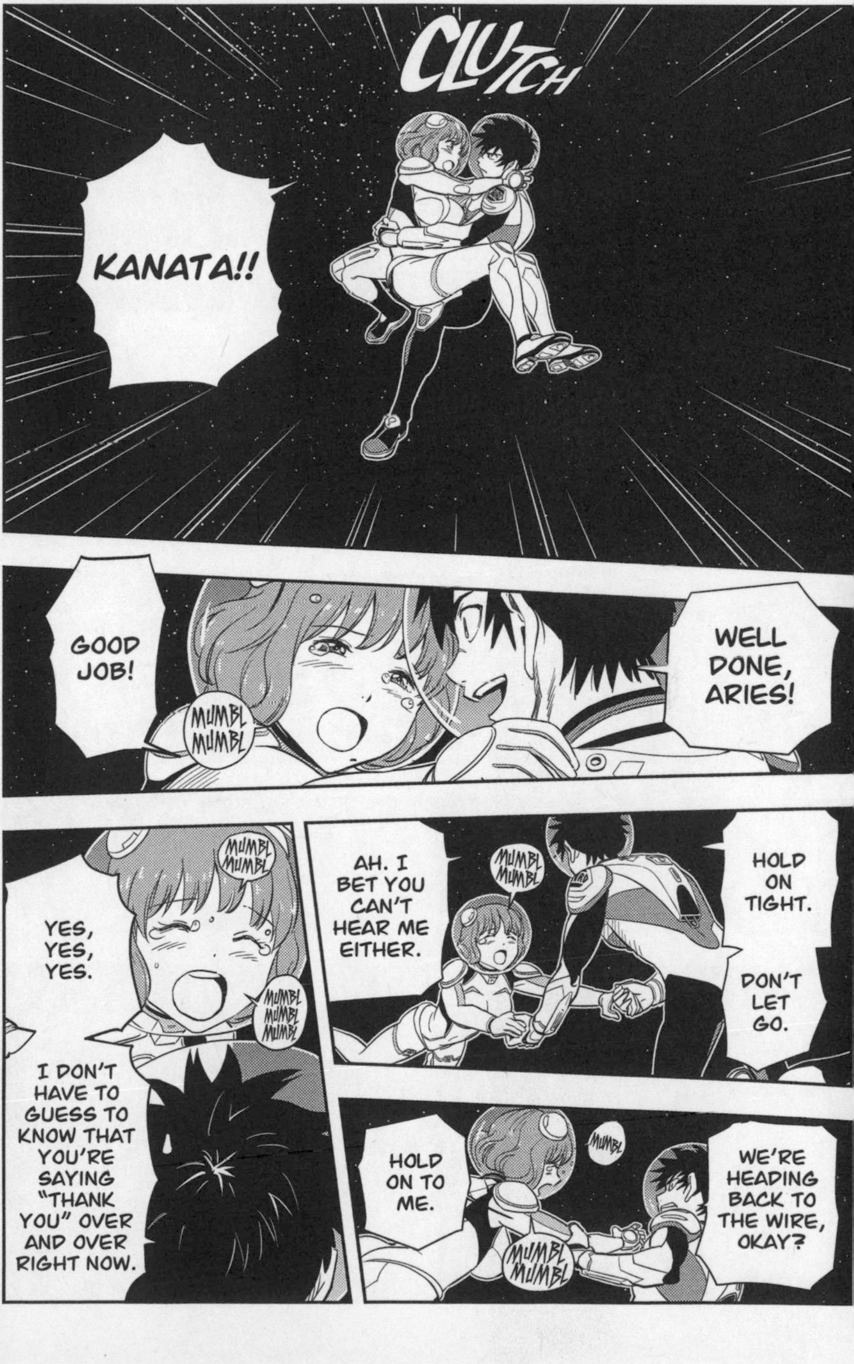
CLUTCH
KANATA!!
WELL DONE, ARIES!
GOOD JOB!
MUMBL MUMBL
HOLD ON TIGHT.
DON'T LET GO.
MUMBL MUMBL
AH. I BET YOU CAN'T HEAR ME EITHER.
WE'RE HEADING BACK TO THE WIRE, OKAY?
MUMBL
HOLD ON TO ME.
MUMBL MUMBL
MUMBL MUMBL
YES, YES, YES.
MUMBL MUMBL MUMBL
I DON'T HAVE TO GUESS TO KNOW THAT YOU'RE SAYING "THANK YOU" OVER AND OVER RIGHT NOW.

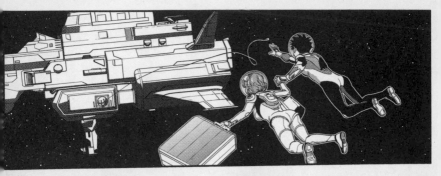

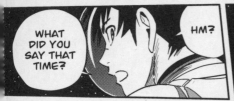

MUMBL MUMBL
HM?
WHAT DID YOU SAY THAT TIME?
"I WAS SO SCARED BEFORE...
"...BUT NOW THAT I HAVE A HAND TO HOLD ON TO...
"...SPACE SUDDENLY LOOKS MUCH MORE BEAUTIFUL TO ME."
THAT'S WHAT I SAID.

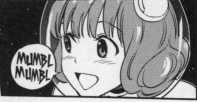

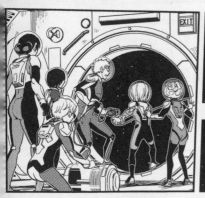

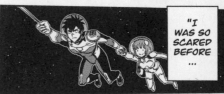

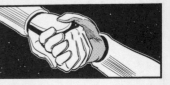

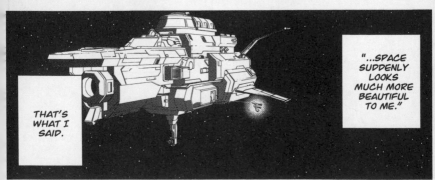

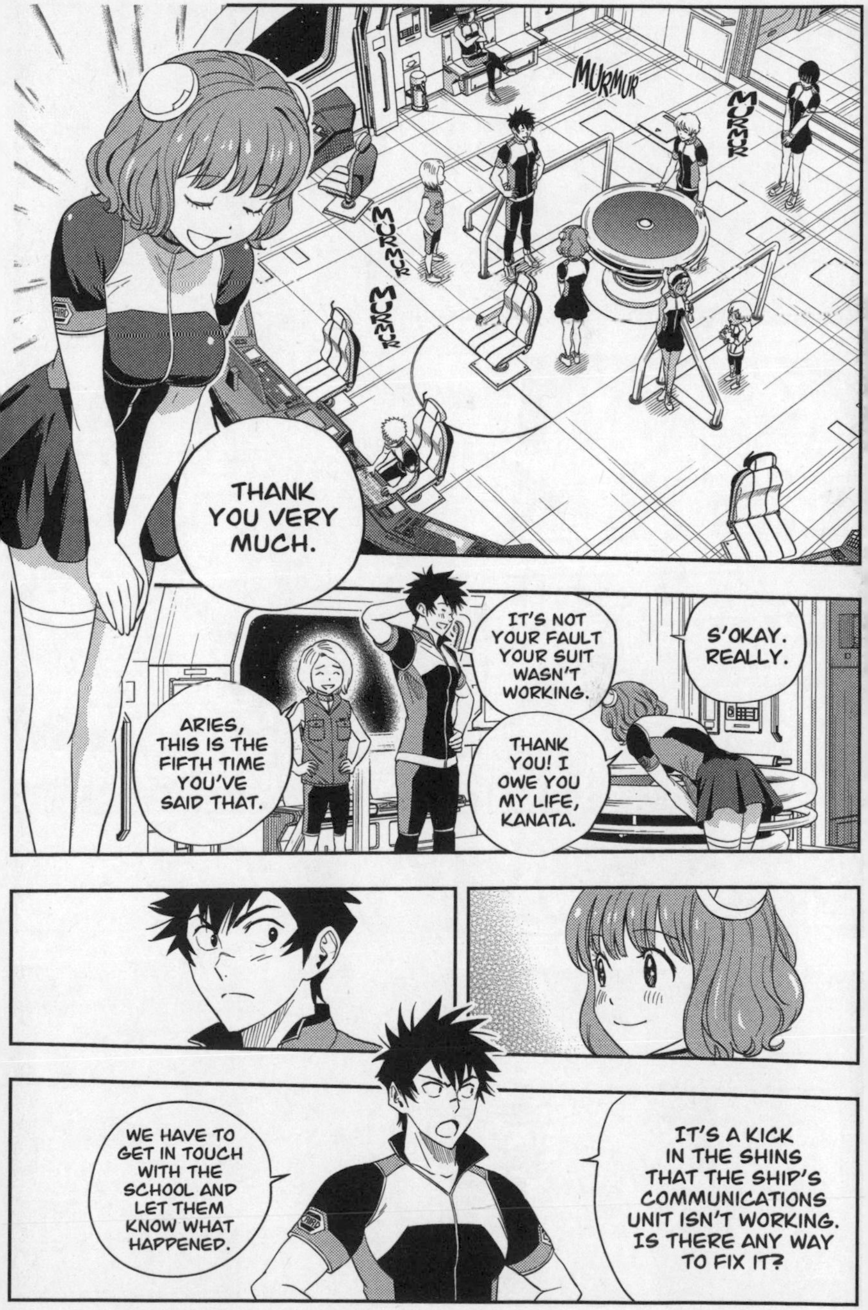
MURMUR
MURMUR
MURMUR
MURMUR
THANK YOU VERY MUCH.
S'OKAY. REALLY.
IT'S NOT YOUR FAULT YOUR SUIT WASN'T WORKING.
THANK YOU! I OWE YOU MY LIFE, KANATA.
ARIES, THIS IS THE FIFTH TIME YOU'VE SAID THAT.
IT'S A KICK IN THE SHINS THAT THE SHIP'S COMMUNICATIONS UNIT ISN'T WORKING. IS THERE ANY WAY TO FIX IT?
WE HAVE TO GET IN TOUCH WITH THE SCHOOL AND LET THEM KNOW WHAT HAPPENED.

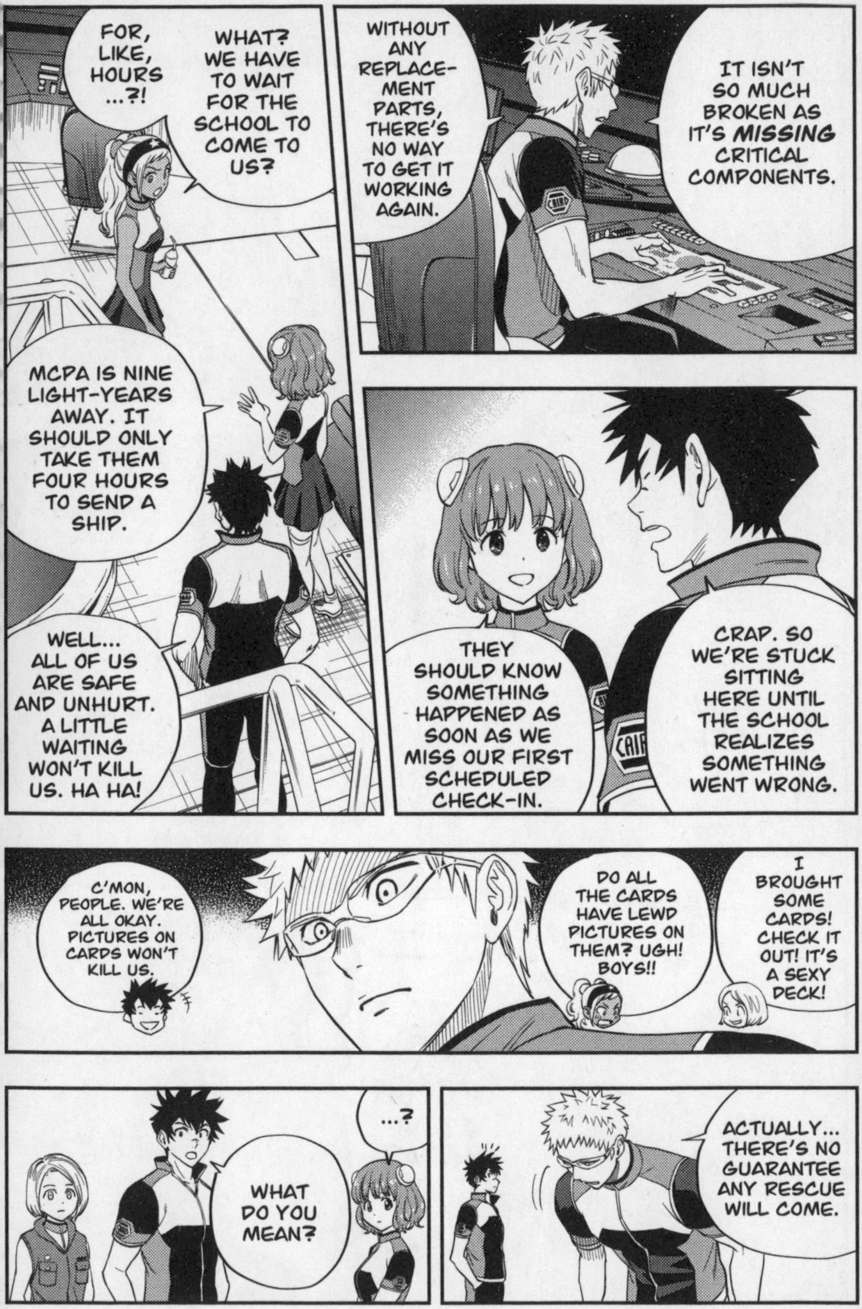
IT ISN'T SO MUCH BROKEN AS IT'S *MISSING* CRITICAL COMPONENTS.
WITHOUT ANY REPLACE-MENT PARTS, THERE'S NO WAY TO GET IT WORKING AGAIN.
CRAP. SO WE'RE STUCK SITTING HERE UNTIL THE SCHOOL REALIZES SOMETHING WENT WRONG.
THEY SHOULD KNOW SOMETHING HAPPENED AS SOON AS WE MISS OUR FIRST SCHEDULED CHECK-IN.
WHAT? WE HAVE TO WAIT FOR THE SCHOOL TO COME TO US?
FOR, LIKE, HOURS ...?!
MCPA IS NINE LIGHT-YEARS AWAY. IT SHOULD ONLY TAKE THEM FOUR HOURS TO SEND A SHIP.
WELL... ALL OF US ARE SAFE AND UNHURT. A LITTLE WAITING WON'T KILL US. HA HA!
I BROUGHT SOME CARDS! CHECK IT OUT! IT'S A SEXY DECK!
DO ALL THE CARDS HAVE LEWD PICTURES ON THEM? UGH! BOYS!!
C'MON, PEOPLE. WE'RE ALL OKAY. PICTURES ON CARDS WON'T KILL US.
ACTUALLY... THERE'S NO GUARANTEE ANY RESCUE WILL COME.
...?
WHAT DO YOU MEAN?

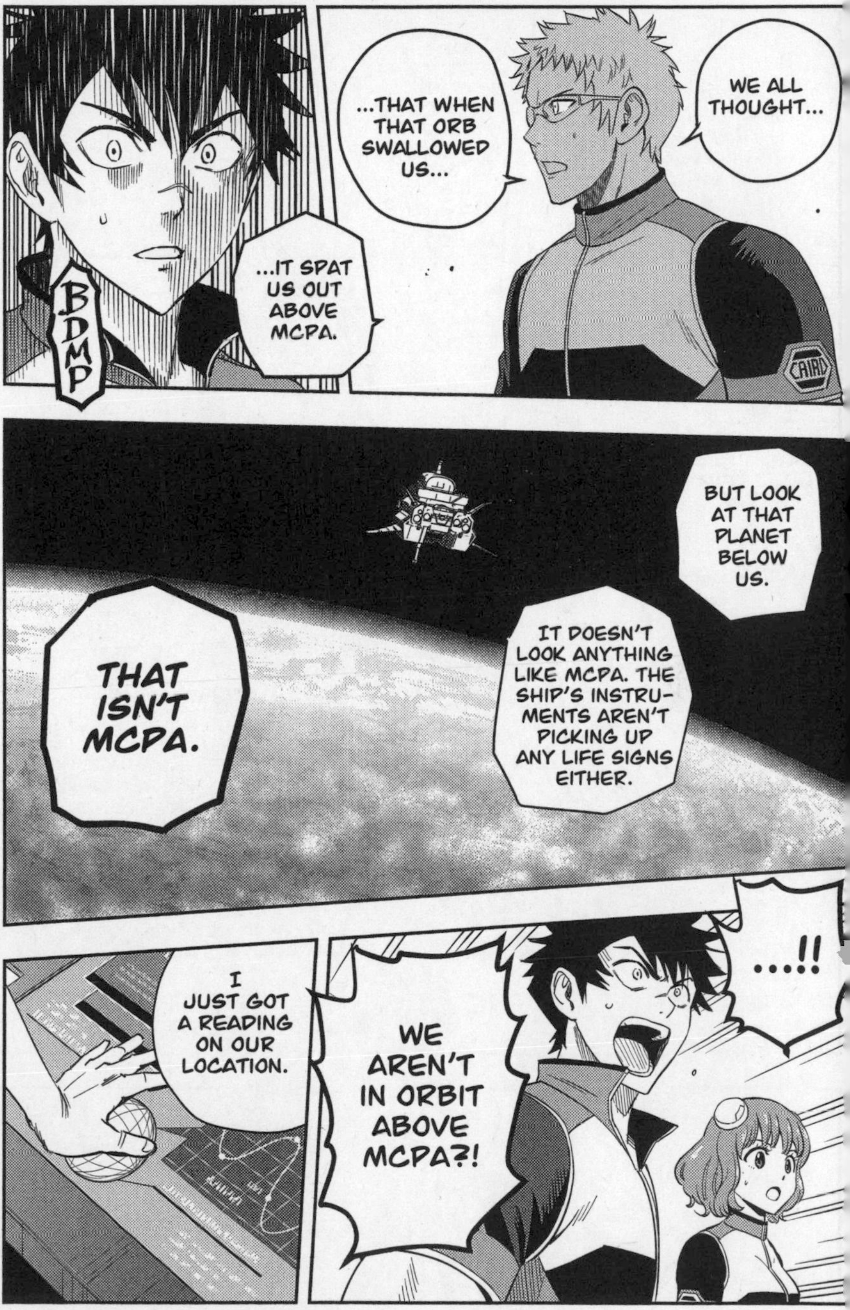
WE ALL THOUGHT...
...THAT WHEN THAT ORB SWALLOWED US...
CAIRD
...IT SPAT US OUT ABOVE MCPA.
BDMP
BUT LOOK AT THAT PLANET BELOW US.
IT DOESN'T LOOK ANYTHING LIKE MCPA. THE SHIP'S INSTRU-MENTS AREN'T PICKING UP ANY LIFE SIGNS EITHER.
THAT ISN'T MCPA.
...!!
WE AREN'T IN ORBIT ABOVE MCPA?!
I JUST GOT A READING ON OUR LOCATION.

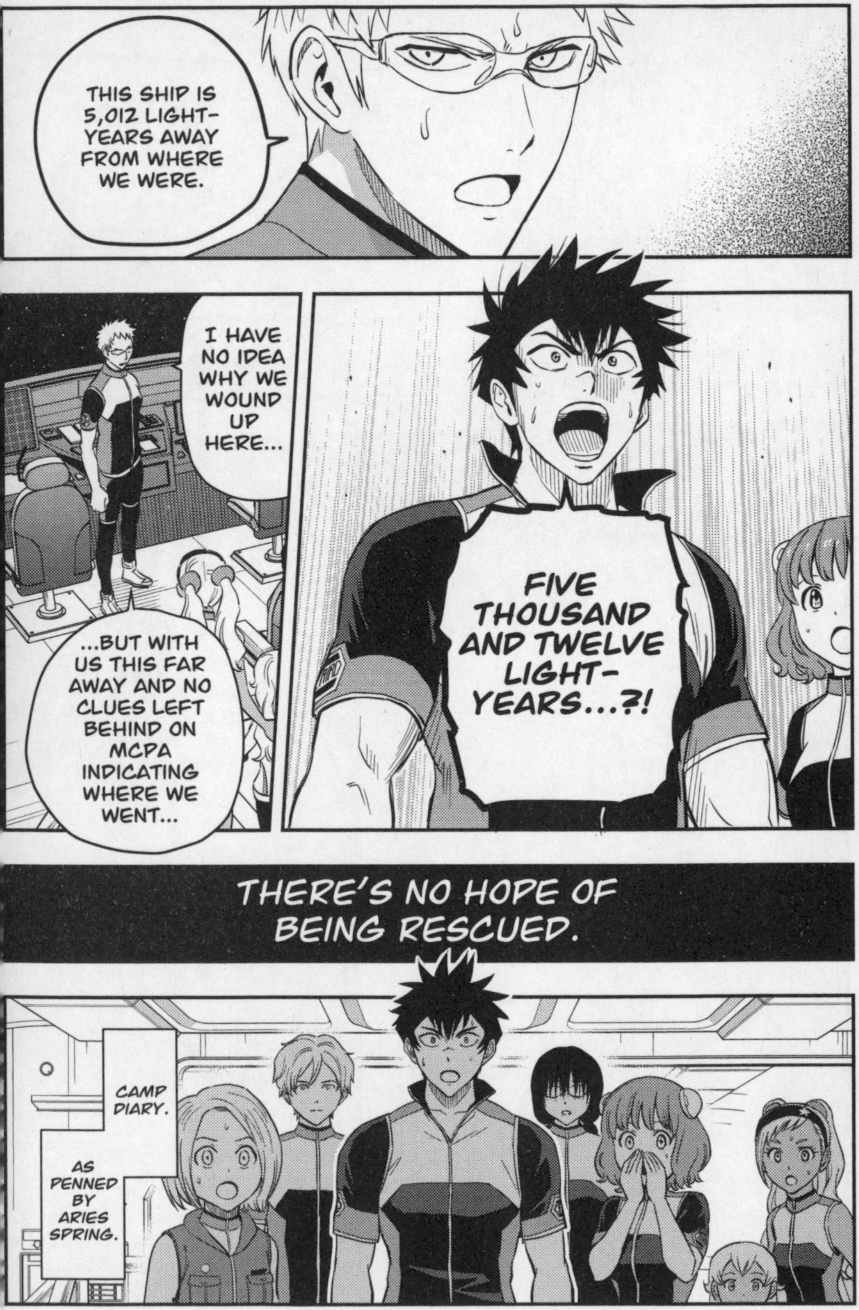
THIS SHIP IS 5,012 LIGHT-YEARS AWAY FROM WHERE WE WERE.
FIVE THOUSAND AND TWELVE LIGHT-YEARS...?!
I HAVE NO IDEA WHY WE WOUND UP HERE...
...BUT WITH US THIS FAR AWAY AND NO CLUES LEFT BEHIND ON MCPA INDICATING WHERE WE WENT...
THERE'S NO HOPE OF BEING RESCUED.
CAMP DIARY.
AS PENNED BY ARIES SPRING.

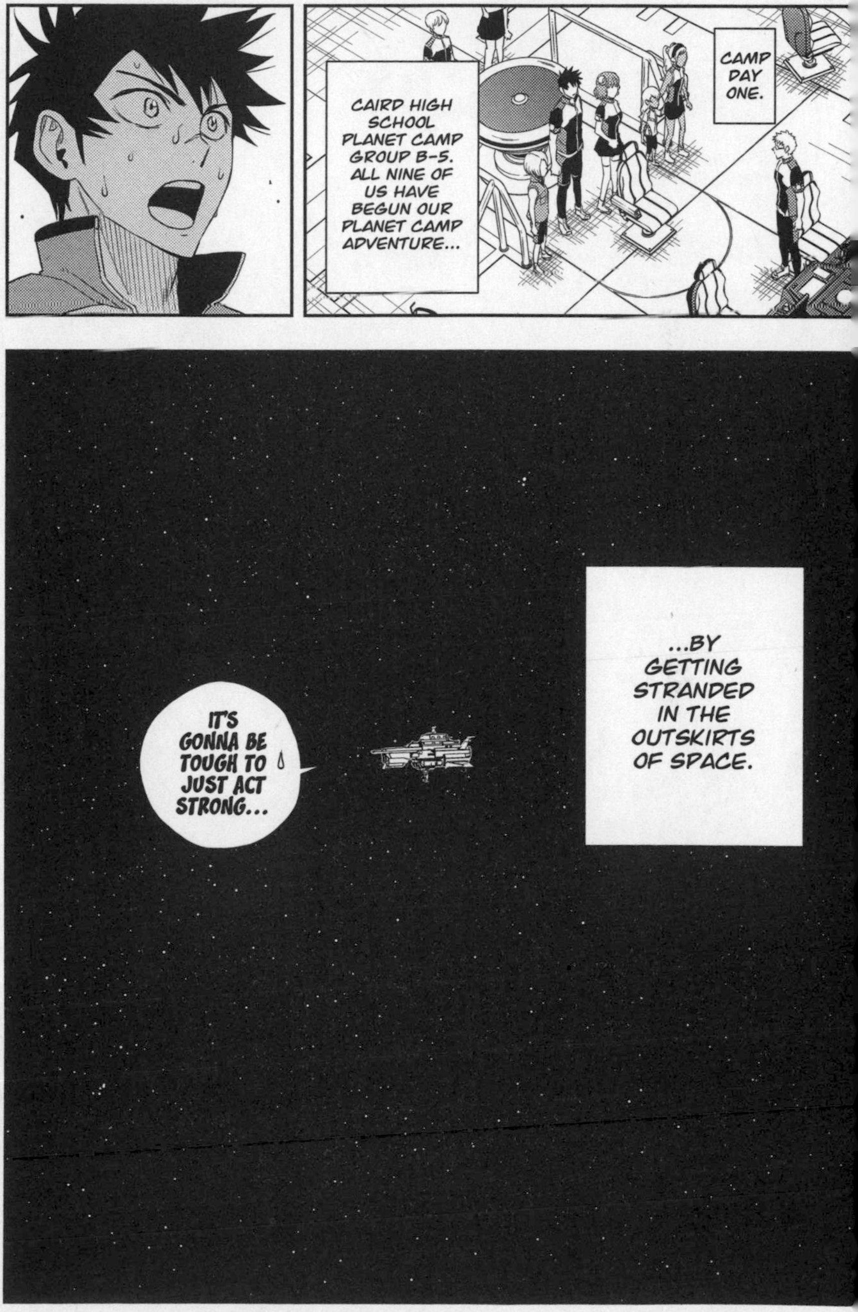
CAMP DAY ONE.
CAIRD HIGH SCHOOL PLANET CAMP GROUP B-5. ALL NINE OF US HAVE BEGUN OUR PLANET CAMP ADVENTURE...
...BY GETTING STRANDED IN THE OUTSKIRTS OF SPACE.
IT'S GONNA BE TOUGH TO JUST ACT STRONG...

Material Collection

01

CRUST SUIT

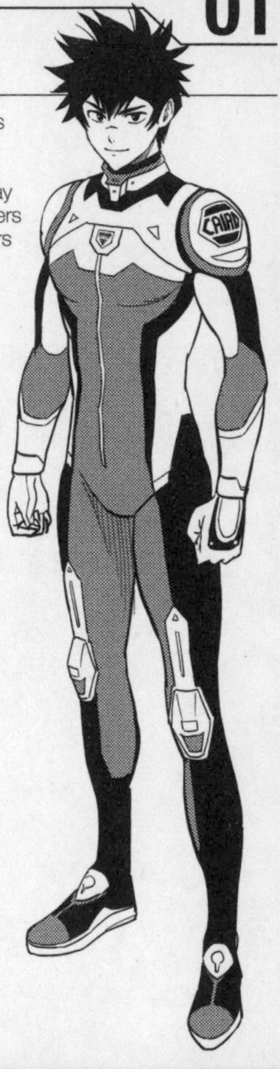

This is a modern space suit made of a special synthetic material that is both hard and flexible. While exceptionally lightweight, the suit still has a fully adjustable internal pressure and temperature system and is also equipped with the necessary systems for short space walks. In this day and age, these suits are as casual as skiwear once was. Various makers have their own designs commercially available, allowing their customers to pick one that fits their sense of fashion.

THRUSTERS

The suits include built-in thruster systems in both wrists and on the back. Control mechanisms are on the palm of each glove.

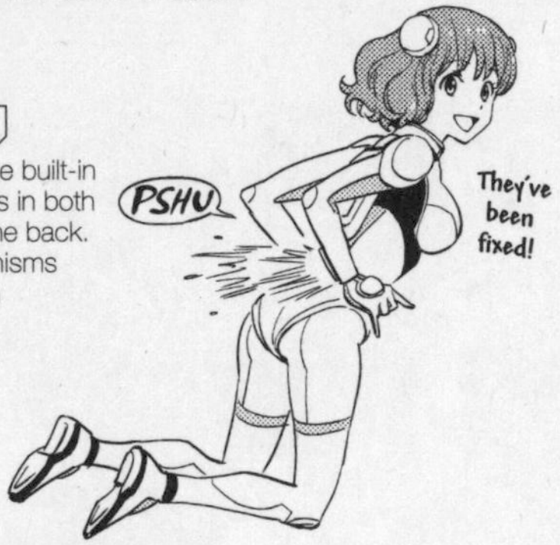
PSHU
They've been fixed!

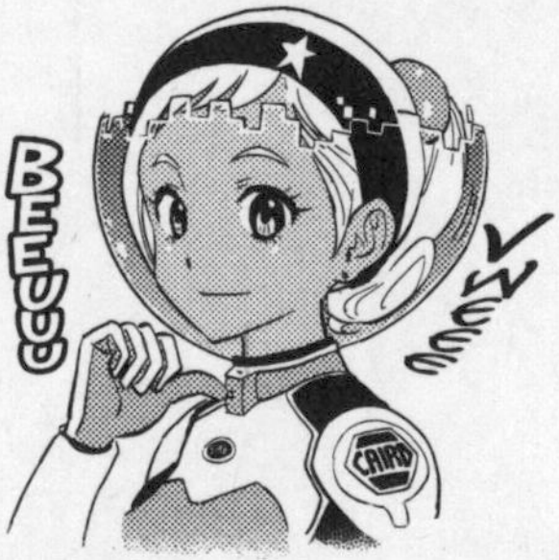
BEEUUU
VWEEEE

HELMET

A clear, bubble-type helmet can be activated by pushing a switch at the neck of the suit. Materializing in less than a second, it automatically sweeps up longer hair into a bundle at its base. Comes with a built-in communication unit.

RIPPER

The ripper is the common clothing-fastener device found in this era. With the press of a button, seams instantly separate or seal back together. Functionally capable of glowing or changing color, rippers are a highly versatile and visible fashion statement.

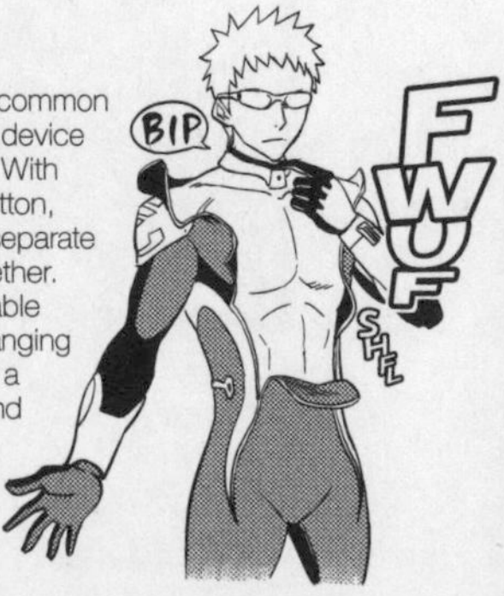
BIP
FWUF
SHL

·GENESIS·

BRANDS

Genesis, Hyperion, SMB and Falken are the four most popular brands.

Hyperion

SMB

FALKEN
New Space Technology

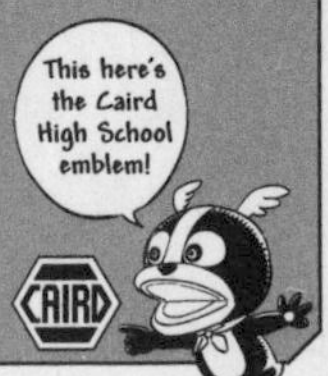
This here's the Caird High School emblem!
CAIRD

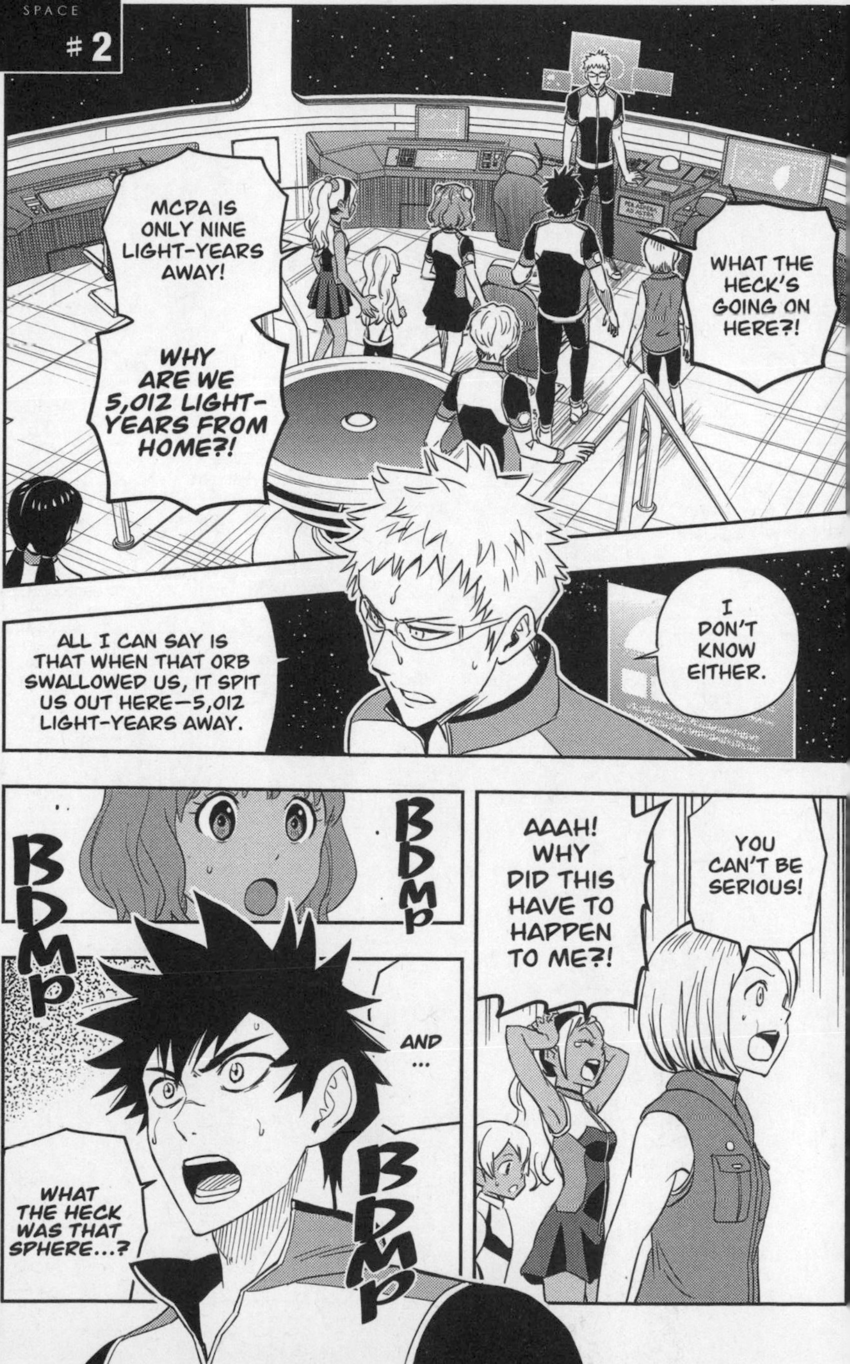
WHAT THE HECK'S GOING ON HERE?!
MCPA IS ONLY NINE LIGHT-YEARS AWAY!
WHY ARE WE 5,012 LIGHT-YEARS FROM HOME?!
I DON'T KNOW EITHER.
ALL I CAN SAY IS THAT WHEN THAT ORB SWALLOWED US, IT SPIT US OUT HERE—5,012 LIGHT-YEARS AWAY.
YOU CAN'T BE SERIOUS!
AAAH! WHY DID THIS HAVE TO HAPPEN TO ME?!
BDMP
BDMP
AND ...
WHAT THE HECK WAS THAT SPHERE...?
BDMP

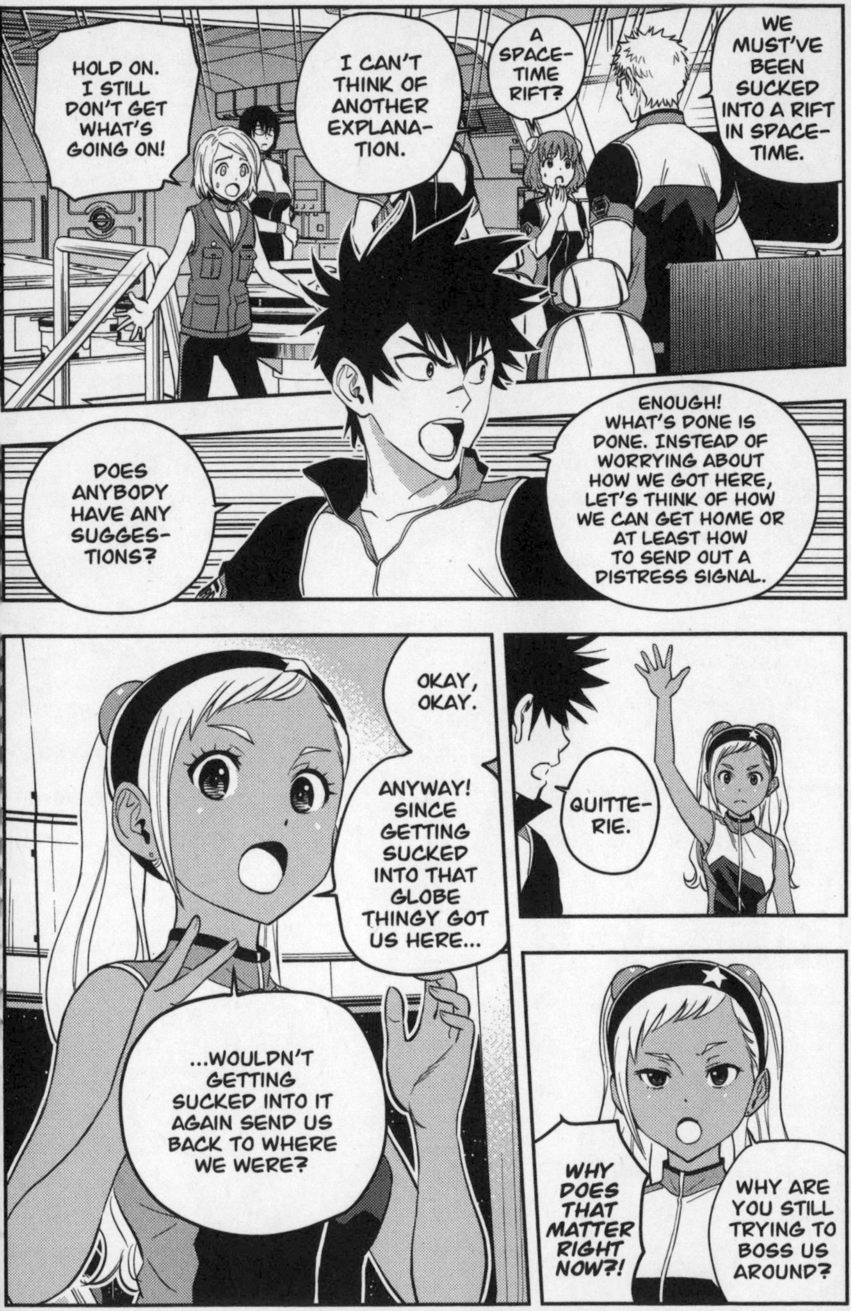
WE MUST'VE BEEN SUCKED INTO A RIFT IN SPACE-TIME.
A SPACE-TIME RIFT?
I CAN'T THINK OF ANOTHER EXPLANATION.
HOLD ON. I STILL DON'T GET WHAT'S GOING ON!
ENOUGH! WHAT'S DONE IS DONE. INSTEAD OF WORRYING ABOUT HOW WE GOT HERE, LET'S THINK OF HOW WE CAN GET HOME OR AT LEAST HOW TO SEND OUT A DISTRESS SIGNAL.
DOES ANYBODY HAVE ANY SUGGESTIONS?
QUITTERIE.
WHY ARE YOU STILL TRYING TO BOSS US AROUND?
WHY DOES THAT MATTER RIGHT NOW?!
OKAY, OKAY.
ANYWAY! SINCE GETTING SUCKED INTO THAT GLOBE THINGY GOT US HERE...
...WOULDN'T GETTING SUCKED INTO IT AGAIN SEND US BACK TO WHERE WE WERE?

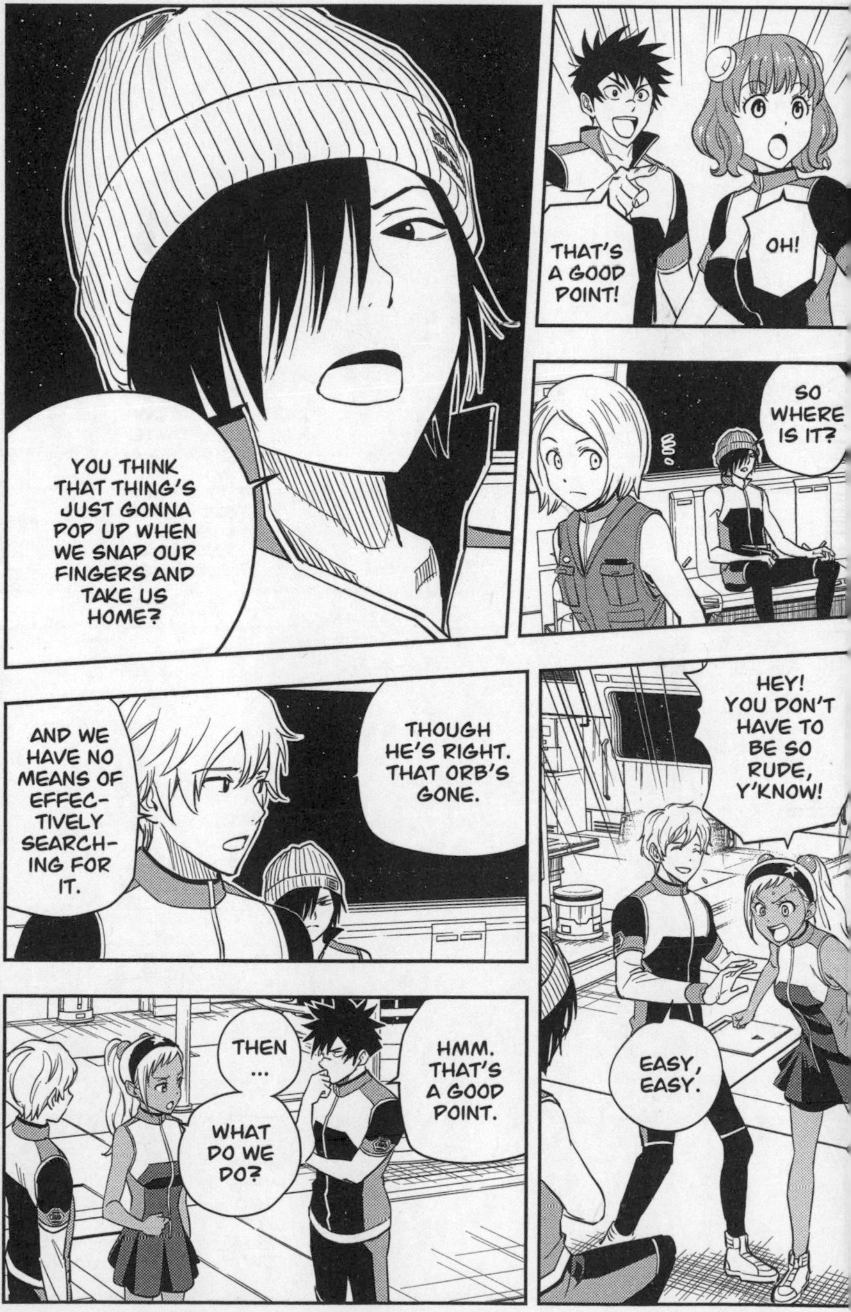
OH!
THAT'S A GOOD POINT!
SO WHERE IS IT?
YOU THINK THAT THING'S JUST GONNA POP UP WHEN WE SNAP OUR FINGERS AND TAKE US HOME?
HEY! YOU DON'T HAVE TO BE SO RUDE, Y'KNOW!
EASY, EASY.
THOUGH HE'S RIGHT. THAT ORB'S GONE.
AND WE HAVE NO MEANS OF EFFEC-TIVELY SEARCH-ING FOR IT.
HMM. THAT'S A GOOD POINT.
THEN ...
WHAT DO WE DO?

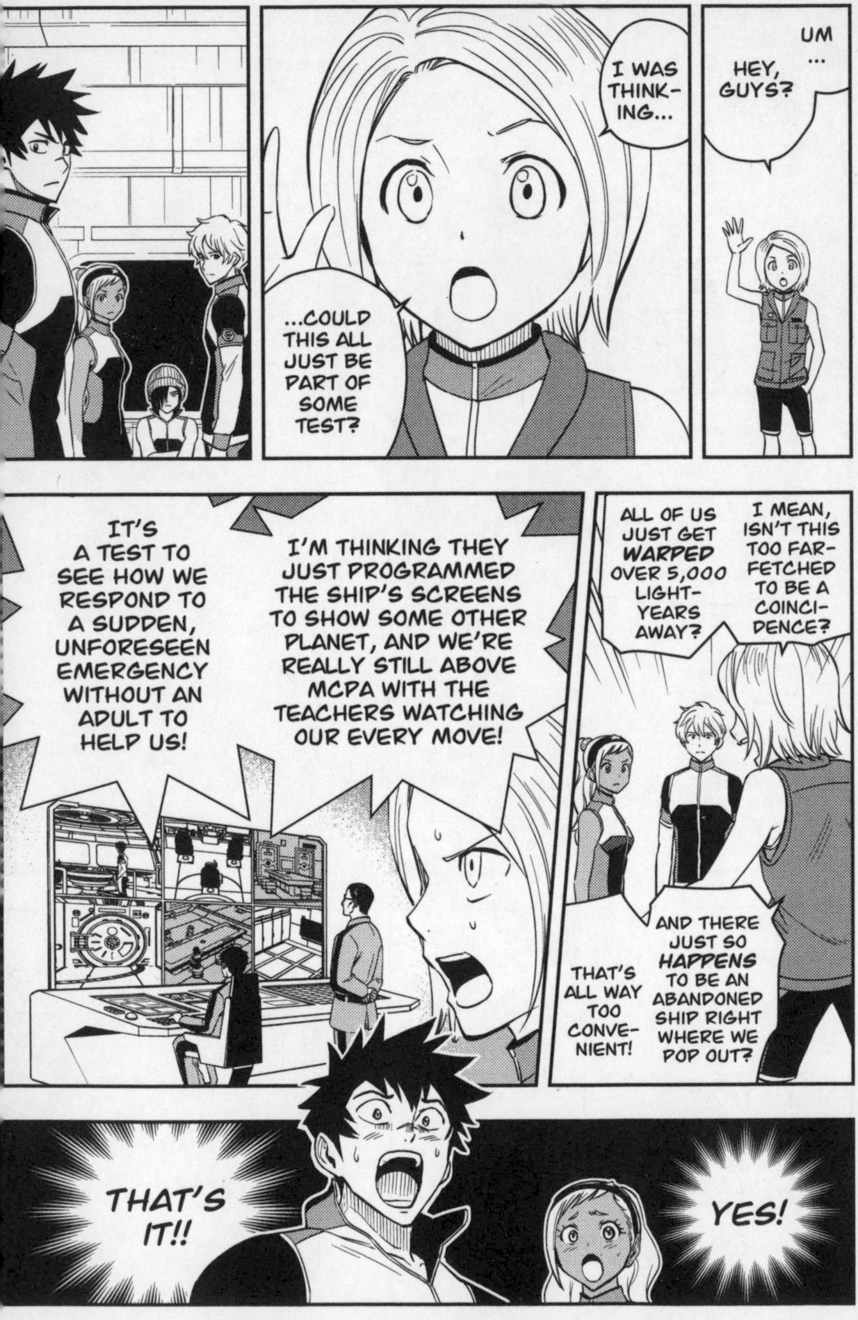
UM ...
HEY, GUYS?
I WAS THINKING...
...COULD THIS ALL JUST BE PART OF SOME TEST?
I MEAN, ISN'T THIS TOO FAR-FETCHED TO BE A COINCIDENCE?
ALL OF US JUST GET WARPED OVER 5,000 LIGHT-YEARS AWAY?
AND THERE JUST SO HAPPENS TO BE AN ABANDONED SHIP RIGHT WHERE WE POP OUT?
THAT'S ALL WAY TOO CONVENIENT!
I'M THINKING THEY JUST PROGRAMMED THE SHIP'S SCREENS TO SHOW SOME OTHER PLANET, AND WE'RE REALLY STILL ABOVE MCPA WITH THE TEACHERS WATCHING OUR EVERY MOVE!
IT'S A TEST TO SEE HOW WE RESPOND TO A SUDDEN, UNFORESEEN EMERGENCY WITHOUT AN ADULT TO HELP US!
YES!
THAT'S IT!!

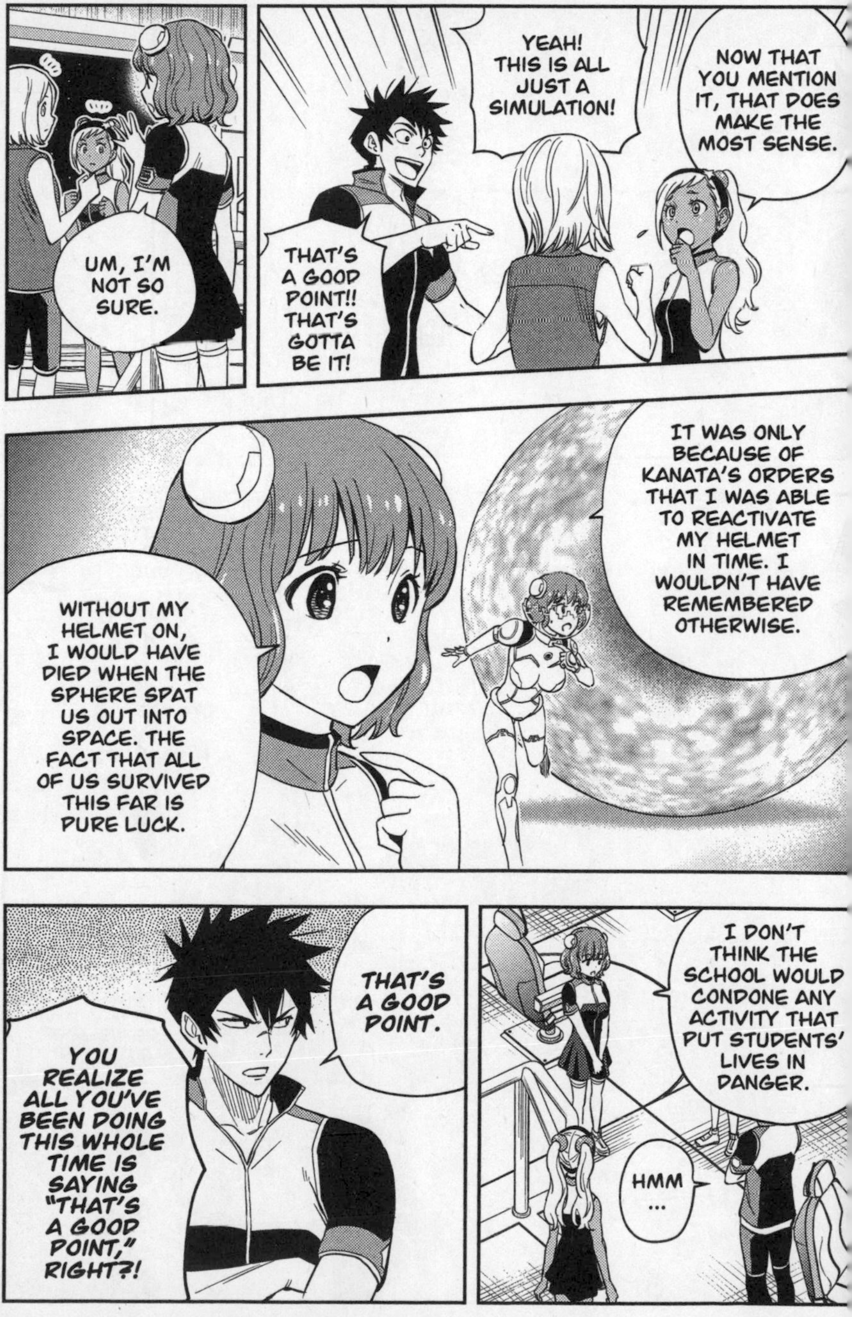
NOW THAT YOU MENTION IT, THAT DOES MAKE THE MOST SENSE.
YEAH! THIS IS ALL JUST A SIMULATION!
THAT'S A GOOD POINT!! THAT'S GOTTA BE IT!
UM, I'M NOT SO SURE.
IT WAS ONLY BECAUSE OF KANATA'S ORDERS THAT I WAS ABLE TO REACTIVATE MY HELMET IN TIME. I WOULDN'T HAVE REMEMBERED OTHERWISE.
WITHOUT MY HELMET ON, I WOULD HAVE DIED WHEN THE SPHERE SPAT US OUT INTO SPACE. THE FACT THAT ALL OF US SURVIVED THIS FAR IS PURE LUCK.
I DON'T THINK THE SCHOOL WOULD CONDONE ANY ACTIVITY THAT PUT STUDENTS' LIVES IN DANGER.
HMM ...
THAT'S A GOOD POINT.
YOU REALIZE ALL YOU'VE BEEN DOING THIS WHOLE TIME IS SAYING "THAT'S A GOOD POINT," RIGHT?!

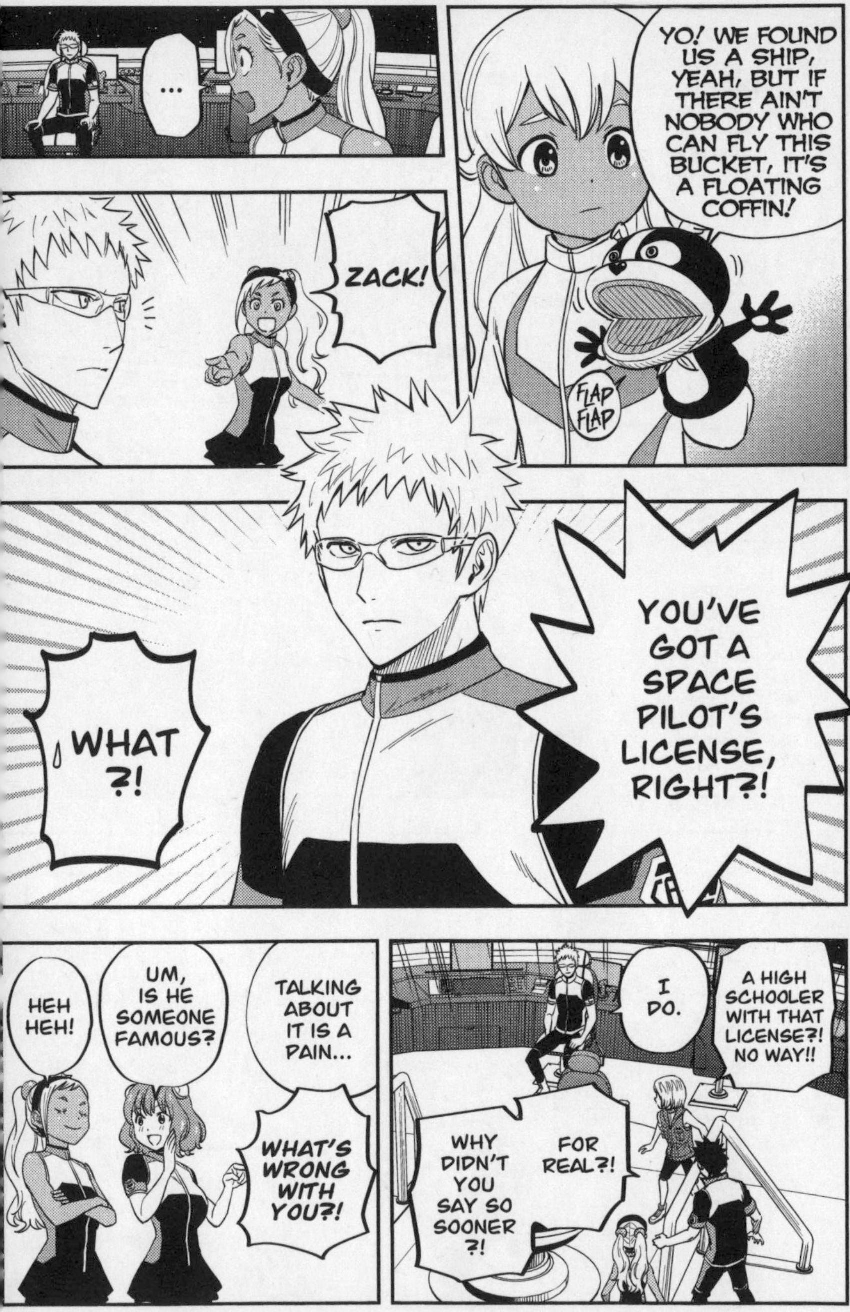
YO! WE FOUND US A SHIP, YEAH, BUT IF THERE AIN'T NOBODY WHO CAN FLY THIS BUCKET, IT'S A FLOATING COFFIN!
FLAP FLAP
...
ZACK!
YOU'VE GOT A SPACE PILOT'S LICENSE, RIGHT?!
WHAT?!
I DO.
A HIGH SCHOOLER WITH THAT LICENSE?! NO WAY!!
FOR REAL?!
WHY DIDN'T YOU SAY SO SOONER?!
TALKING ABOUT IT IS A PAIN...
WHAT'S WRONG WITH YOU?!
UM, IS HE SOMEONE FAMOUS?
HEH HEH!

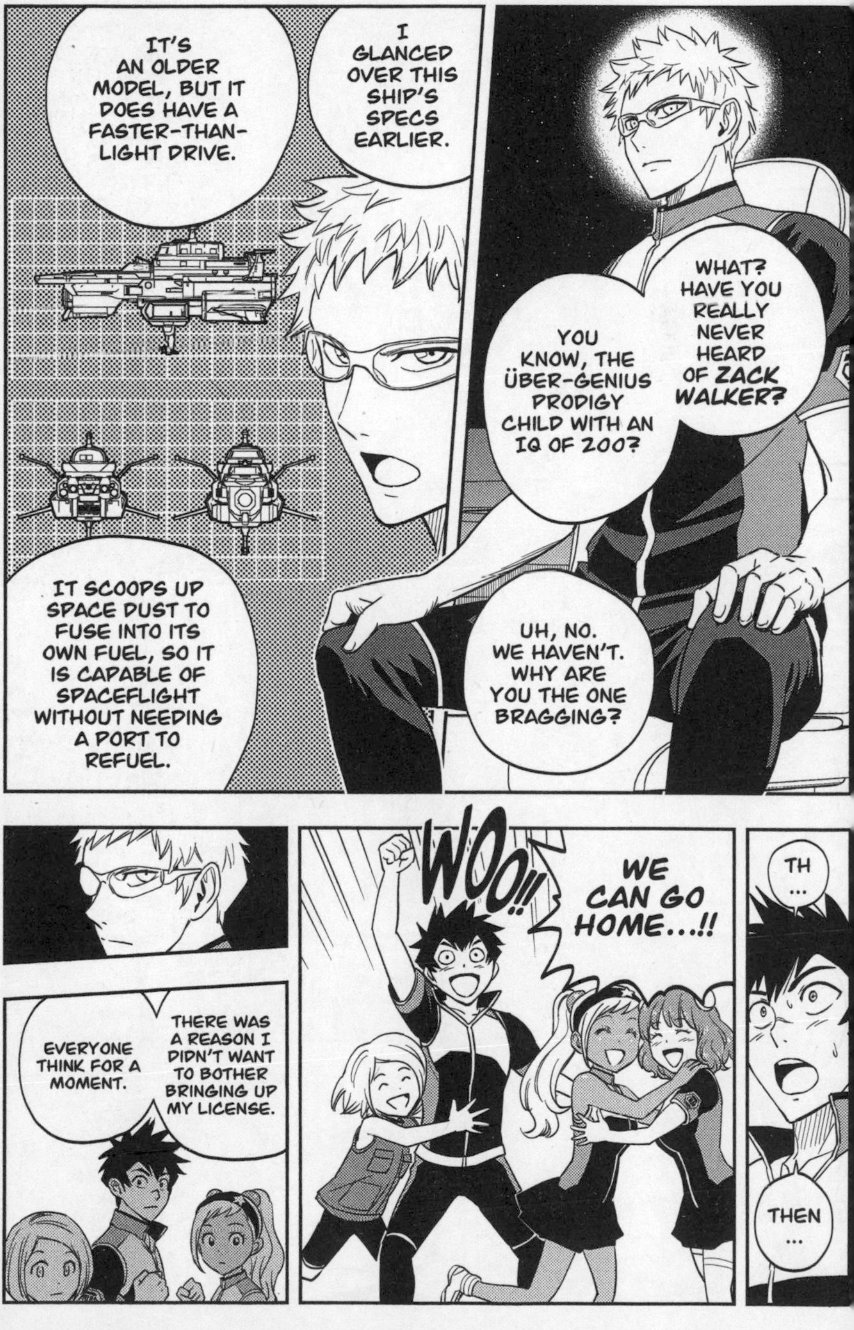
WHAT? HAVE YOU REALLY NEVER HEARD OF ZACK WALKER?
YOU KNOW, THE ÜBER-GENIUS PRODIGY CHILD WITH AN IQ OF 200?
UH, NO. WE HAVEN'T. WHY ARE YOU THE ONE BRAGGING?
I GLANCED OVER THIS SHIP'S SPECS EARLIER.
IT'S AN OLDER MODEL, BUT IT DOES HAVE A FASTER-THAN-LIGHT DRIVE.
IT SCOOPS UP SPACE DUST TO FUSE INTO ITS OWN FUEL, SO IT IS CAPABLE OF SPACEFLIGHT WITHOUT NEEDING A PORT TO REFUEL.
TH...
THEN...
WOO!!
WE CAN GO HOME...!!
THERE WAS A REASON I DIDN'T WANT TO BOTHER BRINGING UP MY LICENSE.
EVERYONE THINK FOR A MOMENT.

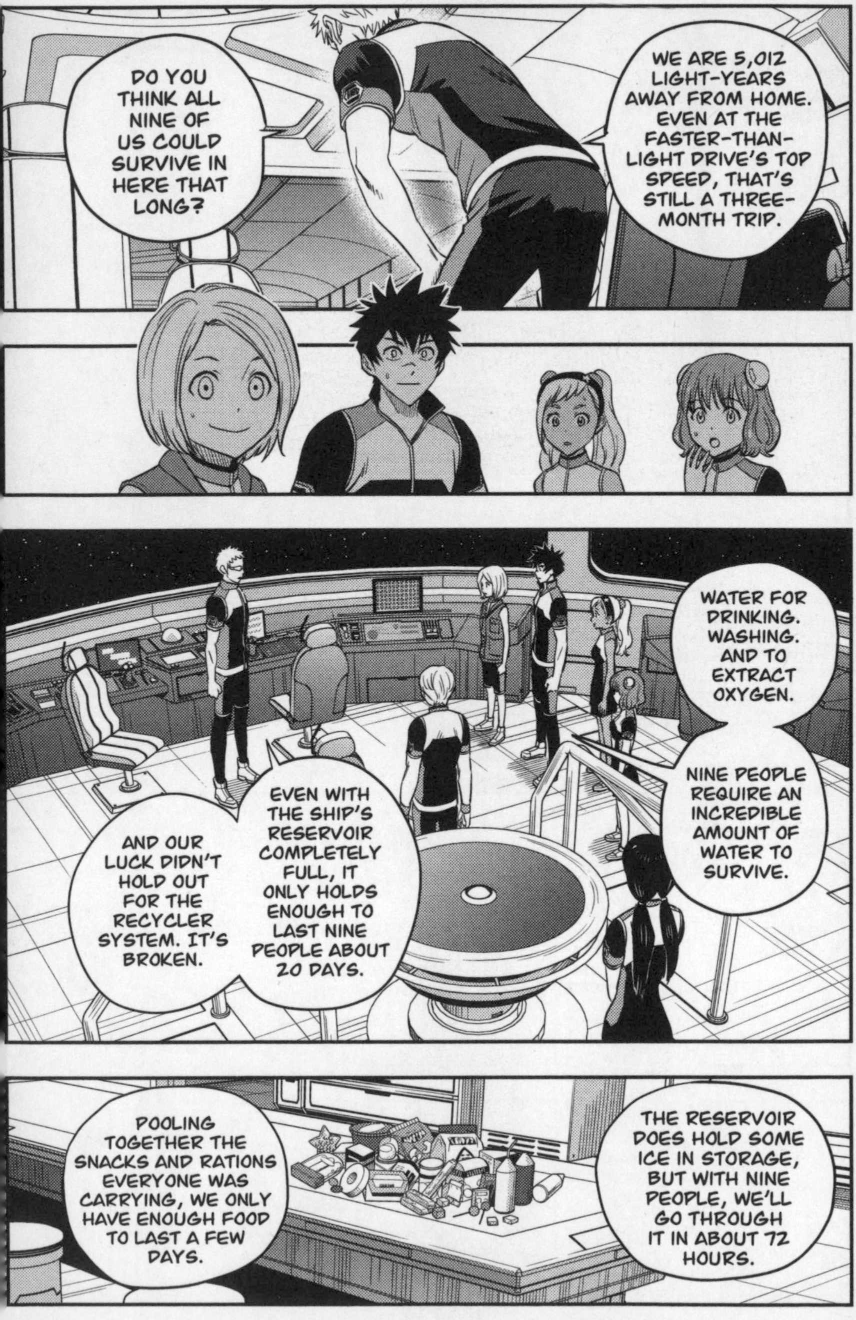
WE ARE 5,012 LIGHT-YEARS AWAY FROM HOME. EVEN AT THE FASTER-THAN-LIGHT DRIVE'S TOP SPEED, THAT'S STILL A THREE-MONTH TRIP.
DO YOU THINK ALL NINE OF US COULD SURVIVE IN HERE THAT LONG?
WATER FOR DRINKING. WASHING. AND TO EXTRACT OXYGEN.
NINE PEOPLE REQUIRE AN INCREDIBLE AMOUNT OF WATER TO SURVIVE.
EVEN WITH THE SHIP'S RESERVOIR COMPLETELY FULL, IT ONLY HOLDS ENOUGH TO LAST NINE PEOPLE ABOUT 20 DAYS.
AND OUR LUCK DIDN'T HOLD OUT FOR THE RECYCLER SYSTEM. IT'S BROKEN.
THE RESERVOIR DOES HOLD SOME ICE IN STORAGE, BUT WITH NINE PEOPLE, WE'LL GO THROUGH IT IN ABOUT 72 HOURS.
POOLING TOGETHER THE SNACKS AND RATIONS EVERYONE WAS CARRYING, WE ONLY HAVE ENOUGH FOOD TO LAST A FEW DAYS.

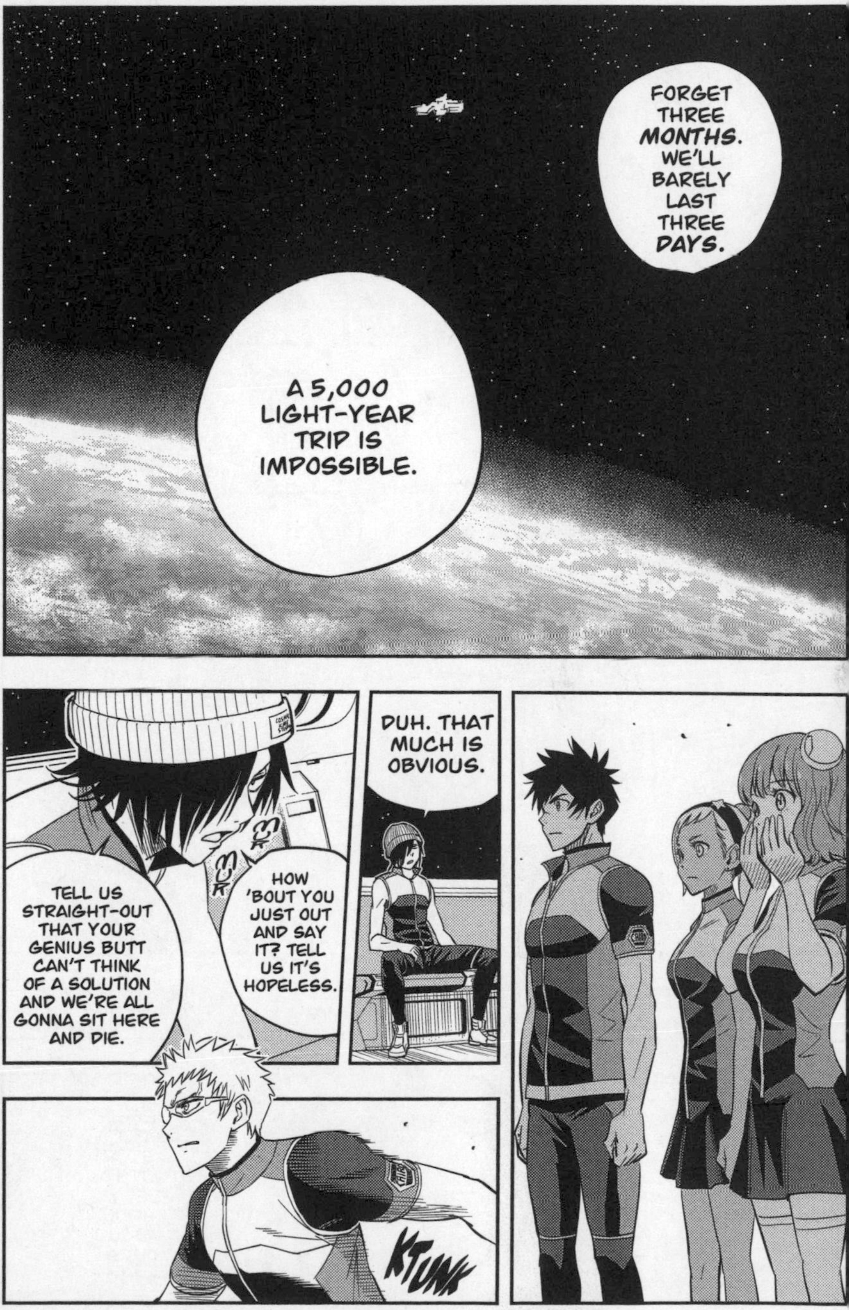
FORGET THREE MONTHS. WE'LL BARELY LAST THREE DAYS.
A 5,000 LIGHT-YEAR TRIP IS IMPOSSIBLE.
DUH. THAT MUCH IS OBVIOUS.
HOW 'BOUT YOU JUST OUT AND SAY IT? TELL US IT'S HOPELESS.
TELL US STRAIGHT-OUT THAT YOUR GENIUS BUTT CAN'T THINK OF A SOLUTION AND WE'RE ALL GONNA SIT HERE AND DIE.
KTUNK

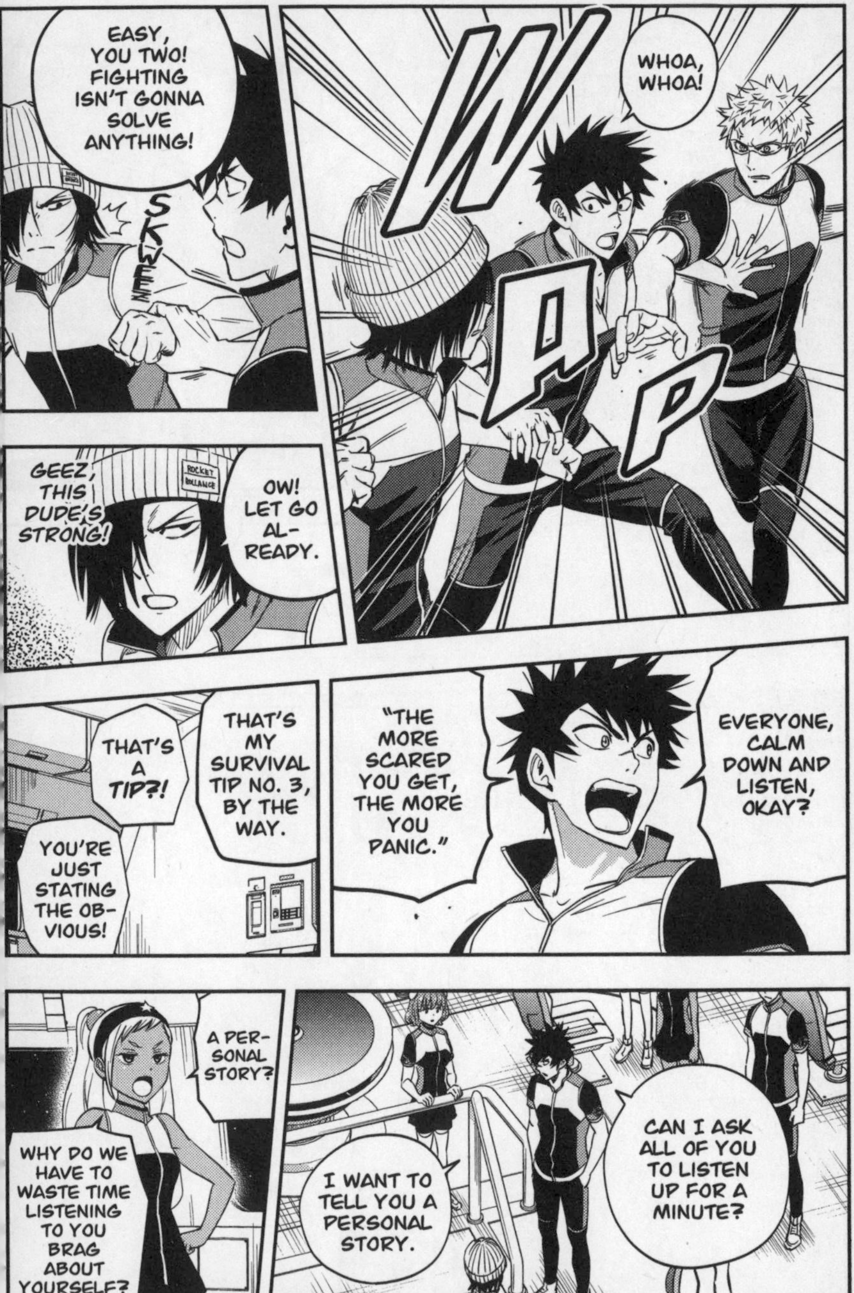
WHOA, WHOA!
WAP
EASY, YOU TWO! FIGHTING ISN'T GONNA SOLVE ANYTHING!
SKWEEZ
OW! LET GO AL-READY.
GEEZ, THIS DUDE'S STRONG!
ROCKET BALANCE
EVERYONE, CALM DOWN AND LISTEN, OKAY?
"THE MORE SCARED YOU GET, THE MORE YOU PANIC."
THAT'S MY SURVIVAL TIP NO. 3, BY THE WAY.
THAT'S A TIP?!
YOU'RE JUST STATING THE OB-VIOUS!
CAN I ASK ALL OF YOU TO LISTEN UP FOR A MINUTE?
I WANT TO TELL YOU A PERSONAL STORY.
A PER-SONAL STORY?
WHY DO WE HAVE TO WASTE TIME LISTENING TO YOU BRAG ABOUT YOURSELF?

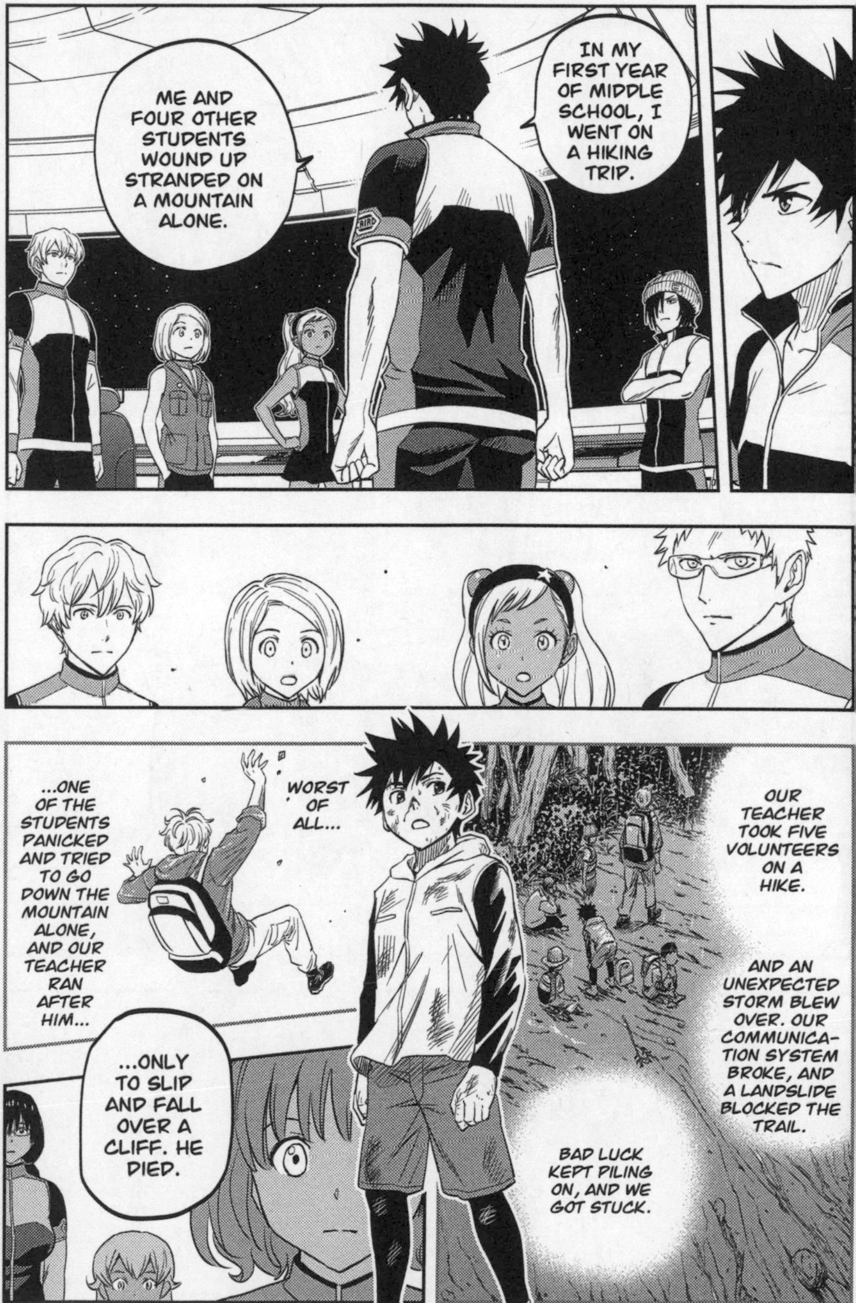
IN MY FIRST YEAR OF MIDDLE SCHOOL, I WENT ON A HIKING TRIP.
ME AND FOUR OTHER STUDENTS WOUND UP STRANDED ON A MOUNTAIN ALONE.
OUR TEACHER TOOK FIVE VOLUNTEERS ON A HIKE.
AND AN UNEXPECTED STORM BLEW OVER. OUR COMMUNICATION SYSTEM BROKE, AND A LANDSLIDE BLOCKED THE TRAIL.
BAD LUCK KEPT PILING ON, AND WE GOT STUCK.
WORST OF ALL...
...ONE OF THE STUDENTS PANICKED AND TRIED TO GO DOWN THE MOUNTAIN ALONE, AND OUR TEACHER RAN AFTER HIM...
...ONLY TO SLIP AND FALL OVER A CLIFF. HE DIED.

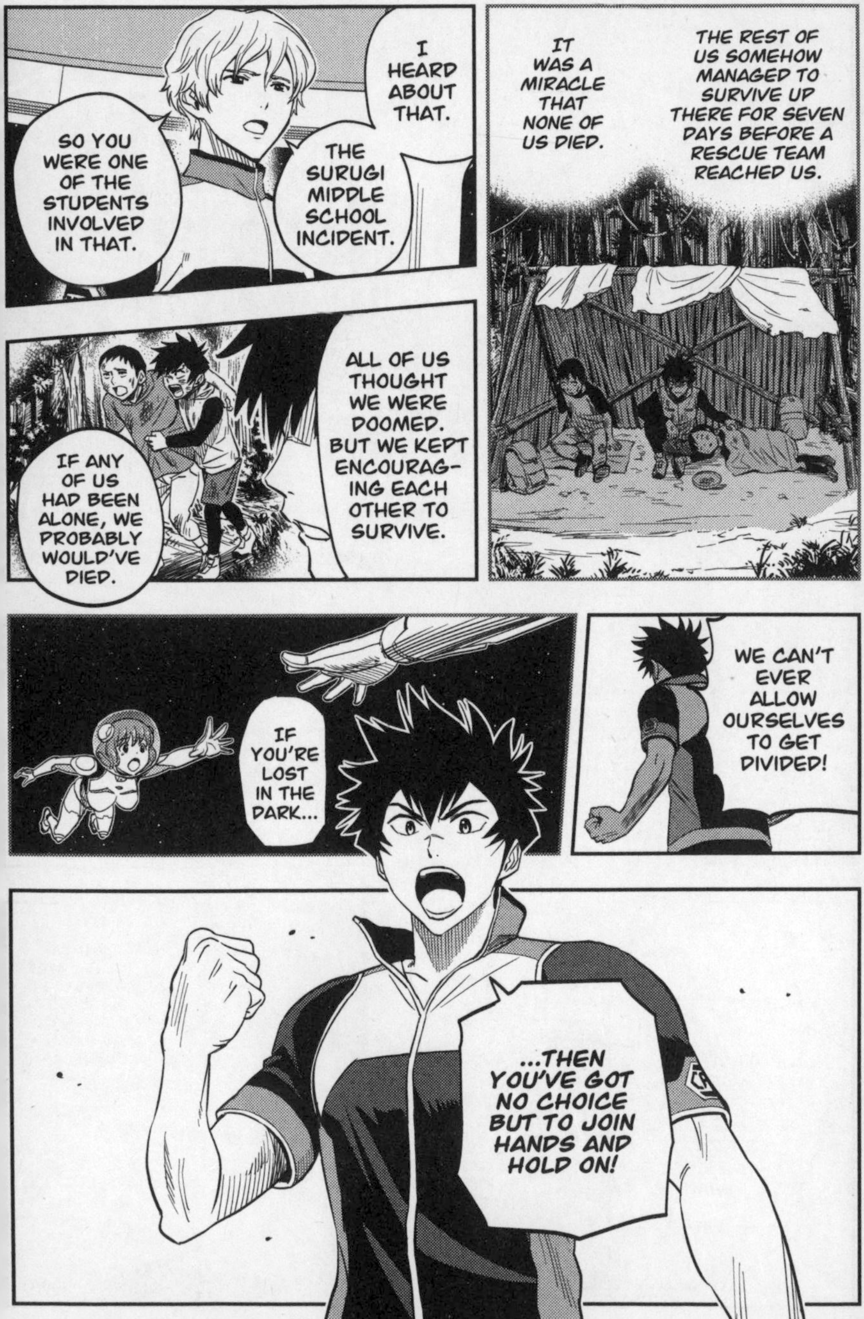
IT WAS A MIRACLE THAT NONE OF US DIED.
THE REST OF US SOMEHOW MANAGED TO SURVIVE UP THERE FOR SEVEN DAYS BEFORE A RESCUE TEAM REACHED US.
I HEARD ABOUT THAT.
THE SURUGI MIDDLE SCHOOL INCIDENT.
SO YOU WERE ONE OF THE STUDENTS INVOLVED IN THAT.
ALL OF US THOUGHT WE WERE DOOMED. BUT WE KEPT ENCOURAG-ING EACH OTHER TO SURVIVE.
IF ANY OF US HAD BEEN ALONE, WE PROBABLY WOULD'VE DIED.
WE CAN'T EVER ALLOW OURSELVES TO GET DIVIDED!
IF YOU'RE LOST IN THE DARK...
...THEN YOU'VE GOT NO CHOICE BUT TO JOIN HANDS AND HOLD ON!

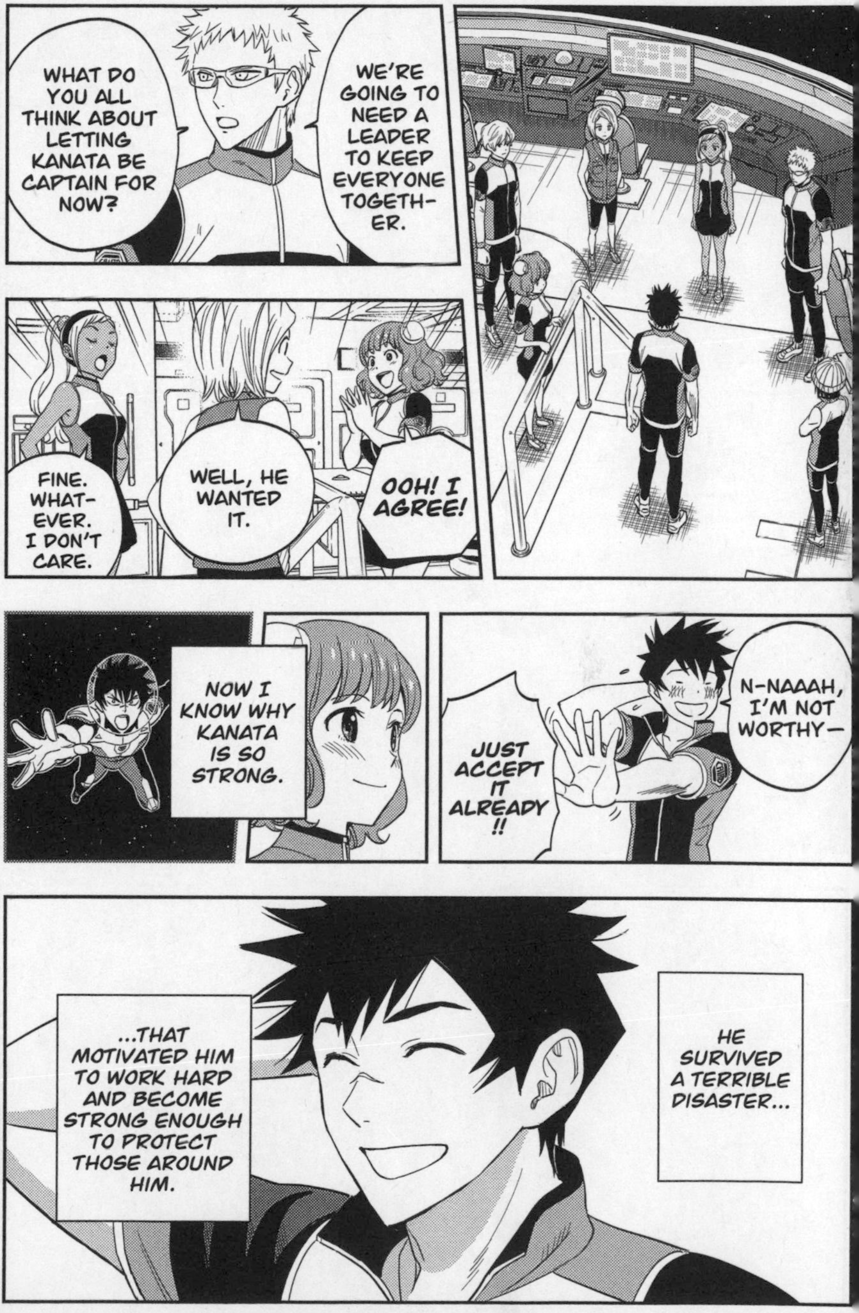
WE'RE GOING TO NEED A LEADER TO KEEP EVERYONE TOGETHER.
WHAT DO YOU ALL THINK ABOUT LETTING KANATA BE CAPTAIN FOR NOW?
OOH! I AGREE!
WELL, HE WANTED IT.
FINE. WHATEVER. I DON'T CARE.
N-NAAAH, I'M NOT WORTHY—
JUST ACCEPT IT ALREADY!!
NOW I KNOW WHY KANATA IS SO STRONG.
HE SURVIVED A TERRIBLE DISASTER...
...THAT MOTIVATED HIM TO WORK HARD AND BECOME STRONG ENOUGH TO PROTECT THOSE AROUND HIM.

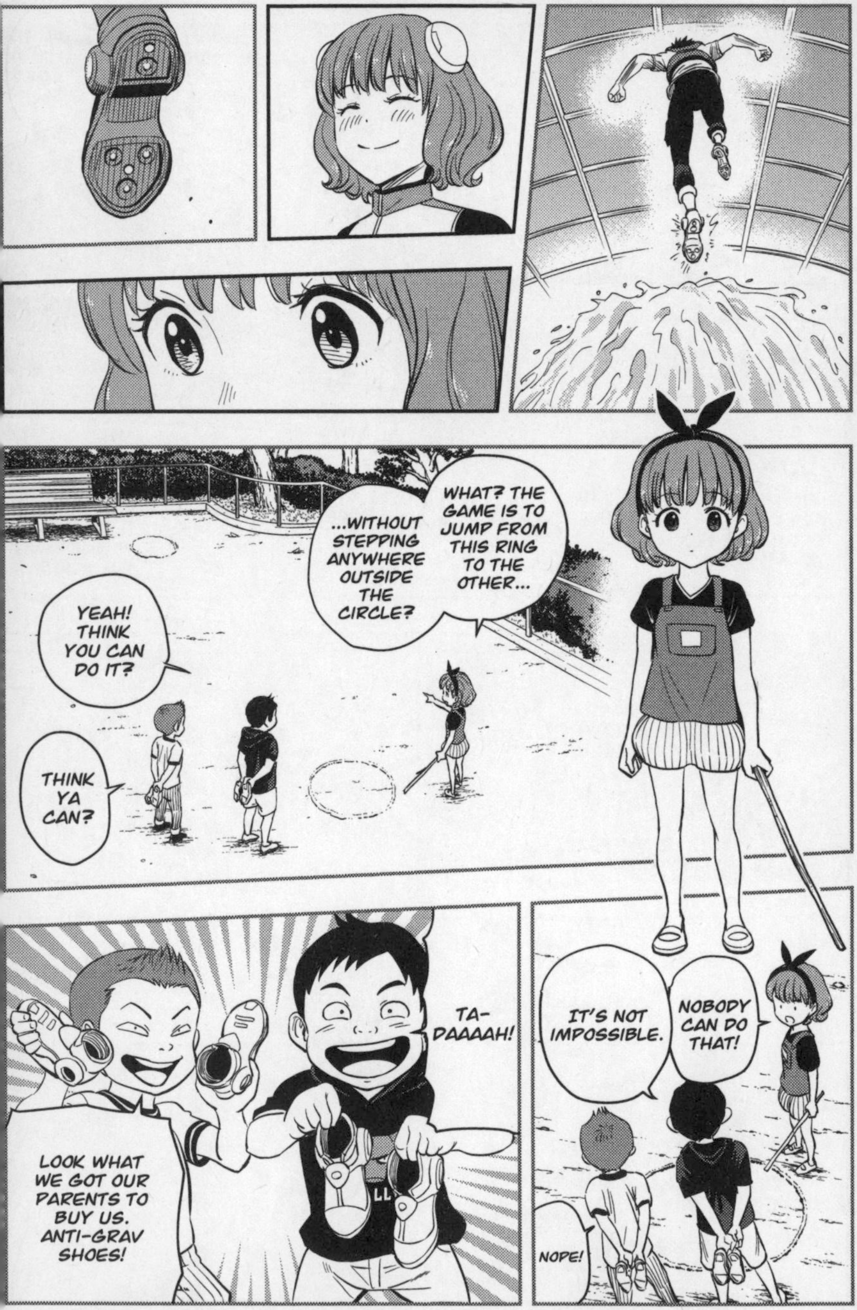
WHAT? THE GAME IS TO JUMP FROM THIS RING TO THE OTHER...
...WITHOUT STEPPING ANYWHERE OUTSIDE THE CIRCLE?
YEAH! THINK YOU CAN DO IT?
THINK YA CAN?
NOBODY CAN DO THAT!
IT'S NOT IMPOSSIBLE.
NOPE!
TA-DAAAAH!
LOOK WHAT WE GOT OUR PARENTS TO BUY US. ANTI-GRAV SHOES!

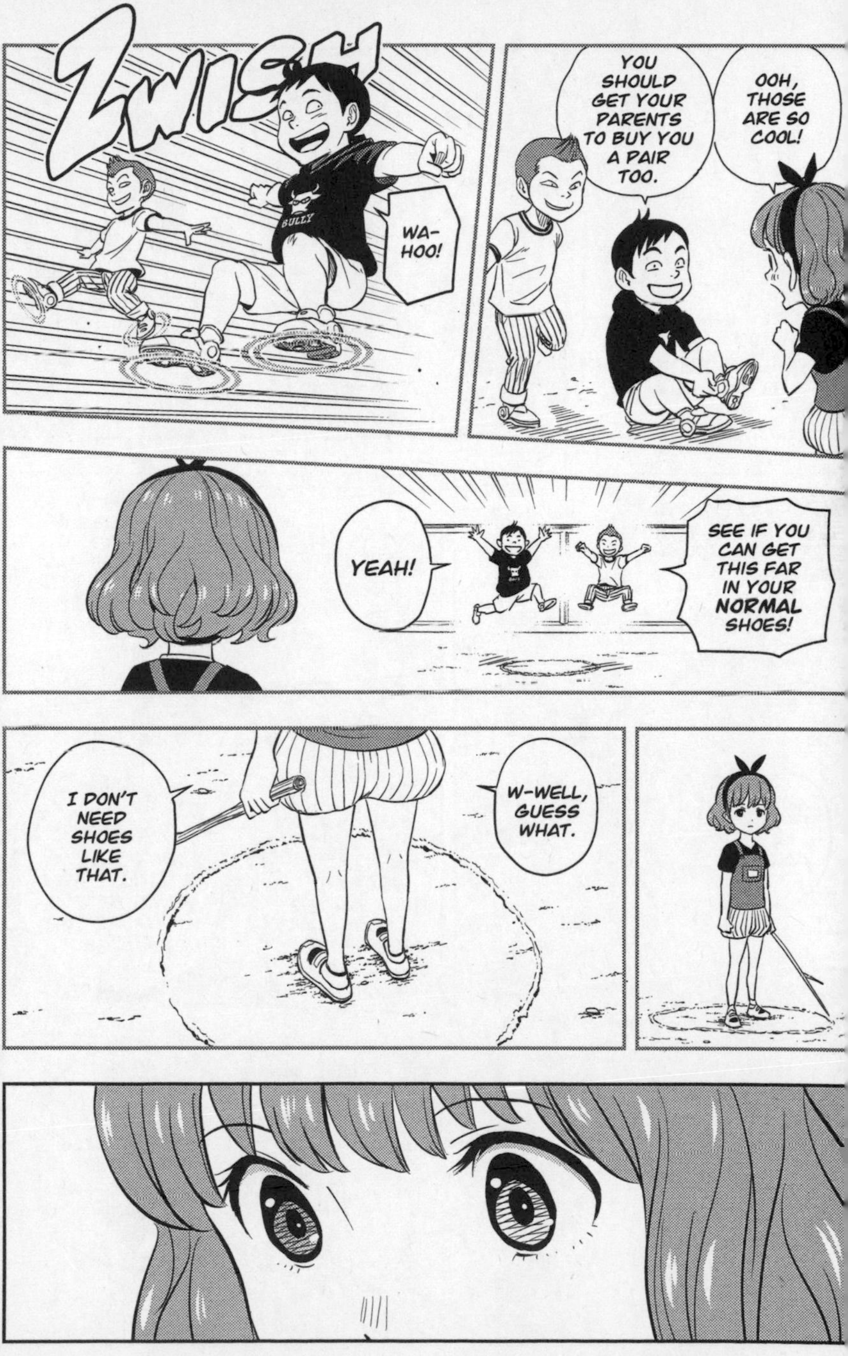
OOH, THOSE ARE SO COOL!
YOU SHOULD GET YOUR PARENTS TO BUY YOU A PAIR TOO.
ZWISH
WA-HOO!
SEE IF YOU CAN GET THIS FAR IN YOUR NORMAL SHOES!
YEAH!
W-WELL, GUESS WHAT.
I DON'T NEED SHOES LIKE THAT.

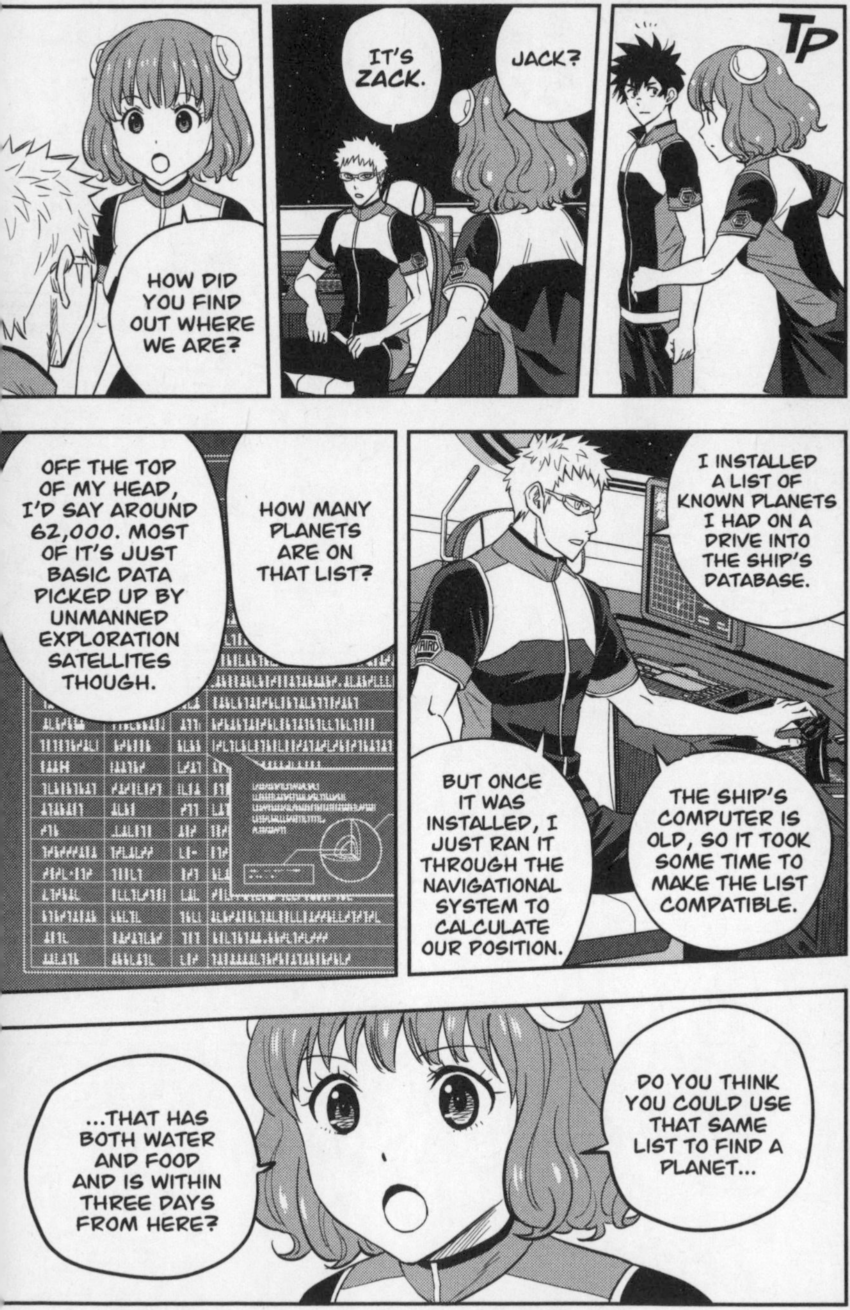
TP
JACK?
IT'S ZACK.
HOW DID YOU FIND OUT WHERE WE ARE?
I INSTALLED A LIST OF KNOWN PLANETS I HAD ON A DRIVE INTO THE SHIP'S DATABASE.
THE SHIP'S COMPUTER IS OLD, SO IT TOOK SOME TIME TO MAKE THE LIST COMPATIBLE.
BUT ONCE IT WAS INSTALLED, I JUST RAN IT THROUGH THE NAVIGATIONAL SYSTEM TO CALCULATE OUR POSITION.
HOW MANY PLANETS ARE ON THAT LIST?
OFF THE TOP OF MY HEAD, I'D SAY AROUND 62,000. MOST OF IT'S JUST BASIC DATA PICKED UP BY UNMANNED EXPLORATION SATELLITES THOUGH.
DO YOU THINK YOU COULD USE THAT SAME LIST TO FIND A PLANET...
...THAT HAS BOTH WATER AND FOOD AND IS WITHIN THREE DAYS FROM HERE?

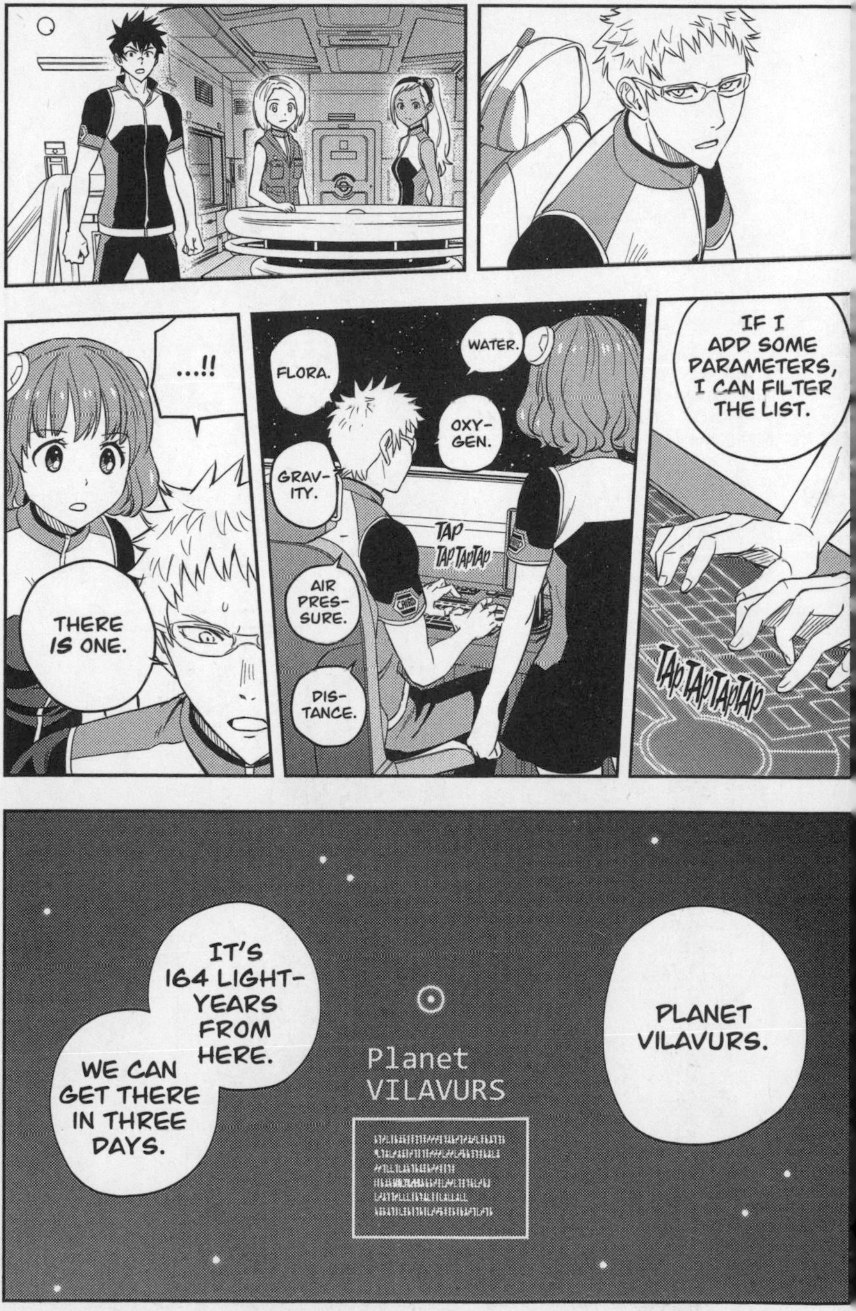
IF I ADD SOME PARAMETERS, I CAN FILTER THE LIST.
TAPTAPTAPTAP
WATER.
OXYGEN.
FLORA.
GRAVITY.
TAP TAP TAP TAP
AIR PRESSURE.
DISTANCE.
...!!
THERE IS ONE.
PLANET VILAVURS.
Planet VILAVURS
IT'S 164 LIGHT-YEARS FROM HERE.
WE CAN GET THERE IN THREE DAYS.

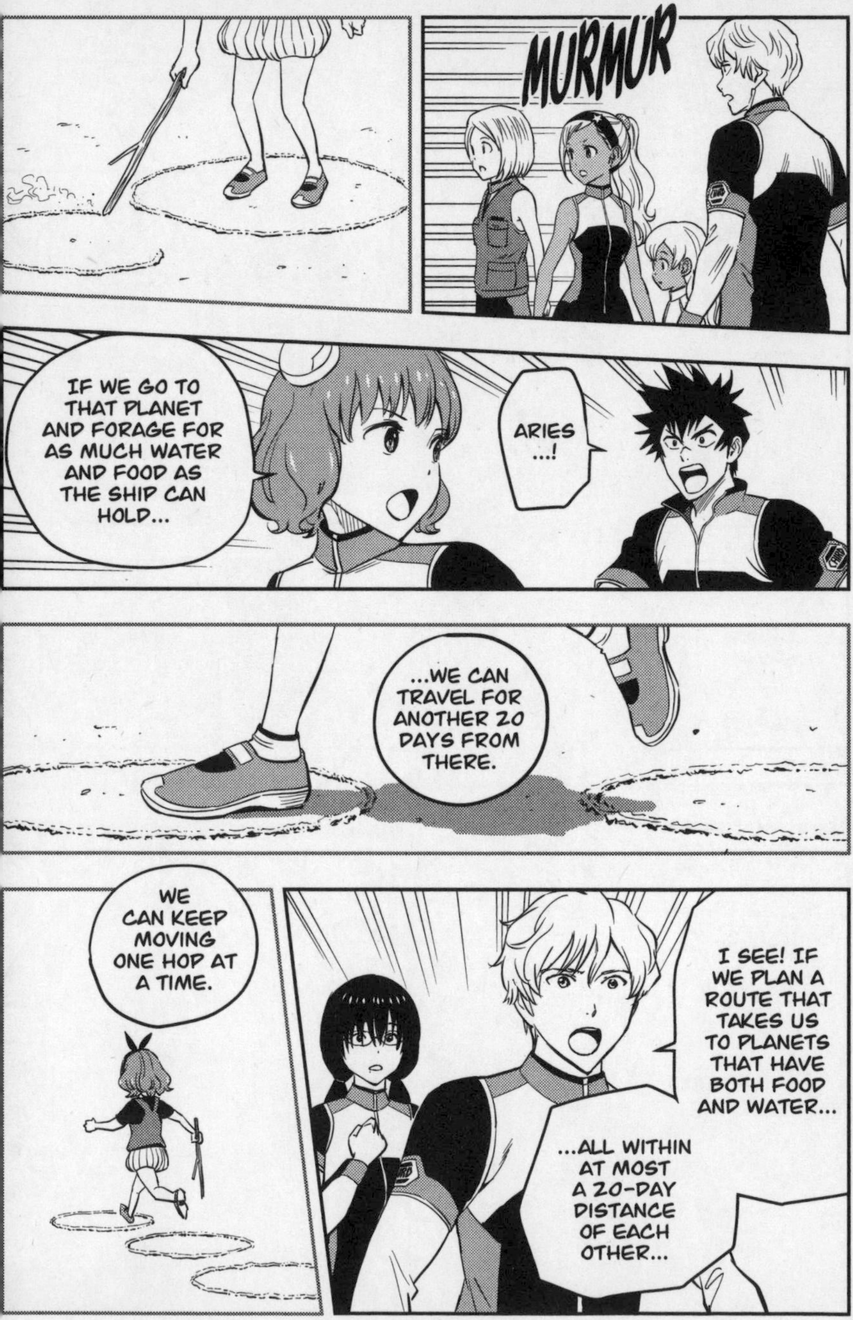
MURMUR
ARIES ...!
IF WE GO TO THAT PLANET AND FORAGE FOR AS MUCH WATER AND FOOD AS THE SHIP CAN HOLD...
...WE CAN TRAVEL FOR ANOTHER 20 DAYS FROM THERE.
I SEE! IF WE PLAN A ROUTE THAT TAKES US TO PLANETS THAT HAVE BOTH FOOD AND WATER...
...ALL WITHIN AT MOST A 20-DAY DISTANCE OF EACH OTHER...
WE CAN KEEP MOVING ONE HOP AT A TIME.

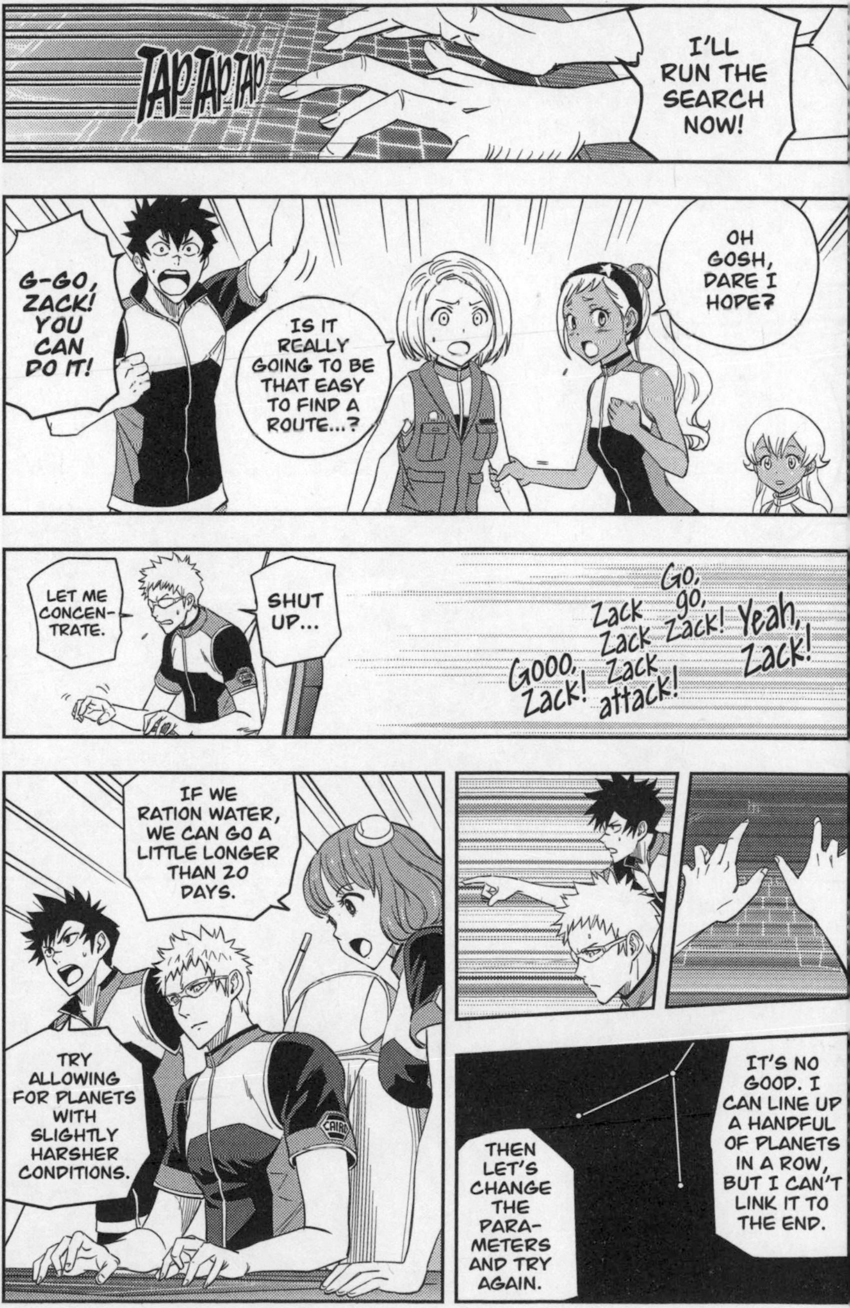
I'LL RUN THE SEARCH NOW!
TAP TAP TAP
OH GOSH, DARE I HOPE?
IS IT REALLY GOING TO BE THAT EASY TO FIND A ROUTE...?
G-GO, ZACK! YOU CAN DO IT!
Yeah, Zack!
Go, go, Zack!
Zack Zack Zack attack!
Gooo, Zack!
SHUT UP...
LET ME CONCENTRATE.
IT'S NO GOOD. I CAN LINE UP A HANDFUL OF PLANETS IN A ROW, BUT I CAN'T LINK IT TO THE END.
THEN LET'S CHANGE THE PARAMETERS AND TRY AGAIN.
IF WE RATION WATER, WE CAN GO A LITTLE LONGER THAN 20 DAYS.
TRY ALLOWING FOR PLANETS WITH SLIGHTLY HARSHER CONDITIONS.

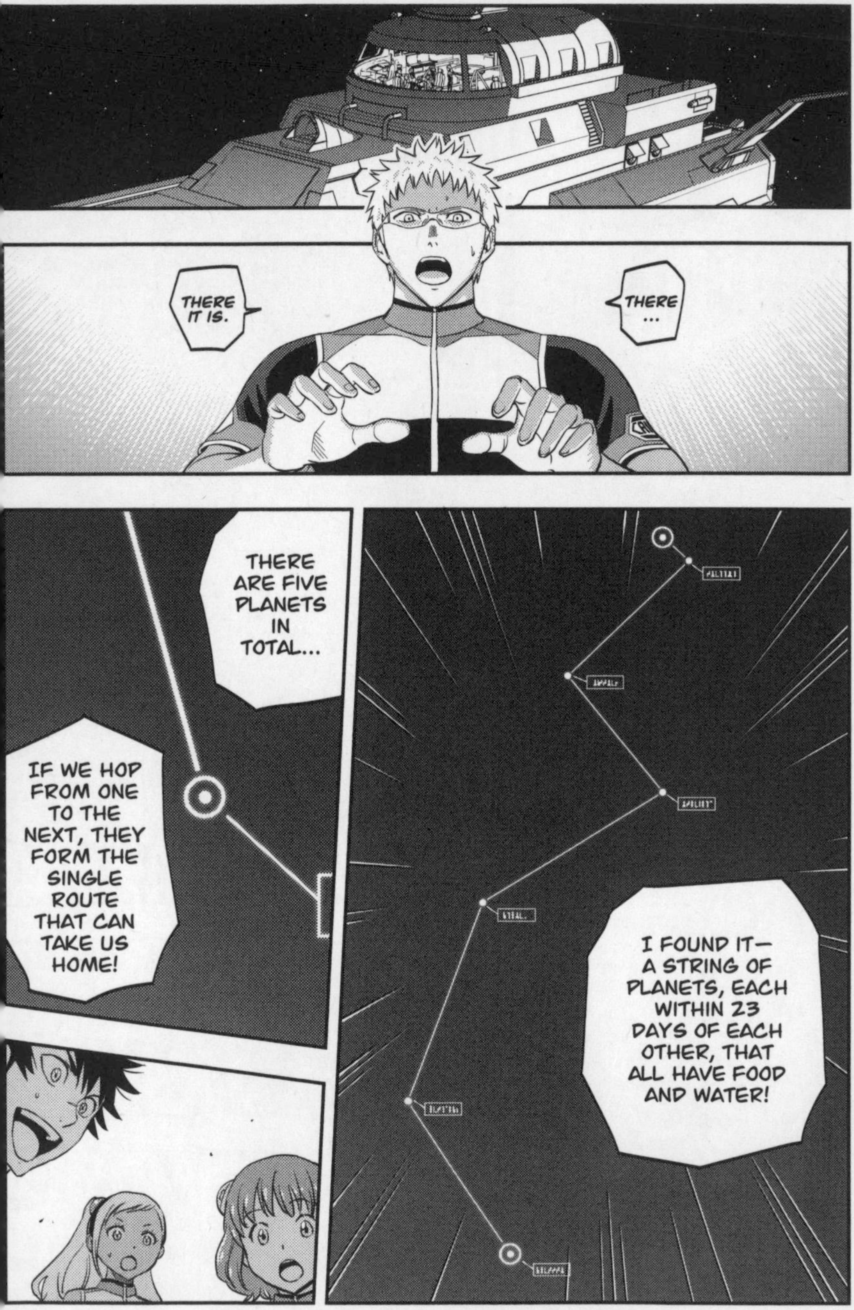
THERE ...
THERE IT IS.
I FOUND IT— A STRING OF PLANETS, EACH WITHIN 23 DAYS OF EACH OTHER, THAT ALL HAVE FOOD AND WATER!
THERE ARE FIVE PLANETS IN TOTAL...
IF WE HOP FROM ONE TO THE NEXT, THEY FORM THE SINGLE ROUTE THAT CAN TAKE US HOME!

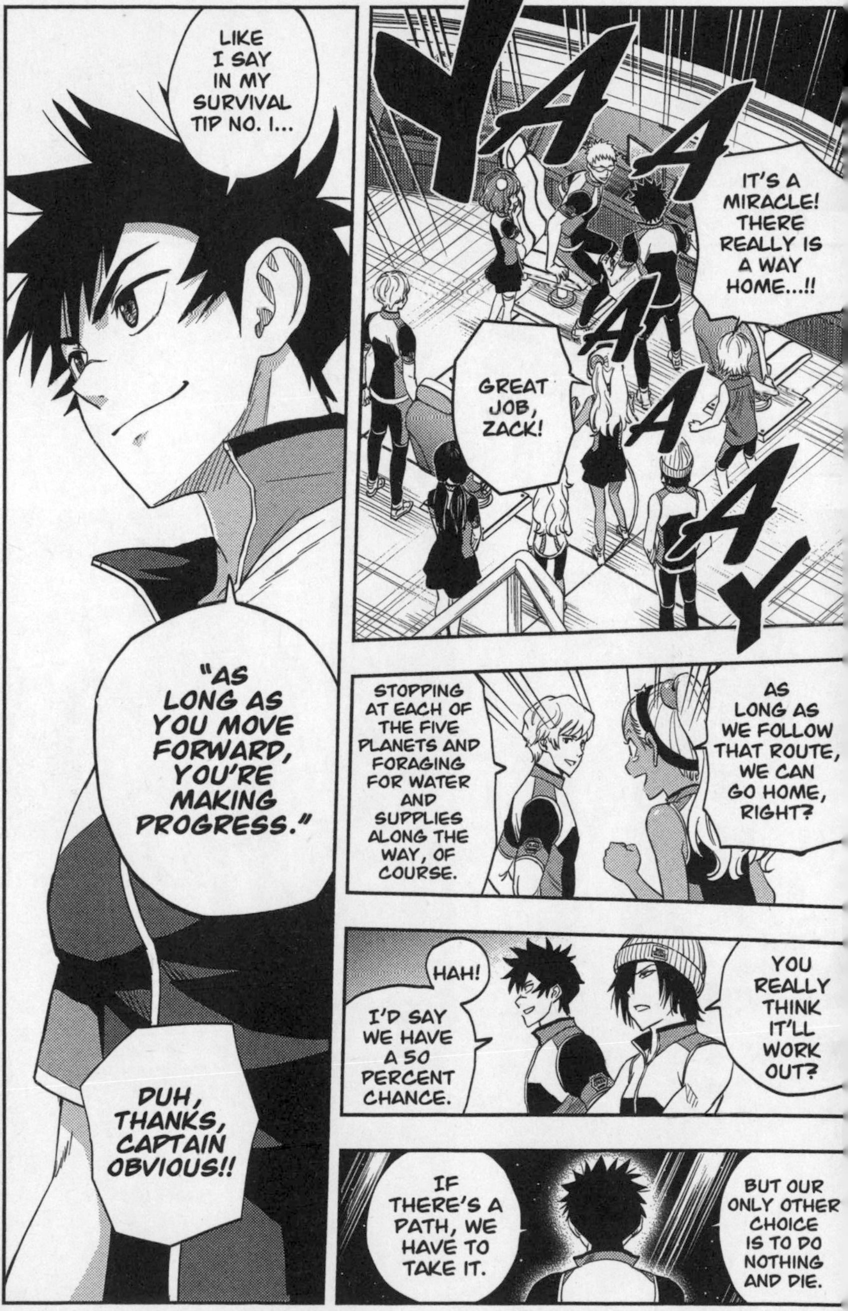
YAAAAAAY
IT'S A MIRACLE! THERE REALLY IS A WAY HOME...!!
GREAT JOB, ZACK!
AS LONG AS WE FOLLOW THAT ROUTE, WE CAN GO HOME, RIGHT?
STOPPING AT EACH OF THE FIVE PLANETS AND FORAGING FOR WATER AND SUPPLIES ALONG THE WAY, OF COURSE.
YOU REALLY THINK IT'LL WORK OUT?
HAH!
I'D SAY WE HAVE A 50 PERCENT CHANCE.
BUT OUR ONLY OTHER CHOICE IS TO DO NOTHING AND DIE.
IF THERE'S A PATH, WE HAVE TO TAKE IT.
LIKE I SAY IN MY SURVIVAL TIP NO. 1...
"AS LONG AS YOU MOVE FORWARD, YOU'RE MAKING PROGRESS."
DUH, THANKS, CAPTAIN OBVIOUS!!

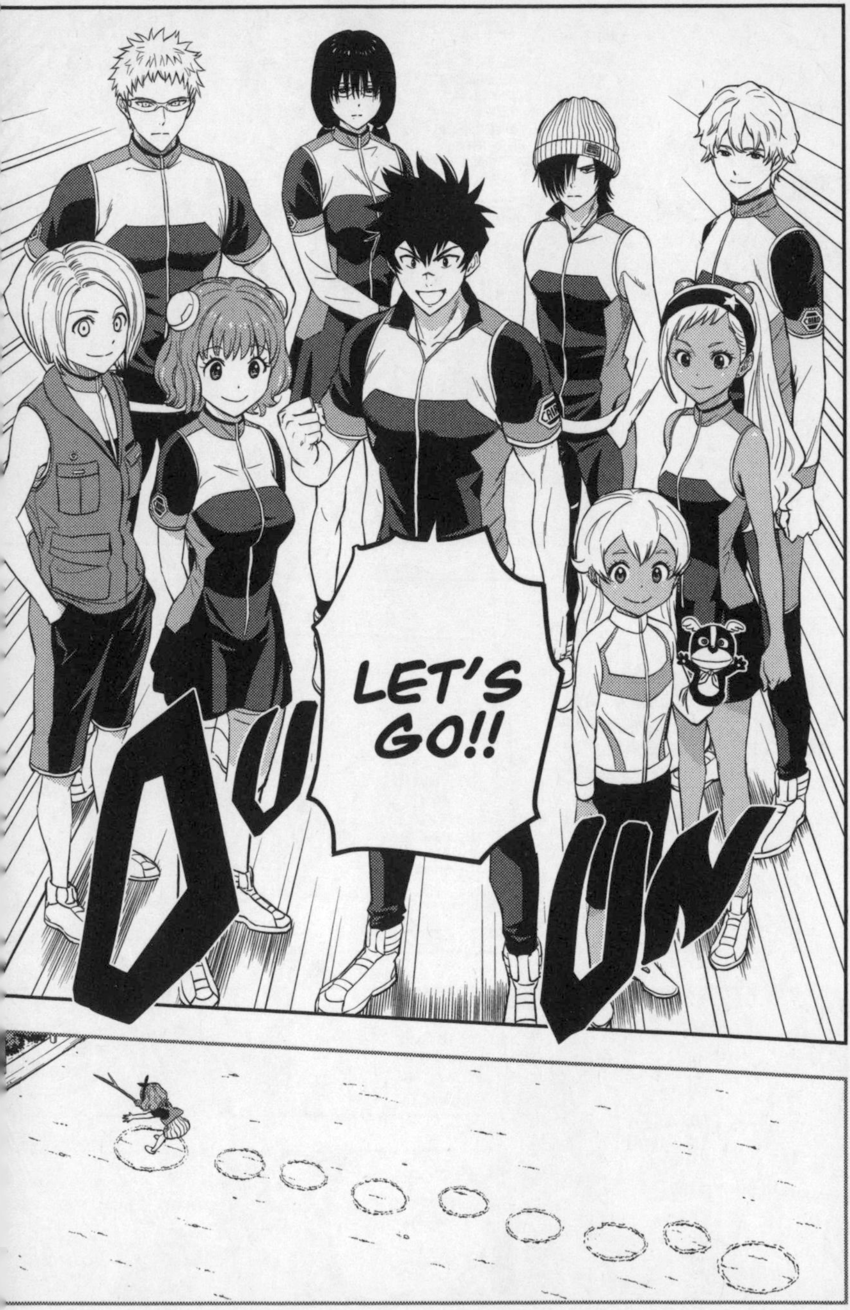
LET'S GO!!
DOON

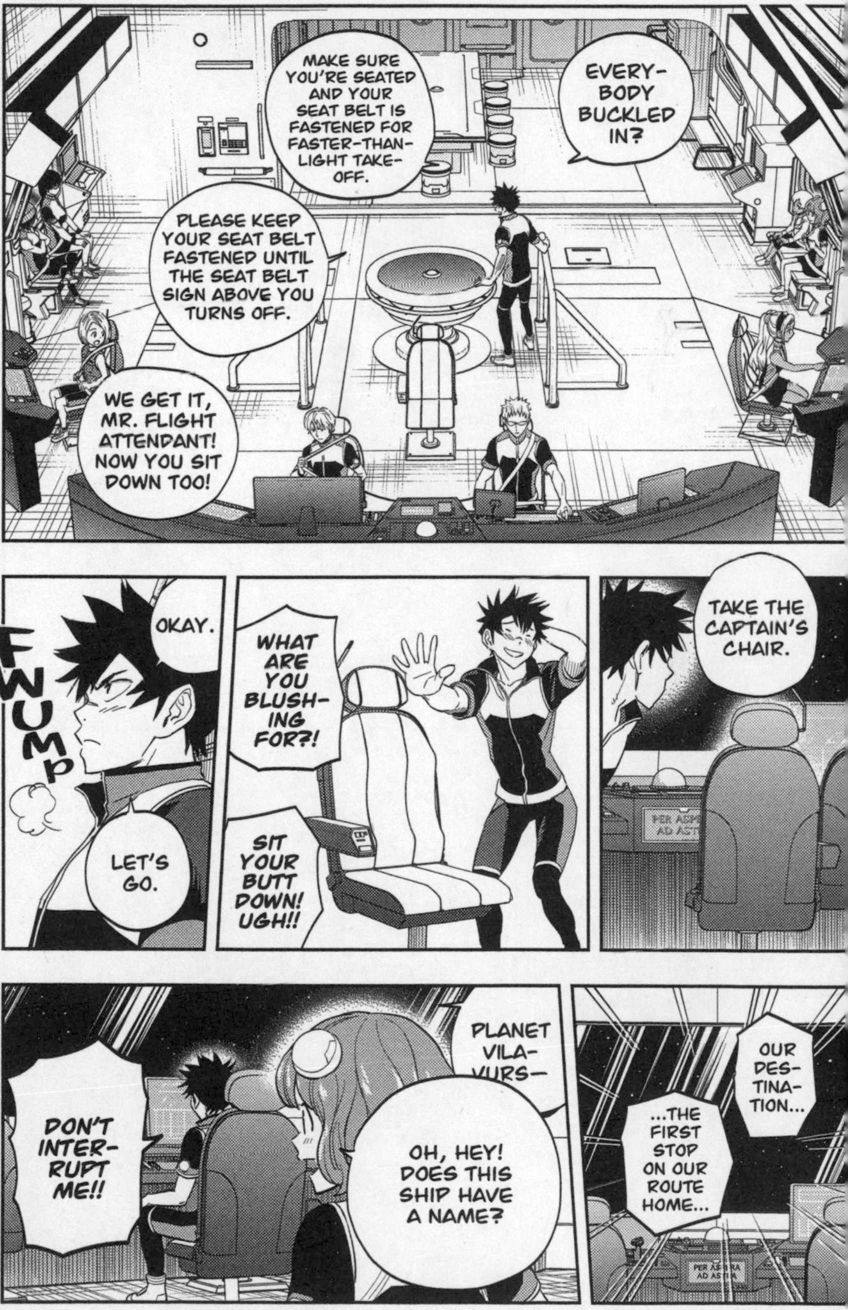
EVERY-BODY BUCKLED IN?
MAKE SURE YOU'RE SEATED AND YOUR SEAT BELT IS FASTENED FOR FASTER-THAN-LIGHT TAKE-OFF.
PLEASE KEEP YOUR SEAT BELT FASTENED UNTIL THE SEAT BELT SIGN ABOVE YOU TURNS OFF.
WE GET IT, MR. FLIGHT ATTENDANT! NOW YOU SIT DOWN TOO!
TAKE THE CAPTAIN'S CHAIR.
WHAT ARE YOU BLUSH-ING FOR?!
SIT YOUR BUTT DOWN! UGH!!
OKAY.
FWUMP
LET'S GO.
OUR DES-TINA-TION...
...THE FIRST STOP ON OUR ROUTE HOME...
PER ASPERA AD ASTRA
PLANET VILA-VURS—
OH, HEY! DOES THIS SHIP HAVE A NAME?
DON'T INTER-RUPT ME!!

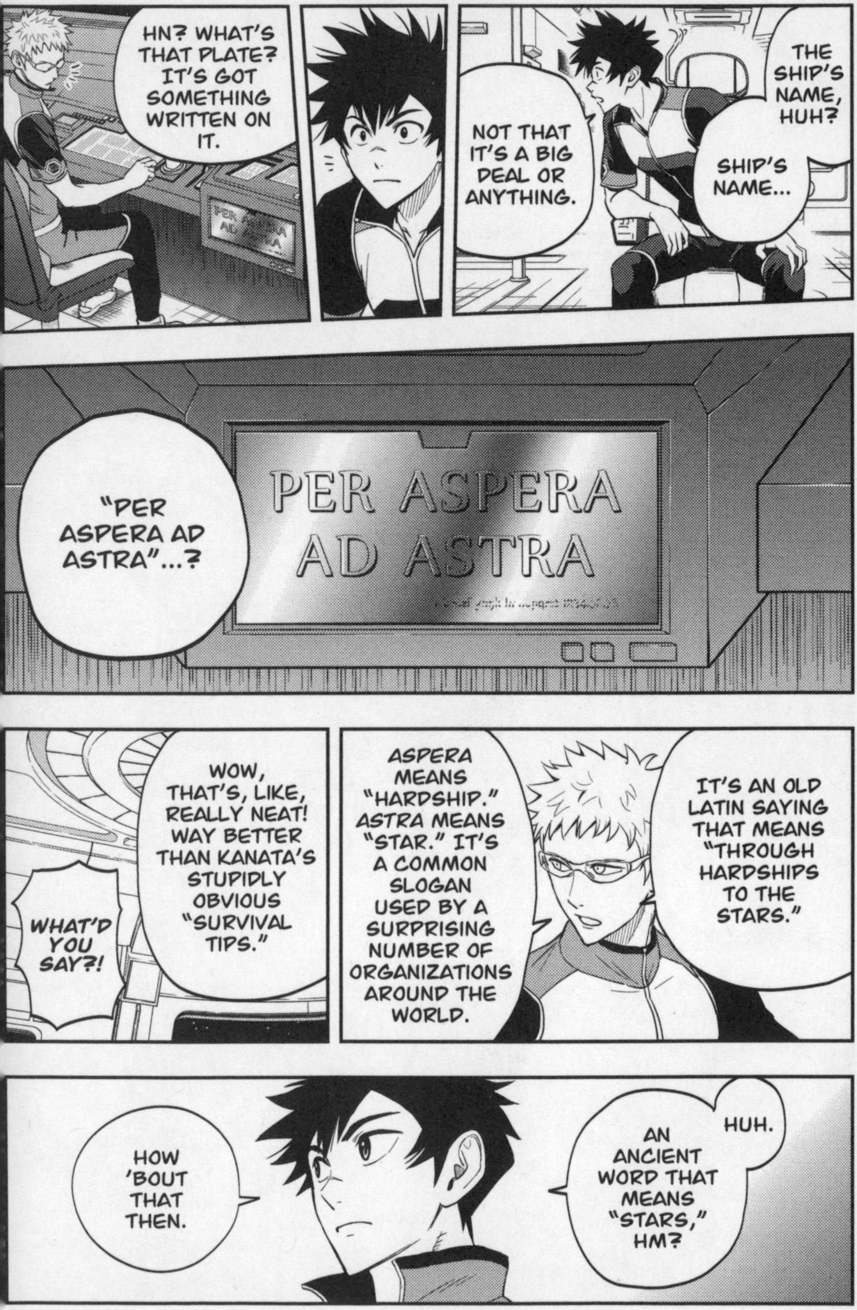
THE SHIP'S NAME, HUH?
SHIP'S NAME...
NOT THAT IT'S A BIG DEAL OR ANYTHING.
HN? WHAT'S THAT PLATE? IT'S GOT SOMETHING WRITTEN ON IT.
PER ASPERA AD ASTRA
“PER ASPERA AD ASTRA”...?
IT'S AN OLD LATIN SAYING THAT MEANS “THROUGH HARDSHIPS TO THE STARS.”
ASPERA MEANS “HARDSHIP.” ASTRA MEANS “STAR.” IT'S A COMMON SLOGAN USED BY A SURPRISING NUMBER OF ORGANIZATIONS AROUND THE WORLD.
WOW, THAT'S, LIKE, REALLY NEAT! WAY BETTER THAN KANATA'S STUPIDLY OBVIOUS “SURVIVAL TIPS.”
WHAT'D YOU SAY?!
HUH.
AN ANCIENT WORD THAT MEANS “STARS,” HM?
HOW 'BOUT THAT THEN.

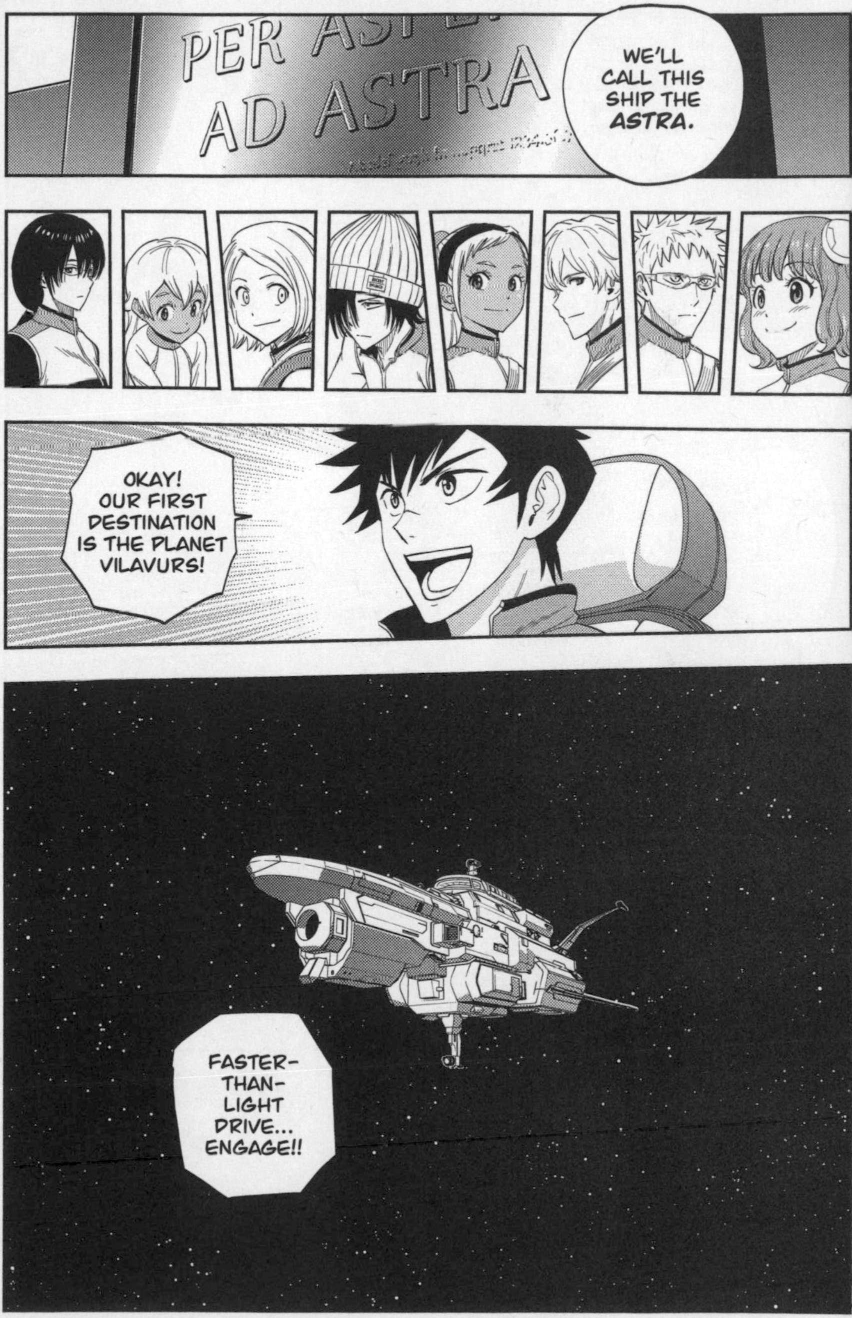
WE'LL CALL THIS SHIP THE ASTRA.
PER
AD ASTRA
OKAY! OUR FIRST DESTINATION IS THE PLANET VILAVURS!
FASTER-THAN-LIGHT DRIVE... ENGAGE!!

THE *ASTRA*

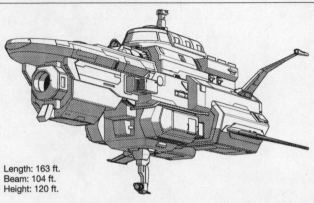

Length: 163 ft.
Beam: 104 ft.
Height: 120 ft.

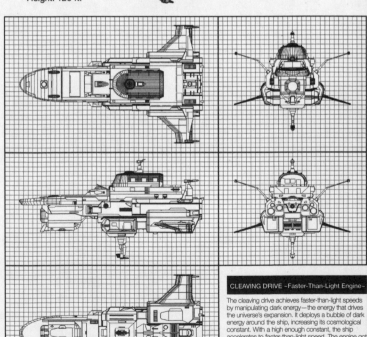

CLEAVING DRIVE ~Faster-Than-Light Engine~

The cleaving drive achieves faster-than-light speeds by manipulating dark energy—the energy that drives the universe's expansion. It deploys a bubble of dark energy around the ship, increasing its cosmological constant. With a high enough constant, the ship accelerates to faster-than-light speed. The engine got its name because it essentially "cleaves" space to reach its destination. The engine absorbs dark energy as it moves through space, turning that energy into fuel.

While the ship is moving at faster-than-light speeds, another field surrounds the interior of the ship, keeping space-time inside of it stationary. This prevents the crew from experiencing time dilation during flight.

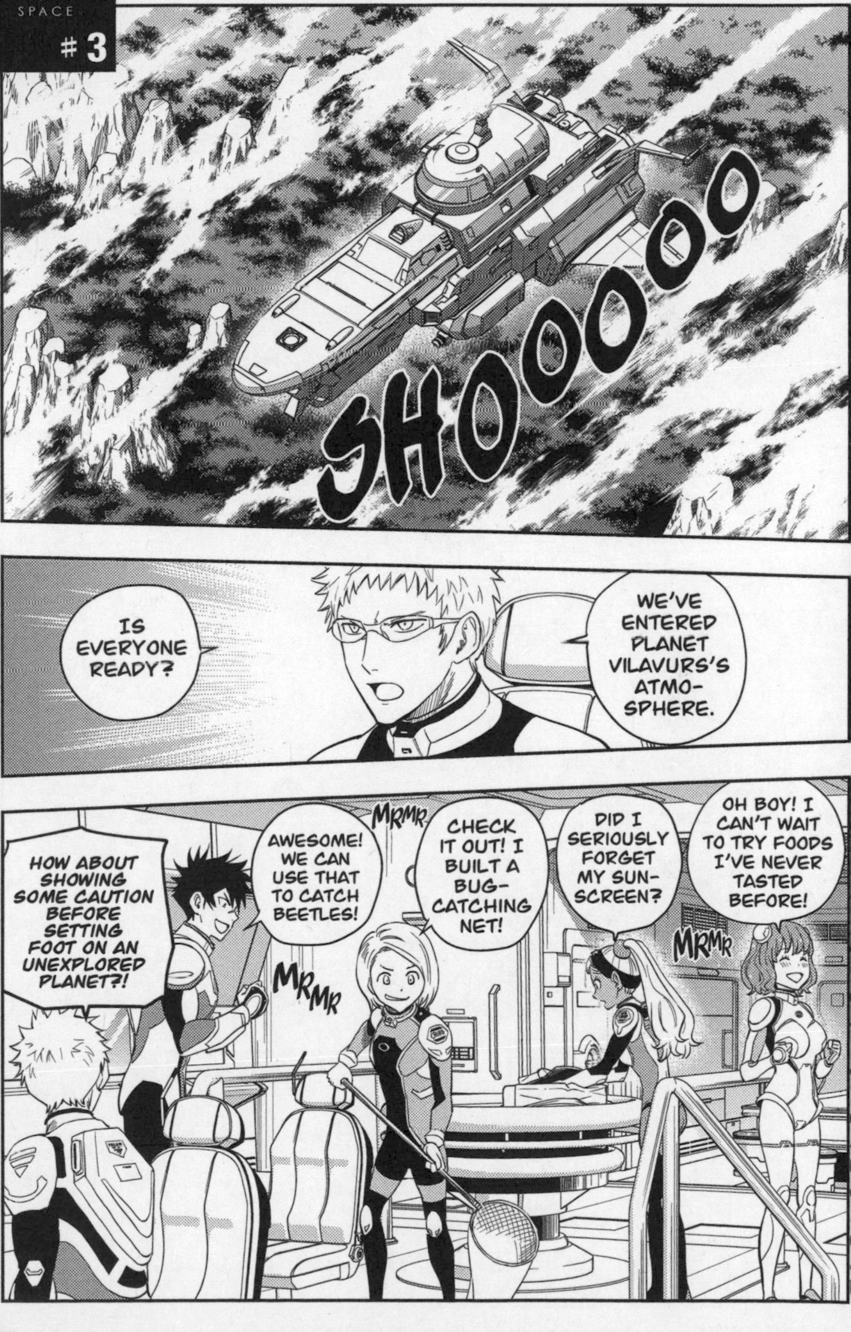
SHOOOOOO
WE'VE ENTERED PLANET VILAVURS'S ATMO-SPHERE.
IS EVERYONE READY?
OH BOY! I CAN'T WAIT TO TRY FOODS I'VE NEVER TASTED BEFORE!
MRMR
DID I SERIOUSLY FORGET MY SUN-SCREEN?
CHECK IT OUT! I BUILT A BUG-CATCHING NET!
MRMR
AWESOME! WE CAN USE THAT TO CATCH BEETLES!
MRMR
HOW ABOUT SHOWING SOME CAUTION BEFORE SETTING FOOT ON AN UNEXPLORED PLANET?!

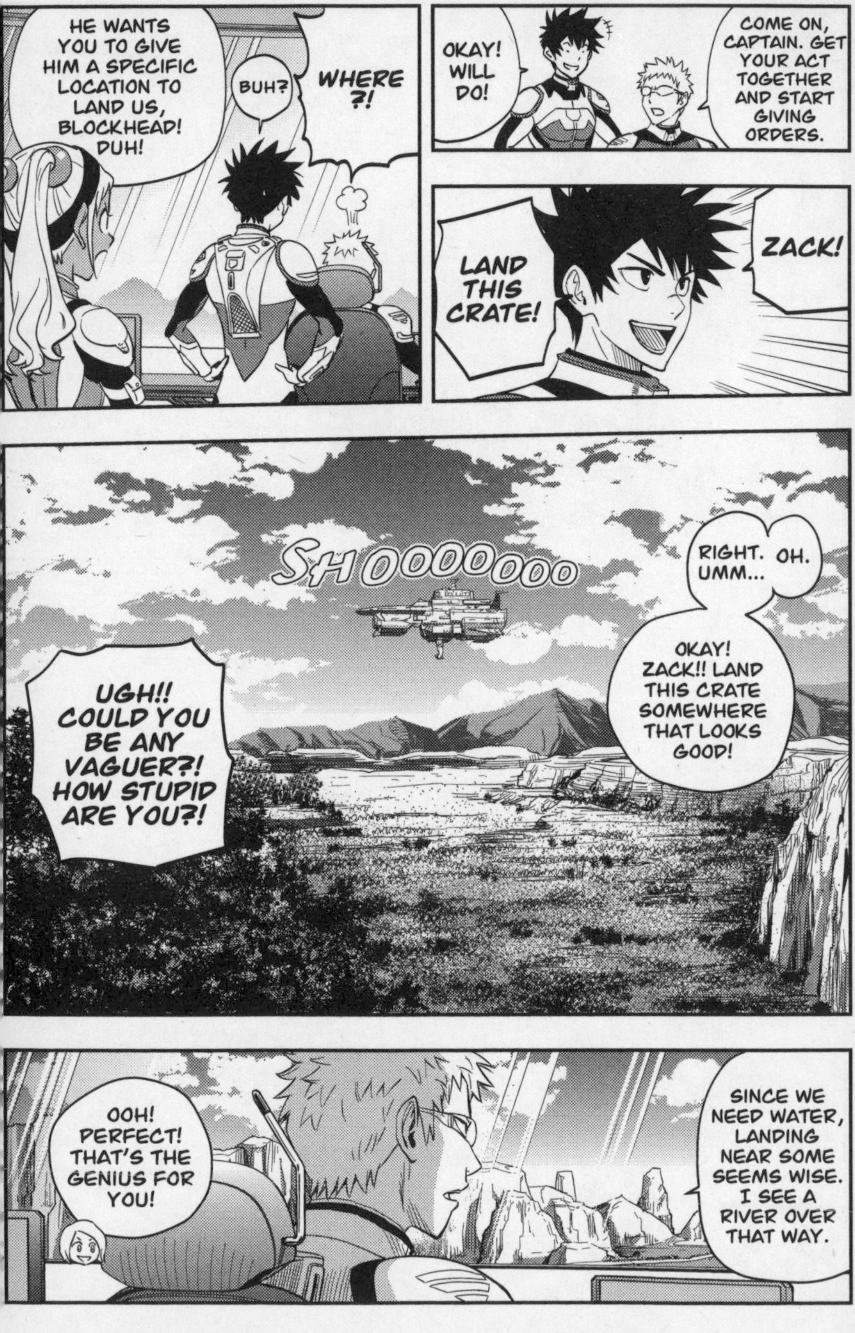
COME ON, CAPTAIN. GET YOUR ACT TOGETHER AND START GIVING ORDERS.
OKAY! WILL DO!
ZACK!
LAND THIS CRATE!
WHERE ?!
BUH?
HE WANTS YOU TO GIVE HIM A SPECIFIC LOCATION TO LAND US, BLOCKHEAD! DUH!
OH.
RIGHT. UMM...
OKAY! ZACK!! LAND THIS CRATE SOMEWHERE THAT LOOKS GOOD!
SHOOOOOOO
UGH!! COULD YOU BE ANY VAGUER?! HOW STUPID ARE YOU?!
SINCE WE NEED WATER, LANDING NEAR SOME SEEMS WISE. I SEE A RIVER OVER THAT WAY.
OOH! PERFECT! THAT'S THE GENIUS FOR YOU!

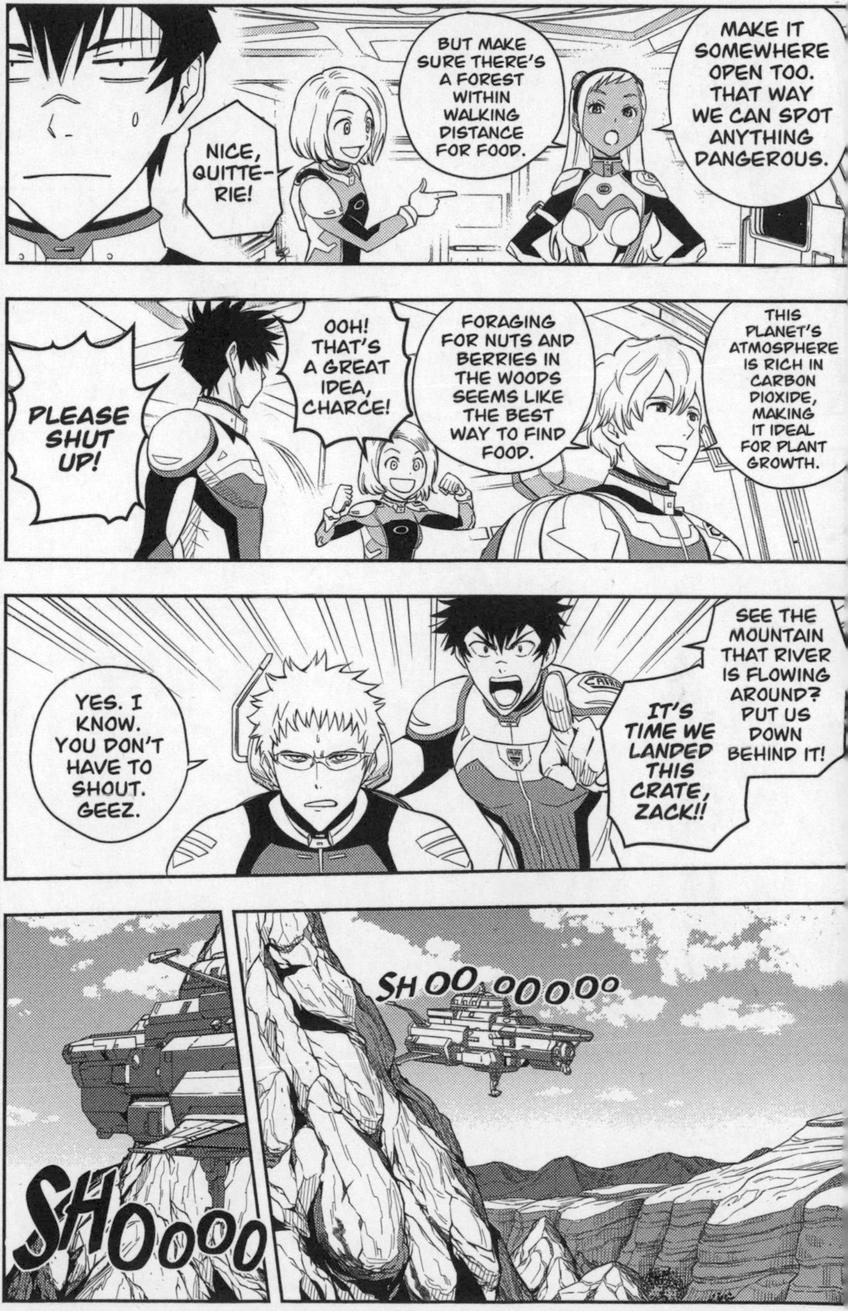
MAKE IT SOMEWHERE OPEN TOO. THAT WAY WE CAN SPOT ANYTHING DANGEROUS.
BUT MAKE SURE THERE'S A FOREST WITHIN WALKING DISTANCE FOR FOOD.
NICE, QUITTE-RIE!
THIS PLANET'S ATMOSPHERE IS RICH IN CARBON DIOXIDE, MAKING IT IDEAL FOR PLANT GROWTH.
FORAGING FOR NUTS AND BERRIES IN THE WOODS SEEMS LIKE THE BEST WAY TO FIND FOOD.
OOH! THAT'S A GREAT IDEA, CHARCE!
PLEASE SHUT UP!
SEE THE MOUNTAIN THAT RIVER IS FLOWING AROUND? PUT US DOWN BEHIND IT!
IT'S TIME WE LANDED THIS CRATE, ZACK!!
YES. I KNOW. YOU DON'T HAVE TO SHOUT. GEEZ.
SHOOOOOOOO
SHOOOO

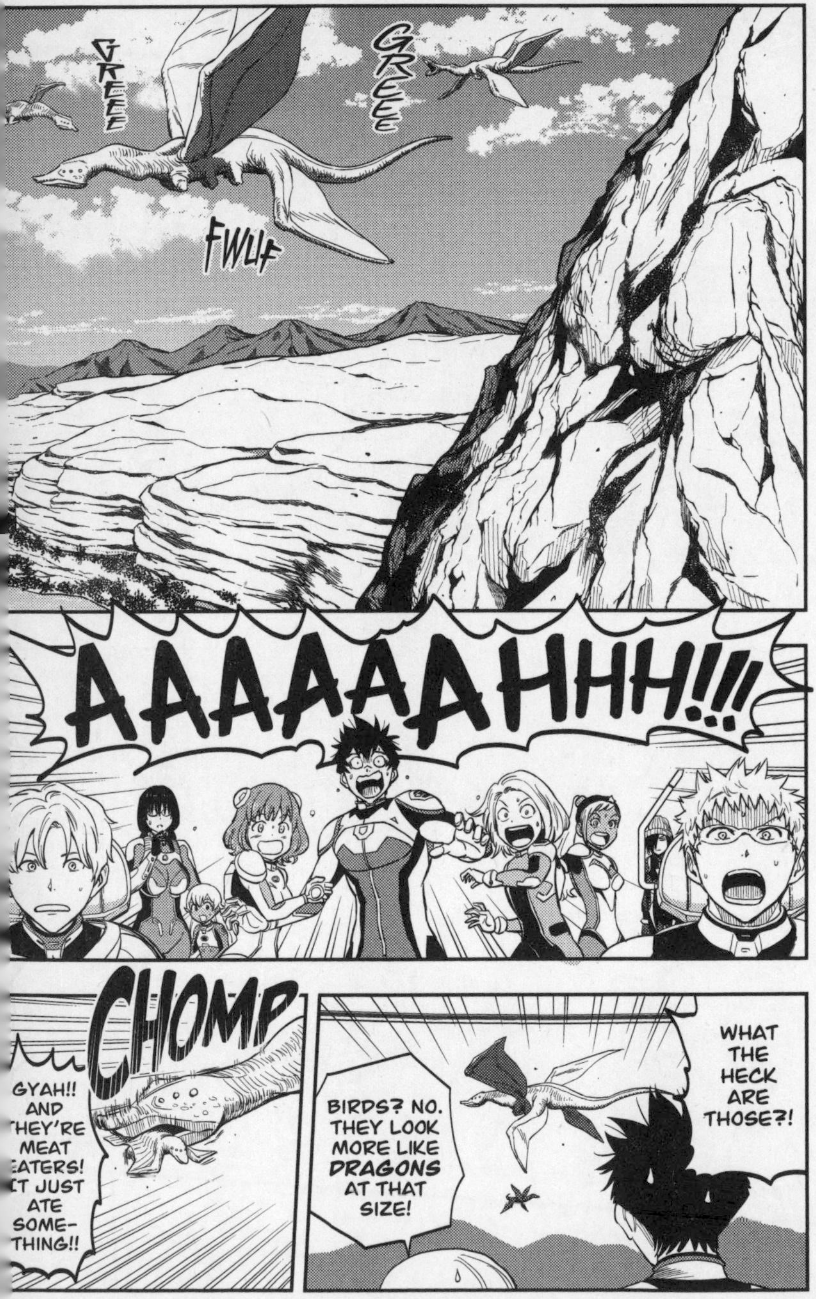
GREEEE
GREEEE
FWUF
AAAAAAHHH!!!
WHAT THE HECK ARE THOSE?!
BIRDS? NO. THEY LOOK MORE LIKE DRAGONS AT THAT SIZE!
CHOMP
GYAH!! AND THEY'RE MEAT EATERS! IT JUST ATE SOMETHING!!

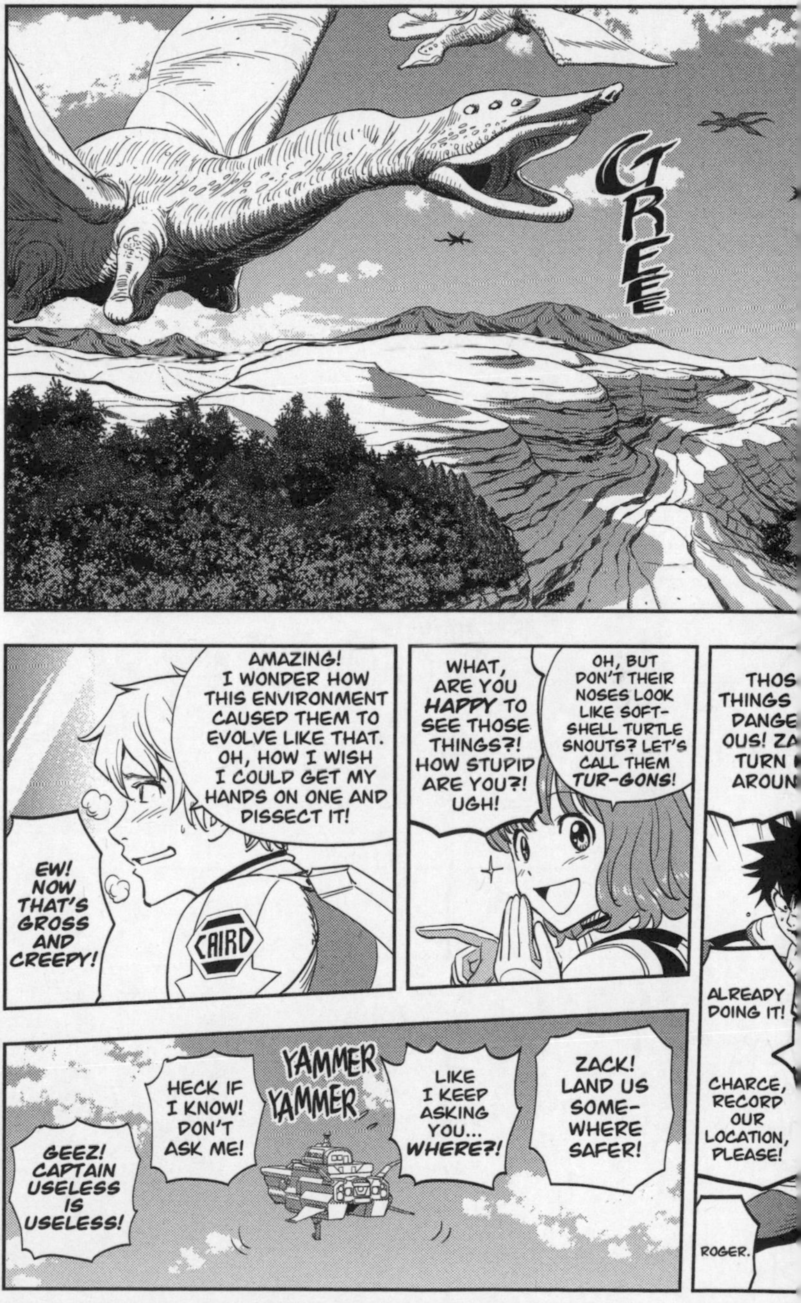
GREE
THOS THINGS DANGE OUS! ZA TURN AROUN
ALREADY DOING IT!
OH, BUT DON'T THEIR NOSES LOOK LIKE SOFT-SHELL TURTLE SNOUTS? LET'S CALL THEM TUR-GONS!
WHAT, ARE YOU HAPPY TO SEE THOSE THINGS?! HOW STUPID ARE YOU?! UGH!
AMAZING! I WONDER HOW THIS ENVIRONMENT CAUSED THEM TO EVOLVE LIKE THAT. OH, HOW I WISH I COULD GET MY HANDS ON ONE AND DISSECT IT!
EW! NOW THAT'S GROSS AND CREEPY!
CAIRD
CHARCE, RECORD OUR LOCATION, PLEASE!
ROGER.
ZACK! LAND US SOME-WHERE SAFER!
LIKE I KEEP ASKING YOU... WHERE?!
YAMMER YAMMER
HECK IF I KNOW! DON'T ASK ME!
GEEZ! CAPTAIN USELESS IS USELESS!

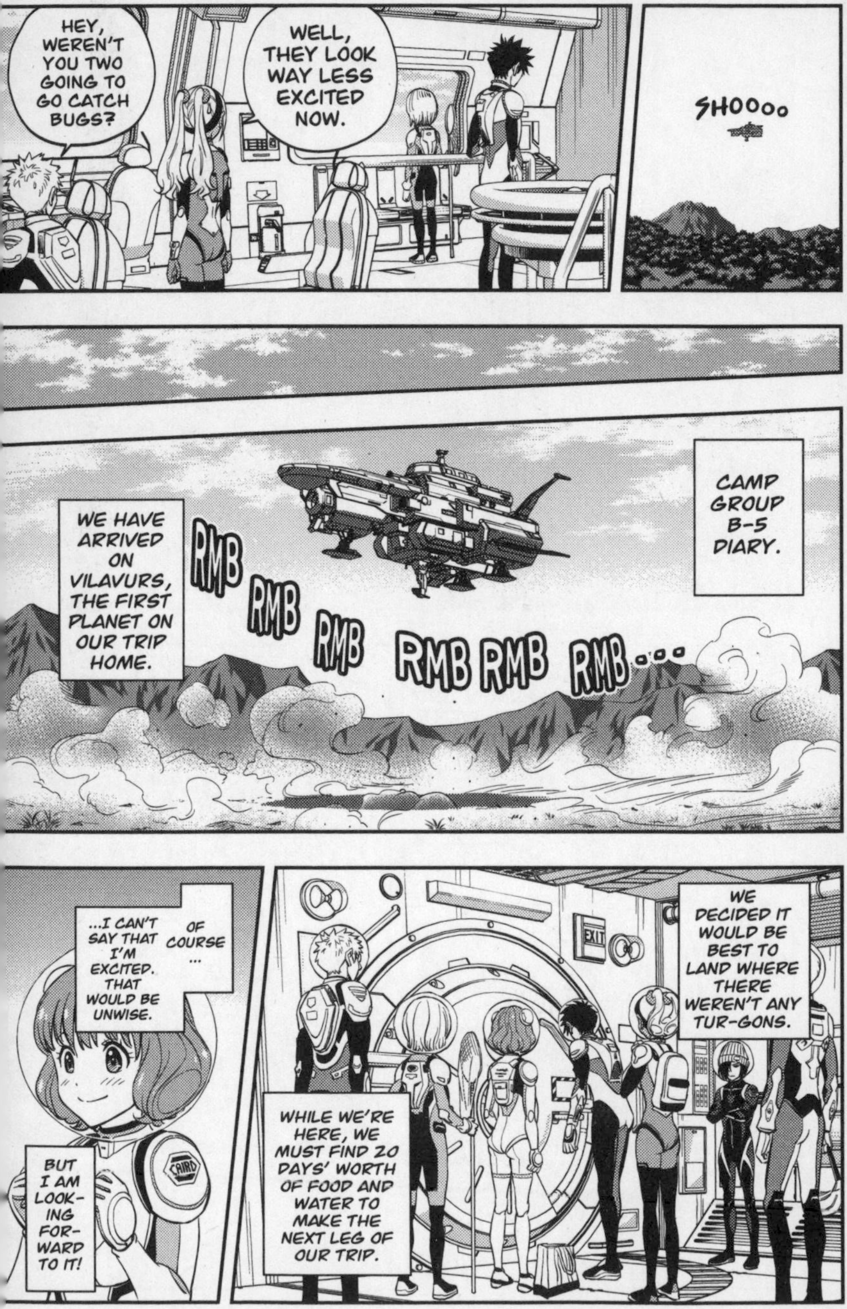
SHOOOo
WELL, THEY LOOK WAY LESS EXCITED NOW.
HEY, WEREN'T YOU TWO GOING TO GO CATCH BUGS?
CAMP GROUP B-5 DIARY.
RMB RMB RMB RMB RMB RMB...
WE HAVE ARRIVED ON VILAVURS, THE FIRST PLANET ON OUR TRIP HOME.
WE DECIDED IT WOULD BE BEST TO LAND WHERE THERE WEREN'T ANY TUR-GONS.
EXIT
WHILE WE'RE HERE, WE MUST FIND 20 DAYS' WORTH OF FOOD AND WATER TO MAKE THE NEXT LEG OF OUR TRIP.
OF COURSE...
...I CAN'T SAY THAT I'M EXCITED. THAT WOULD BE UNWISE.
BUT I AM LOOK-ING FOR-WARD TO IT!
CAIRD

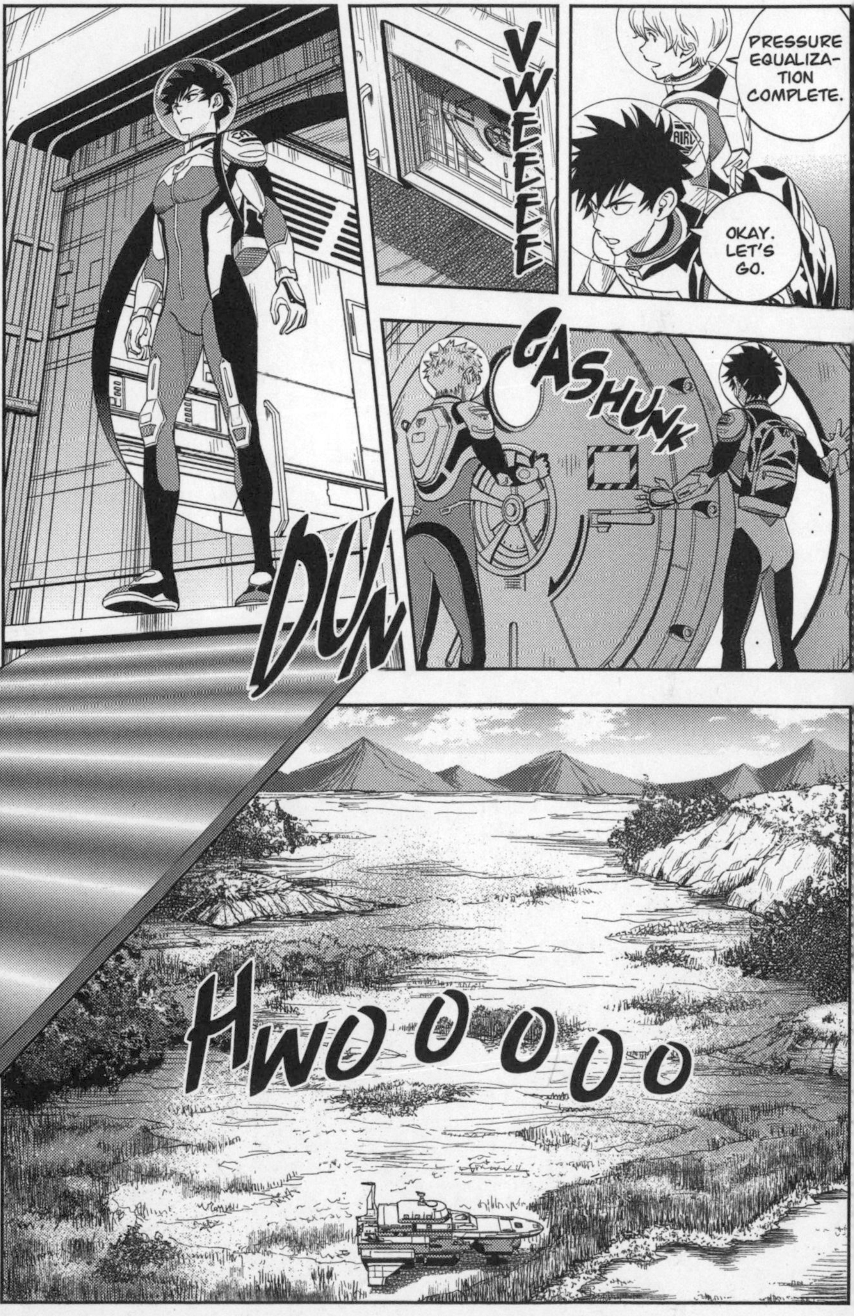
PRESSURE EQUALIZATION COMPLETE.
OKAY. LET'S GO.
VWEEEE
GASHUNK
DUN
HWOOOOOO

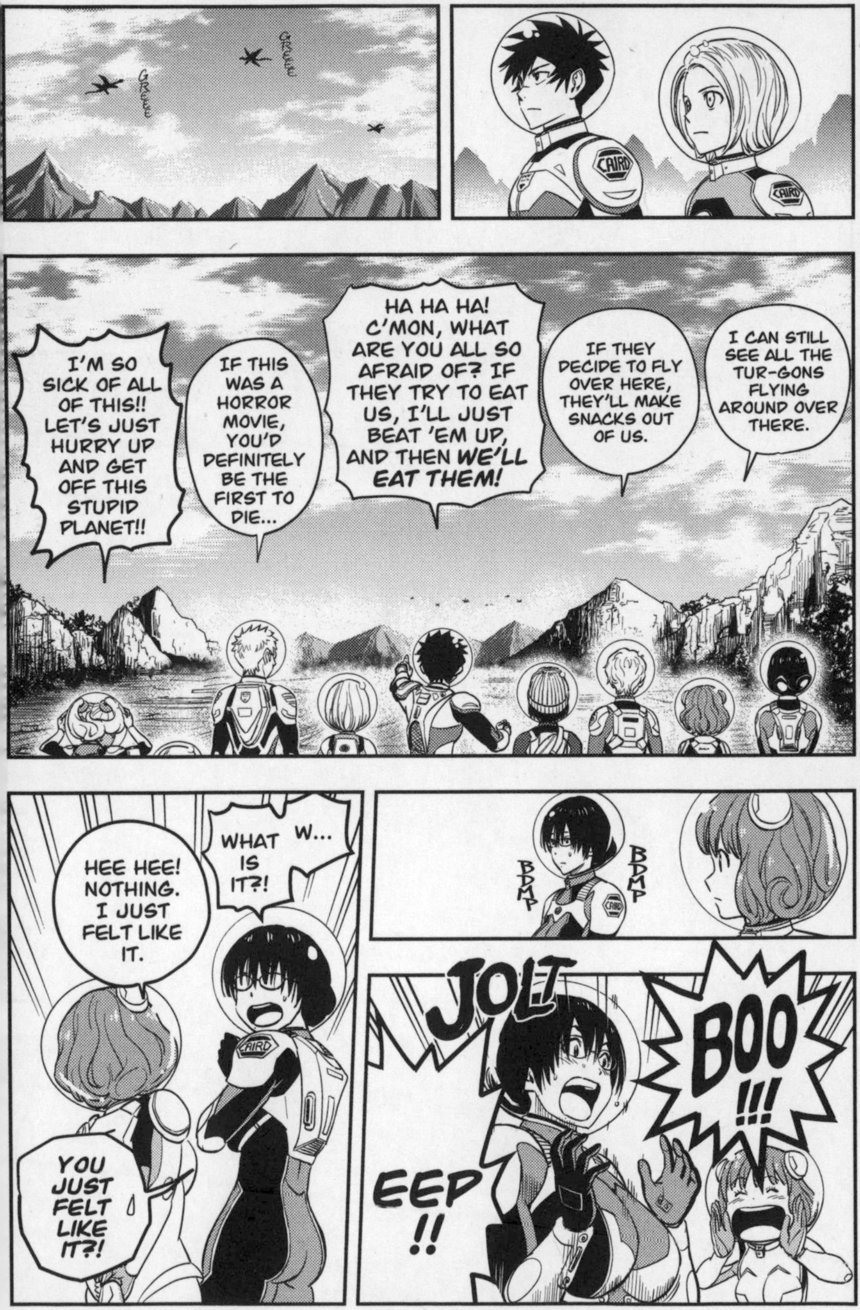
GREEE
GREEE
I CAN STILL SEE ALL THE TUR-GONS FLYING AROUND OVER THERE.
IF THEY DECIDE TO FLY OVER HERE, THEY'LL MAKE SNACKS OUT OF US.
HA HA HA! C'MON, WHAT ARE YOU ALL SO AFRAID OF? IF THEY TRY TO EAT US, I'LL JUST BEAT 'EM UP, AND THEN ***WE'LL EAT THEM!***
IF THIS WAS A HORROR MOVIE, YOU'D DEFINITELY BE THE FIRST TO DIE...
I'M SO SICK OF ALL OF THIS!! LET'S JUST HURRY UP AND GET OFF THIS STUPID PLANET!!
BDMP
BDMP
BOO!!!
JOLT
EEP!!
W...
WHAT IS IT?!
HEE HEE! NOTHING. I JUST FELT LIKE IT.
YOU JUST FELT LIKE IT?!

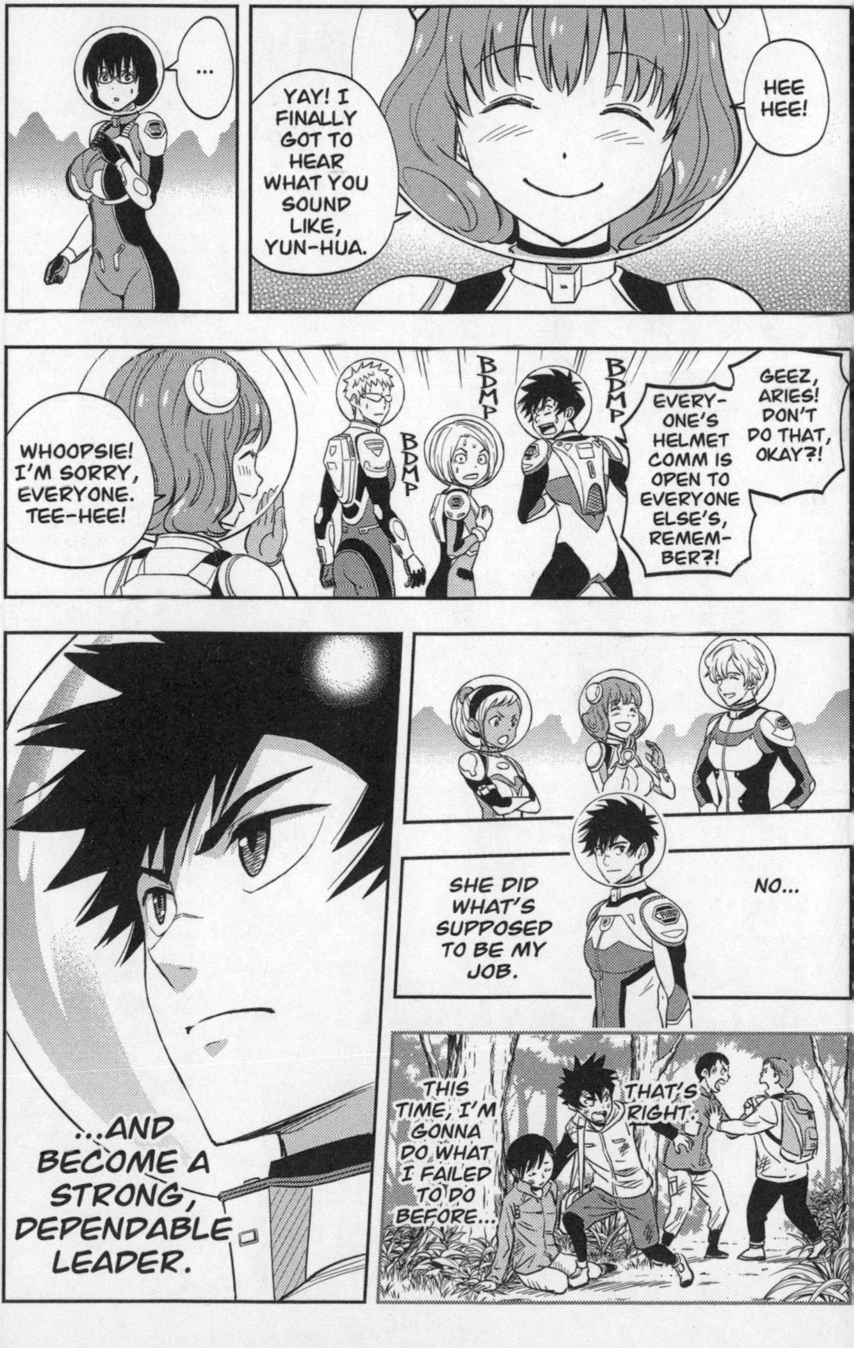
HEE HEE!
YAY! I FINALLY GOT TO HEAR WHAT YOU SOUND LIKE, YUN-HUA.
...
GEEZ, ARIES! DON'T DO THAT, OKAY?!
EVERYONE'S HELMET COMM IS OPEN TO EVERYONE ELSE'S, REMEMBER?!
BDMP
BDMP
BDMP
WHOOPSIE! I'M SORRY, EVERYONE. TEE-HEE!
NO...
SHE DID WHAT'S SUPPOSED TO BE MY JOB.
THAT'S RIGHT.
THIS TIME, I'M GONNA DO WHAT I FAILED TO DO BEFORE...
...AND BECOME A STRONG, DEPENDABLE LEADER.

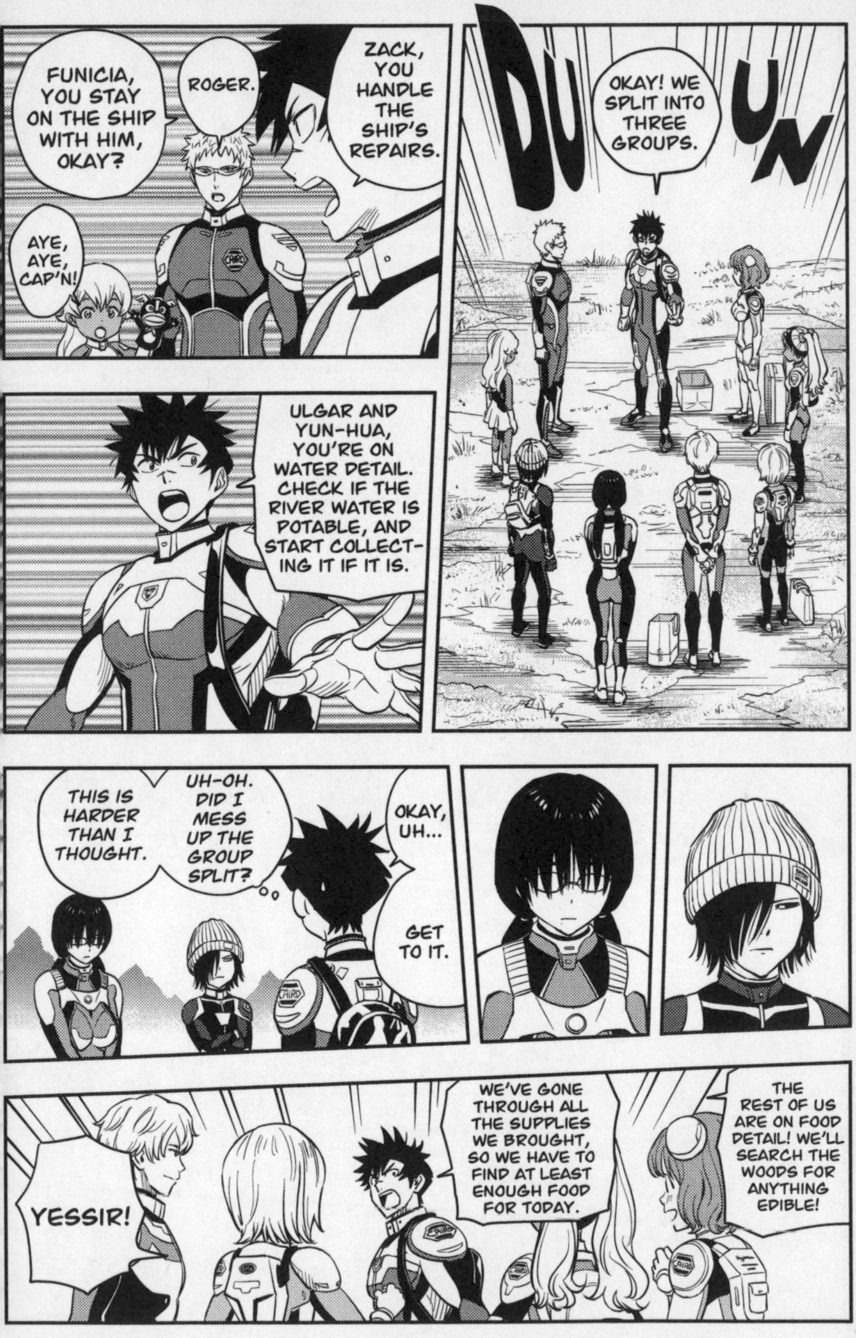
DUUN
OKAY! WE SPLIT INTO THREE GROUPS.
ZACK, YOU HANDLE THE SHIP'S REPAIRS.
ROGER.
FUNICIA, YOU STAY ON THE SHIP WITH HIM, OKAY?
AYE, AYE, CAP'N!
ULGAR AND YUN-HUA, YOU'RE ON WATER DETAIL. CHECK IF THE RIVER WATER IS POTABLE, AND START COLLECTING IT IF IT IS.
OKAY, UH...
UH-OH. DID I MESS UP THE GROUP SPLIT?
THIS IS HARDER THAN I THOUGHT.
GET TO IT.
THE REST OF US ARE ON FOOD DETAIL! WE'LL SEARCH THE WOODS FOR ANYTHING EDIBLE!
WE'VE GONE THROUGH ALL THE SUPPLIES WE BROUGHT, SO WE HAVE TO FIND AT LEAST ENOUGH FOOD FOR TODAY.
YESSIR!

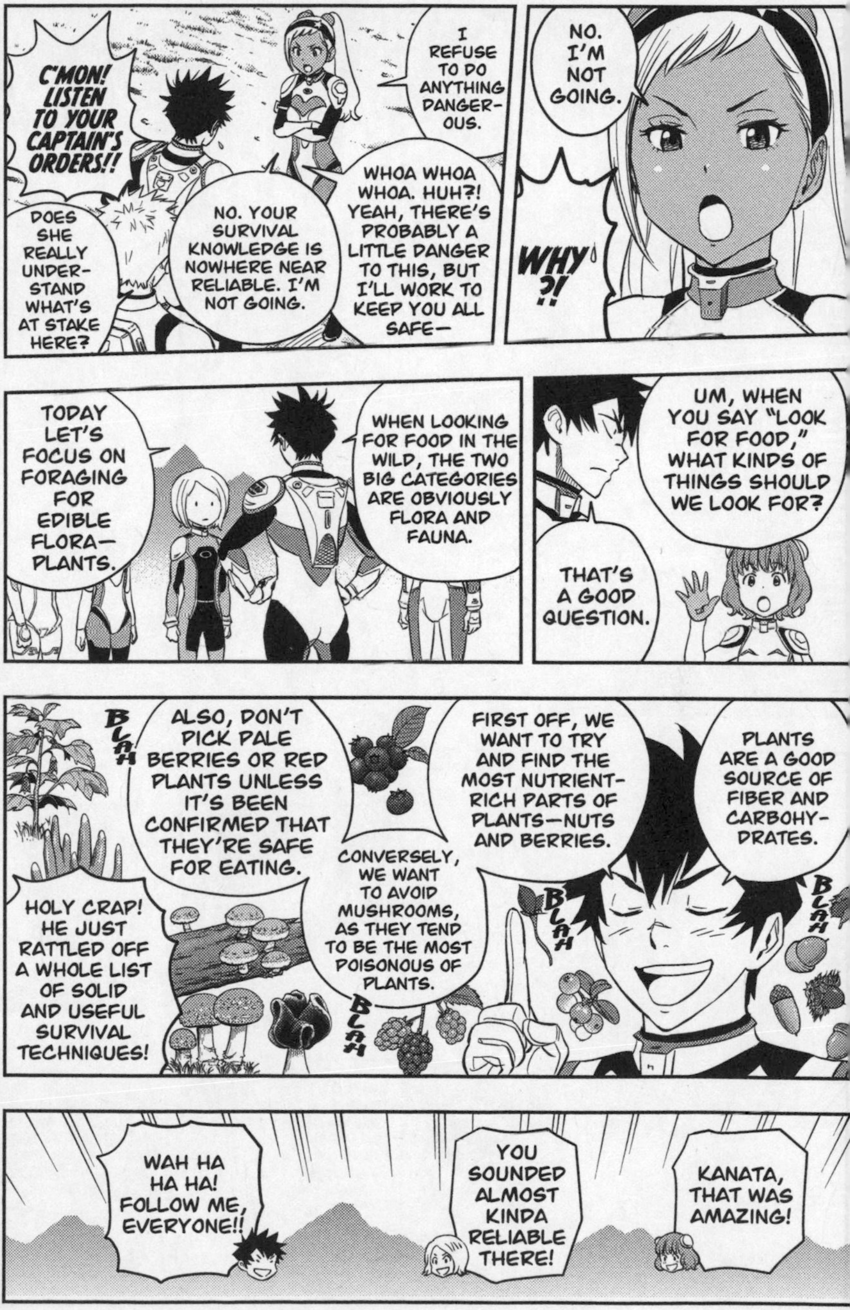
NO. I'M NOT GOING.
WHY?!
I REFUSE TO DO ANYTHING DANGER-OUS.
C'MON! LISTEN TO YOUR CAPTAIN'S ORDERS!!
WHOA WHOA WHOA. HUH?! YEAH, THERE'S PROBABLY A LITTLE DANGER TO THIS, BUT I'LL WORK TO KEEP YOU ALL SAFE—
NO. YOUR SURVIVAL KNOWLEDGE IS NOWHERE NEAR RELIABLE. I'M NOT GOING.
DOES SHE REALLY UNDER-STAND WHAT'S AT STAKE HERE?
UM, WHEN YOU SAY "LOOK FOR FOOD," WHAT KINDS OF THINGS SHOULD WE LOOK FOR?
THAT'S A GOOD QUESTION.
WHEN LOOKING FOR FOOD IN THE WILD, THE TWO BIG CATEGORIES ARE OBVIOUSLY FLORA AND FAUNA.
TODAY LET'S FOCUS ON FORAGING FOR EDIBLE FLORA—PLANTS.
PLANTS ARE A GOOD SOURCE OF FIBER AND CARBOHY-DRATES.
BLAH
FIRST OFF, WE WANT TO TRY AND FIND THE MOST NUTRIENT-RICH PARTS OF PLANTS—NUTS AND BERRIES.
BLAH
ALSO, DON'T PICK PALE BERRIES OR RED PLANTS UNLESS IT'S BEEN CONFIRMED THAT THEY'RE SAFE FOR EATING.
BLAH
CONVERSELY, WE WANT TO AVOID MUSHROOMS, AS THEY TEND TO BE THE MOST POISONOUS OF PLANTS.
BLAH
HOLY CRAP! HE JUST RATTLED OFF A WHOLE LIST OF SOLID AND USEFUL SURVIVAL TECHNIQUES!
KANATA, THAT WAS AMAZING!
YOU SOUNDED ALMOST KINDA RELIABLE THERE!
WAH HA HA HA! FOLLOW ME, EVERYONE!!

HECK IF I KNOW! DON'T ASK ME!!

I'm sorry, okay?!

WHICH OF THESE COUNT AS NUTS AND WHICH AS BERRIES?

SKTR. SKTR.

WRIGGL-WRIGGL

...

UH, KANA-TA?

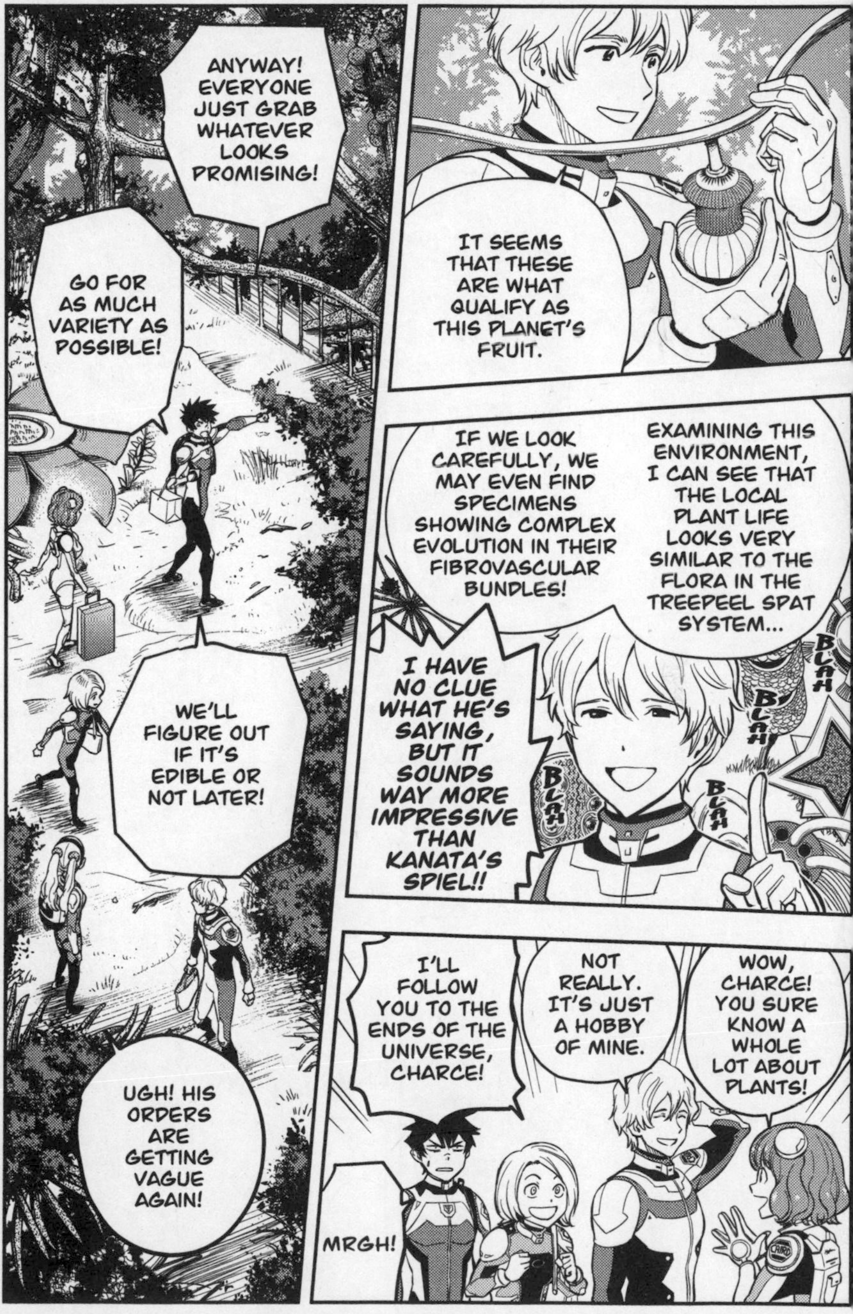
IT SEEMS THAT THESE ARE WHAT QUALIFY AS THIS PLANET'S FRUIT.
EXAMINING THIS ENVIRONMENT, I CAN SEE THAT THE LOCAL PLANT LIFE LOOKS VERY SIMILAR TO THE FLORA IN THE TREEPEEL SPAT SYSTEM...
IF WE LOOK CAREFULLY, WE MAY EVEN FIND SPECIMENS SHOWING COMPLEX EVOLUTION IN THEIR FIBROVASCULAR BUNDLES!
BLAH
BLAH
BLAH
BLAH
I HAVE NO CLUE WHAT HE'S SAYING, BUT IT SOUNDS WAY MORE IMPRESSIVE THAN KANATA'S SPIEL!!
WOW, CHARCE! YOU SURE KNOW A WHOLE LOT ABOUT PLANTS!
NOT REALLY. IT'S JUST A HOBBY OF MINE.
I'LL FOLLOW YOU TO THE ENDS OF THE UNIVERSE, CHARCE!
MRGH!
ANYWAY! EVERYONE JUST GRAB WHATEVER LOOKS PROMISING!
GO FOR AS MUCH VARIETY AS POSSIBLE!
WE'LL FIGURE OUT IF IT'S EDIBLE OR NOT LATER!
UGH! HIS ORDERS ARE GETTING VAGUE AGAIN!

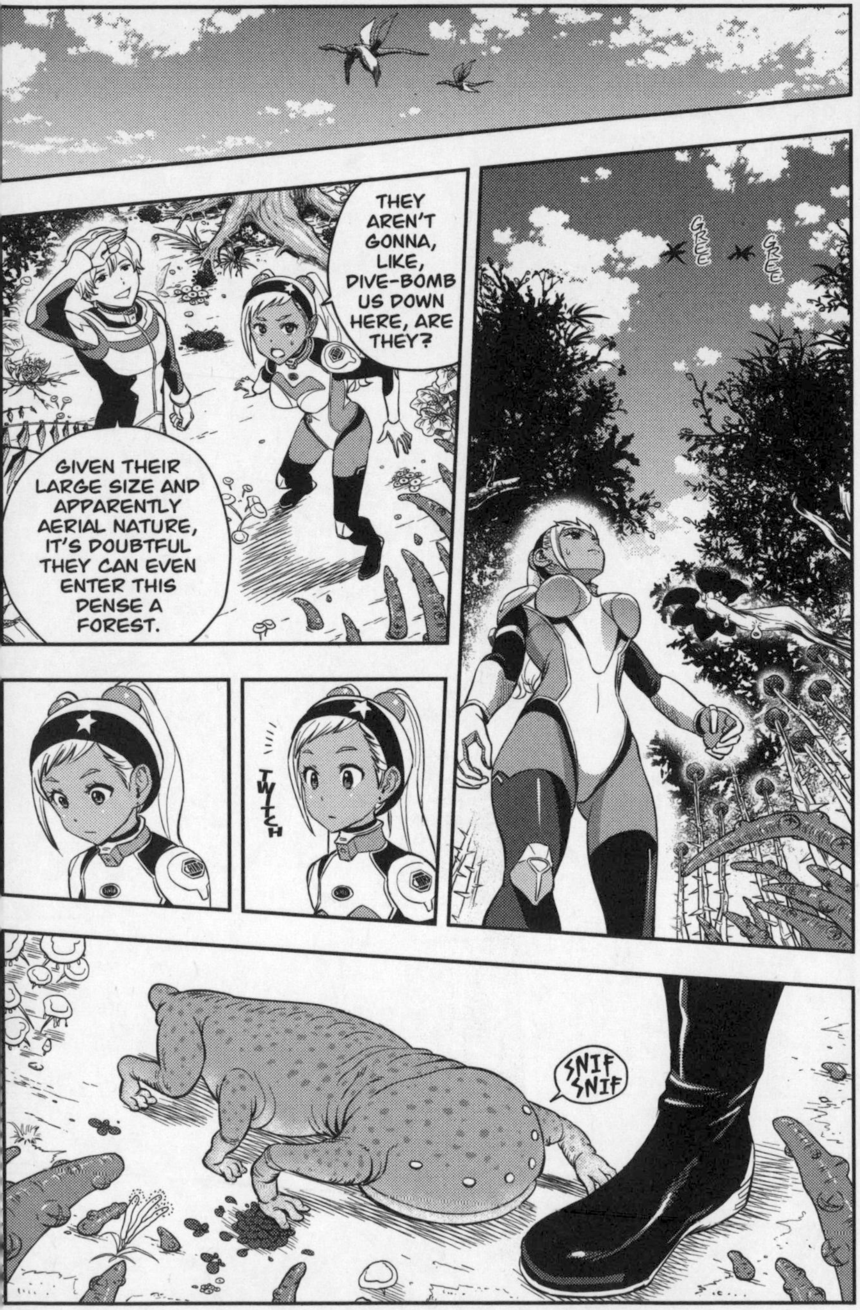
GREE GREE
THEY AREN'T GONNA, LIKE, DIVE-BOMB US DOWN HERE, ARE THEY?
GIVEN THEIR LARGE SIZE AND APPARENTLY AERIAL NATURE, IT'S DOUBTFUL THEY CAN EVEN ENTER THIS DENSE A FOREST.
TWITCH
SNIF SNIF

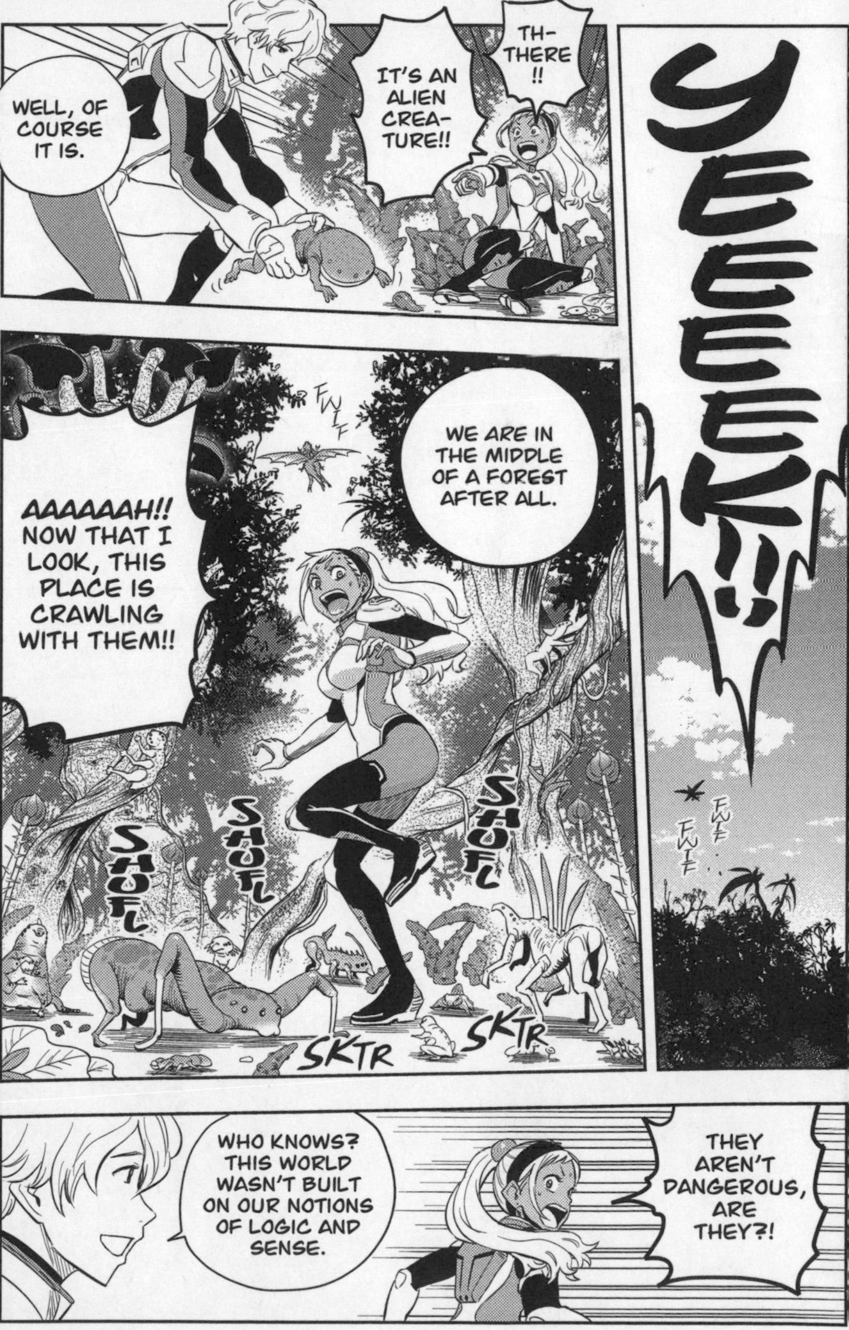
YEEEEEK!!
FWIF FWIF
TH-THERE!!
IT'S AN ALIEN CREATURE!!
WELL, OF COURSE IT IS.
WE ARE IN THE MIDDLE OF A FOREST AFTER ALL.
FWIF
AAAAAAH!! NOW THAT I LOOK, THIS PLACE IS CRAWLING WITH THEM!!
SHUFL
SHUFL
SHUFL
SKTR
SKTR
THEY AREN'T DANGEROUS, ARE THEY?!
WHO KNOWS? THIS WORLD WASN'T BUILT ON OUR NOTIONS OF LOGIC AND SENSE.

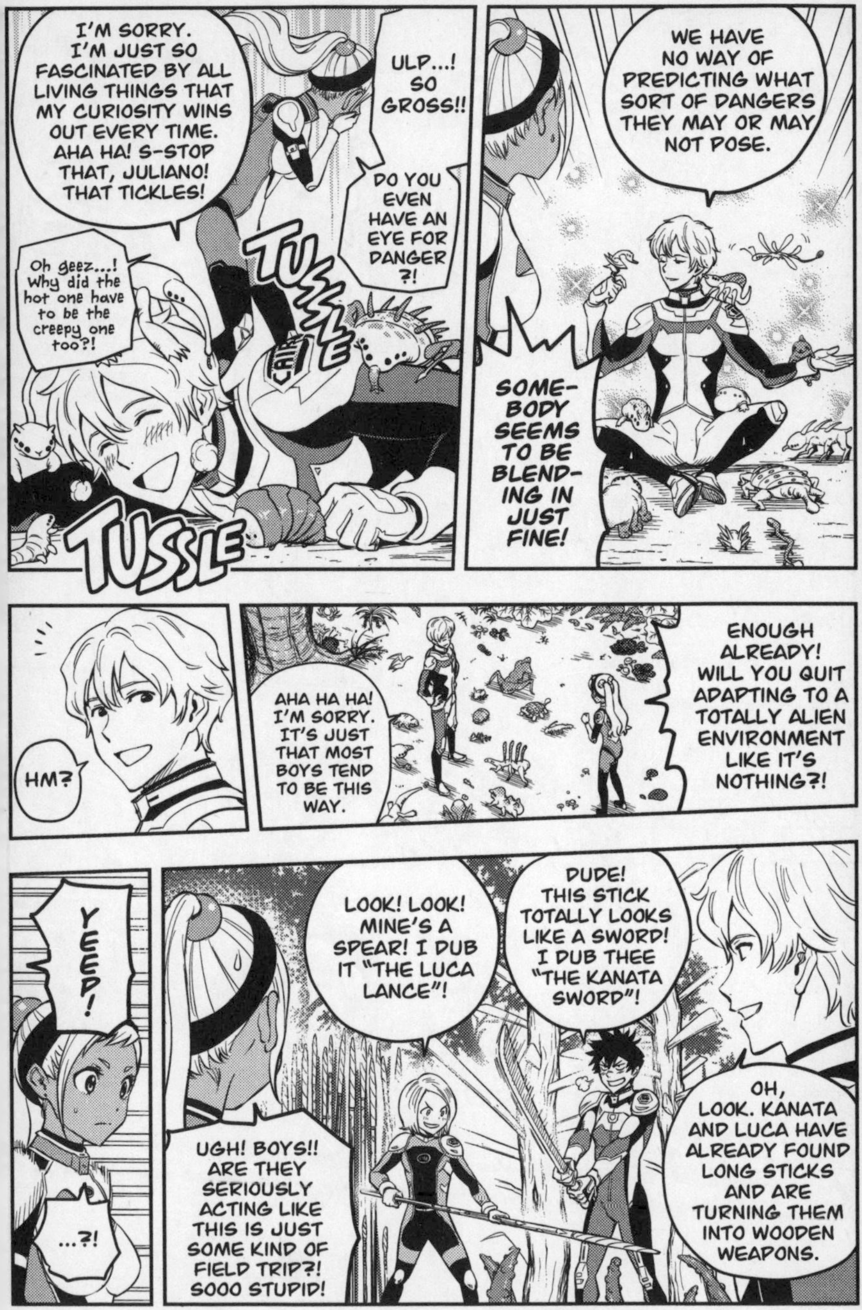
WE HAVE NO WAY OF PREDICTING WHAT SORT OF DANGERS THEY MAY OR MAY NOT POSE.
SOMEBODY SEEMS TO BE BLENDING IN JUST FINE!
ULP...! SO GROSS!!
DO YOU EVEN HAVE AN EYE FOR DANGER?!
I'M SORRY. I'M JUST SO FASCINATED BY ALL LIVING THINGS THAT MY CURIOSITY WINS OUT EVERY TIME. AHA HA! S-STOP THAT, JULIANO! THAT TICKLES!
TUSSLE
Oh geez...! Why did the hot one have to be the creepy one too?!
TUSSLE
ENOUGH ALREADY! WILL YOU QUIT ADAPTING TO A TOTALLY ALIEN ENVIRONMENT LIKE IT'S NOTHING?!
AHA HA HA! I'M SORRY. IT'S JUST THAT MOST BOYS TEND TO BE THIS WAY.
HM?
OH, LOOK. KANATA AND LUCA HAVE ALREADY FOUND LONG STICKS AND ARE TURNING THEM INTO WOODEN WEAPONS.
DUDE! THIS STICK TOTALLY LOOKS LIKE A SWORD! I DUB THEE "THE KANATA SWORD"!
LOOK! LOOK! MINE'S A SPEAR! I DUB IT "THE LUCA LANCE"!
UGH! BOYS!! ARE THEY SERIOUSLY ACTING LIKE THIS IS JUST SOME KIND OF FIELD TRIP?! SOOO STUPID!
YEEP!
...?!

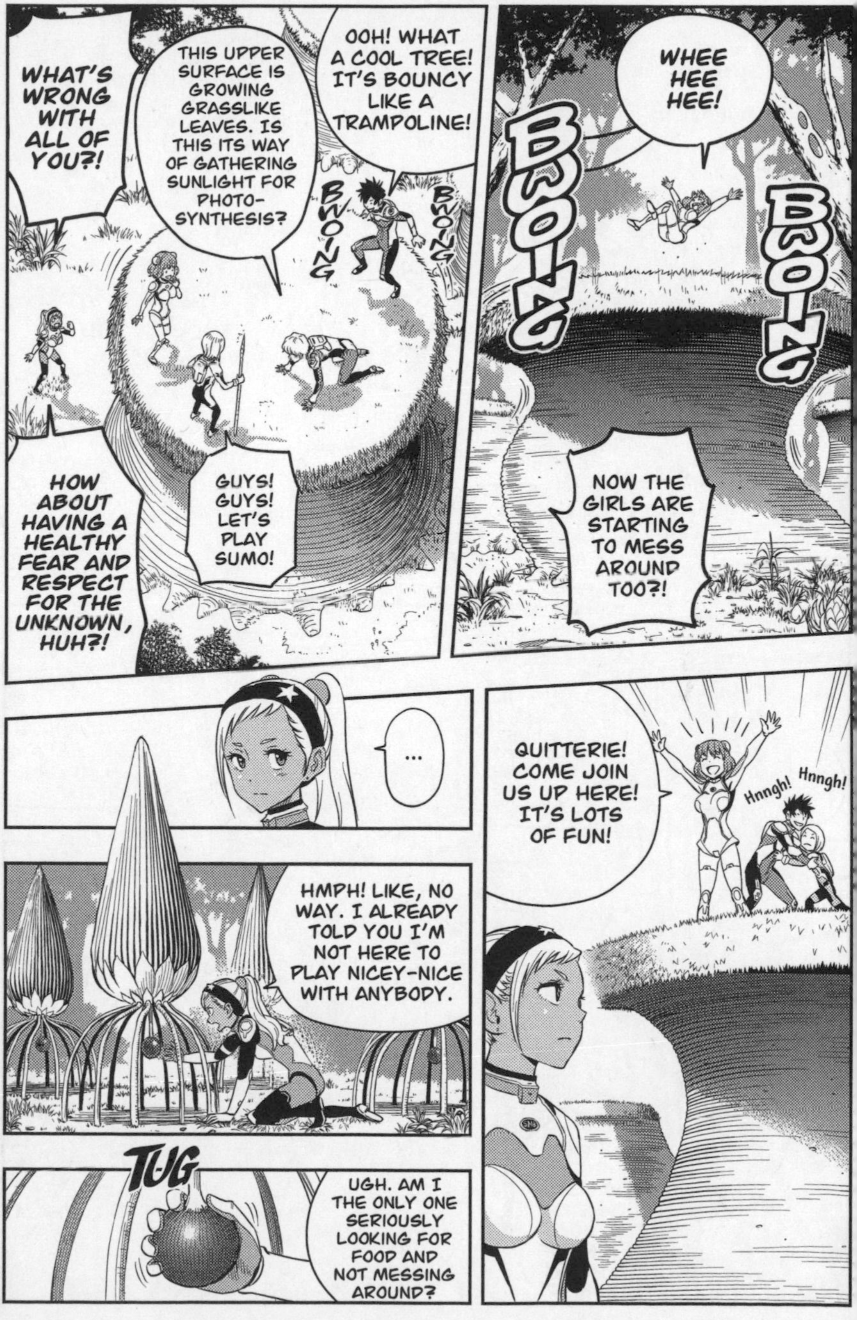
WHEE HEE HEE!
BWOING
BWOING
NOW THE GIRLS ARE STARTING TO MESS AROUND TOO?!
OOH! WHAT A COOL TREE! IT'S BOUNCY LIKE A TRAMPOLINE!
THIS UPPER SURFACE IS GROWING GRASSLIKE LEAVES. IS THIS ITS WAY OF GATHERING SUNLIGHT FOR PHOTO-SYNTHESIS?
WHAT'S WRONG WITH ALL OF YOU?!
BWOING
BWOING
GUYS! GUYS! LET'S PLAY SUMO!
HOW ABOUT HAVING A HEALTHY FEAR AND RESPECT FOR THE UNKNOWN, HUH?!
QUITTERIE! COME JOIN US UP HERE! IT'S LOTS OF FUN!
Hnngh!
Hnngh!
...
HMPH! LIKE, NO WAY. I ALREADY TOLD YOU I'M NOT HERE TO PLAY NICEY-NICE WITH ANYBODY.
TUG
UGH. AM I THE ONLY ONE SERIOUSLY LOOKING FOR FOOD AND NOT MESSING AROUND?

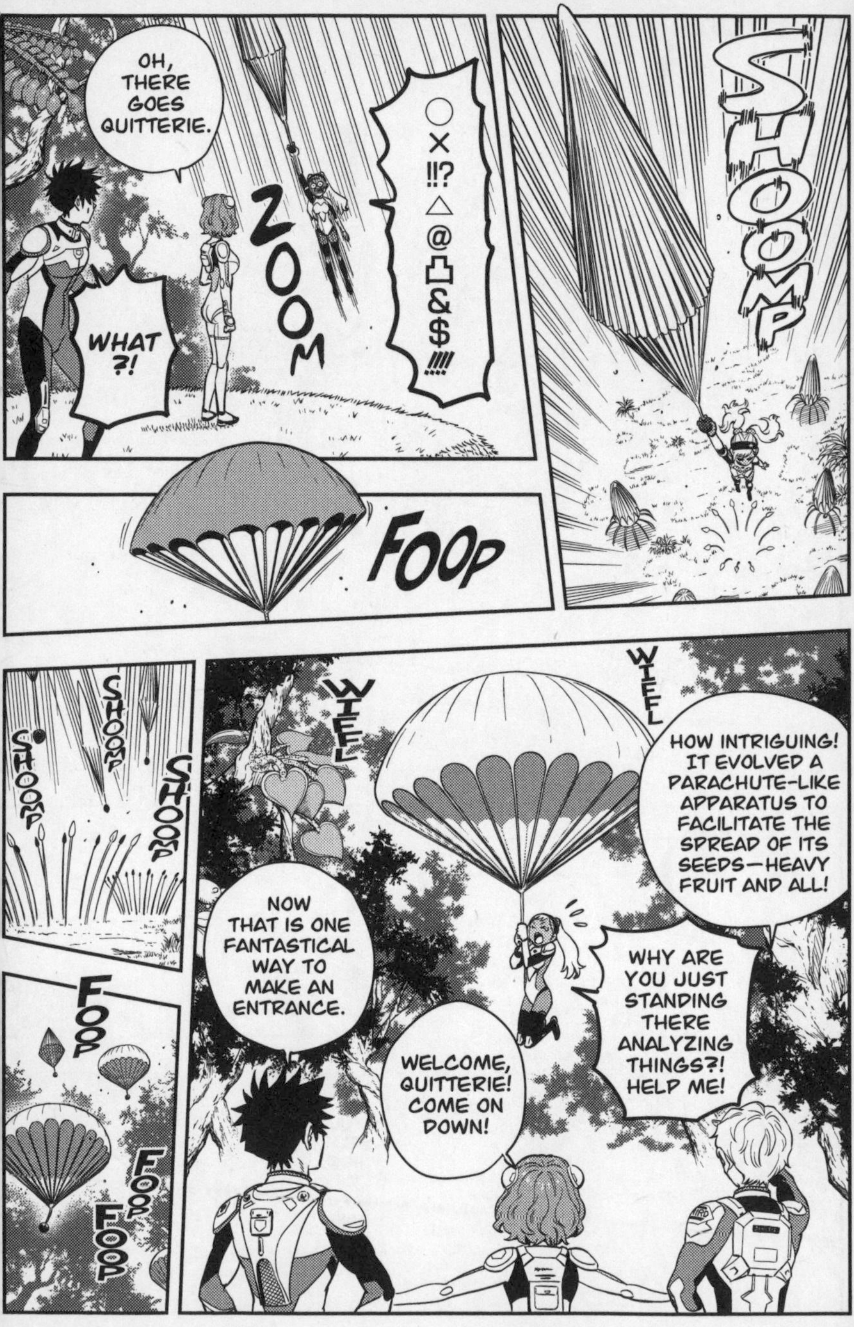
SHOOMP
○×!!?△@凸&$!!!!
ZOOM
OH, THERE GOES QUITTERIE.
WHAT?!
FOOP
WIFFL
HOW INTRIGUING! IT EVOLVED A PARACHUTE-LIKE APPARATUS TO FACILITATE THE SPREAD OF ITS SEEDS—HEAVY FRUIT AND ALL!
WIFFL
WHY ARE YOU JUST STANDING THERE ANALYZING THINGS?! HELP ME!
NOW THAT IS ONE FANTASTICAL WAY TO MAKE AN ENTRANCE.
WELCOME, QUITTERIE! COME ON DOWN!
SHOOMP
SHOOMP
SHOOMP
FOOP
FOOP
FOOP

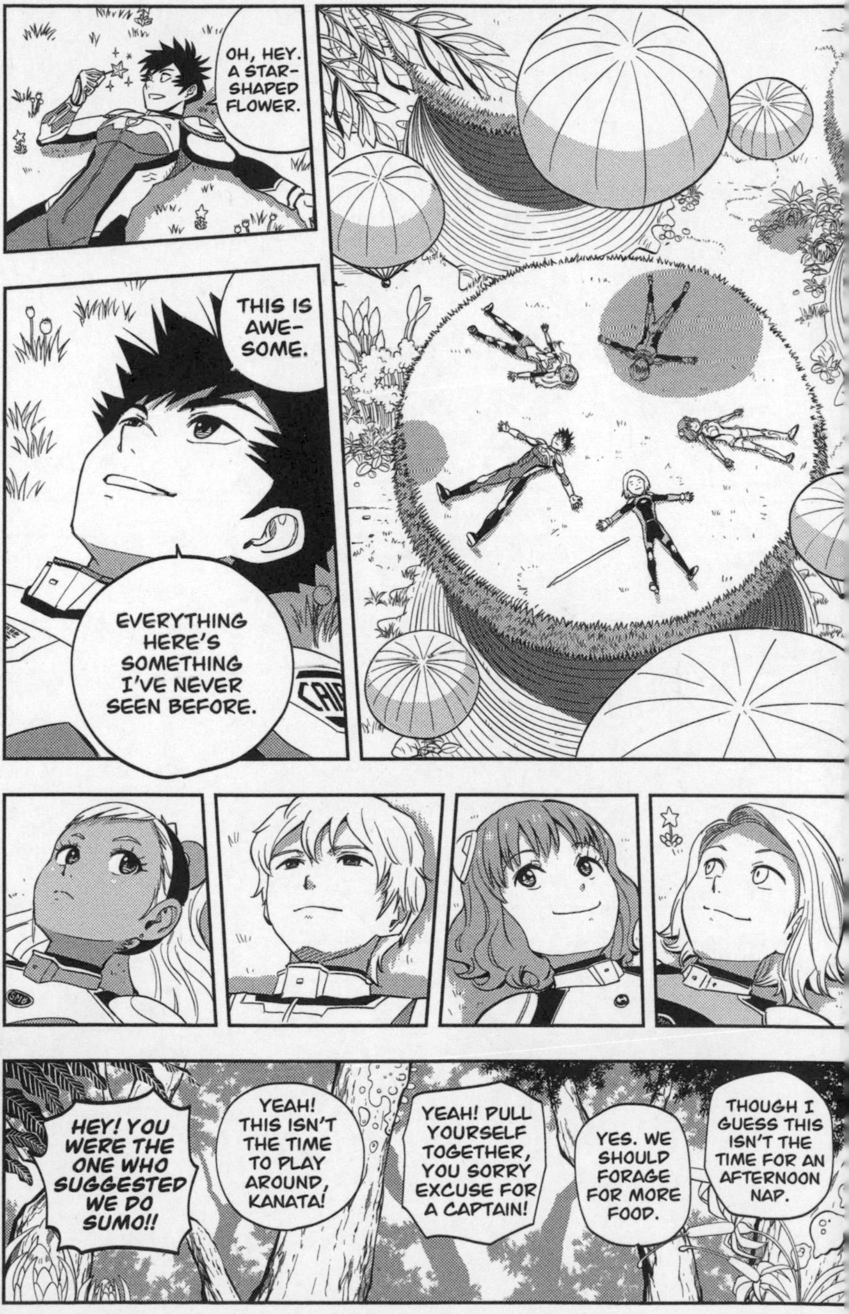
OH, HEY. A STAR-SHAPED FLOWER.
THIS IS AWESOME.
EVERYTHING HERE'S SOMETHING I'VE NEVER SEEN BEFORE.
THOUGH I GUESS THIS ISN'T THE TIME FOR AN AFTERNOON NAP.
YES. WE SHOULD FORAGE FOR MORE FOOD.
YEAH! PULL YOURSELF TOGETHER, YOU SORRY EXCUSE FOR A CAPTAIN!
YEAH! THIS ISN'T THE TIME TO PLAY AROUND, KANATA!
HEY! YOU WERE THE ONE WHO SUGGESTED WE DO SUMO!!

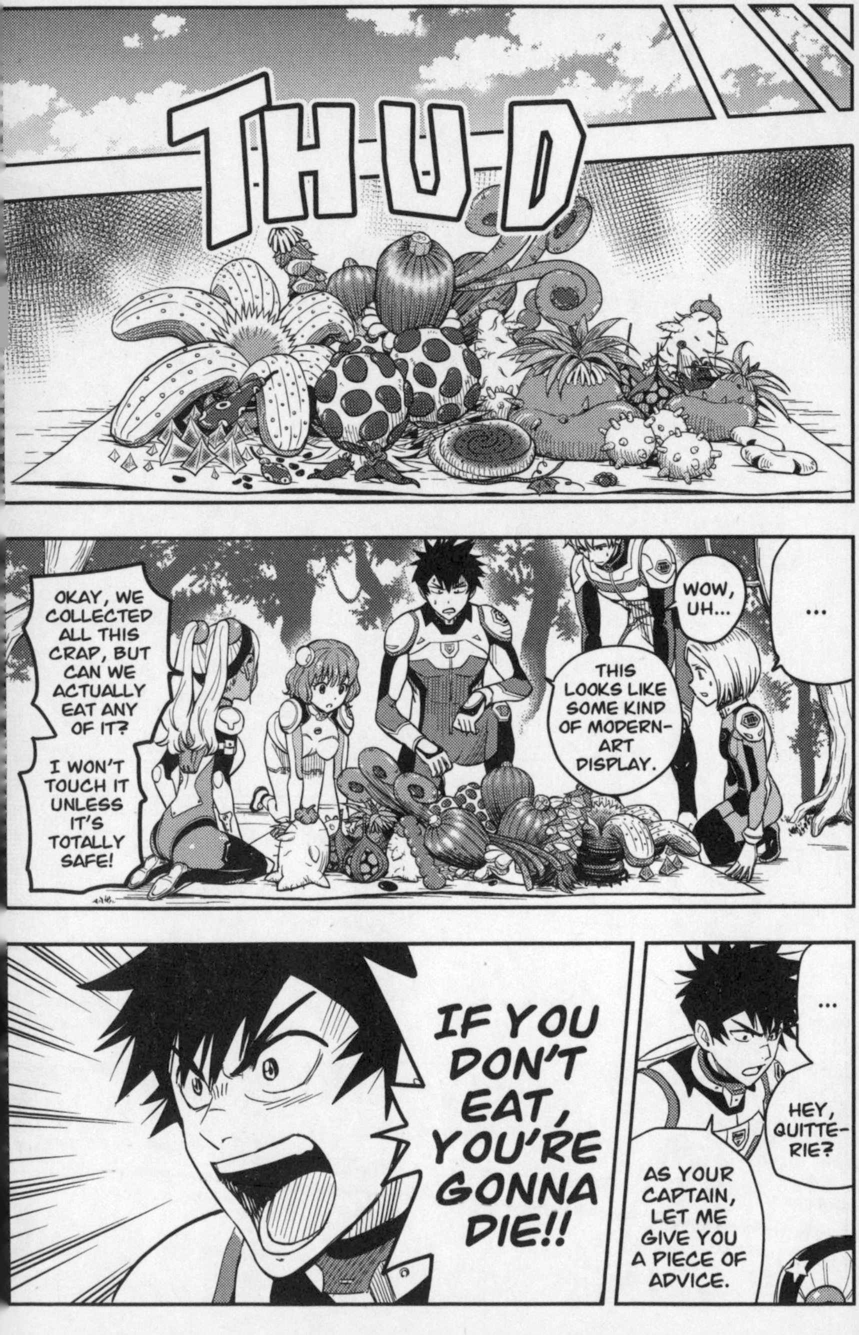
THUD
...
WOW, UH...
THIS LOOKS LIKE SOME KIND OF MODERN-ART DISPLAY.
OKAY, WE COLLECTED ALL THIS CRAP, BUT CAN WE ACTUALLY EAT ANY OF IT?
I WON'T TOUCH IT UNLESS IT'S TOTALLY SAFE!
...
HEY, QUITTERIE?
AS YOUR CAPTAIN, LET ME GIVE YOU A PIECE OF ADVICE.
IF YOU DON'T EAT, YOU'RE GONNA DIE!!

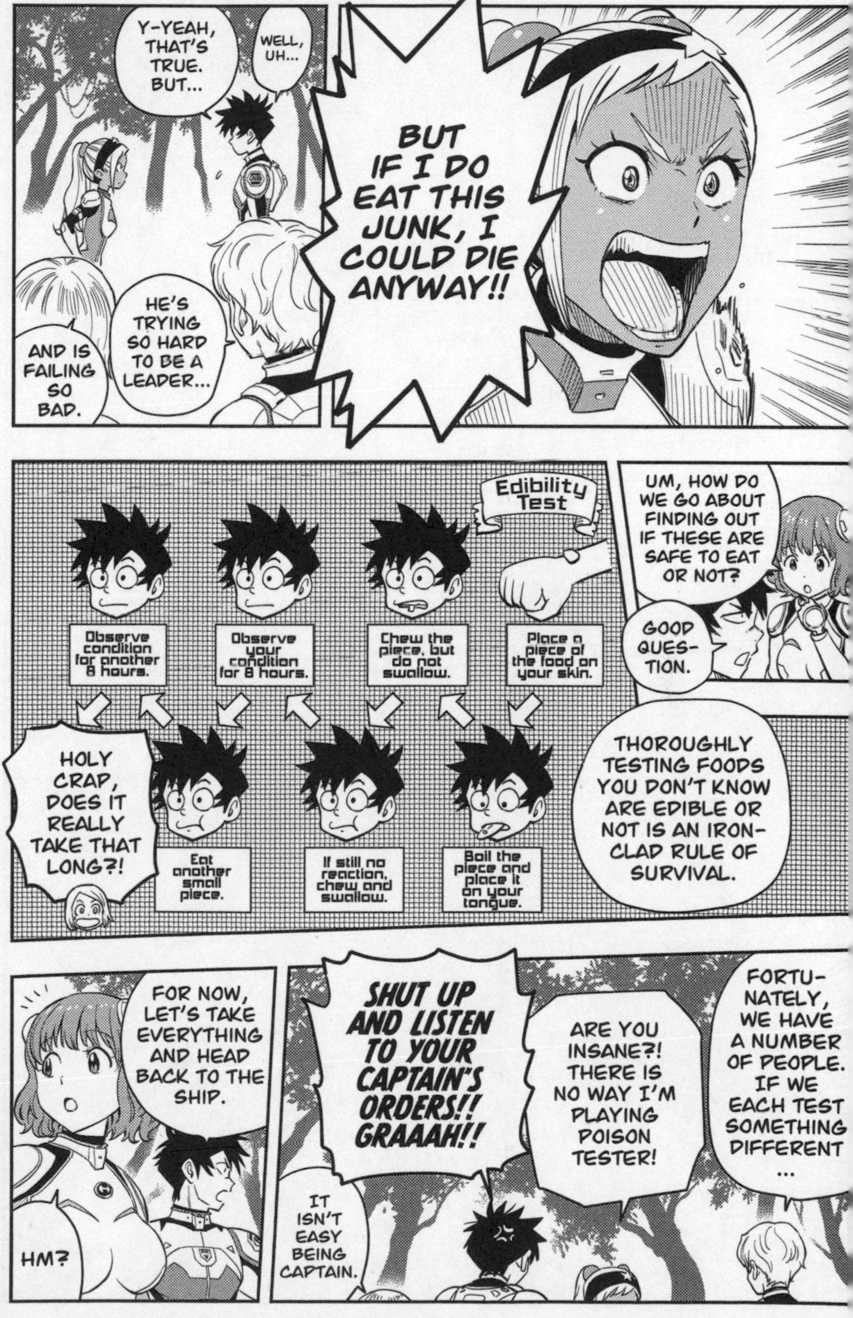
BUT IF I DO EAT THIS JUNK, I COULD DIE ANYWAY!!
WELL, UH...
Y-YEAH, THAT'S TRUE. BUT...
HE'S TRYING SO HARD TO BE A LEADER...
AND IS FAILING SO BAD.
UM, HOW DO WE GO ABOUT FINDING OUT IF THESE ARE SAFE TO EAT OR NOT?
GOOD QUES-TION.
THOROUGHLY TESTING FOODS YOU DON'T KNOW ARE EDIBLE OR NOT IS AN IRON-CLAD RULE OF SURVIVAL.
Edibility Test
Place a piece of the food on your skin.
Chew the piece, but do not swallow.
Observe your condition for 8 hours.
Observe condition for another 8 hours.
Boil the piece and place it on your tongue.
If still no reaction, chew and swallow.
Eat another small piece.
HOLY CRAP, DOES IT REALLY TAKE THAT LONG?!
FORTU-NATELY, WE HAVE A NUMBER OF PEOPLE. IF WE EACH TEST SOMETHING DIFFERENT ...
ARE YOU INSANE?! THERE IS NO WAY I'M PLAYING POISON TESTER!
SHUT UP AND LISTEN TO YOUR CAPTAIN'S ORDERS!! GRAAAH!!
IT ISN'T EASY BEING CAPTAIN.
FOR NOW, LET'S TAKE EVERYTHING AND HEAD BACK TO THE SHIP.
HM?

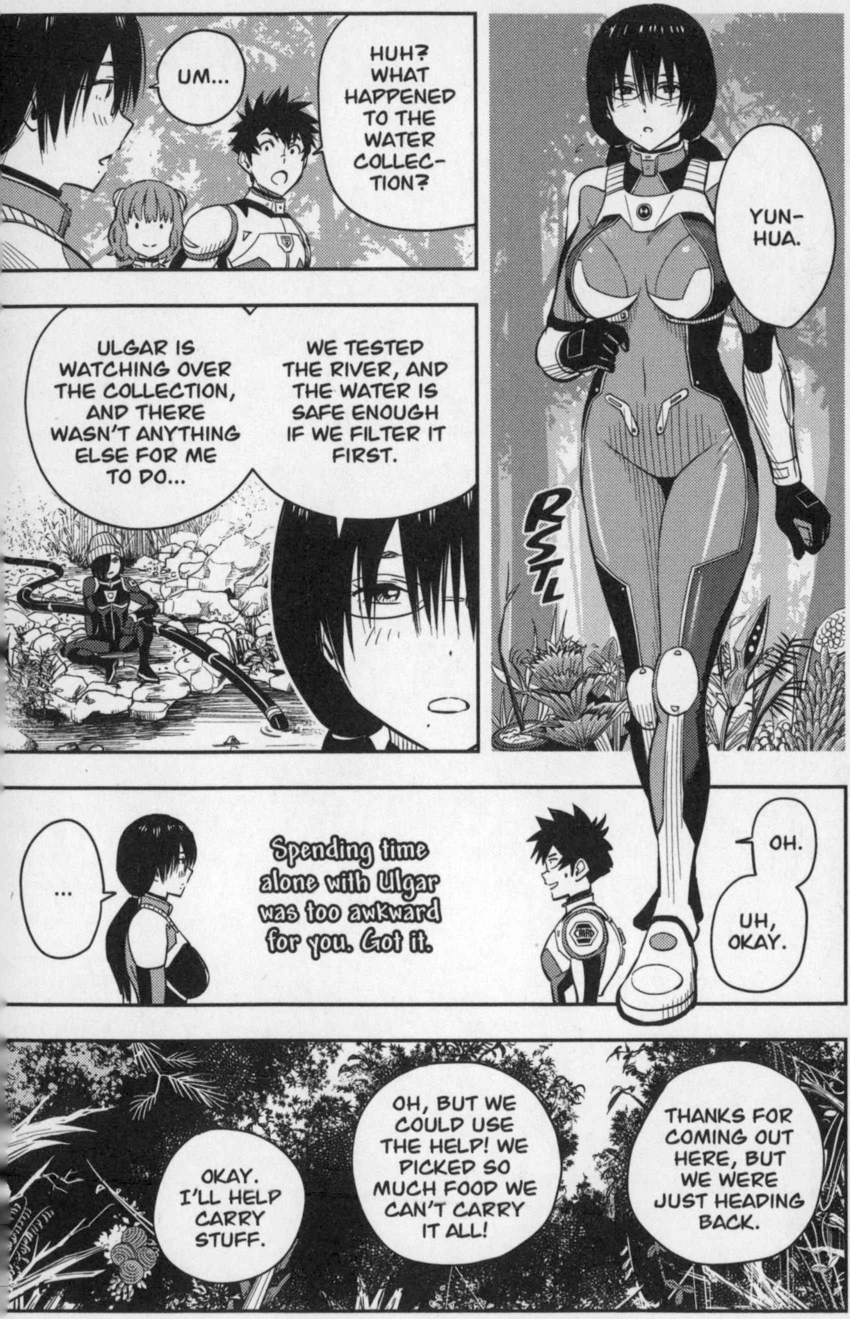
YUN-HUA.
RSTL
HUH? WHAT HAPPENED TO THE WATER COLLECTION?
UM...
WE TESTED THE RIVER, AND THE WATER IS SAFE ENOUGH IF WE FILTER IT FIRST.
ULGAR IS WATCHING OVER THE COLLECTION, AND THERE WASN'T ANYTHING ELSE FOR ME TO DO...
OH.
UH, OKAY.
Spending time alone with Ulgar was too awkward for you. Got it.
...
THANKS FOR COMING OUT HERE, BUT WE WERE JUST HEADING BACK.
OH, BUT WE COULD USE THE HELP! WE PICKED SO MUCH FOOD WE CAN'T CARRY IT ALL!
OKAY. I'LL HELP CARRY STUFF.

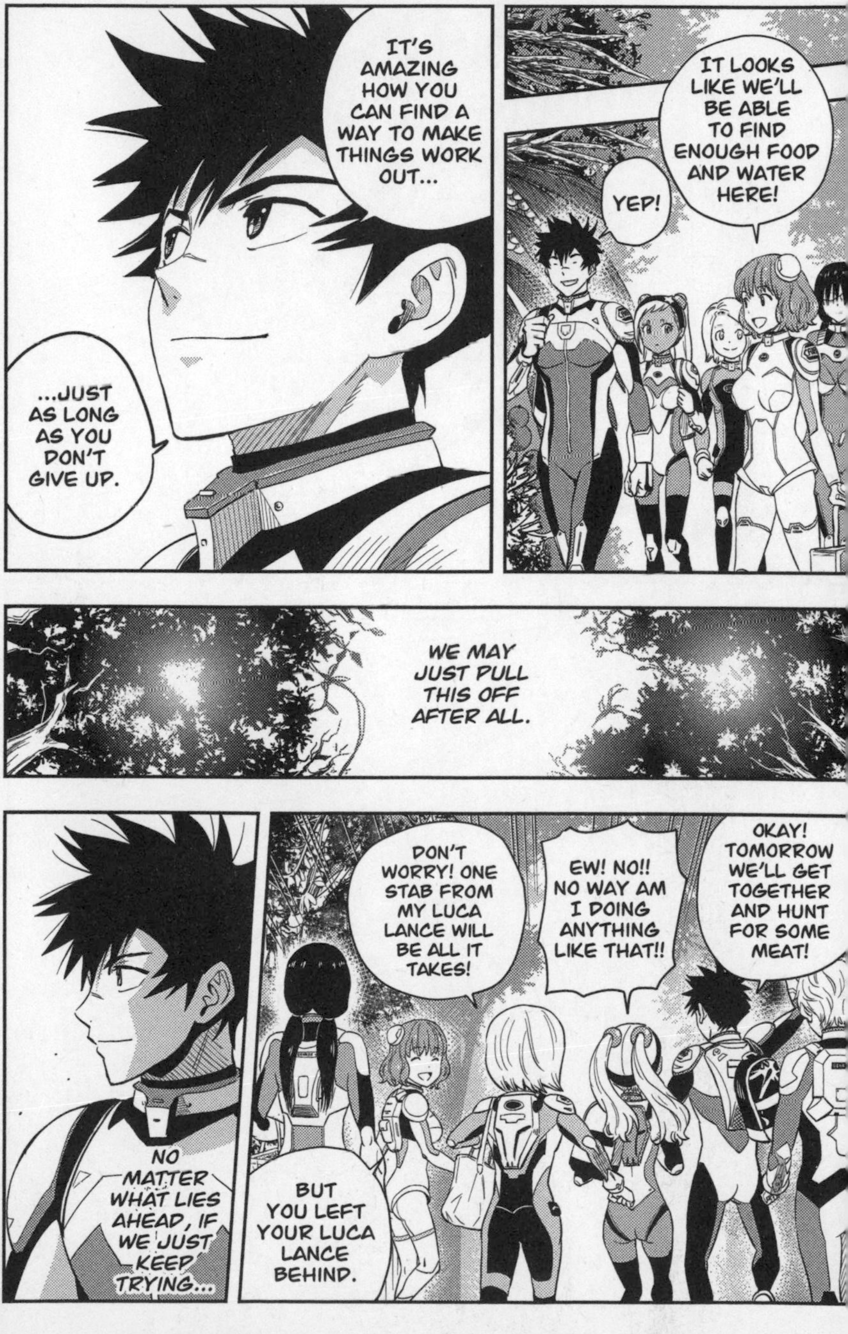
IT LOOKS LIKE WE'LL BE ABLE TO FIND ENOUGH FOOD AND WATER HERE!
YEP!
IT'S AMAZING HOW YOU CAN FIND A WAY TO MAKE THINGS WORK OUT...
...JUST AS LONG AS YOU DON'T GIVE UP.
WE MAY JUST PULL THIS OFF AFTER ALL.
OKAY! TOMORROW WE'LL GET TOGETHER AND HUNT FOR SOME MEAT!
EW! NO!! NO WAY AM I DOING ANYTHING LIKE THAT!!
DON'T WORRY! ONE STAB FROM MY LUCA LANCE WILL BE ALL IT TAKES!
BUT YOU LEFT YOUR LUCA LANCE BEHIND.
NO MATTER WHAT LIES AHEAD, IF WE JUST KEEP TRYING...

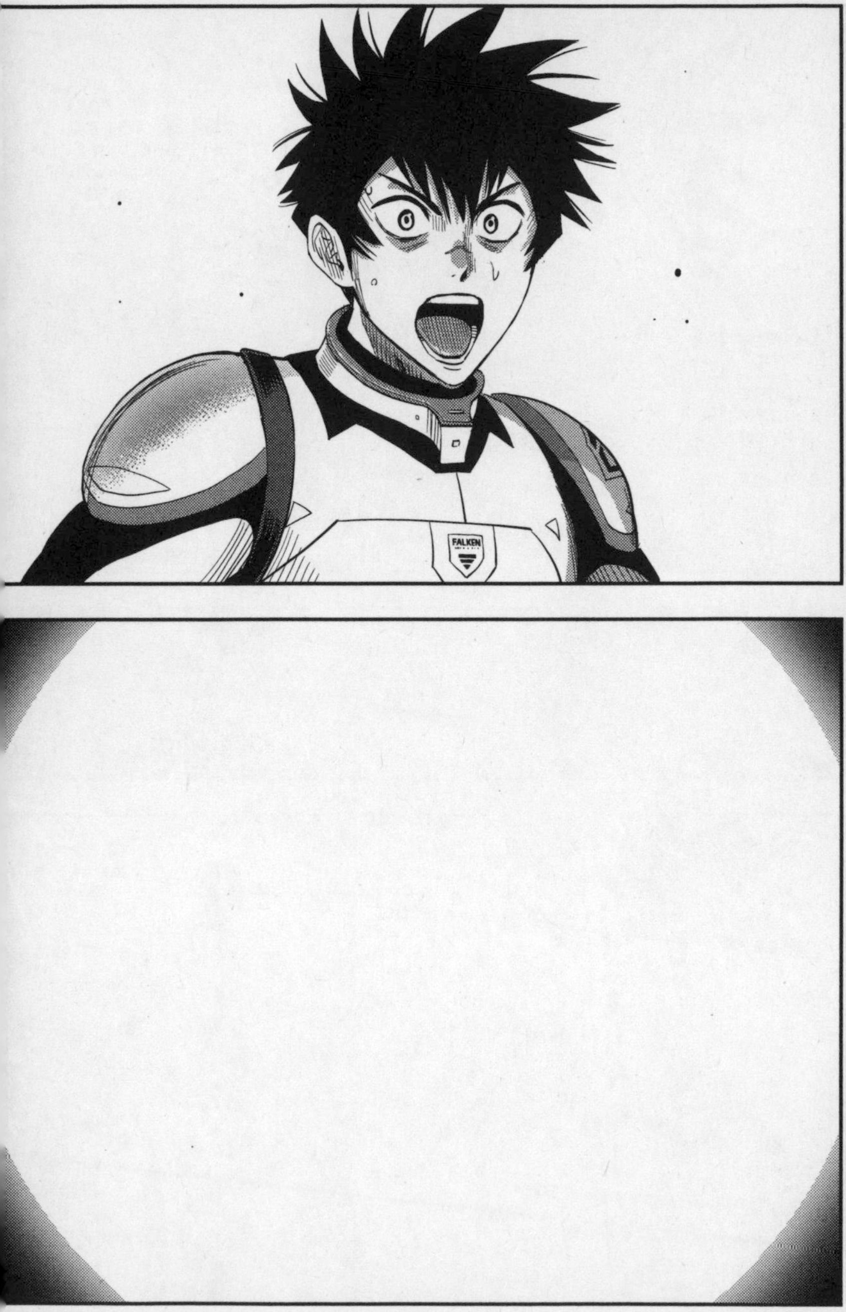
FALKEN

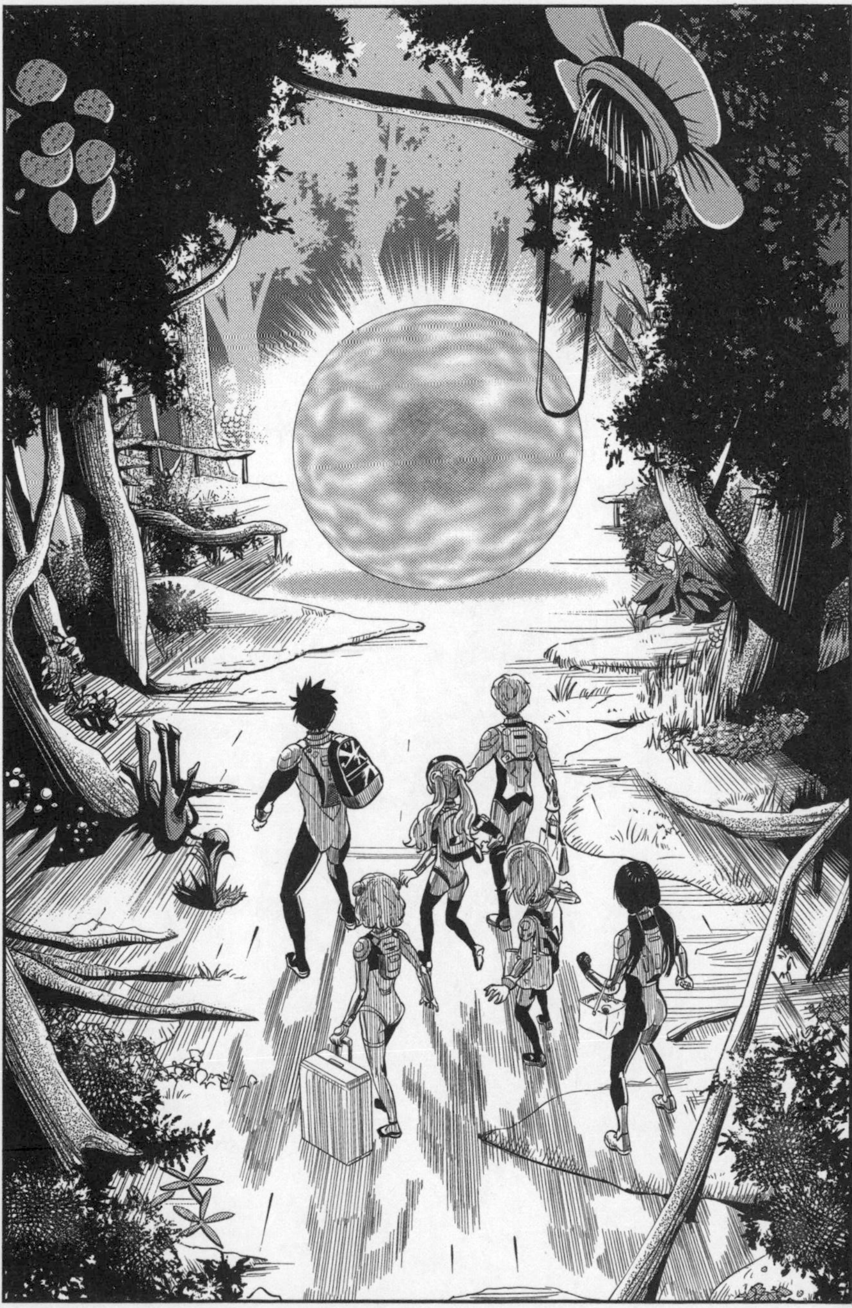

HARACTER HEIGHT CHART

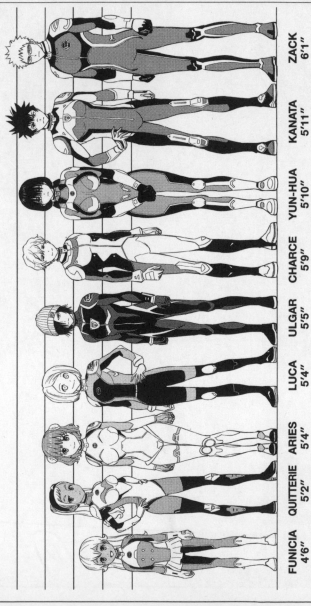

ZACK
6'1"

KANATA
5'11"

YUN-HUA
5'10"

CHARCE
5'9"

ULGAR
5'5"

LUCA
5'4"

ARIES
5'4"

QUITTERIE
5'2"

FUNICIA
4'6"

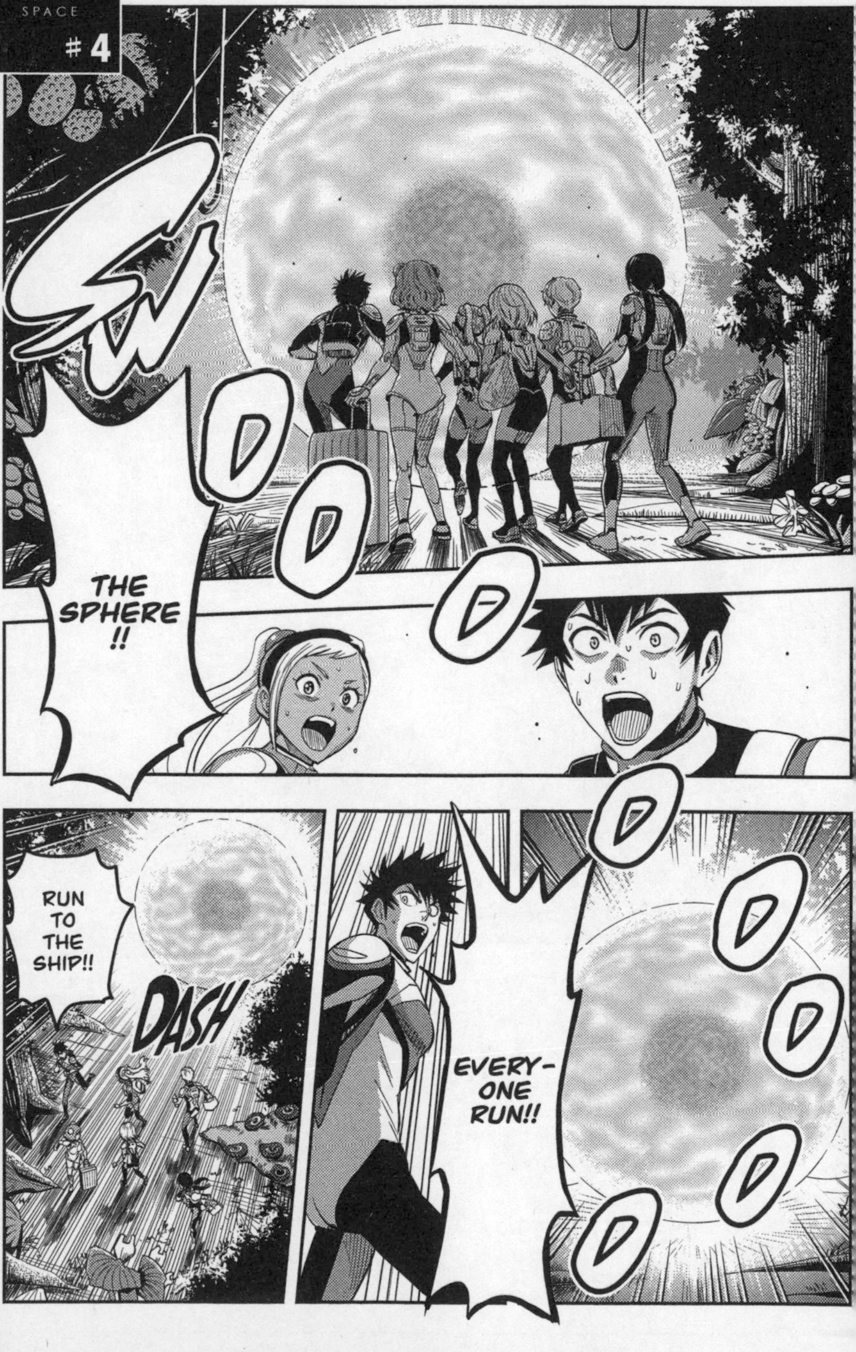
SWOOOOOOOO
THE SPHERE!!
EVERY-ONE RUN!!
RUN TO THE SHIP!!
DASH

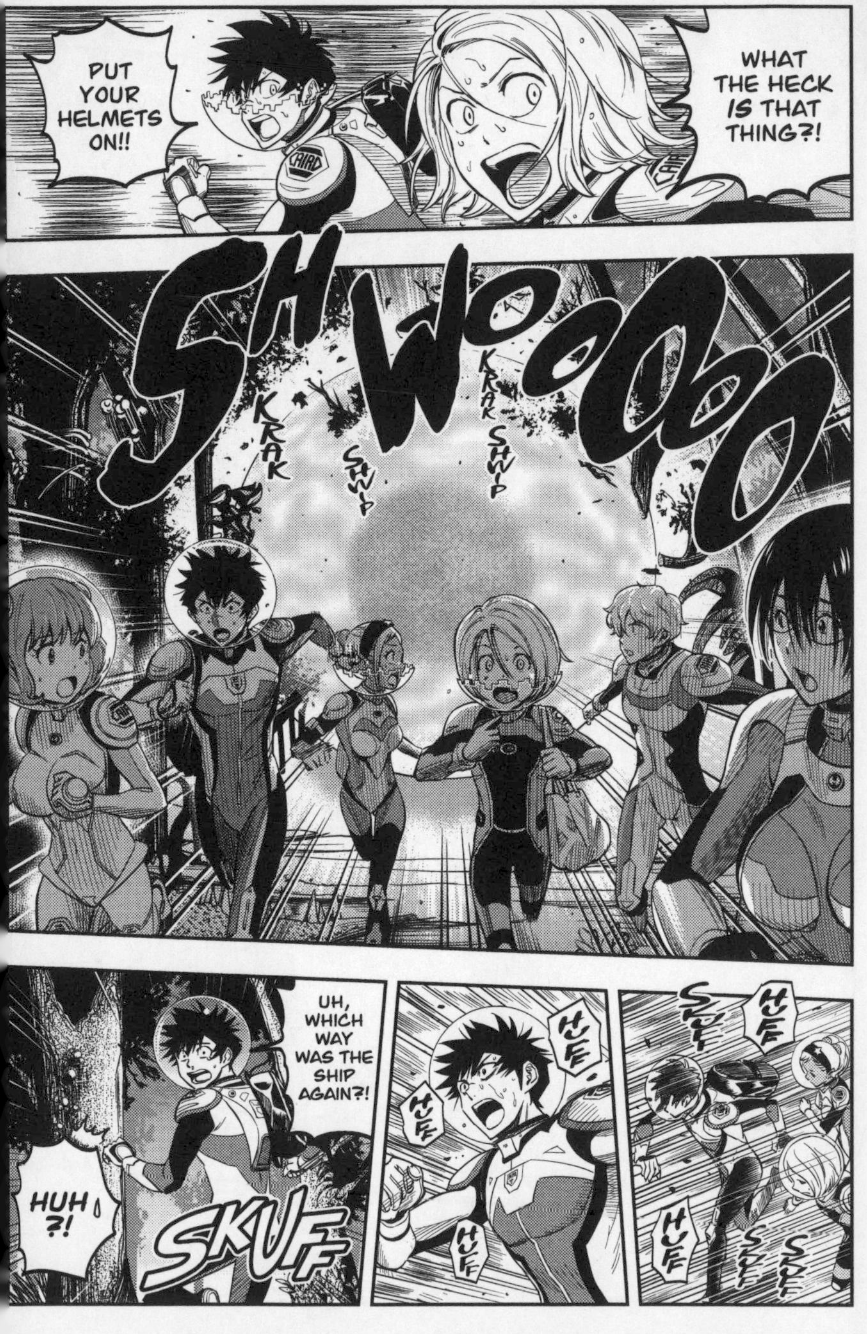
WHAT THE HECK IS THAT THING?!
PUT YOUR HELMETS ON!!
SHWOOOOOO
KRAK KRAK
SHWIP
KRAK
SHWIP
HUFF
SKUFF
HUFF
SKUFF
SKUFF
HUFF
HUFF
HUFF
HUFF
UH, WHICH WAY WAS THE SHIP AGAIN?!
HUH?!
SKUFF

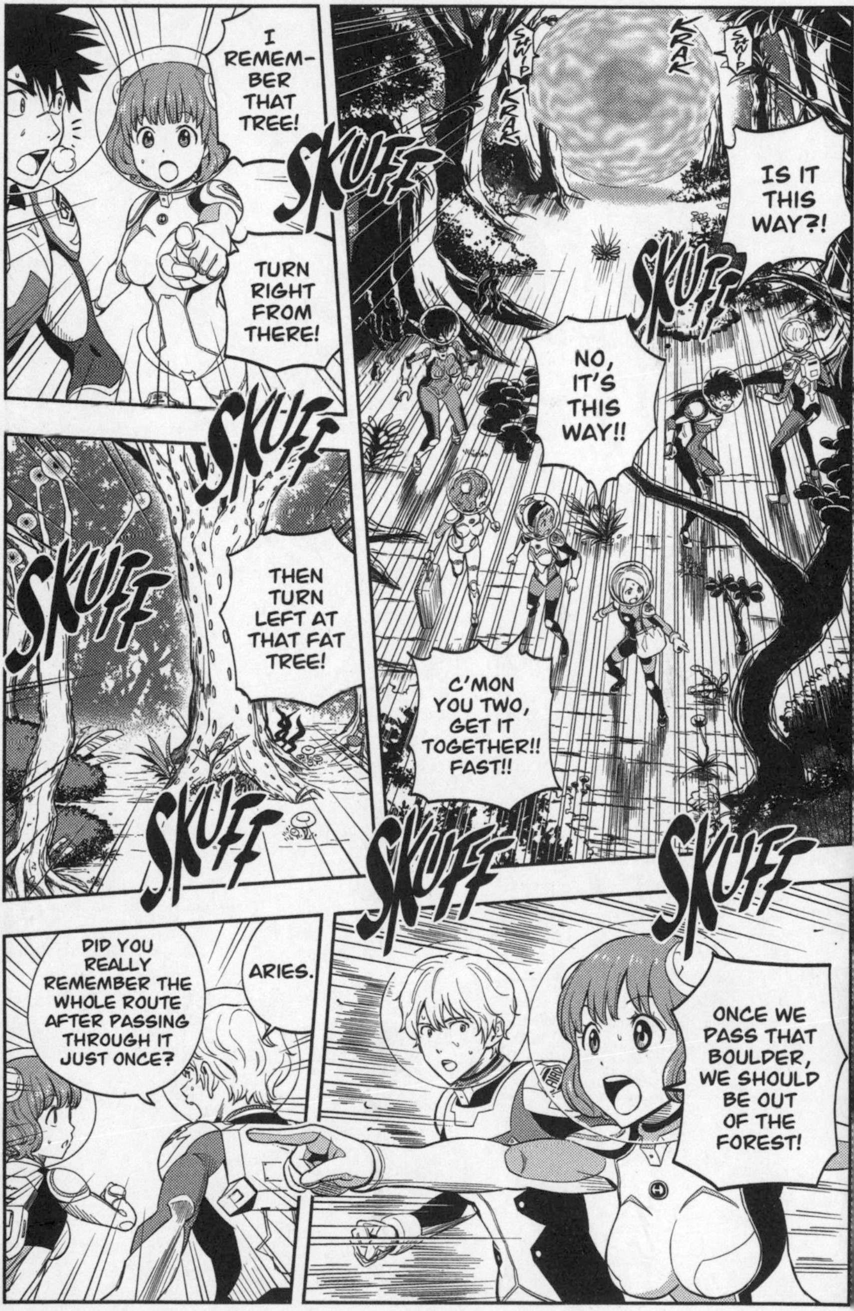
SHWIP
KRAK
KRAK
SHWIP
IS IT THIS WAY?!
SKUFF
NO, IT'S THIS WAY!!
C'MON YOU TWO, GET IT TOGETHER!! FAST!!
SKUFF
SKUFF
I REMEMBER THAT TREE!
SKUFF
TURN RIGHT FROM THERE!
SKUFF
SKUFF
THEN TURN LEFT AT THAT FAT TREE!
SKUFF
SKUFF
ONCE WE PASS THAT BOULDER, WE SHOULD BE OUT OF THE FOREST!
ARIES.
DID YOU REALLY REMEMBER THE WHOLE ROUTE AFTER PASSING THROUGH IT JUST ONCE?

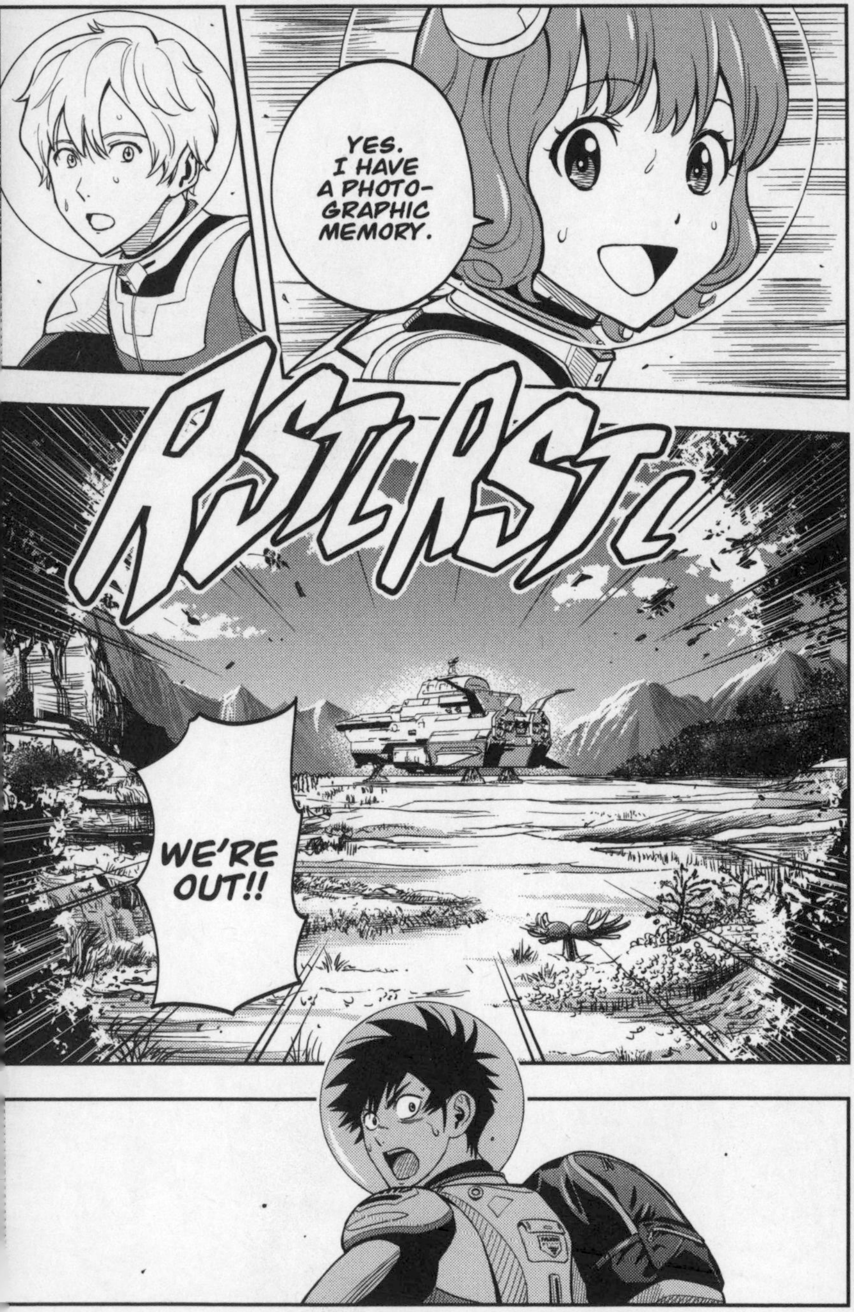
YES. I HAVE A PHOTO-GRAPHIC MEMORY.
RSTLRSTL
WE'RE OUT!!

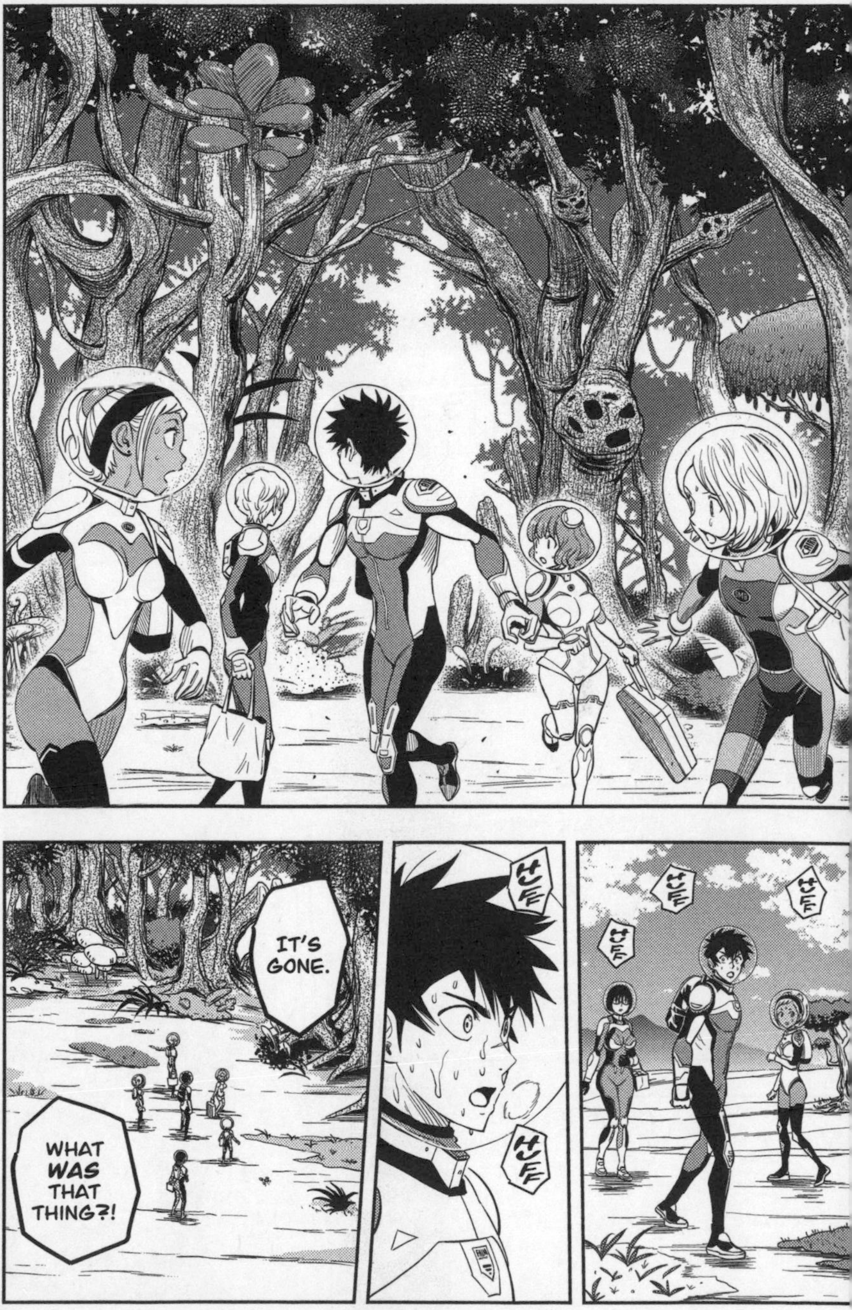

HUFF
HUFF
HUFF
HUFF
HUFF
IT'S GONE.
WHAT WAS THAT THING?!

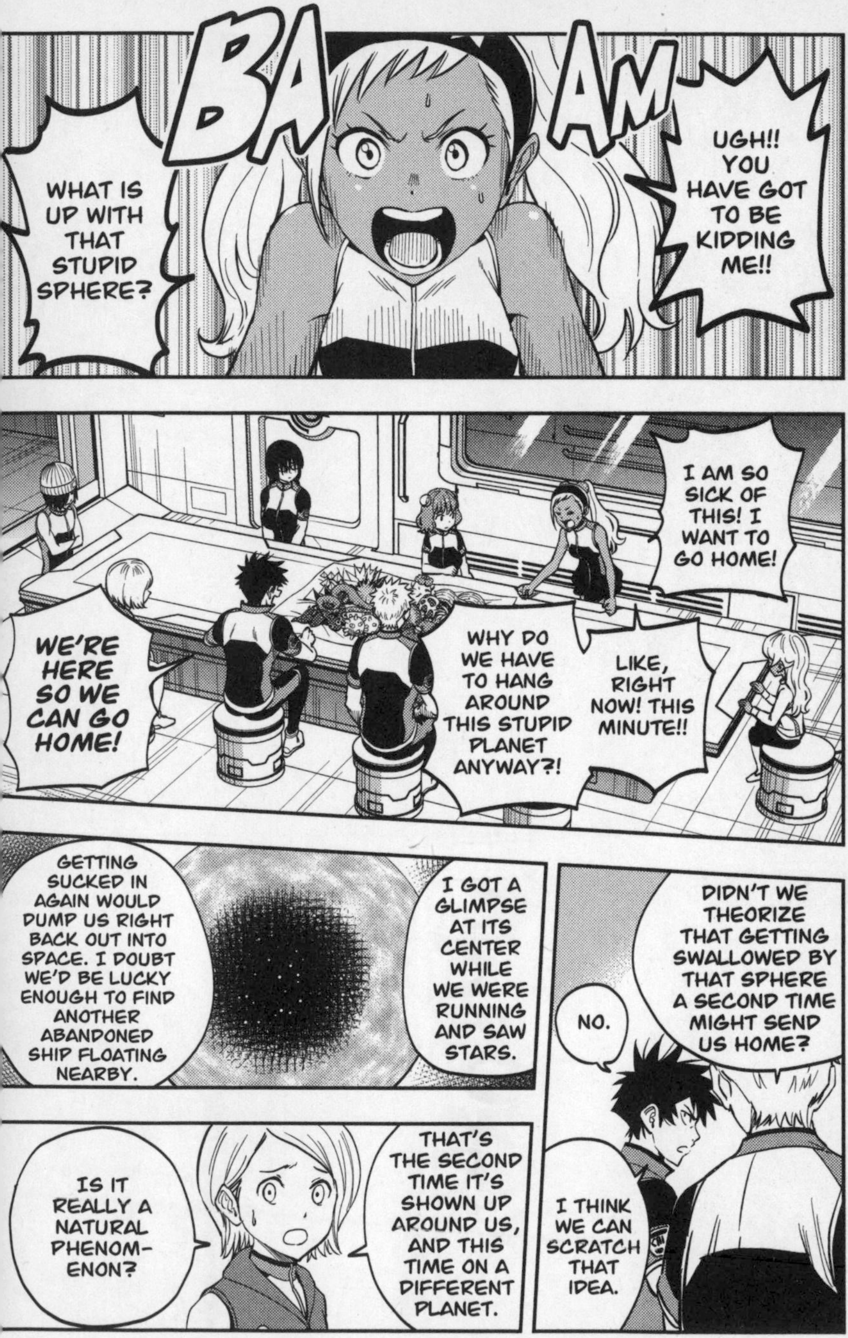
BAAM
UGH!! YOU HAVE GOT TO BE KIDDING ME!!
WHAT IS UP WITH THAT STUPID SPHERE?
I AM SO SICK OF THIS! I WANT TO GO HOME!
LIKE, RIGHT NOW! THIS MINUTE!!
WHY DO WE HAVE TO HANG AROUND THIS STUPID PLANET ANYWAY?!
WE'RE HERE SO WE CAN GO HOME!
DIDN'T WE THEORIZE THAT GETTING SWALLOWED BY THAT SPHERE A SECOND TIME MIGHT SEND US HOME?
NO.
I THINK WE CAN SCRATCH THAT IDEA.
I GOT A GLIMPSE AT ITS CENTER WHILE WE WERE RUNNING AND SAW STARS.
GETTING SUCKED IN AGAIN WOULD DUMP US RIGHT BACK OUT INTO SPACE. I DOUBT WE'D BE LUCKY ENOUGH TO FIND ANOTHER ABANDONED SHIP FLOATING NEARBY.
THAT'S THE SECOND TIME IT'S SHOWN UP AROUND US, AND THIS TIME ON A DIFFERENT PLANET.
IS IT REALLY A NATURAL PHENOM-ENON?

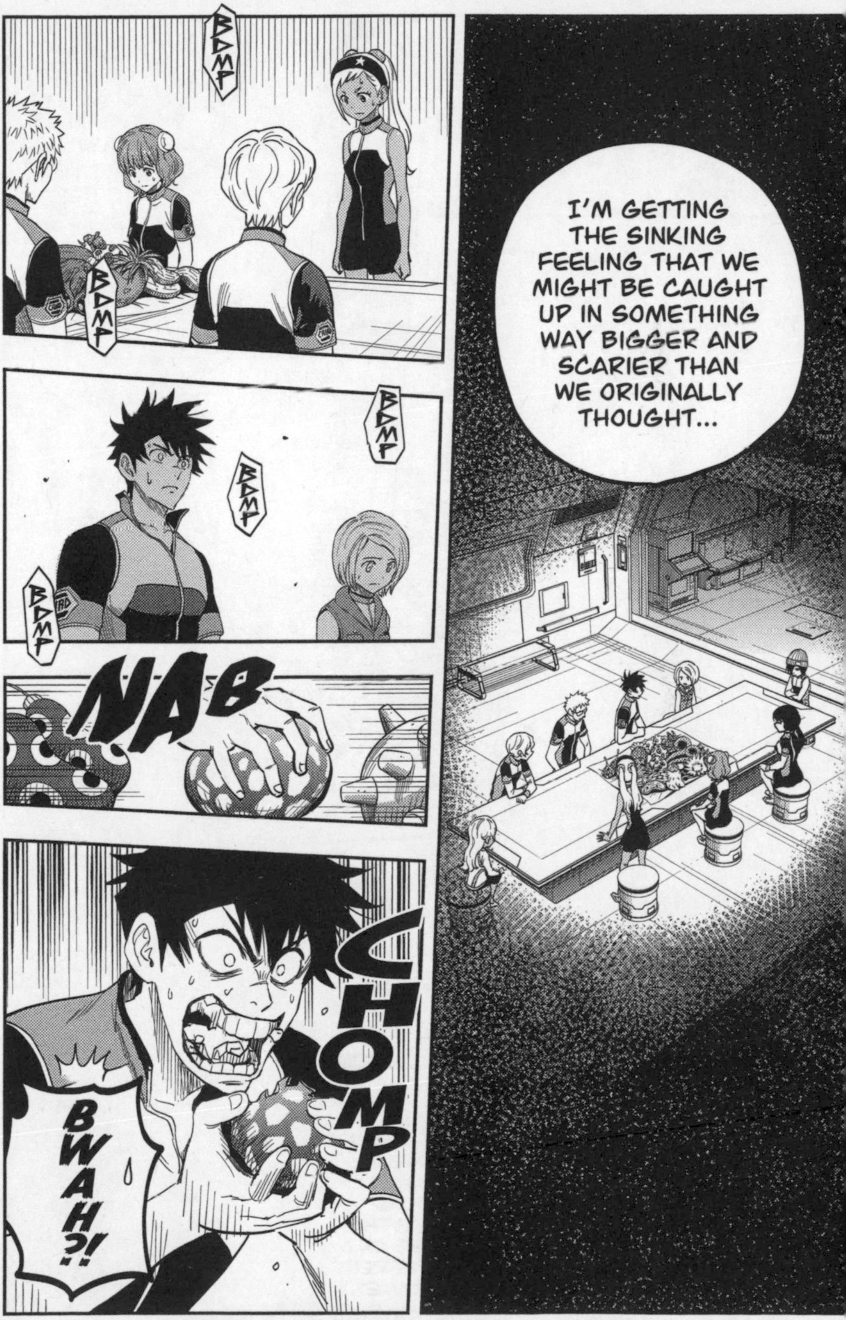
I'M GETTING THE SINKING FEELING THAT WE MIGHT BE CAUGHT UP IN SOMETHING WAY BIGGER AND SCARIER THAN WE ORIGINALLY THOUGHT...
BDMP
BDMP
BDMP
BDMP
BDMP
NAB
CHOMP
BWAH?!

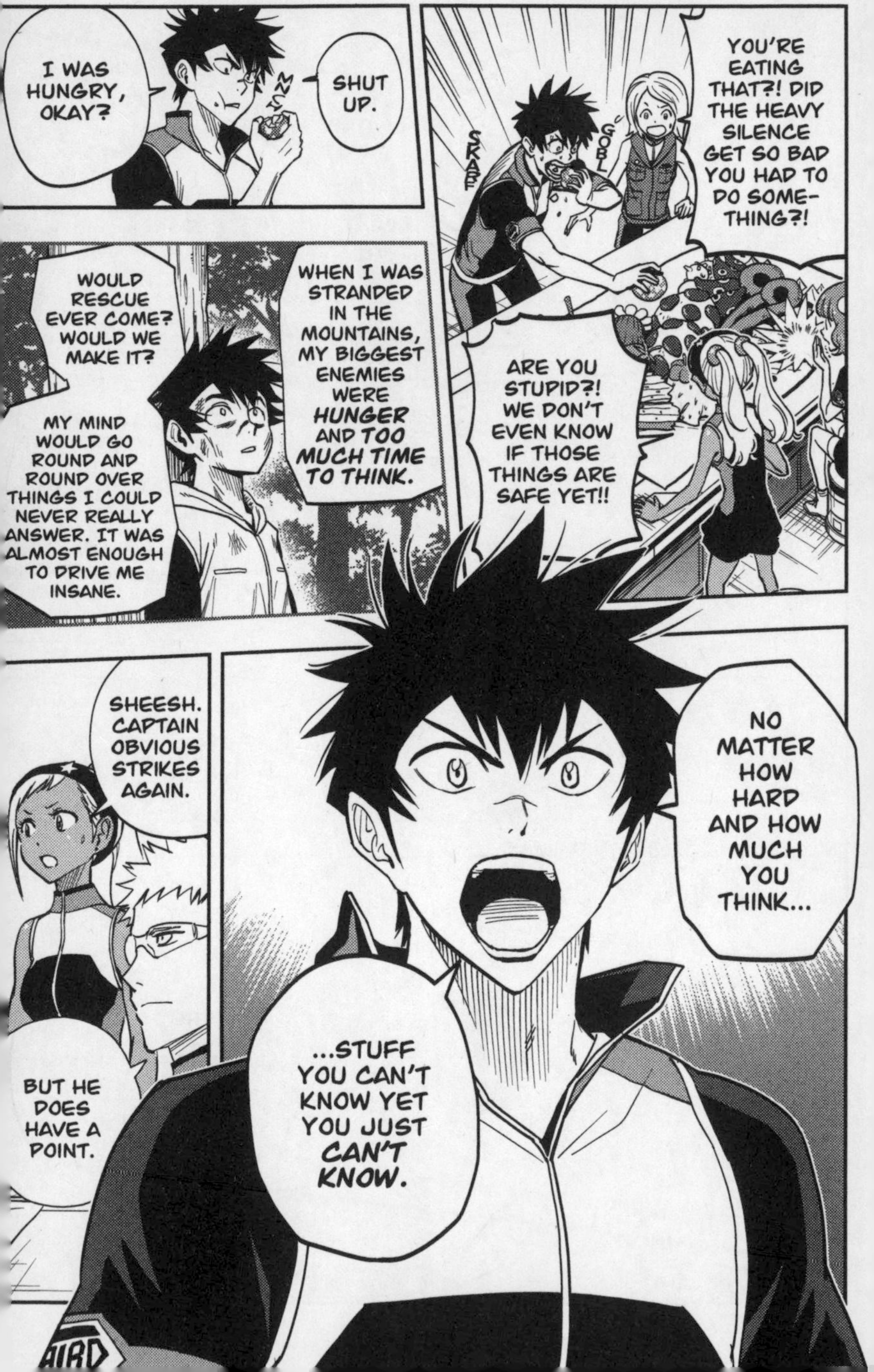
YOU'RE EATING THAT?! DID THE HEAVY SILENCE GET SO BAD YOU HAD TO DO SOME-THING?!
GOBL
SKARF
ARE YOU STUPID?! WE DON'T EVEN KNOW IF THOSE THINGS ARE SAFE YET!!
SHUT UP.
MNCH
I WAS HUNGRY, OKAY?
WHEN I WAS STRANDED IN THE MOUNTAINS, MY BIGGEST ENEMIES WERE HUNGER AND TOO MUCH TIME TO THINK.
WOULD RESCUE EVER COME? WOULD WE MAKE IT?
MY MIND WOULD GO ROUND AND ROUND OVER THINGS I COULD NEVER REALLY ANSWER. IT WAS ALMOST ENOUGH TO DRIVE ME INSANE.
NO MATTER HOW HARD AND HOW MUCH YOU THINK...
...STUFF YOU CAN'T KNOW YET YOU JUST CAN'T KNOW.
SHEESH. CAPTAIN OBVIOUS STRIKES AGAIN.
BUT HE DOES HAVE A POINT.

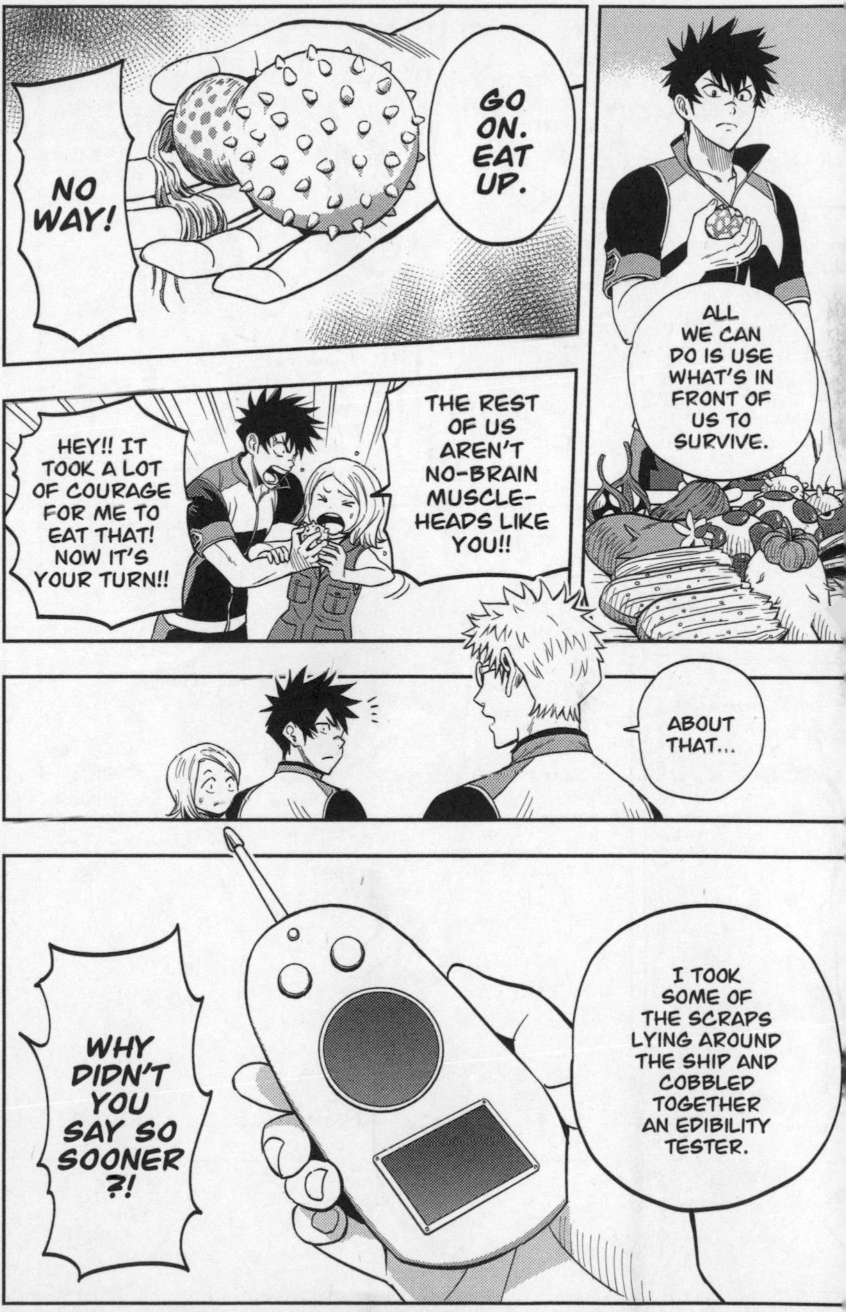
ALL WE CAN DO IS USE WHAT'S IN FRONT OF US TO SURVIVE.
GO ON. EAT UP.
NO WAY!
THE REST OF US AREN'T NO-BRAIN MUSCLE-HEADS LIKE YOU!!
HEY!! IT TOOK A LOT OF COURAGE FOR ME TO EAT THAT! NOW IT'S YOUR TURN!!
ABOUT THAT...
I TOOK SOME OF THE SCRAPS LYING AROUND THE SHIP AND COBBLED TOGETHER AN EDIBILITY TESTER.
WHY DIDN'T YOU SAY SO SOONER?!

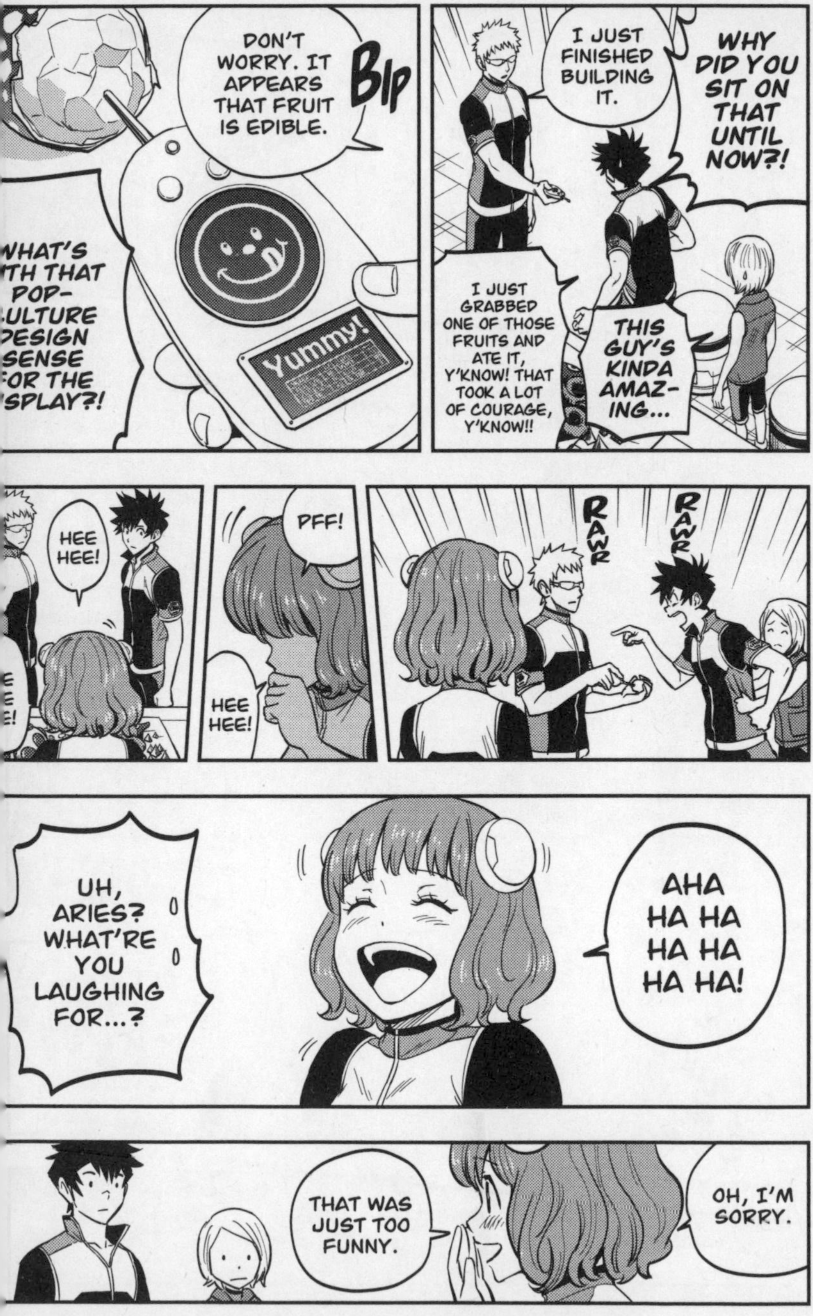
I JUST FINISHED BUILDING IT.
WHY DID YOU SIT ON THAT UNTIL NOW?!
I JUST GRABBED ONE OF THOSE FRUITS AND ATE IT, Y'KNOW! THAT TOOK A LOT OF COURAGE, Y'KNOW!!
THIS GUY'S KINDA AMAZ-ING...
BLIP
DON'T WORRY. IT APPEARS THAT FRUIT IS EDIBLE.
Yummy!
WHAT'S TH THAT POP- ULTURE ESIGN SENSE OR THE SPLAY?!
RAWR
RAWR
PFF!
HEE HEE!
HEE HEE!
AHA HA HA HA HA HA HA!
UH, ARIES? WHAT'RE YOU LAUGHING FOR...?
OH, I'M SORRY.
THAT WAS JUST TOO FUNNY.

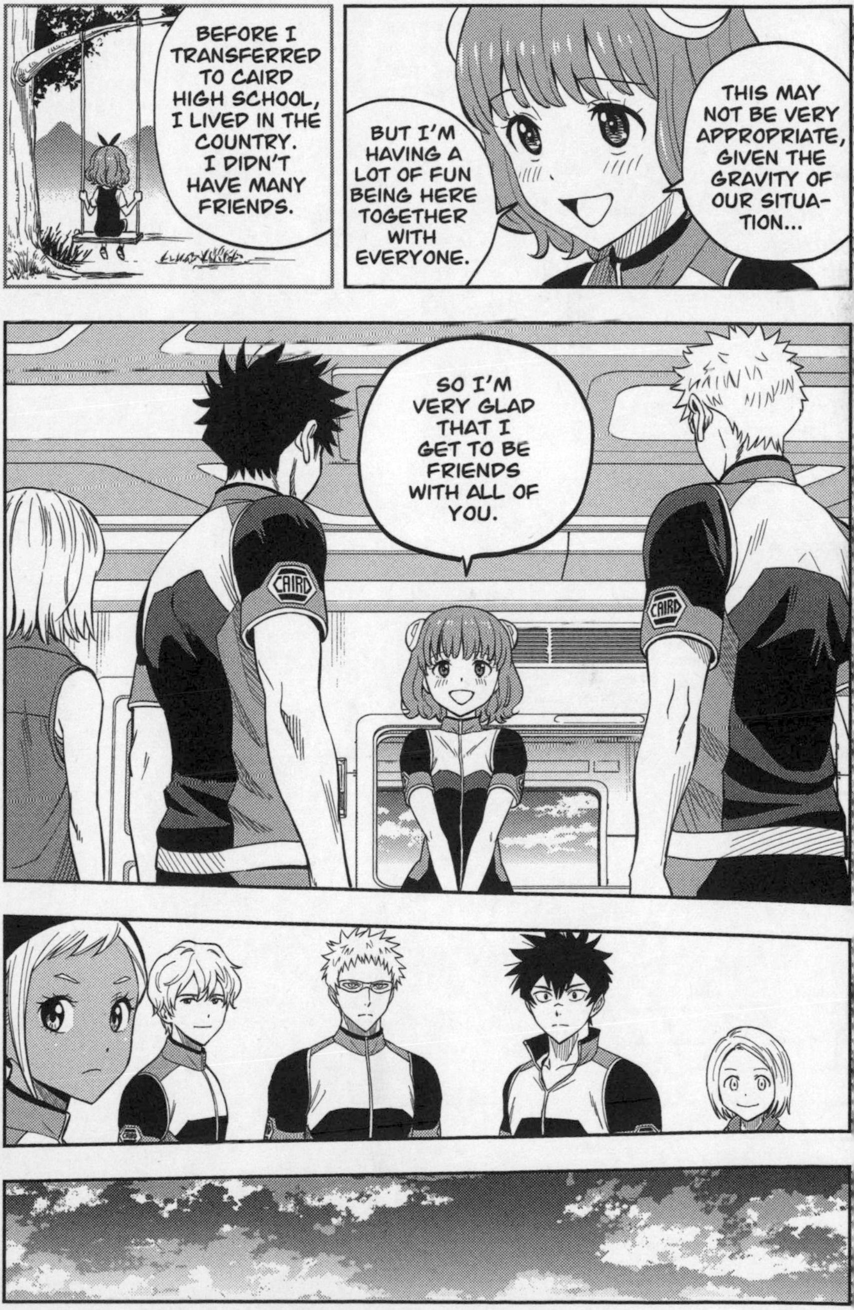
THIS MAY NOT BE VERY APPROPRIATE, GIVEN THE GRAVITY OF OUR SITUA-TION...
BUT I'M HAVING A LOT OF FUN BEING HERE TOGETHER WITH EVERYONE.
BEFORE I TRANSFERRED TO CAIRD HIGH SCHOOL, I LIVED IN THE COUNTRY. I DIDN'T HAVE MANY FRIENDS.
SO I'M VERY GLAD THAT I GET TO BE FRIENDS WITH ALL OF YOU.
CAIRD
CAIRD

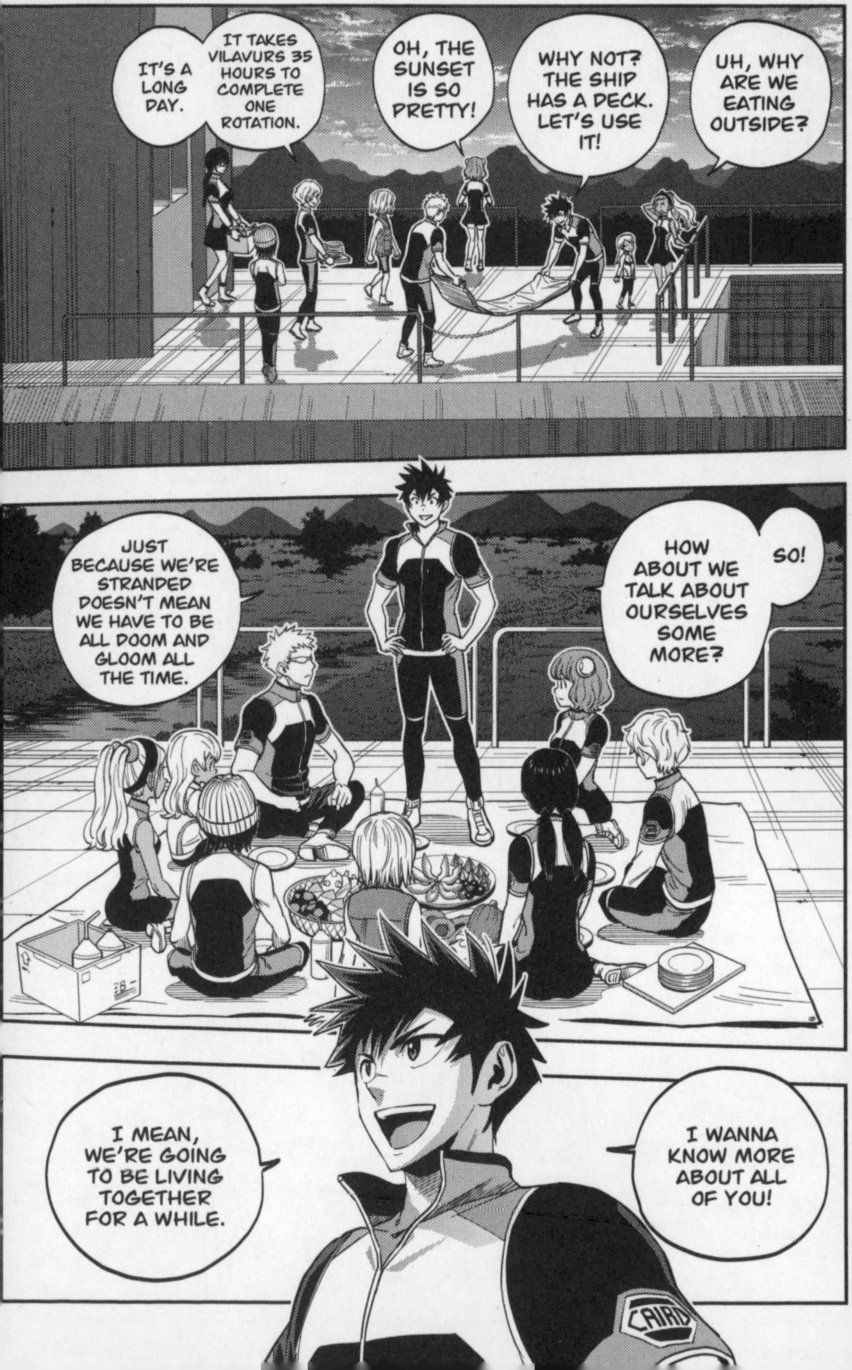
UH, WHY ARE WE EATING OUTSIDE?
WHY NOT? THE SHIP HAS A DECK. LET'S USE IT!
OH, THE SUNSET IS SO PRETTY!
IT TAKES VILAVURS 35 HOURS TO COMPLETE ONE ROTATION.
IT'S A LONG DAY.
SO!
HOW ABOUT WE TALK ABOUT OURSELVES SOME MORE?
JUST BECAUSE WE'RE STRANDED DOESN'T MEAN WE HAVE TO BE ALL DOOM AND GLOOM ALL THE TIME.
I WANNA KNOW MORE ABOUT ALL OF YOU!
I MEAN, WE'RE GOING TO BE LIVING TOGETHER FOR A WHILE.
CAIRD

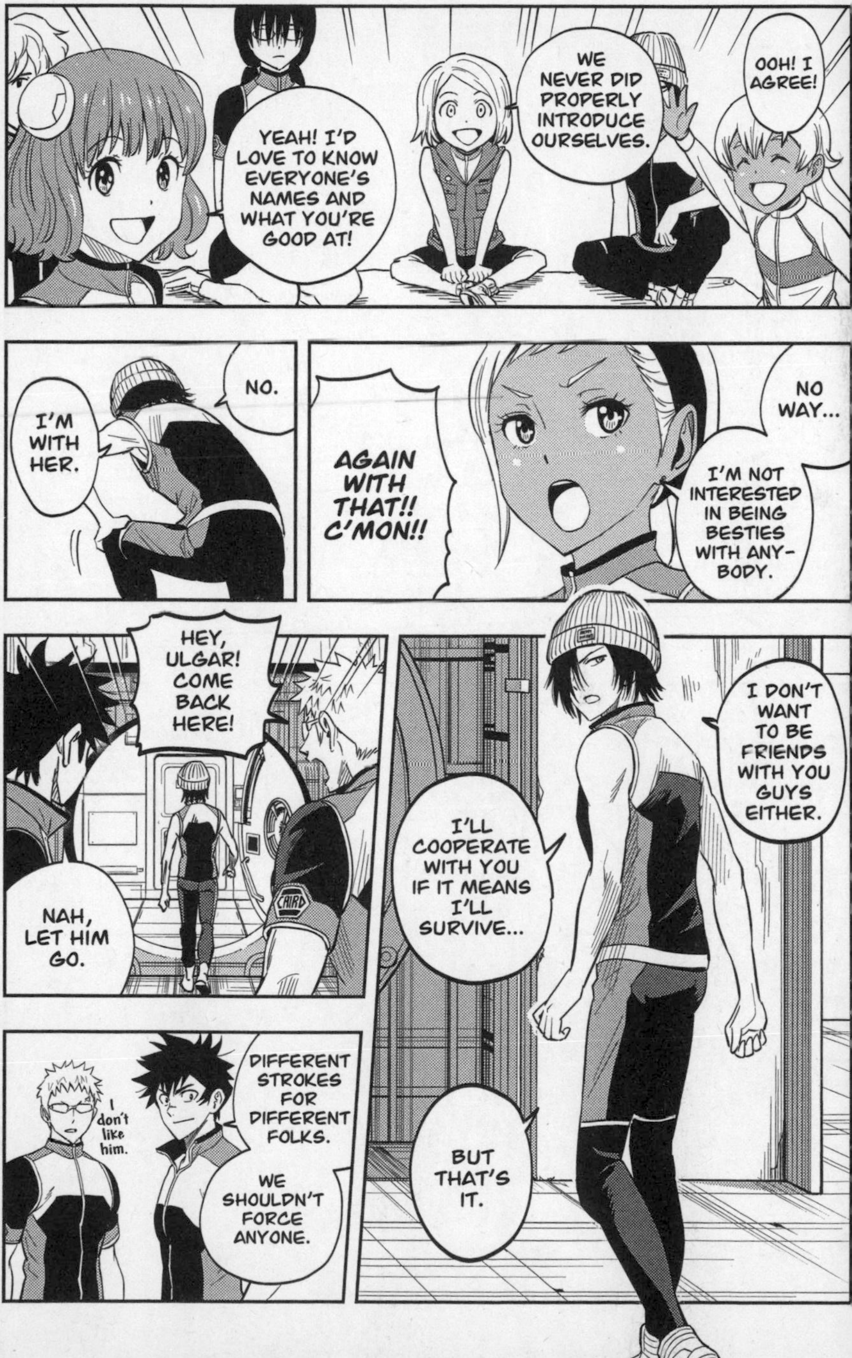
OOH! I AGREE!
WE NEVER DID PROPERLY INTRODUCE OURSELVES.
YEAH! I'D LOVE TO KNOW EVERYONE'S NAMES AND WHAT YOU'RE GOOD AT!
NO WAY...
I'M NOT INTERESTED IN BEING BESTIES WITH ANY-BODY.
AGAIN WITH THAT!! C'MON!!
NO.
I'M WITH HER.
I DON'T WANT TO BE FRIENDS WITH YOU GUYS EITHER.
I'LL COOPERATE WITH YOU IF IT MEANS I'LL SURVIVE...
BUT THAT'S IT.
HEY, ULGAR! COME BACK HERE!
NAH, LET HIM GO.
DIFFERENT STROKES FOR DIFFERENT FOLKS.
WE SHOULDN'T FORCE ANYONE.
I don't like him.

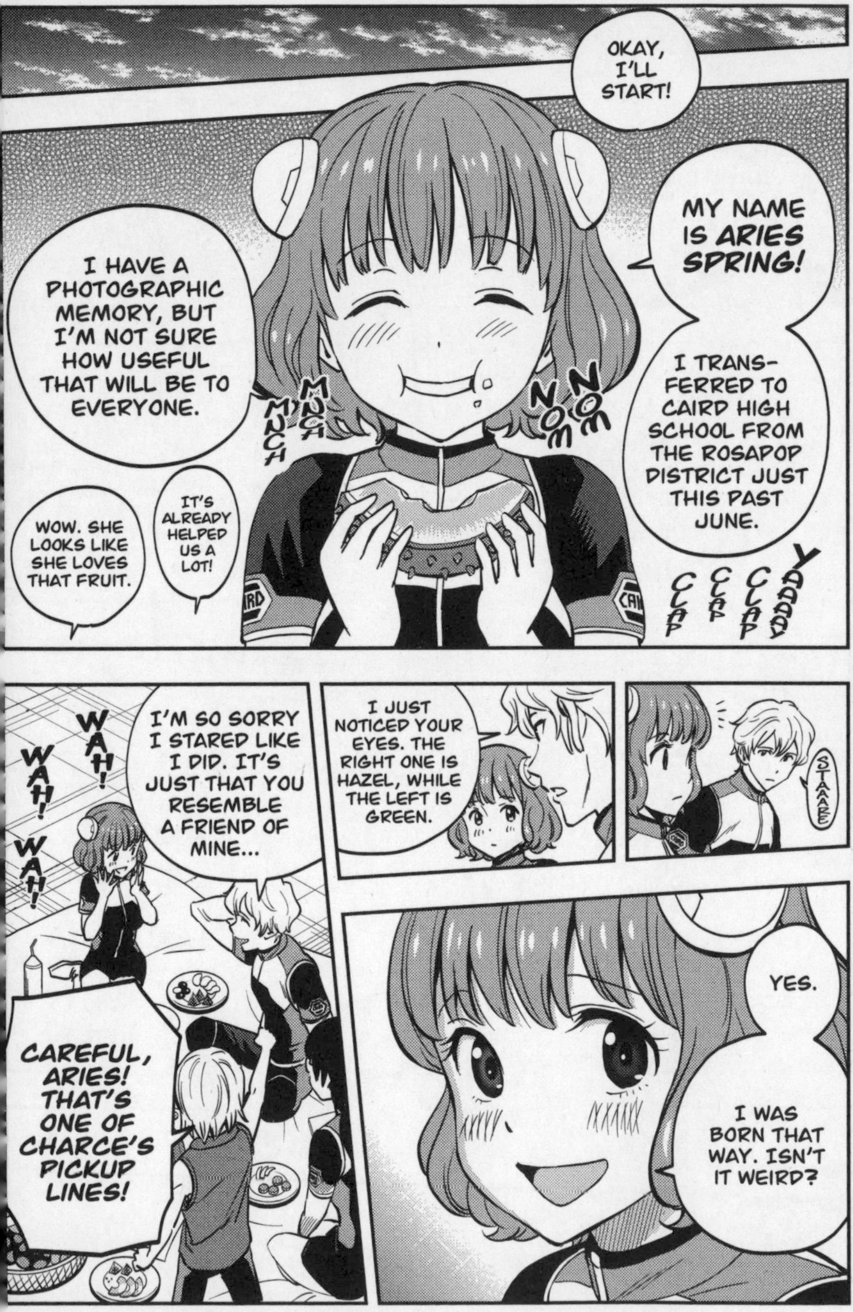
OKAY, I'LL START!
MY NAME IS ARIES SPRING!
I TRANS-FERRED TO CAIRD HIGH SCHOOL FROM THE ROSAPOP DISTRICT JUST THIS PAST JUNE.
CLAP CLAP CLAP YAAAAAY
NOM NOM
MUNCH MUNCH
I HAVE A PHOTOGRAPHIC MEMORY, BUT I'M NOT SURE HOW USEFUL THAT WILL BE TO EVERYONE.
IT'S ALREADY HELPED US A LOT!
WOW. SHE LOOKS LIKE SHE LOVES THAT FRUIT.
STAAARE
I JUST NOTICED YOUR EYES. THE RIGHT ONE IS HAZEL, WHILE THE LEFT IS GREEN.
YES.
I WAS BORN THAT WAY. ISN'T IT WEIRD?
I'M SO SORRY I STARED LIKE I DID. IT'S JUST THAT YOU RESEMBLE A FRIEND OF MINE...
WAH! WAH! WAH!
CAREFUL, ARIES! THAT'S ONE OF CHARCE'S PICKUP LINES!

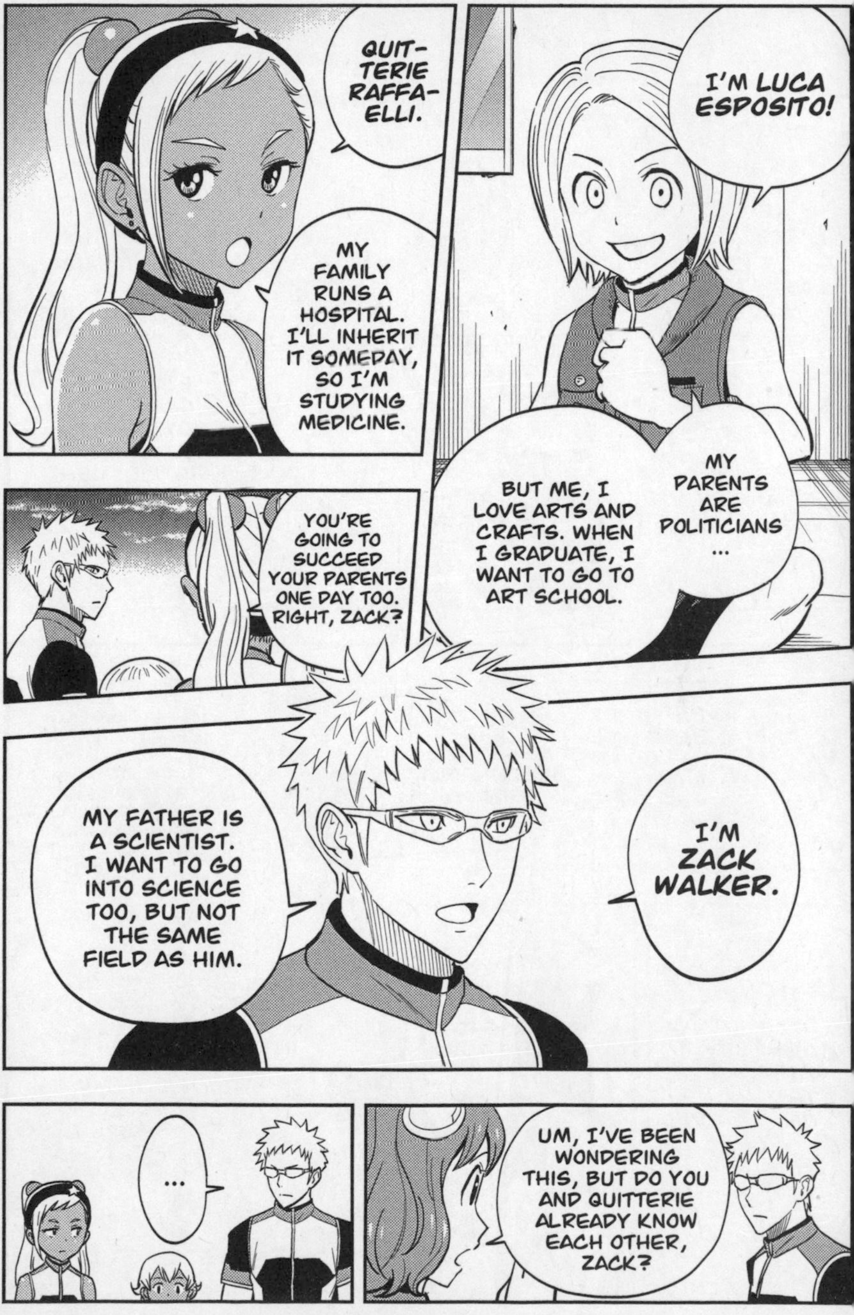
I'M LUCA ESPOSITO!
MY PARENTS ARE POLITICIANS...
BUT ME, I LOVE ARTS AND CRAFTS. WHEN I GRADUATE, I WANT TO GO TO ART SCHOOL.
QUIT-TERIE RAFFA-ELLI.
MY FAMILY RUNS A HOSPITAL. I'LL INHERIT IT SOMEDAY, SO I'M STUDYING MEDICINE.
YOU'RE GOING TO SUCCEED YOUR PARENTS ONE DAY TOO. RIGHT, ZACK?
I'M ZACK WALKER.
MY FATHER IS A SCIENTIST. I WANT TO GO INTO SCIENCE TOO, BUT NOT THE SAME FIELD AS HIM.
UM, I'VE BEEN WONDERING THIS, BUT DO YOU AND QUITTERIE ALREADY KNOW EACH OTHER, ZACK?
...

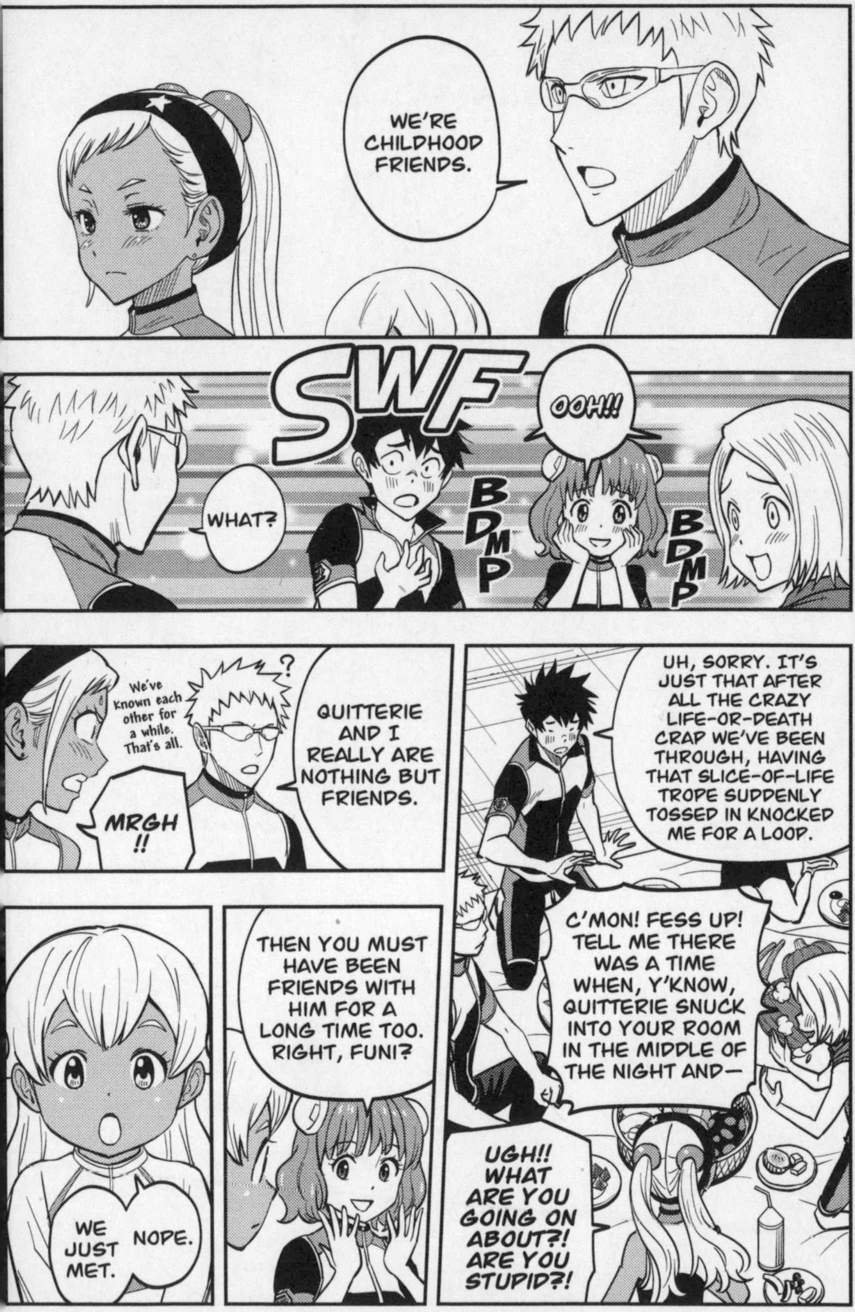
WE'RE CHILDHOOD FRIENDS.
OOH!!
SWF
BDMP
BDMP
WHAT?
UH, SORRY. IT'S JUST THAT AFTER ALL THE CRAZY LIFE-OR-DEATH CRAP WE'VE BEEN THROUGH, HAVING THAT SLICE-OF-LIFE TROPE SUDDENLY TOSSED IN KNOCKED ME FOR A LOOP.
C'MON! FESS UP! TELL ME THERE WAS A TIME WHEN, Y'KNOW, QUITTERIE SNUCK INTO YOUR ROOM IN THE MIDDLE OF THE NIGHT AND—
UGH!! WHAT ARE YOU GOING ON ABOUT?! ARE YOU STUPID?!
?
QUITTERIE AND I REALLY ARE NOTHING BUT FRIENDS.
We've known each other for a while. That's all.
MRGH!!
THEN YOU MUST HAVE BEEN FRIENDS WITH HIM FOR A LONG TIME TOO. RIGHT, FUNI?
NOPE.
WE JUST MET.

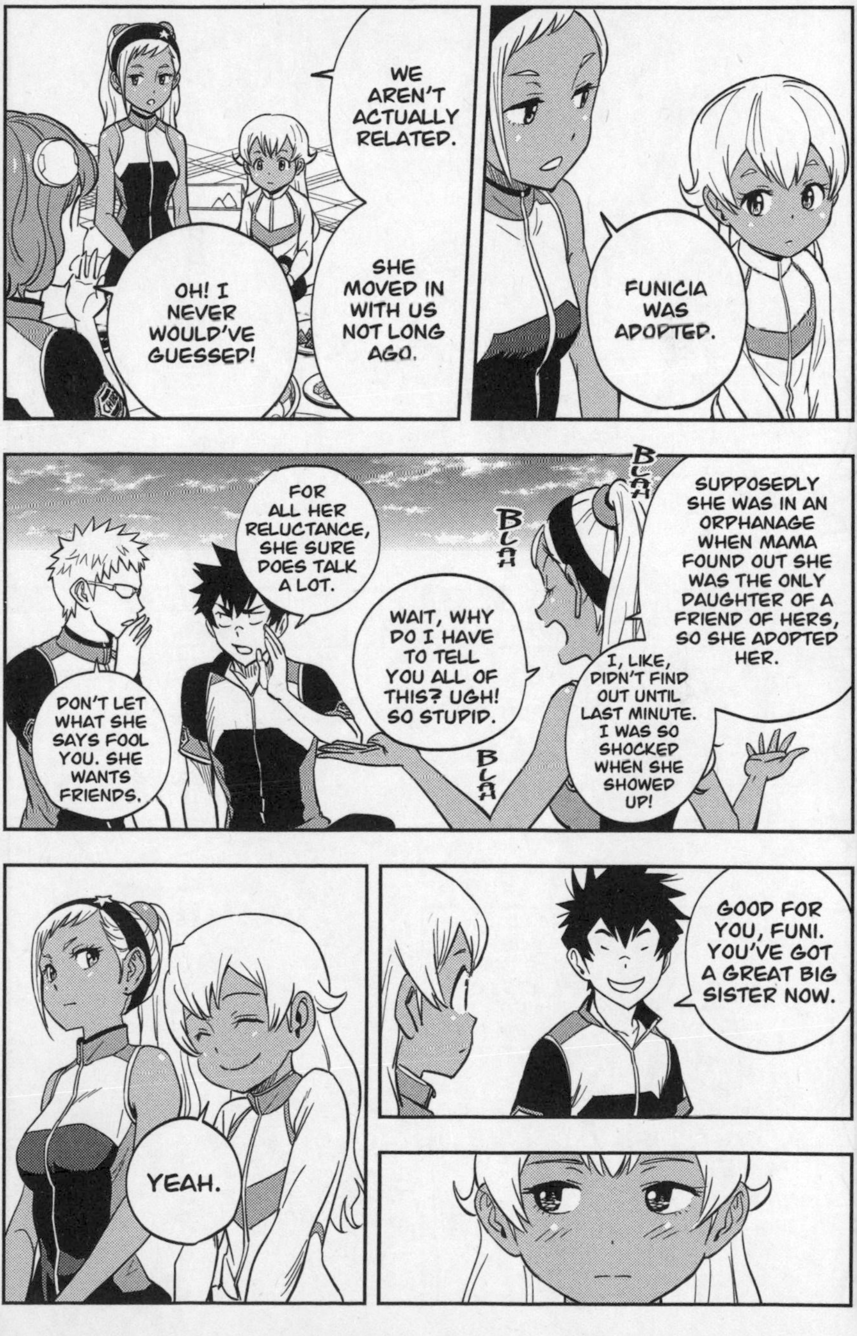
FUNICIA WAS ADOPTED.
WE AREN'T ACTUALLY RELATED.
SHE MOVED IN WITH US NOT LONG AGO.
OH! I NEVER WOULD'VE GUESSED!
BLAH
SUPPOSEDLY SHE WAS IN AN ORPHANAGE WHEN MAMA FOUND OUT SHE WAS THE ONLY DAUGHTER OF A FRIEND OF HERS, SO SHE ADOPTED HER.
BLAH
I, LIKE, DIDN'T FIND OUT UNTIL LAST MINUTE. I WAS SO SHOCKED WHEN SHE SHOWED UP!
WAIT, WHY DO I HAVE TO TELL YOU ALL OF THIS? UGH! SO STUPID.
BLAH
FOR ALL HER RELUCTANCE, SHE SURE DOES TALK A LOT.
DON'T LET WHAT SHE SAYS FOOL YOU. SHE WANTS FRIENDS.
GOOD FOR YOU, FUNI. YOU'VE GOT A GREAT BIG SISTER NOW.
YEAH.

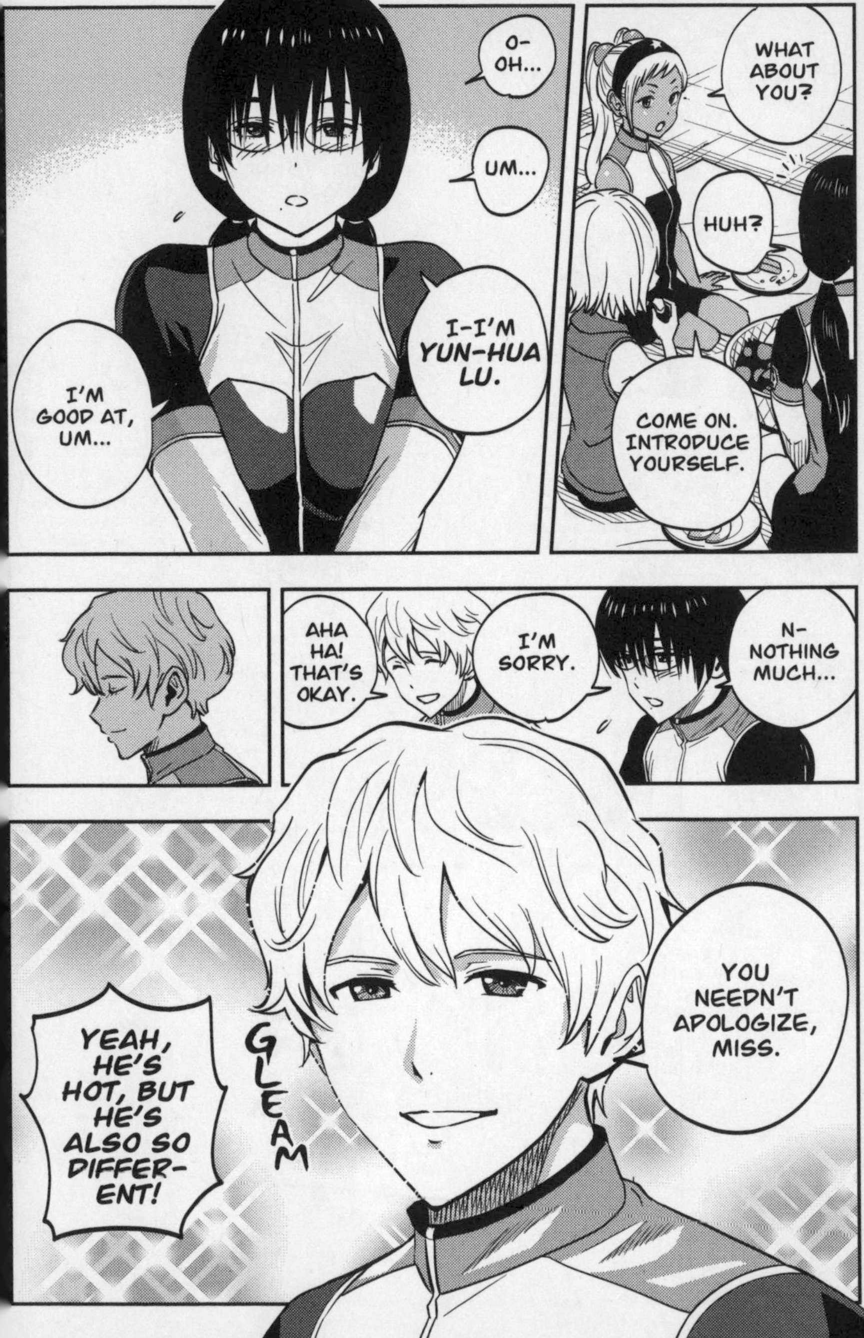
WHAT ABOUT YOU?
HUH?
COME ON. INTRODUCE YOURSELF.
O-OH...
UM...
I-I'M YUN-HUA LU.
I'M GOOD AT, UM...
N-NOTHING MUCH...
I'M SORRY.
AHA HA! THAT'S OKAY.
YOU NEEDN'T APOLOGIZE, MISS.
GLEAM
YEAH, HE'S HOT, BUT HE'S ALSO SO DIFFER-ENT!

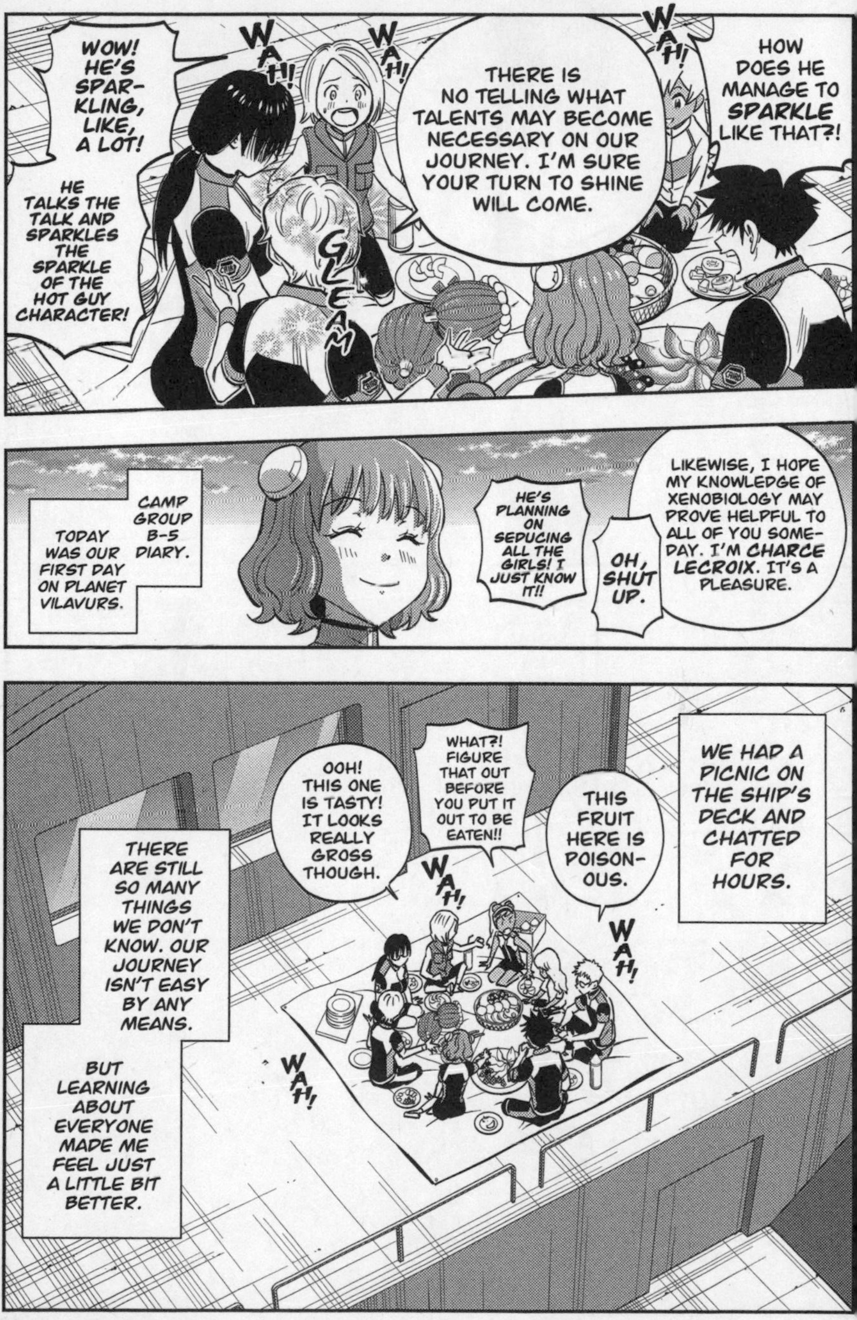
HOW DOES HE MANAGE TO SPARKLE LIKE THAT?!
WAH!
THERE IS NO TELLING WHAT TALENTS MAY BECOME NECESSARY ON OUR JOURNEY. I'M SURE YOUR TURN TO SHINE WILL COME.
WAH!
GLEAM
WAH!
WOW! HE'S SPARKLING, LIKE, A LOT!
HE TALKS THE TALK AND SPARKLES THE SPARKLE OF THE HOT GUY CHARACTER!
LIKEWISE, I HOPE MY KNOWLEDGE OF XENOBIOLOGY MAY PROVE HELPFUL TO ALL OF YOU SOMEDAY. I'M CHARCE LECROIX. IT'S A PLEASURE.
OH, SHUT UP.
HE'S PLANNING ON SEDUCING ALL THE GIRLS! I JUST KNOW IT!!
CAMP GROUP B-5 DIARY.
TODAY WAS OUR FIRST DAY ON PLANET VILAVURS.
WE HAD A PICNIC ON THE SHIP'S DECK AND CHATTED FOR HOURS.
THIS FRUIT HERE IS POISONOUS.
WHAT?! FIGURE THAT OUT BEFORE YOU PUT IT OUT TO BE EATEN!!
OOH! THIS ONE IS TASTY! IT LOOKS REALLY GROSS THOUGH.
WAH!
WAH!
WAH!
THERE ARE STILL SO MANY THINGS WE DON'T KNOW. OUR JOURNEY ISN'T EASY BY ANY MEANS.
BUT LEARNING ABOUT EVERYONE MADE ME FEEL JUST A LITTLE BIT BETTER.

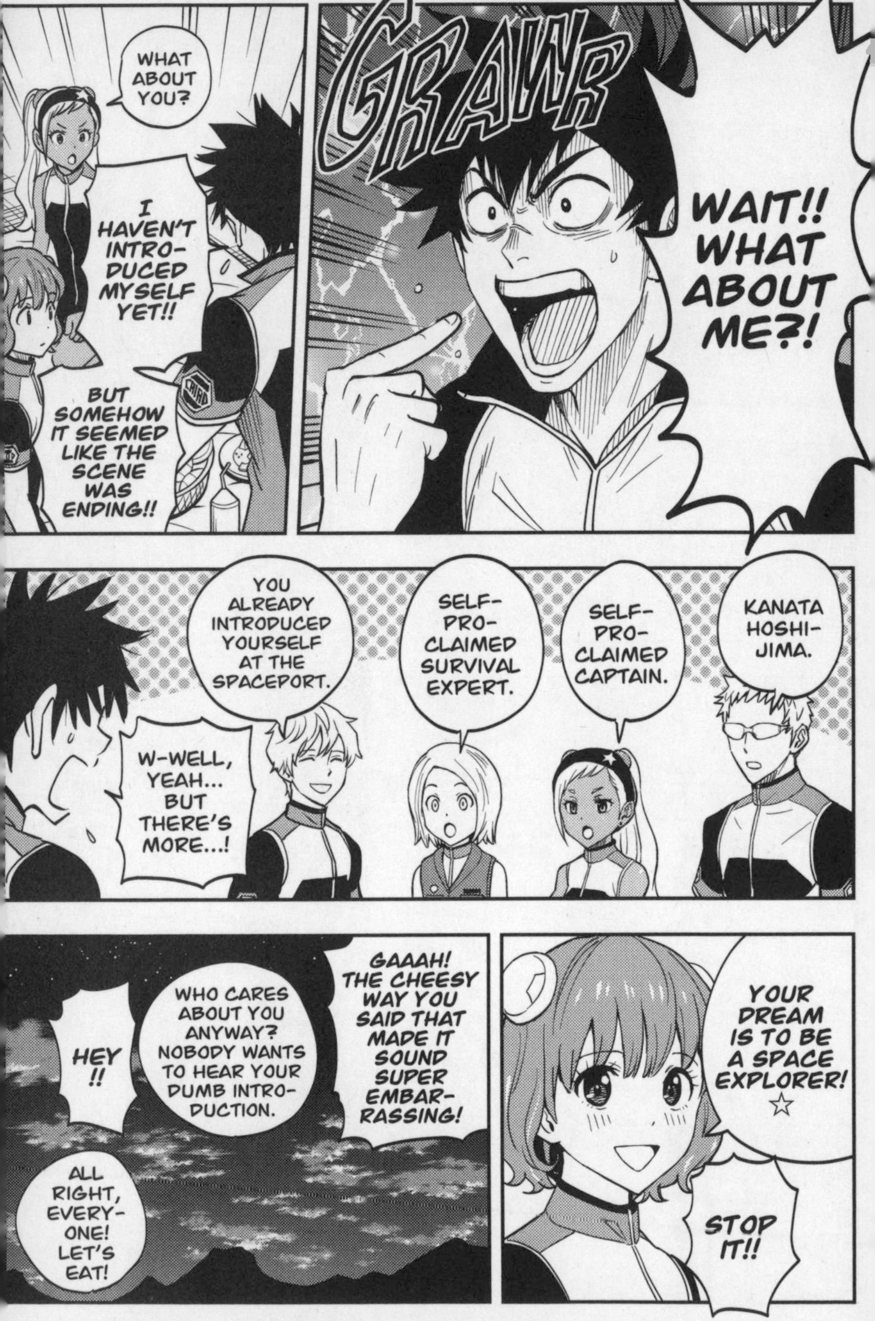
GRAWR
WAIT!! WHAT ABOUT ME?!
WHAT ABOUT YOU?
I HAVEN'T INTRODUCED MYSELF YET!!
BUT SOMEHOW IT SEEMED LIKE THE SCENE WAS ENDING!!
KANATA HOSHIJIMA.
SELF-PROCLAIMED CAPTAIN.
SELF-PROCLAIMED SURVIVAL EXPERT.
YOU ALREADY INTRODUCED YOURSELF AT THE SPACEPORT.
W-WELL, YEAH... BUT THERE'S MORE...!
YOUR DREAM IS TO BE A SPACE EXPLORER! ☆
STOP IT!!
GAAAH! THE CHEESY WAY YOU SAID THAT MADE IT SOUND SUPER EMBARRASSING!
WHO CARES ABOUT YOU ANYWAY? NOBODY WANTS TO HEAR YOUR DUMB INTRODUCTION.
HEY!!
ALL RIGHT, EVERYONE! LET'S EAT!

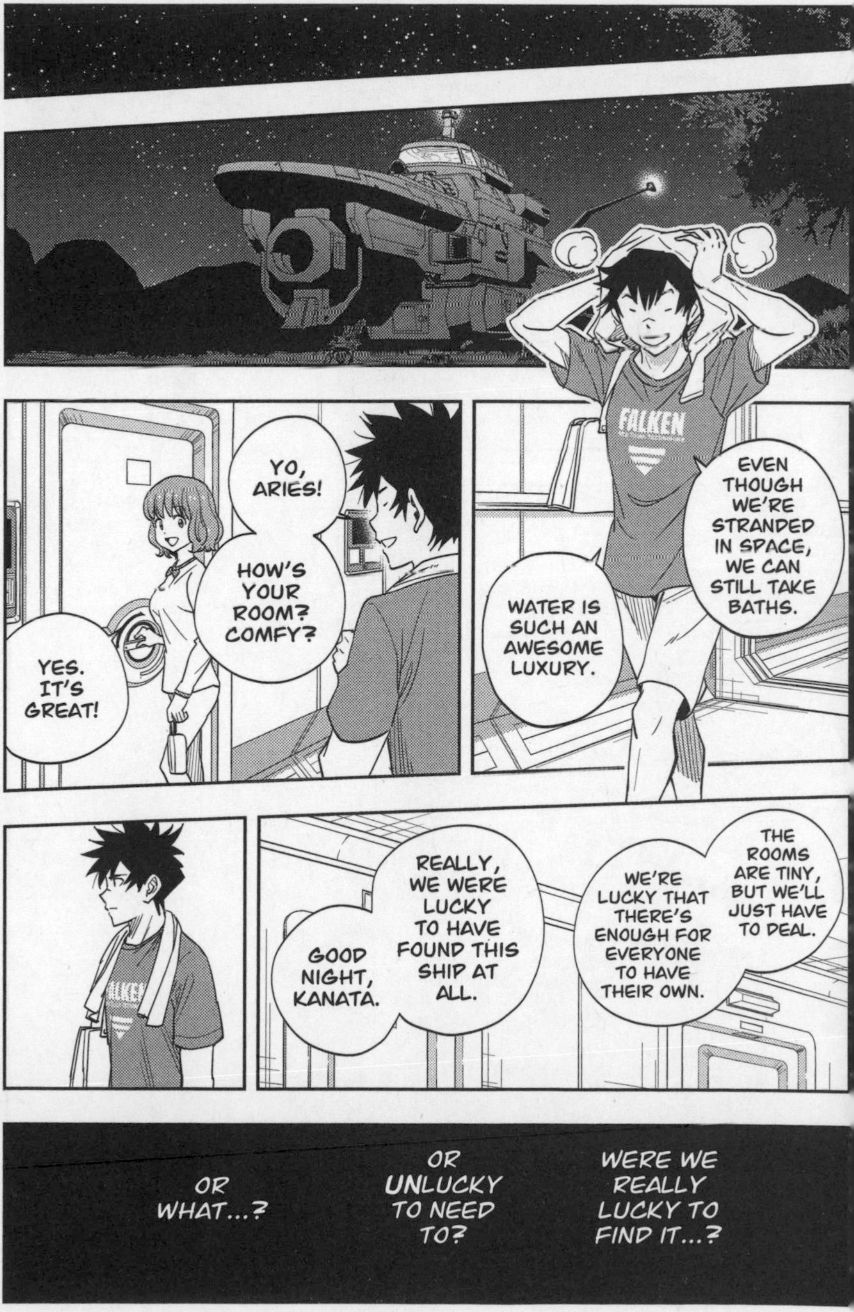
FALKEN
EVEN THOUGH WE'RE STRANDED IN SPACE, WE CAN STILL TAKE BATHS.
WATER IS SUCH AN AWESOME LUXURY.
YO, ARIES!
HOW'S YOUR ROOM? COMFY?
YES. IT'S GREAT!
THE ROOMS ARE TINY, BUT WE'LL JUST HAVE TO DEAL.
WE'RE LUCKY THAT THERE'S ENOUGH FOR EVERYONE TO HAVE THEIR OWN.
REALLY, WE WERE LUCKY TO HAVE FOUND THIS SHIP AT ALL.
GOOD NIGHT, KANATA.
WERE WE REALLY LUCKY TO FIND IT...?
OR UNLUCKY TO NEED TO?
OR WHAT...?

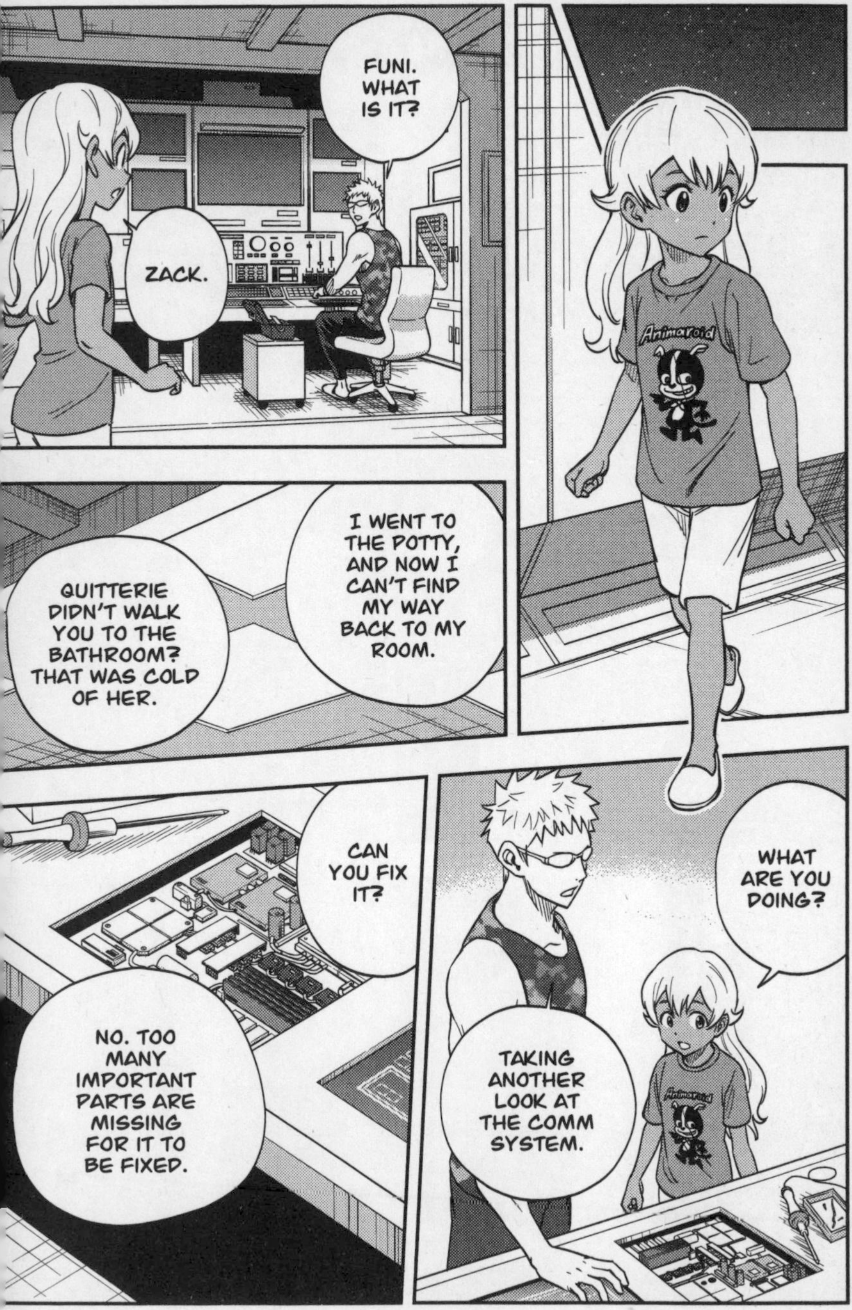
FUNI. WHAT IS IT?
ZACK.
I WENT TO THE POTTY, AND NOW I CAN'T FIND MY WAY BACK TO MY ROOM.
QUITTERIE DIDN'T WALK YOU TO THE BATHROOM? THAT WAS COLD OF HER.
WHAT ARE YOU DOING?
TAKING ANOTHER LOOK AT THE COMM SYSTEM.
CAN YOU FIX IT?
NO. TOO MANY IMPORTANT PARTS ARE MISSING FOR IT TO BE FIXED.
Animaroid

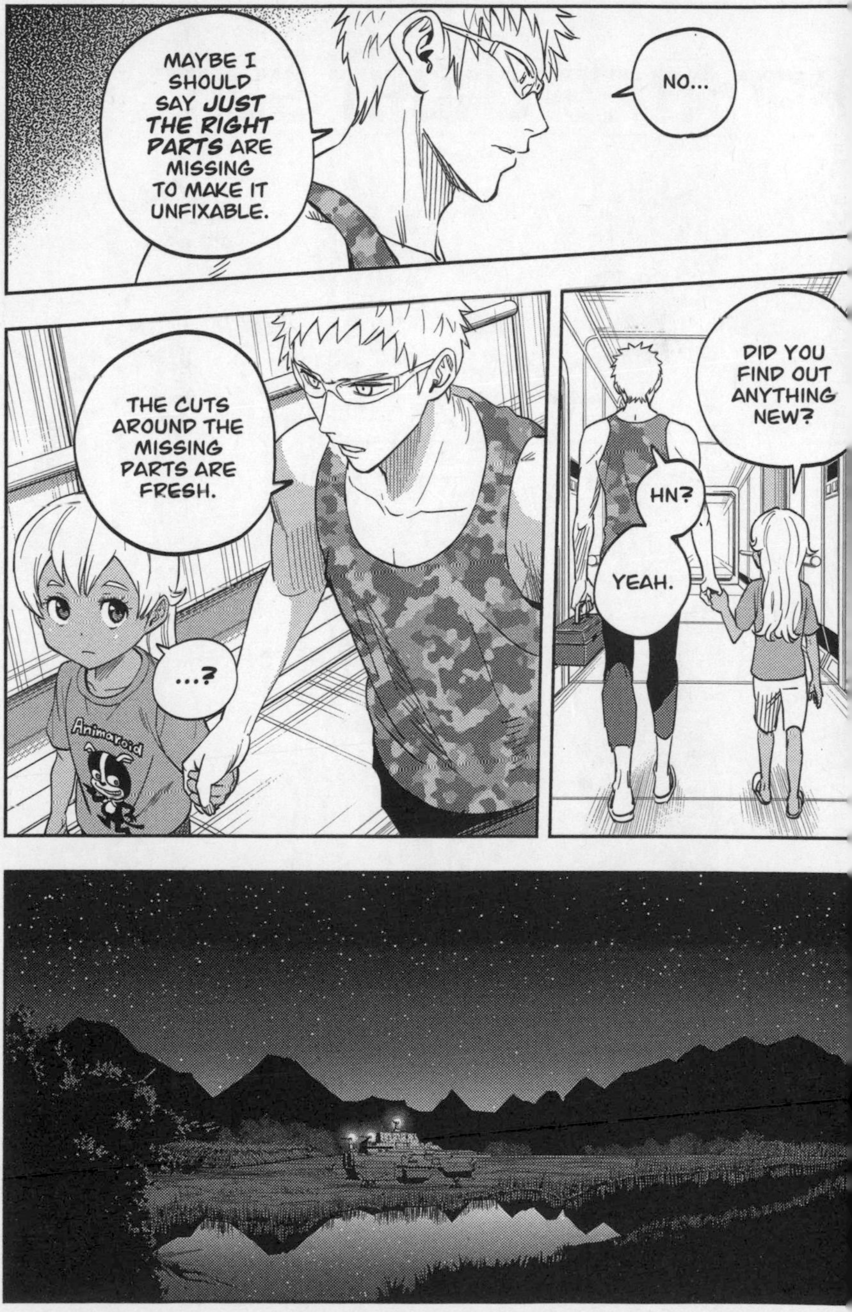
NO...
MAYBE I SHOULD SAY JUST THE RIGHT PARTS ARE MISSING TO MAKE IT UNFIXABLE.
DID YOU FIND OUT ANYTHING NEW?
HN?
YEAH.
THE CUTS AROUND THE MISSING PARTS ARE FRESH.
...?
Animaroid

Material Collection
Costume Design **04**

KANATA'S CRUST SUIT

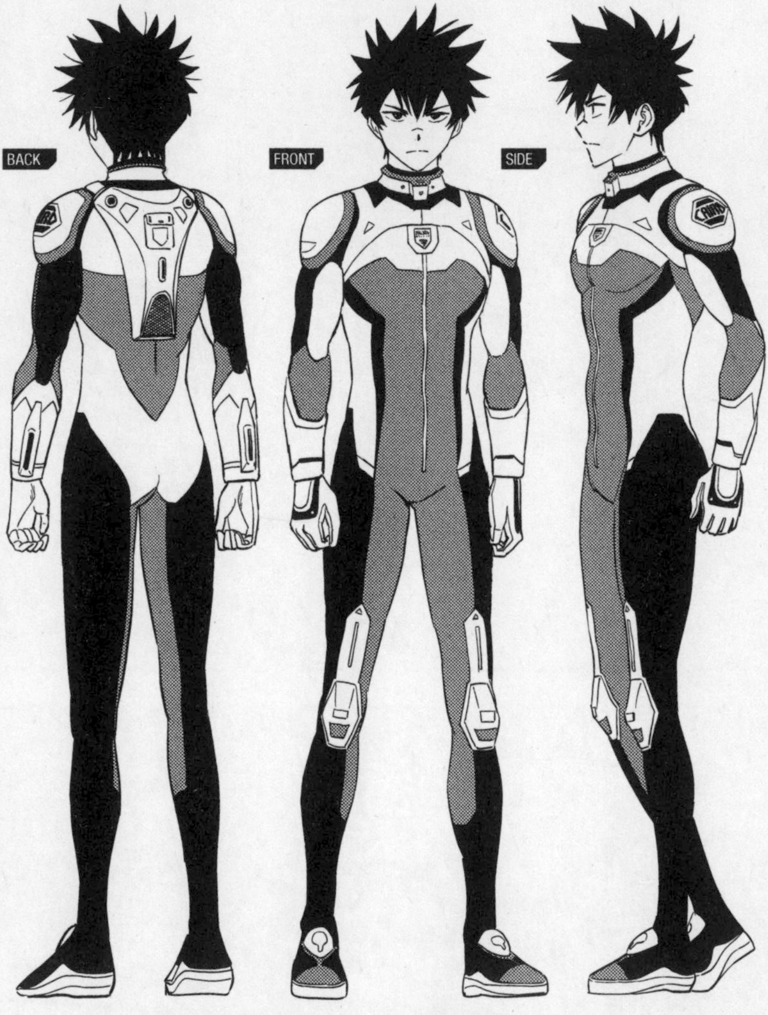
BACK
FRONT
SIDE

A standard men's crust suit by Falken.

Red and blue.

A hand-me-down from his late teacher, it has an older design.

It's a standard model designed for maximum athletic performance.

ASTRA
LOST IN
SPACE

#5

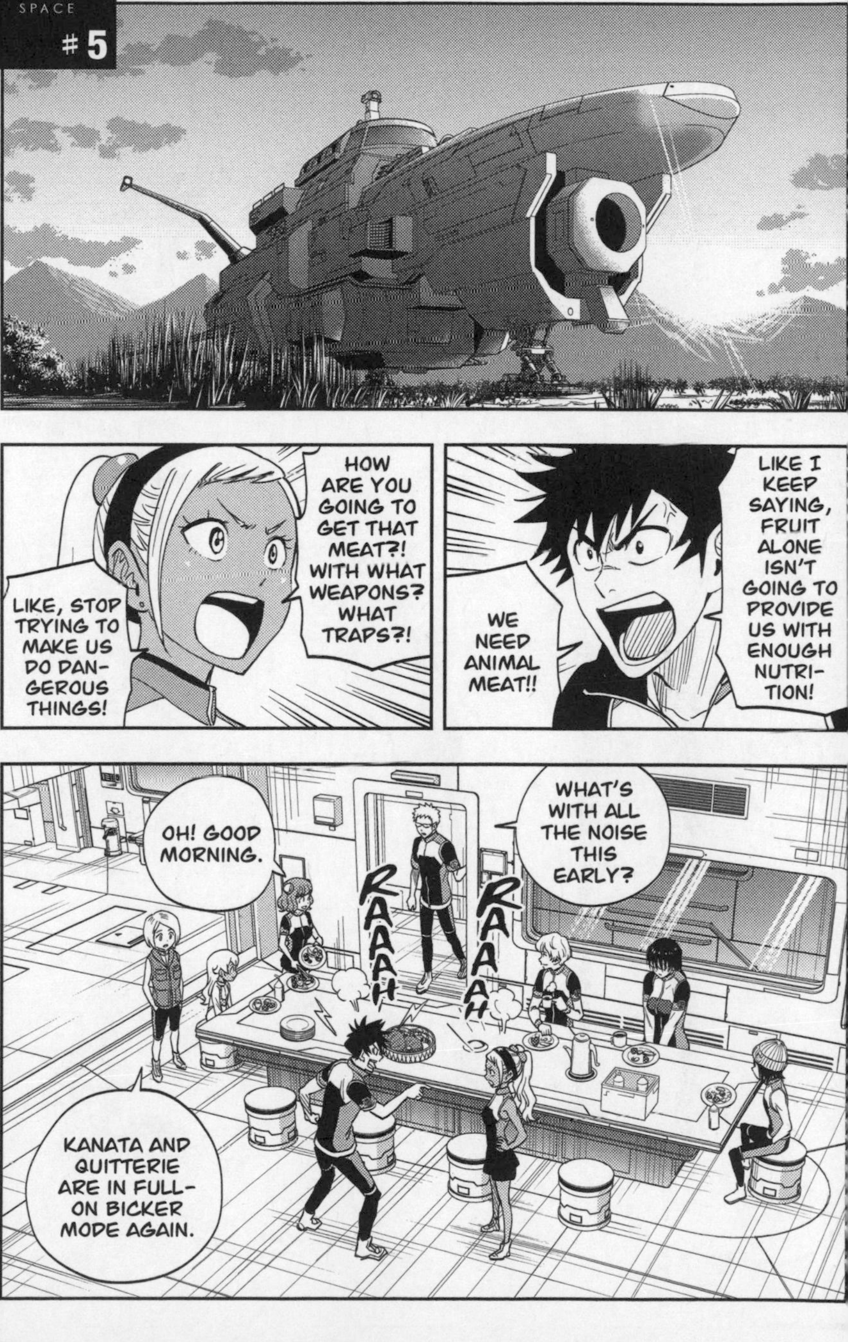
LIKE I KEEP SAYING, FRUIT ALONE ISN'T GOING TO PROVIDE US WITH ENOUGH NUTRITION!
WE NEED ANIMAL MEAT!!
HOW ARE YOU GOING TO GET THAT MEAT?! WITH WHAT WEAPONS? WHAT TRAPS?!
LIKE, STOP TRYING TO MAKE US DO DANGEROUS THINGS!
WHAT'S WITH ALL THE NOISE THIS EARLY?
RAAAAH
RAAAAH
OH! GOOD MORNING.
KANATA AND QUITTERIE ARE IN FULL-ON BICKER MODE AGAIN.

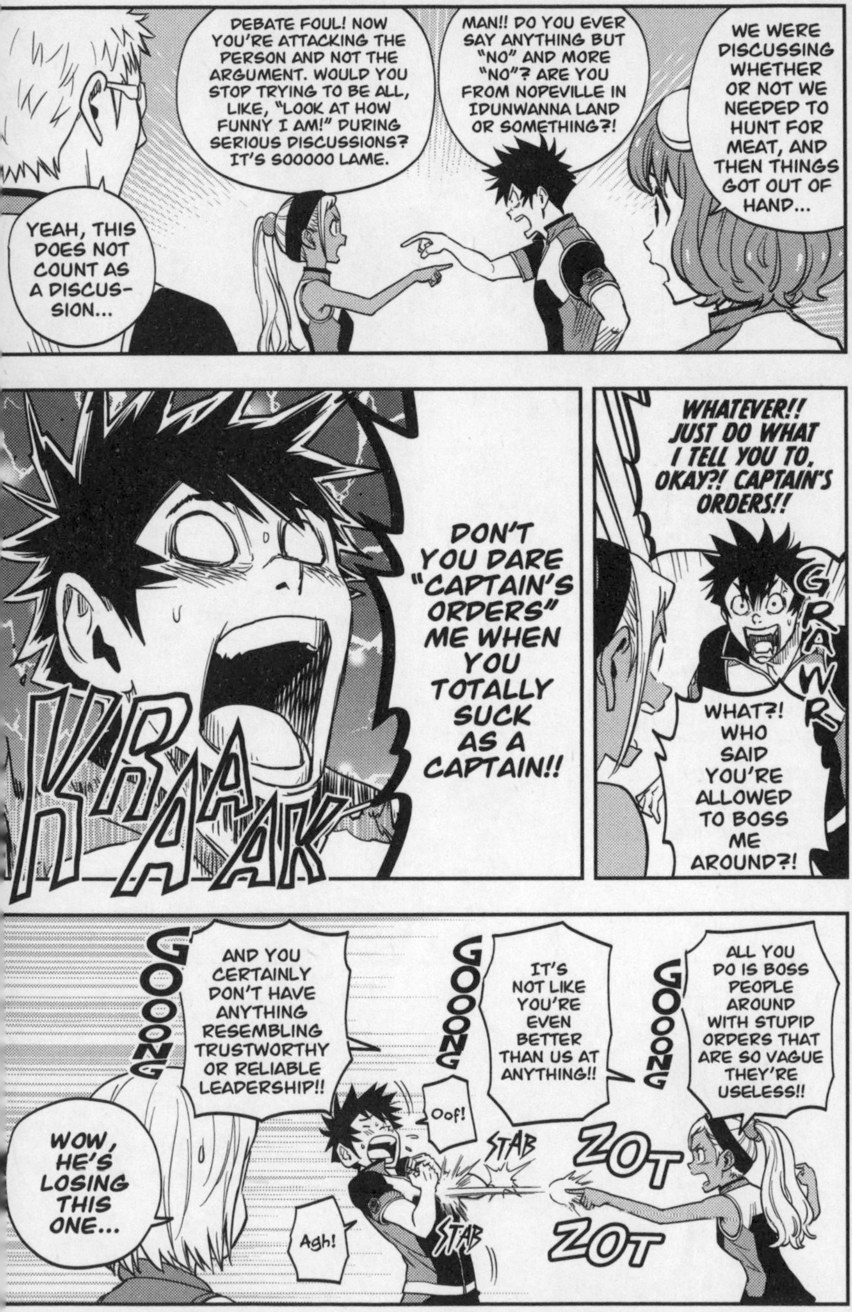
WE WERE DISCUSSING WHETHER OR NOT WE NEEDED TO HUNT FOR MEAT, AND THEN THINGS GOT OUT OF HAND...
MAN!! DO YOU EVER SAY ANYTHING BUT "NO" AND MORE "NO"? ARE YOU FROM NOPEVILLE IN IDUNWANNA LAND OR SOMETHING?!
DEBATE FOUL! NOW YOU'RE ATTACKING THE PERSON AND NOT THE ARGUMENT. WOULD YOU STOP TRYING TO BE ALL, LIKE, "LOOK AT HOW FUNNY I AM!" DURING SERIOUS DISCUSSIONS? IT'S SOOOOO LAME.
YEAH, THIS DOES NOT COUNT AS A DISCUS-SION...
WHATEVER!! JUST DO WHAT I TELL YOU TO, OKAY?! CAPTAIN'S ORDERS!!
GRAWR
WHAT?! WHO SAID YOU'RE ALLOWED TO BOSS ME AROUND?!
DON'T YOU DARE "CAPTAIN'S ORDERS" ME WHEN YOU TOTALLY SUCK AS A CAPTAIN!!
KRAAAAK
ALL YOU DO IS BOSS PEOPLE AROUND WITH STUPID ORDERS THAT ARE SO VAGUE THEY'RE USELESS!!
GOOOONG
ZOT
IT'S NOT LIKE YOU'RE EVEN BETTER THAN US AT ANYTHING!!
GOOOONG
STAB
Oof!
AND YOU CERTAINLY DON'T HAVE ANYTHING RESEMBLING TRUSTWORTHY OR RELIABLE LEADERSHIP!!
GOOOONG
ZOT
STAB
Agh!
WOW, HE'S LOSING THIS ONE...

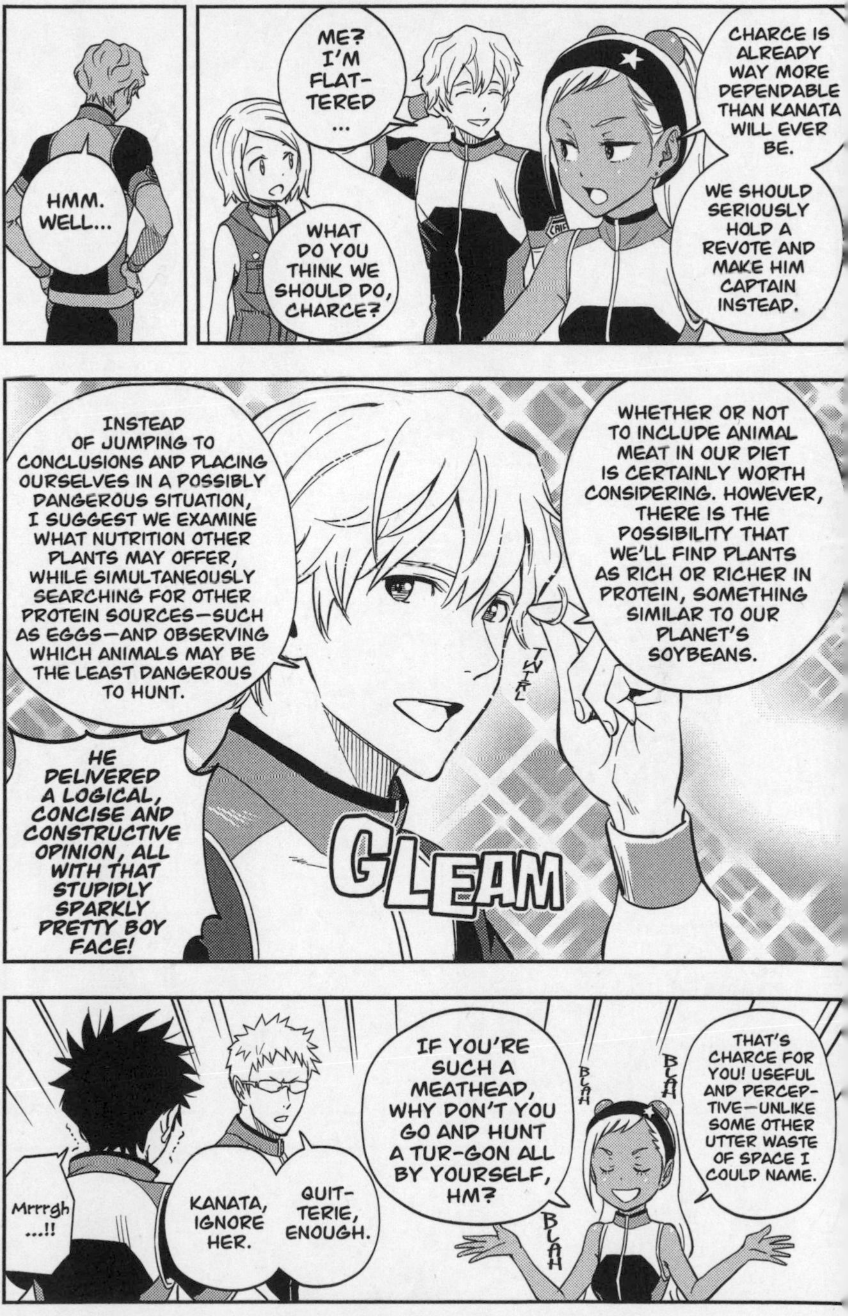
CHARCE IS ALREADY WAY MORE DEPENDABLE THAN KANATA WILL EVER BE.
WE SHOULD SERIOUSLY HOLD A REVOTE AND MAKE HIM CAPTAIN INSTEAD.
ME? I'M FLAT-TERED...
WHAT DO YOU THINK WE SHOULD DO, CHARCE?
HMM. WELL...
WHETHER OR NOT TO INCLUDE ANIMAL MEAT IN OUR DIET IS CERTAINLY WORTH CONSIDERING. HOWEVER, THERE IS THE POSSIBILITY THAT WE'LL FIND PLANTS AS RICH OR RICHER IN PROTEIN, SOMETHING SIMILAR TO OUR PLANET'S SOYBEANS.
INSTEAD OF JUMPING TO CONCLUSIONS AND PLACING OURSELVES IN A POSSIBLY DANGEROUS SITUATION, I SUGGEST WE EXAMINE WHAT NUTRITION OTHER PLANTS MAY OFFER, WHILE SIMULTANEOUSLY SEARCHING FOR OTHER PROTEIN SOURCES—SUCH AS EGGS—AND OBSERVING WHICH ANIMALS MAY BE THE LEAST DANGEROUS TO HUNT.
TWIRL
GLEAM
HE DELIVERED A LOGICAL, CONCISE AND CONSTRUCTIVE OPINION, ALL WITH THAT STUPIDLY SPARKLY PRETTY BOY FACE!
THAT'S CHARCE FOR YOU! USEFUL AND PERCEP-TIVE—UNLIKE SOME OTHER UTTER WASTE OF SPACE I COULD NAME.
BLAH
BLAH
IF YOU'RE SUCH A MEATHEAD, WHY DON'T YOU GO AND HUNT A TUR-GON ALL BY YOURSELF, HM?
BLAH
QUIT-TERIE, ENOUGH.
KANATA, IGNORE HER.
Mrrrgh ...!!

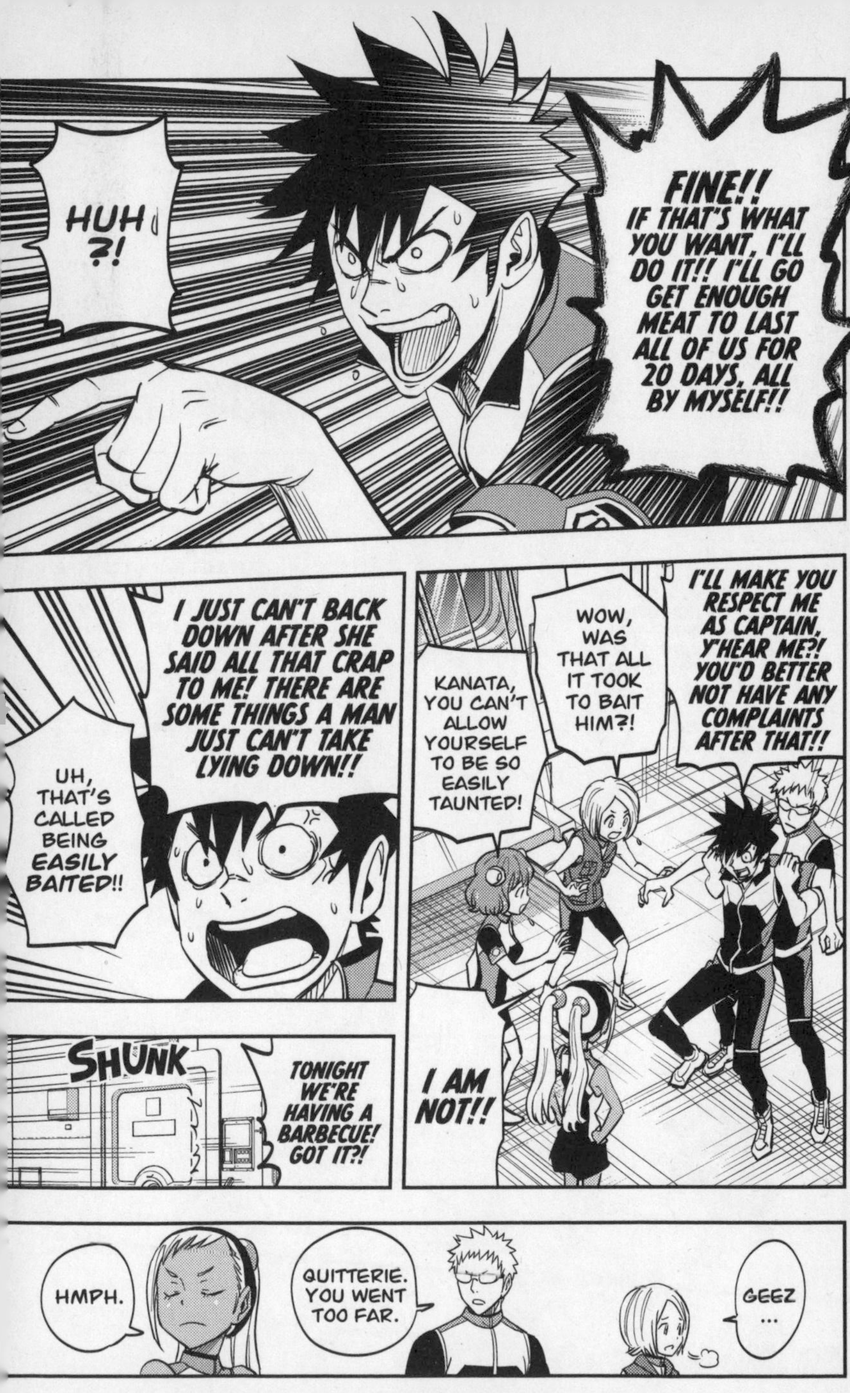
FINE!! IF THAT'S WHAT YOU WANT, I'LL DO IT!! I'LL GO GET ENOUGH MEAT TO LAST ALL OF US FOR 20 DAYS, ALL BY MYSELF!!
HUH ?!
I'LL MAKE YOU RESPECT ME AS CAPTAIN, Y'HEAR ME?! YOU'D BETTER NOT HAVE ANY COMPLAINTS AFTER THAT!!
WOW, WAS THAT ALL IT TOOK TO BAIT HIM?!
KANATA, YOU CAN'T ALLOW YOURSELF TO BE SO EASILY TAUNTED!
I AM NOT!!
I JUST CAN'T BACK DOWN AFTER SHE SAID ALL THAT CRAP TO ME! THERE ARE SOME THINGS A MAN JUST CAN'T TAKE LYING DOWN!!
UH, THAT'S CALLED BEING EASILY BAITED!!
SHUNK
TONIGHT WE'RE HAVING A BARBECUE! GOT IT?!
GEEZ ...
QUITTERIE. YOU WENT TOO FAR.
HMPH.

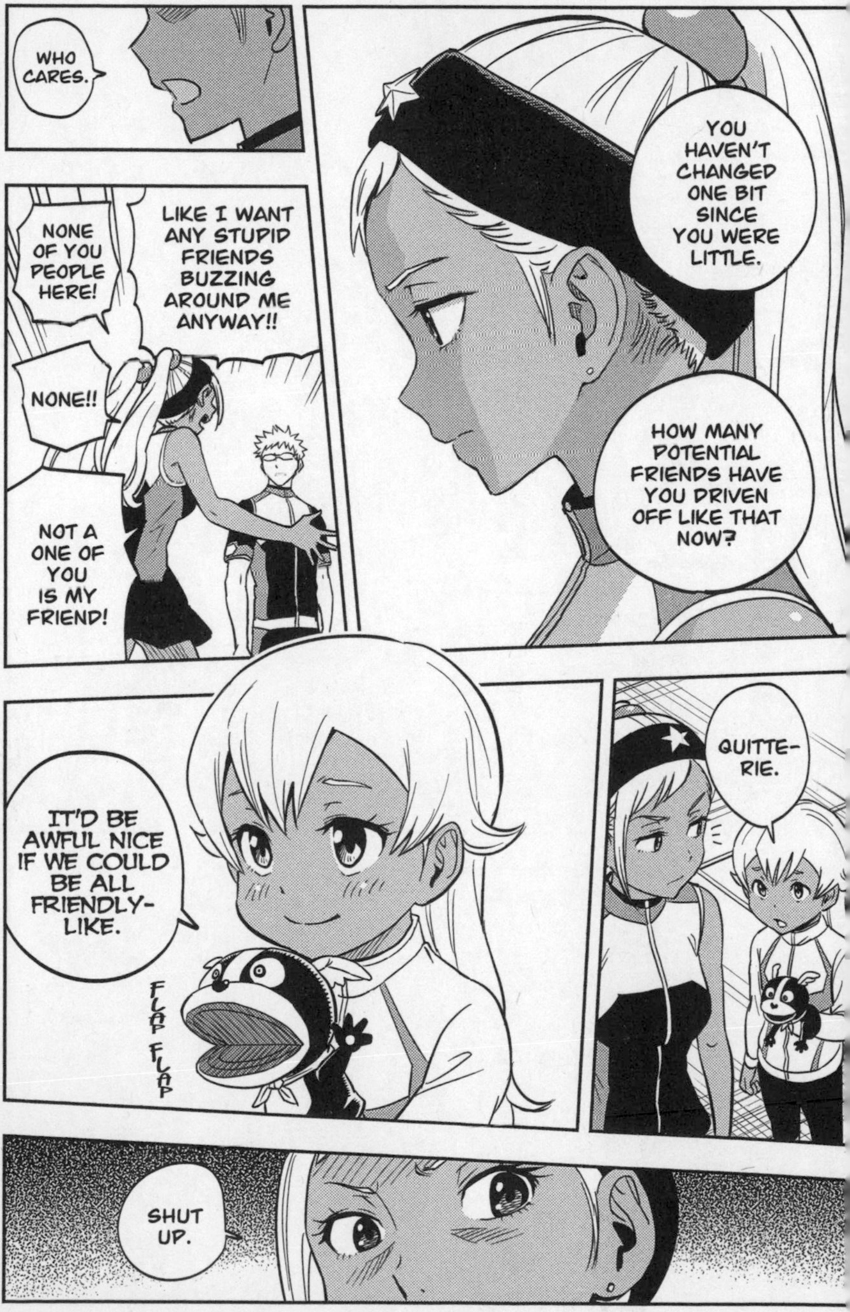
YOU HAVEN'T CHANGED ONE BIT SINCE YOU WERE LITTLE.
HOW MANY POTENTIAL FRIENDS HAVE YOU DRIVEN OFF LIKE THAT NOW?
WHO CARES.
LIKE I WANT ANY STUPID FRIENDS BUZZING AROUND ME ANYWAY!!
NONE OF YOU PEOPLE HERE!
NONE!!
NOT A ONE OF YOU IS MY FRIEND!
QUITTE-RIE.
IT'D BE AWFUL NICE IF WE COULD BE ALL FRIENDLY-LIKE.
FLAP FLAP
SHUT UP.

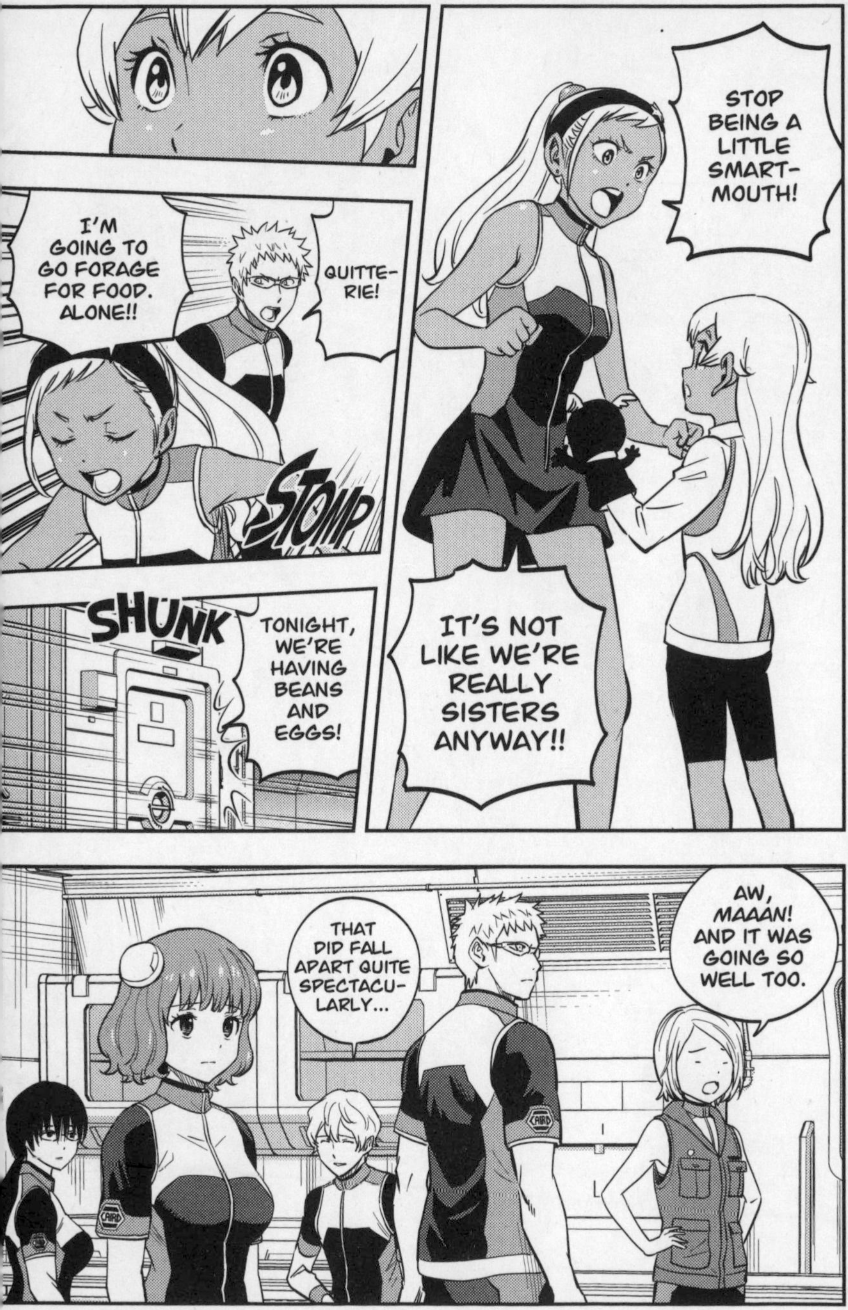
STOP BEING A LITTLE SMART-MOUTH!
IT'S NOT LIKE WE'RE REALLY SISTERS ANYWAY!!
QUITTE-RIE!
I'M GOING TO GO FORAGE FOR FOOD. ALONE!!
STOMP
SHUNK
TONIGHT, WE'RE HAVING BEANS AND EGGS!
AW, MAAAN! AND IT WAS GOING SO WELL TOO.
THAT DID FALL APART QUITE SPECTACU-LARLY...

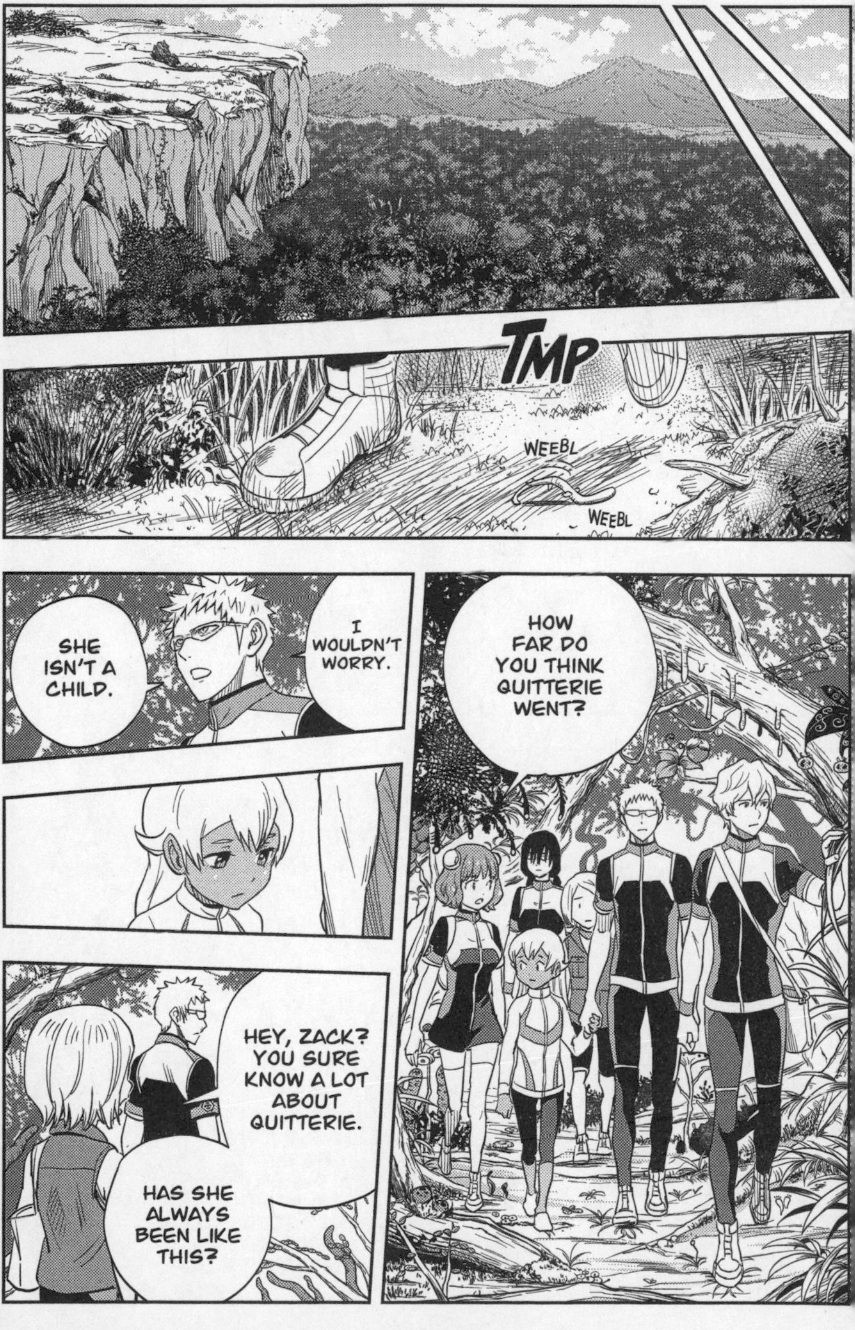
TMP
WEEBL
WEEBL
HOW FAR DO YOU THINK QUITTERIE WENT?
I WOULDN'T WORRY.
SHE ISN'T A CHILD.
HEY, ZACK? YOU SURE KNOW A LOT ABOUT QUITTERIE.
HAS SHE ALWAYS BEEN LIKE THIS?

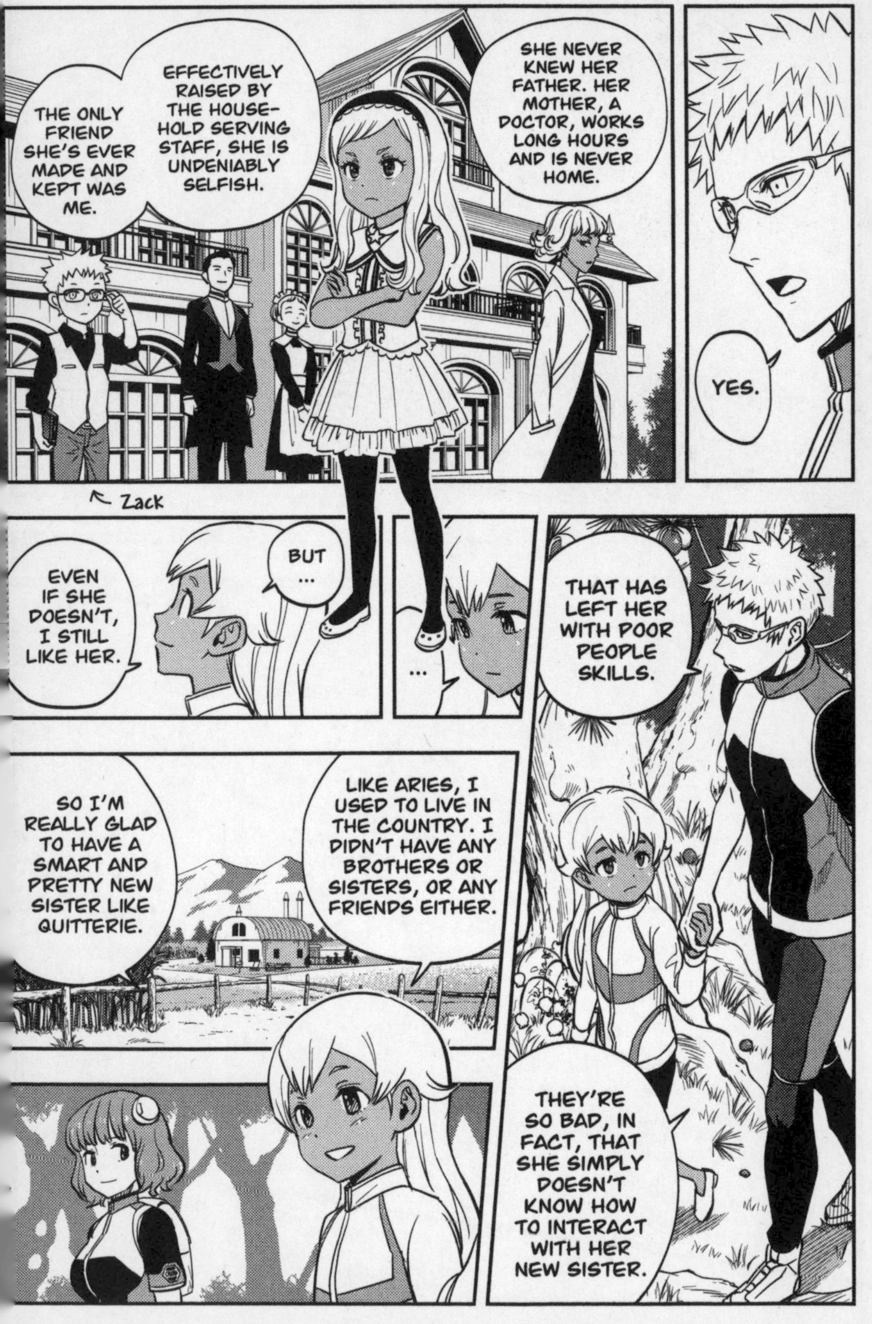
YES.
SHE NEVER KNEW HER FATHER. HER MOTHER, A DOCTOR, WORKS LONG HOURS AND IS NEVER HOME.
EFFECTIVELY RAISED BY THE HOUSE-HOLD SERVING STAFF, SHE IS UNDENIABLY SELFISH.
THE ONLY FRIEND SHE'S EVER MADE AND KEPT WAS ME.
Zack
THAT HAS LEFT HER WITH POOR PEOPLE SKILLS.
THEY'RE SO BAD, IN FACT, THAT SHE SIMPLY DOESN'T KNOW HOW TO INTERACT WITH HER NEW SISTER.
...
BUT ...
EVEN IF SHE DOESN'T, I STILL LIKE HER.
LIKE ARIES, I USED TO LIVE IN THE COUNTRY. I DIDN'T HAVE ANY BROTHERS OR SISTERS, OR ANY FRIENDS EITHER.
SO I'M REALLY GLAD TO HAVE A SMART AND PRETTY NEW SISTER LIKE QUITTERIE.

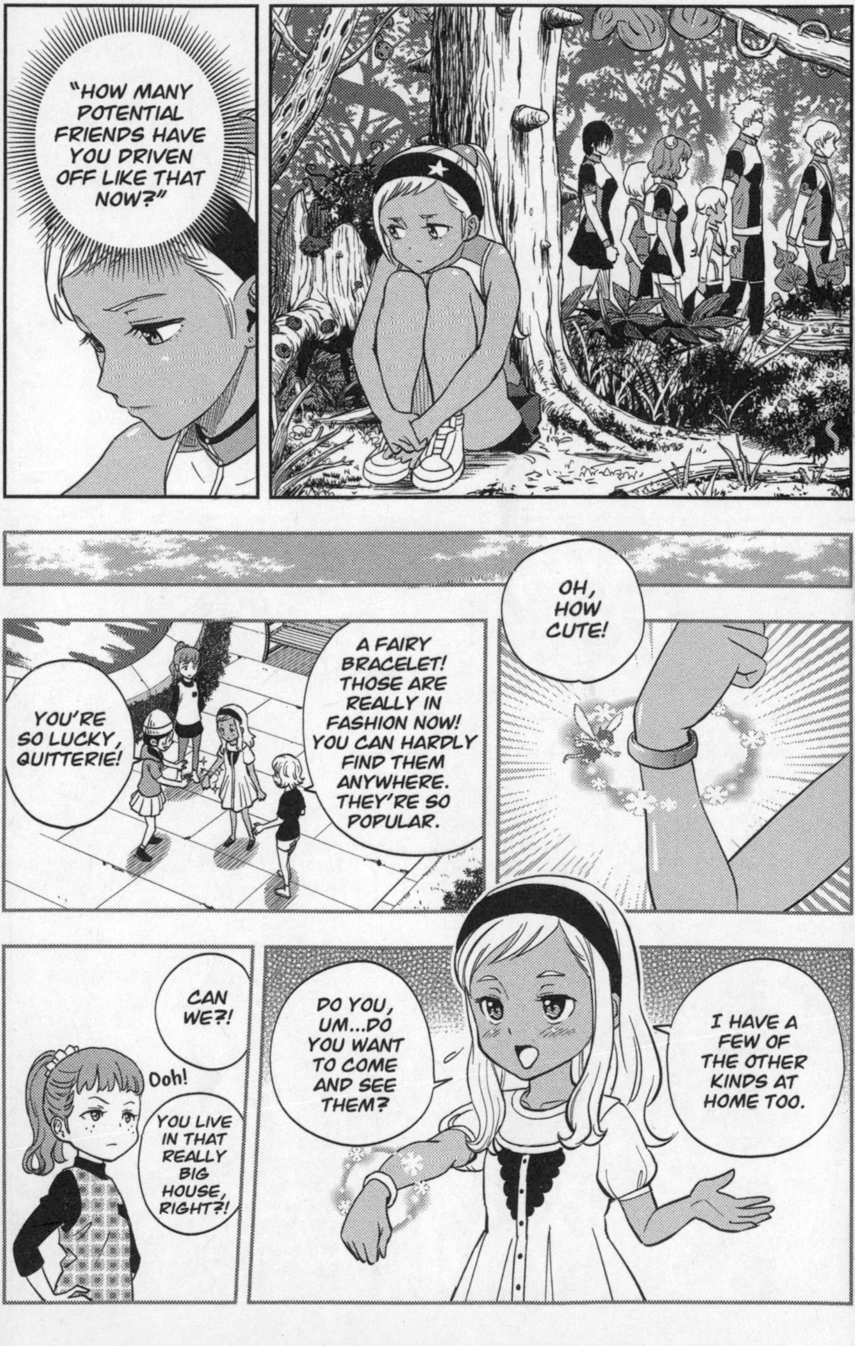
"HOW MANY POTENTIAL FRIENDS HAVE YOU DRIVEN OFF LIKE THAT NOW?"
OH, HOW CUTE!
A FAIRY BRACELET! THOSE ARE REALLY IN FASHION NOW! YOU CAN HARDLY FIND THEM ANYWHERE. THEY'RE SO POPULAR.
YOU'RE SO LUCKY, QUITTERIE!
I HAVE A FEW OF THE OTHER KINDS AT HOME TOO.
DO YOU, UM...DO YOU WANT TO COME AND SEE THEM?
CAN WE?!
Ooh!
YOU LIVE IN THAT REALLY BIG HOUSE, RIGHT?!

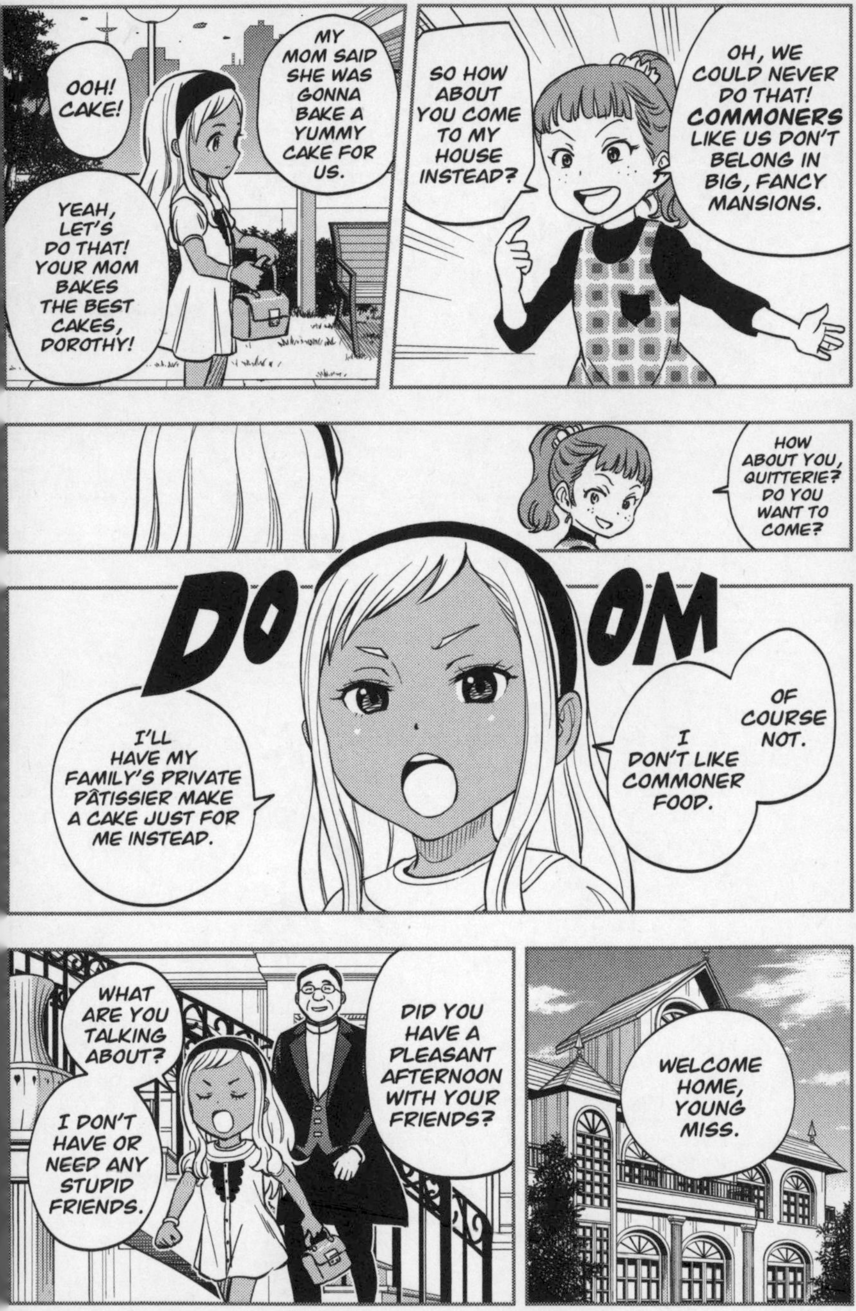
OH, WE COULD NEVER DO THAT! COMMONERS LIKE US DON'T BELONG IN BIG, FANCY MANSIONS.
SO HOW ABOUT YOU COME TO MY HOUSE INSTEAD?
MY MOM SAID SHE WAS GONNA BAKE A YUMMY CAKE FOR US.
OOH! CAKE!
YEAH, LET'S DO THAT! YOUR MOM BAKES THE BEST CAKES, DOROTHY!
HOW ABOUT YOU, QUITTERIE? DO YOU WANT TO COME?
DOOM
OF COURSE NOT.
I DON'T LIKE COMMONER FOOD.
I'LL HAVE MY FAMILY'S PRIVATE PÂTISSIER MAKE A CAKE JUST FOR ME INSTEAD.
WELCOME HOME, YOUNG MISS.
DID YOU HAVE A PLEASANT AFTERNOON WITH YOUR FRIENDS?
WHAT ARE YOU TALKING ABOUT?
I DON'T HAVE OR NEED ANY STUPID FRIENDS.

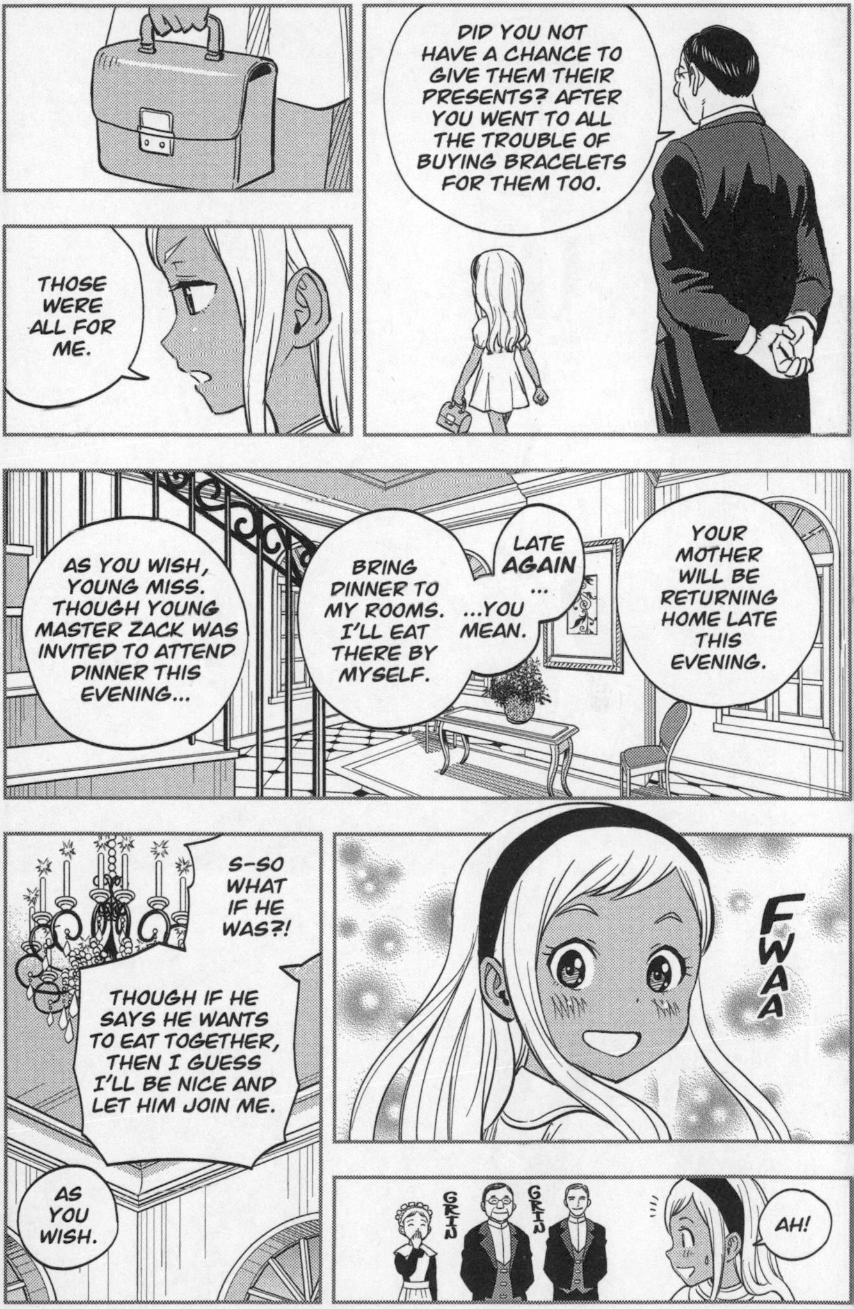
DID YOU NOT HAVE A CHANCE TO GIVE THEM THEIR PRESENTS? AFTER YOU WENT TO ALL THE TROUBLE OF BUYING BRACELETS FOR THEM TOO.
THOSE WERE ALL FOR ME.
YOUR MOTHER WILL BE RETURNING HOME LATE THIS EVENING.
LATE AGAIN ...
...YOU MEAN.
BRING DINNER TO MY ROOMS. I'LL EAT THERE BY MYSELF.
AS YOU WISH, YOUNG MISS. THOUGH YOUNG MASTER ZACK WAS INVITED TO ATTEND DINNER THIS EVENING...
FWAA
GRIN
GRIN
AH!
S-SO WHAT IF HE WAS?!
THOUGH IF HE SAYS HE WANTS TO EAT TOGETHER, THEN I GUESS I'LL BE NICE AND LET HIM JOIN ME.
AS YOU WISH.

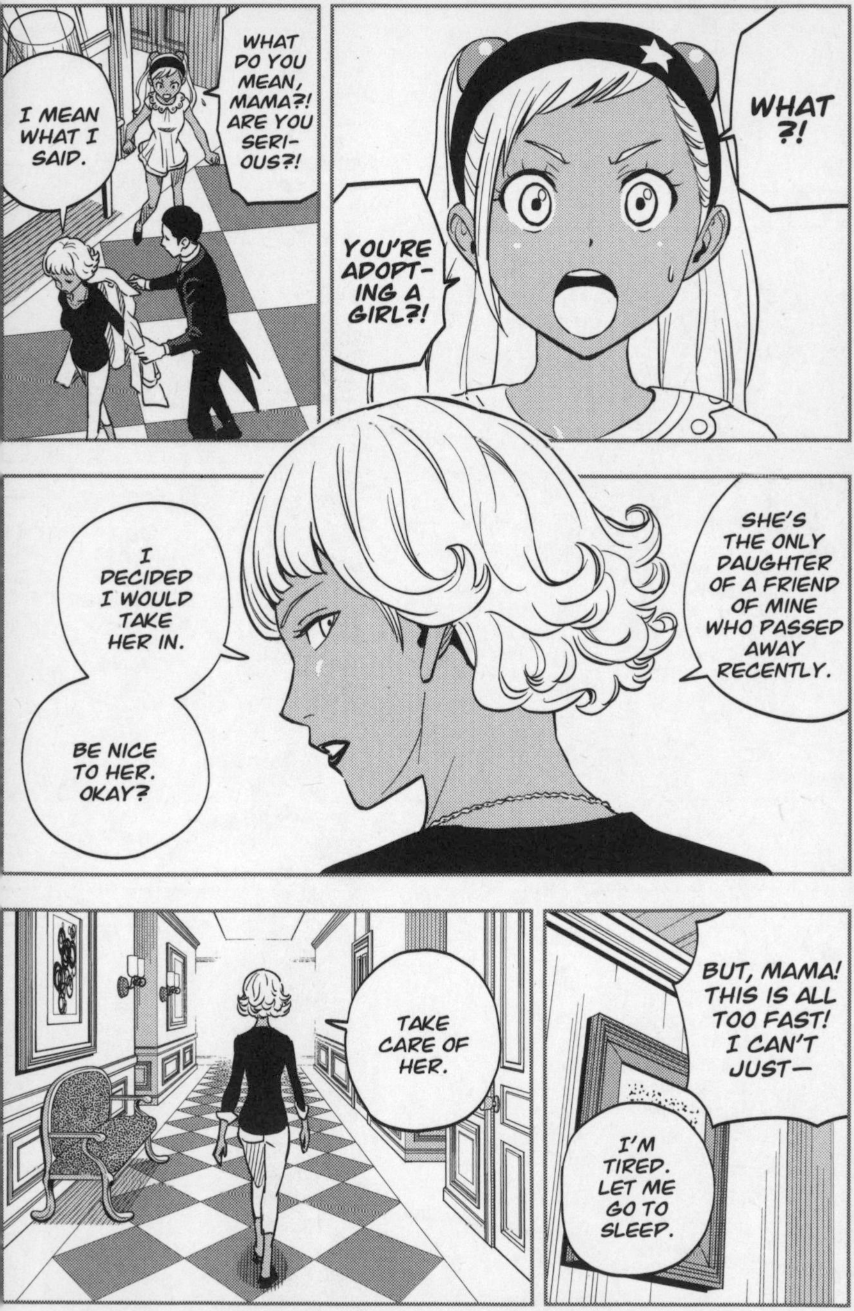
WHAT?!
YOU'RE ADOPTING A GIRL?!
WHAT DO YOU MEAN, MAMA?! ARE YOU SERIOUS?!
I MEAN WHAT I SAID.
SHE'S THE ONLY DAUGHTER OF A FRIEND OF MINE WHO PASSED AWAY RECENTLY.
I DECIDED I WOULD TAKE HER IN.
BE NICE TO HER. OKAY?
BUT, MAMA! THIS IS ALL TOO FAST! I CAN'T JUST—
I'M TIRED. LET ME GO TO SLEEP.
TAKE CARE OF HER.

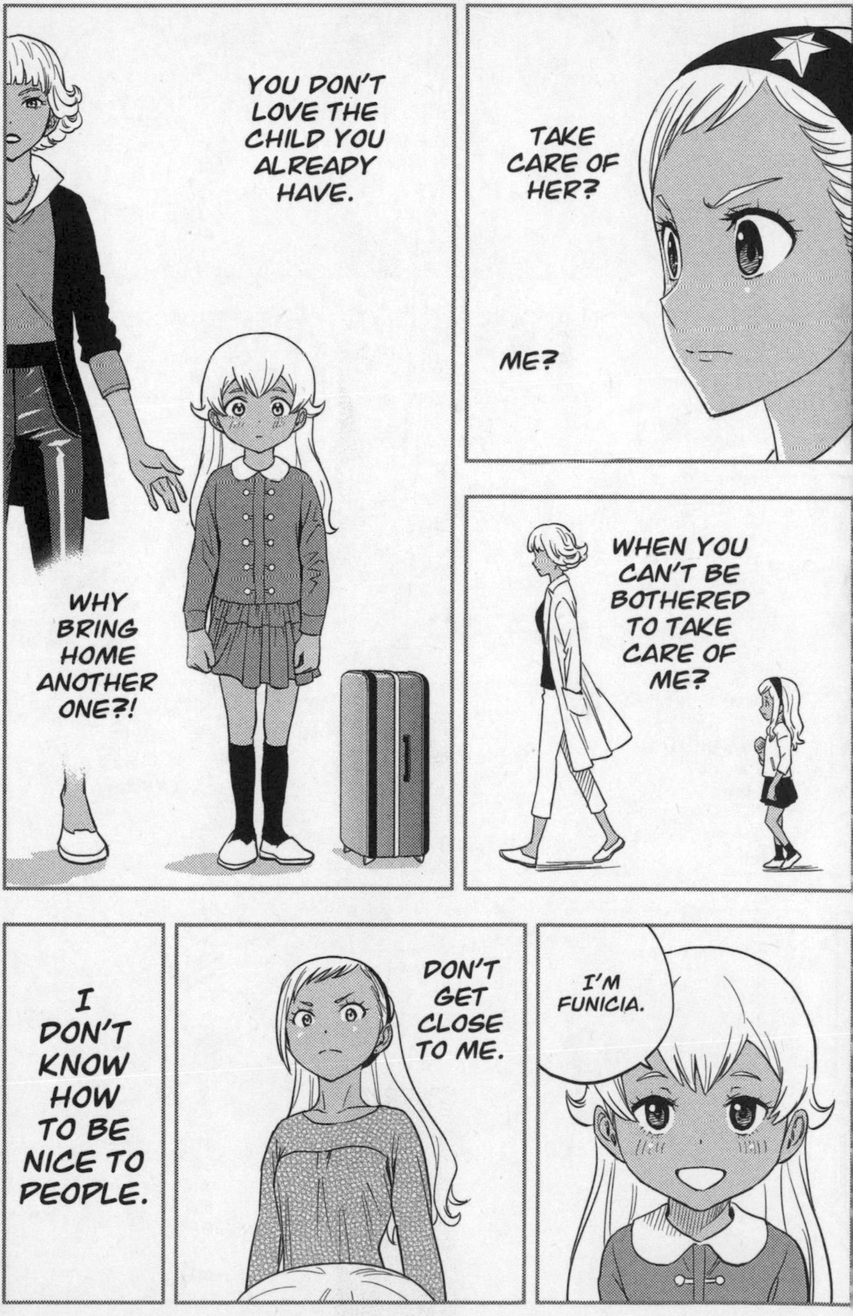
TAKE CARE OF HER?
ME?
WHEN YOU CAN'T BE BOTHERED TO TAKE CARE OF ME?
YOU DON'T LOVE THE CHILD YOU ALREADY HAVE.
WHY BRING HOME ANOTHER ONE?!
I'M FUNICIA.
DON'T GET CLOSE TO ME.
I DON'T KNOW HOW TO BE NICE TO PEOPLE.

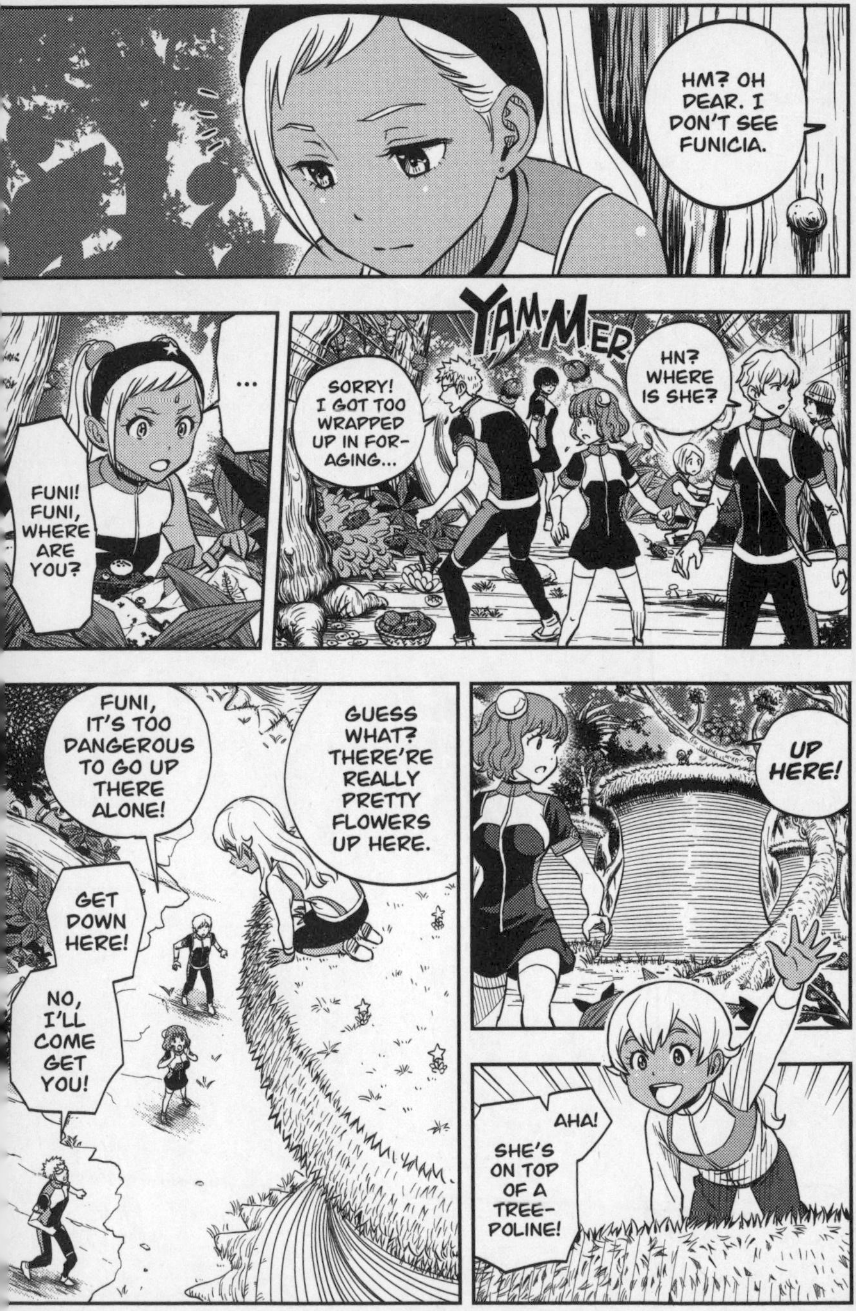
HM? OH DEAR. I DON'T SEE FUNICIA.
YAMMER
HN? WHERE IS SHE?
SORRY! I GOT TOO WRAPPED UP IN FOR-AGING...
...
FUNI! FUNI, WHERE ARE YOU?
UP HERE!
AHA!
SHE'S ON TOP OF A TREE-POLINE!
GUESS WHAT? THERE'RE REALLY PRETTY FLOWERS UP HERE.
FUNI, IT'S TOO DANGEROUS TO GO UP THERE ALONE!
GET DOWN HERE!
NO, I'LL COME GET YOU!

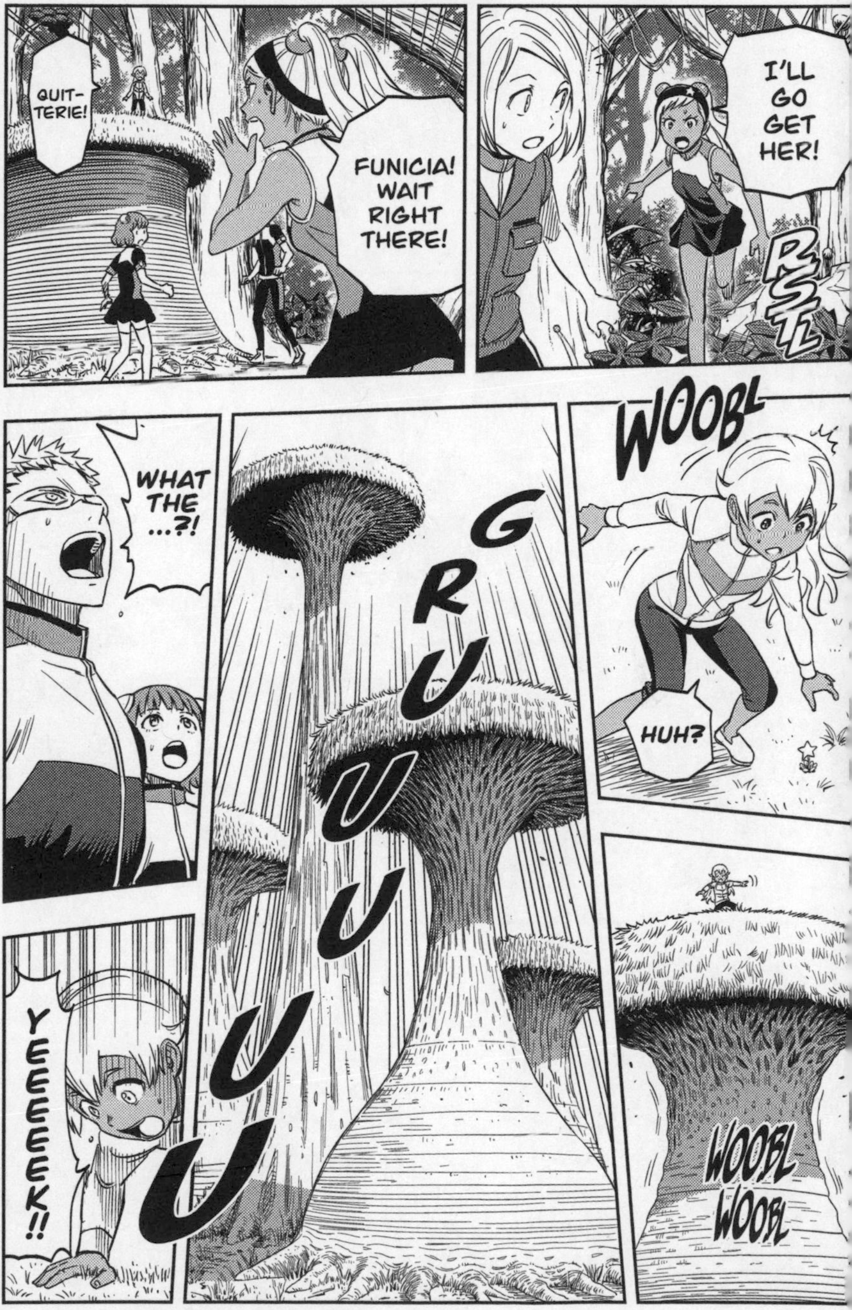
I'LL GO GET HER!
RSTL
FUNICIA! WAIT RIGHT THERE!
QUIT-TERIE!
WOOBL
HUH?
WOOBL WOOBL
GRUUUUUUU
WHAT THE ...?!
YEEEEEK!!

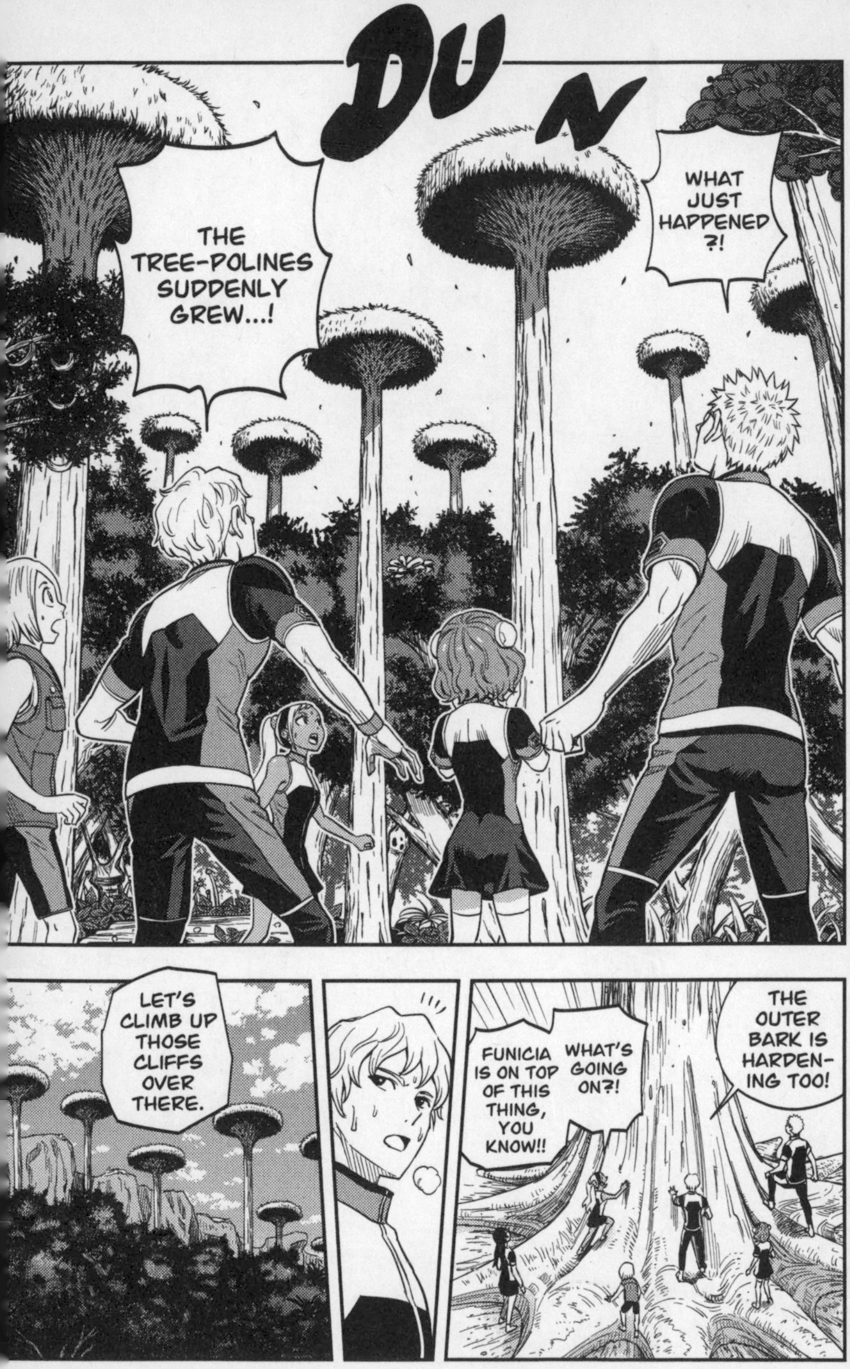
DUN
WHAT JUST HAPPENED?!
THE TREE-POLINES SUDDENLY GREW...!
THE OUTER BARK IS HARDEN-ING TOO!
WHAT'S GOING ON?!
FUNICIA IS ON TOP OF THIS THING, YOU KNOW!!
LET'S CLIMB UP THOSE CLIFFS OVER THERE.

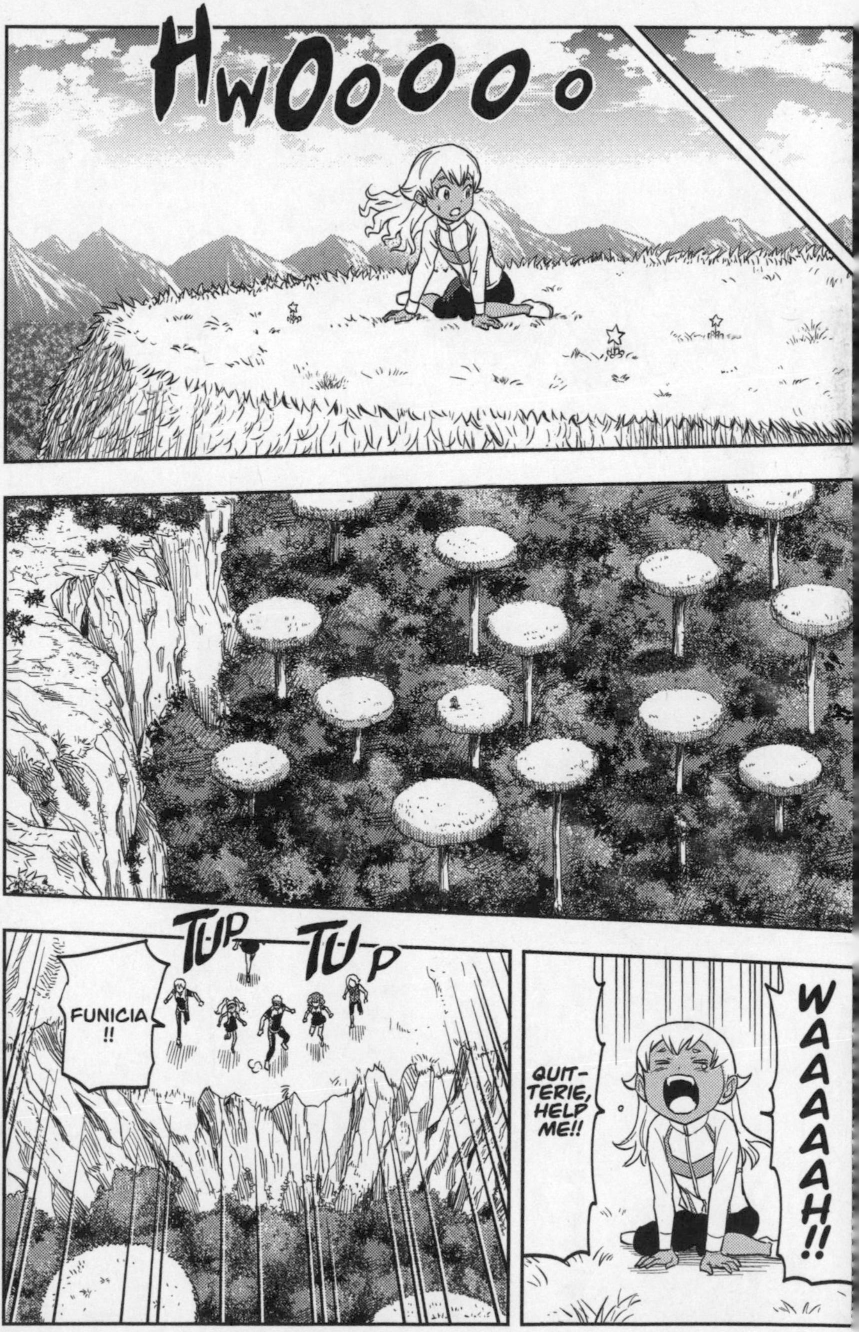
HWOOOOO
WAAAAAH!!
QUIT-TERIE, HELP ME!!
TU-P TU-P
FUNICIA!!

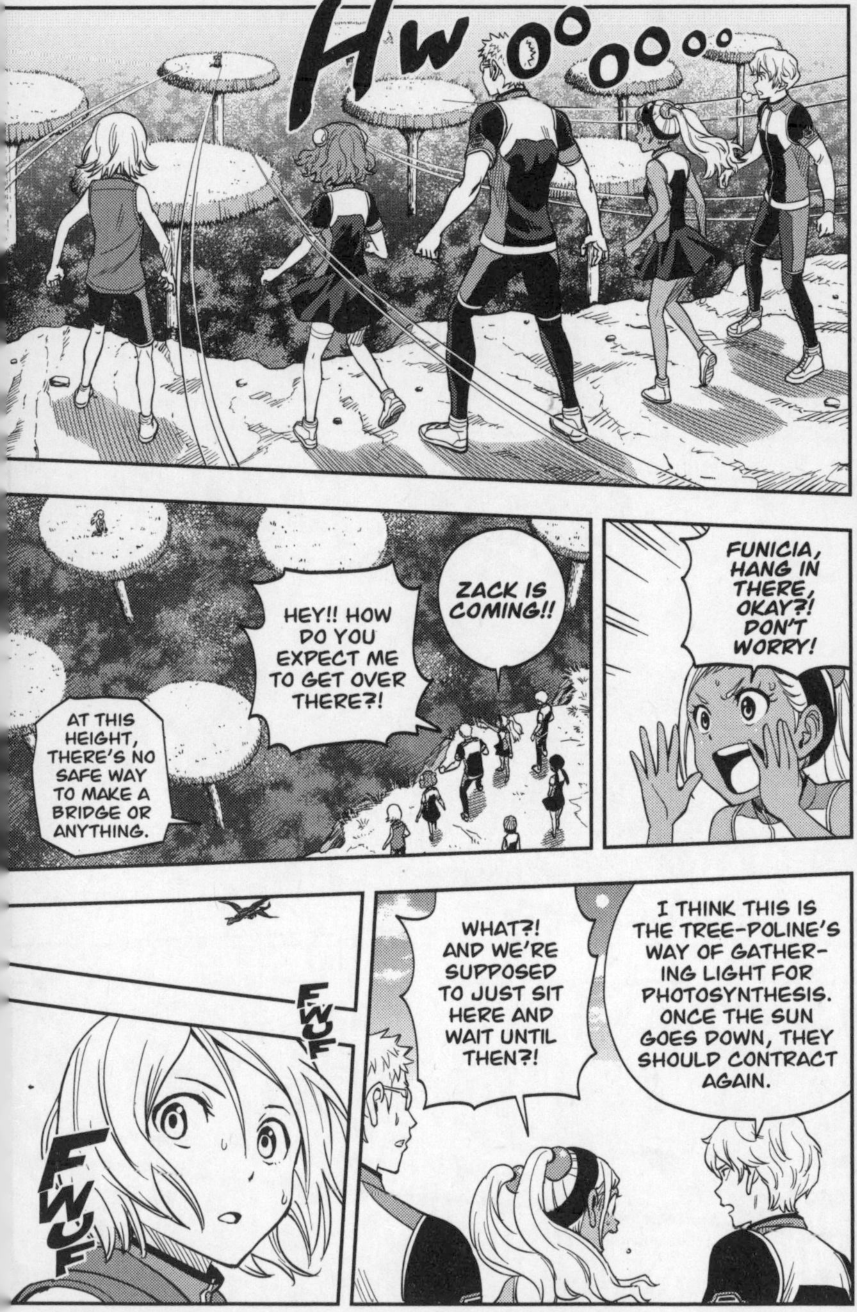
HWOOOOOO
FUNICIA, HANG IN THERE, OKAY?! DON'T WORRY!
ZACK IS COMING!!
HEY!! HOW DO YOU EXPECT ME TO GET OVER THERE?!
AT THIS HEIGHT, THERE'S NO SAFE WAY TO MAKE A BRIDGE OR ANYTHING.
I THINK THIS IS THE TREE-POLINE'S WAY OF GATHERING LIGHT FOR PHOTOSYNTHESIS. ONCE THE SUN GOES DOWN, THEY SHOULD CONTRACT AGAIN.
WHAT?! AND WE'RE SUPPOSED TO JUST SIT HERE AND WAIT UNTIL THEN?!
FWUF
FWUF

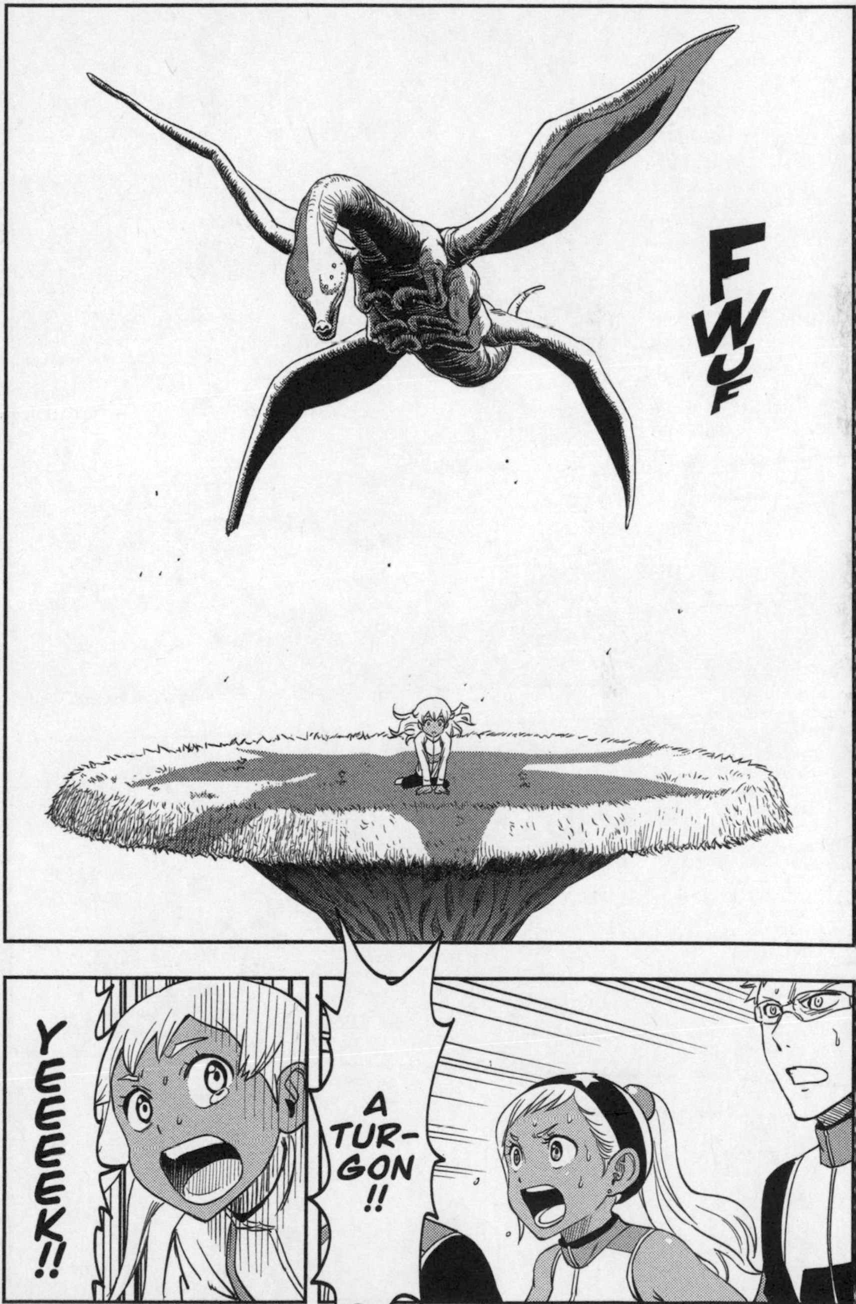
FWUF
A TUR-GON!!
YEEEEK!!

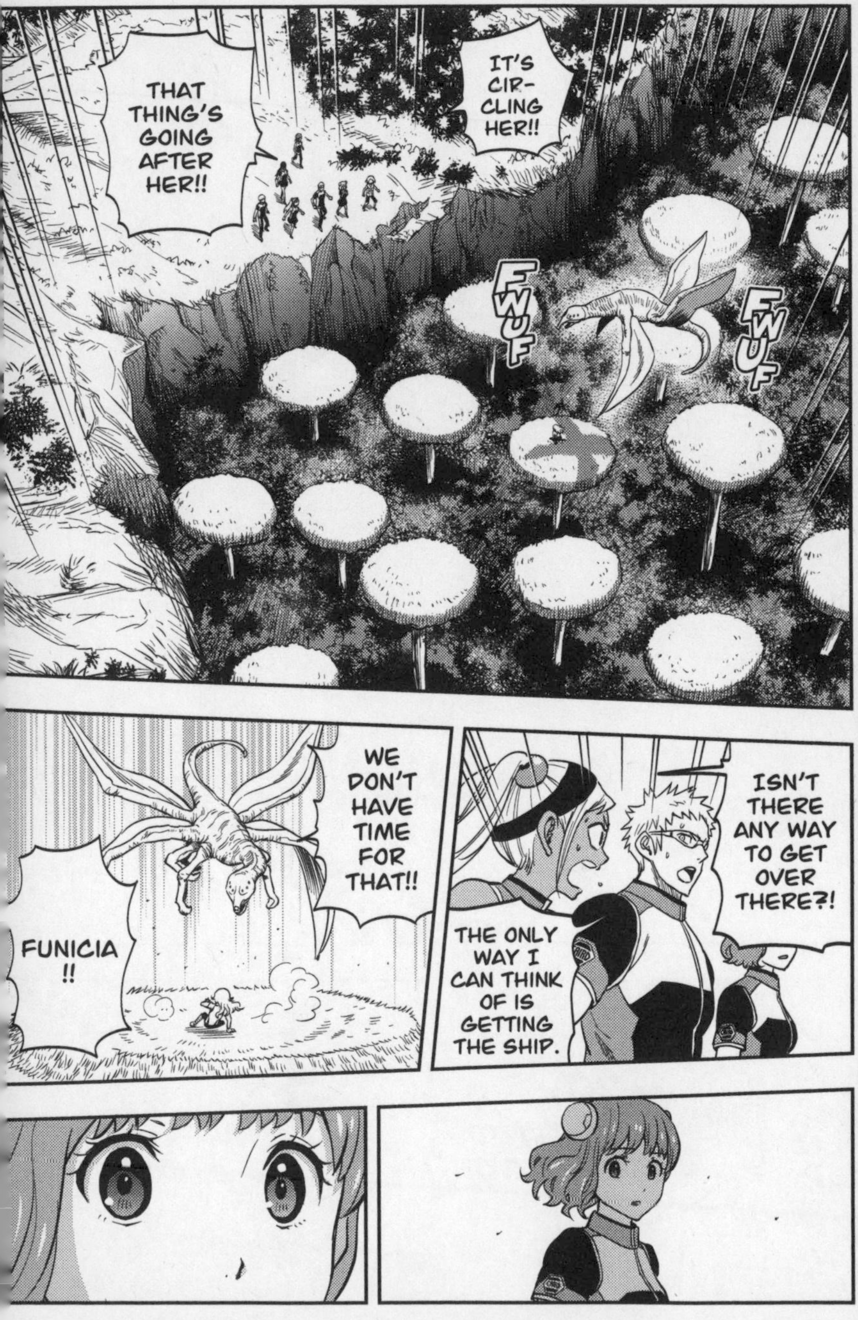
IT'S CIR-CLING HER!!
THAT THING'S GOING AFTER HER!!
FWUF
FWUF
ISN'T THERE ANY WAY TO GET OVER THERE?!
THE ONLY WAY I CAN THINK OF IS GETTING THE SHIP.
WE DON'T HAVE TIME FOR THAT!!
FUNICIA !!

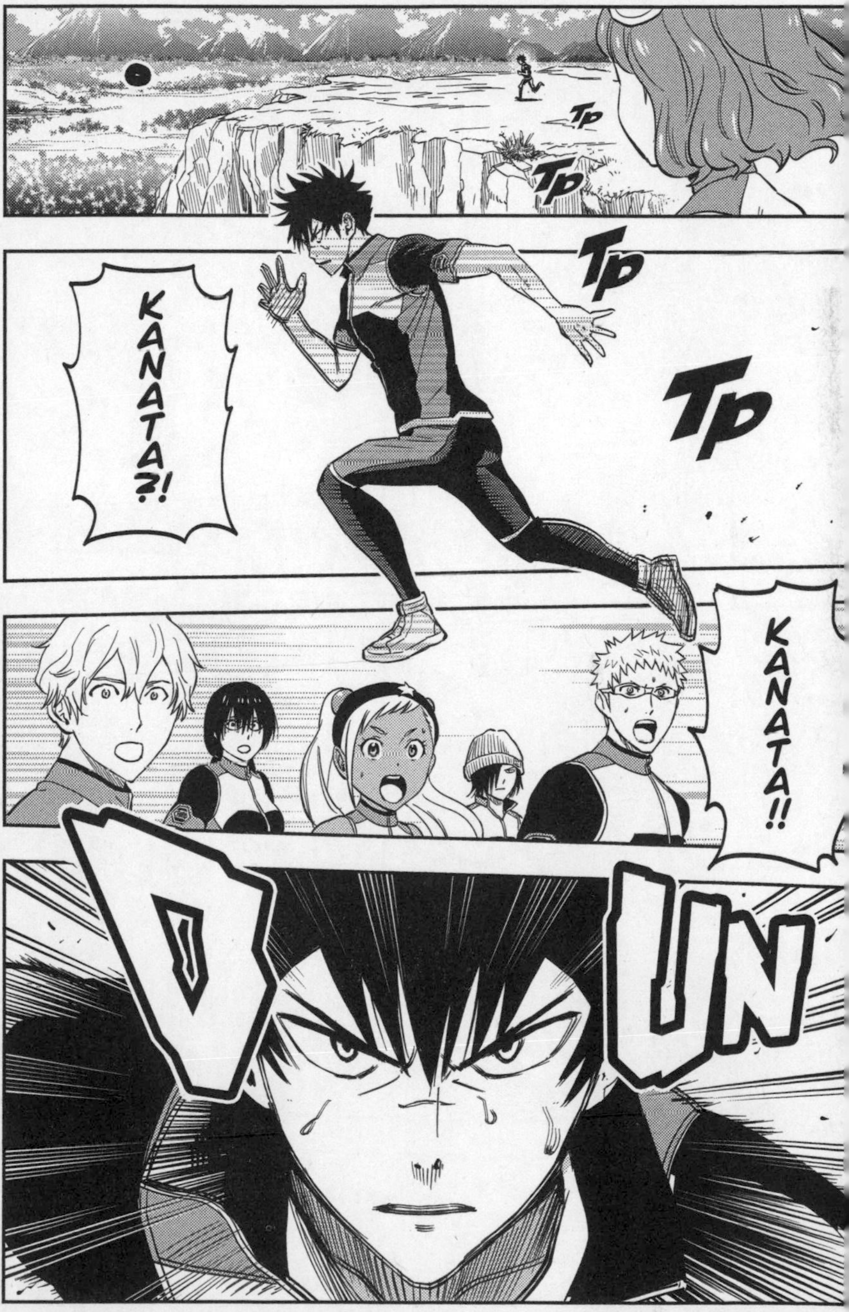

Tp
Tp
Tp
Tp
KANATA?!
KANATA!!
DUN

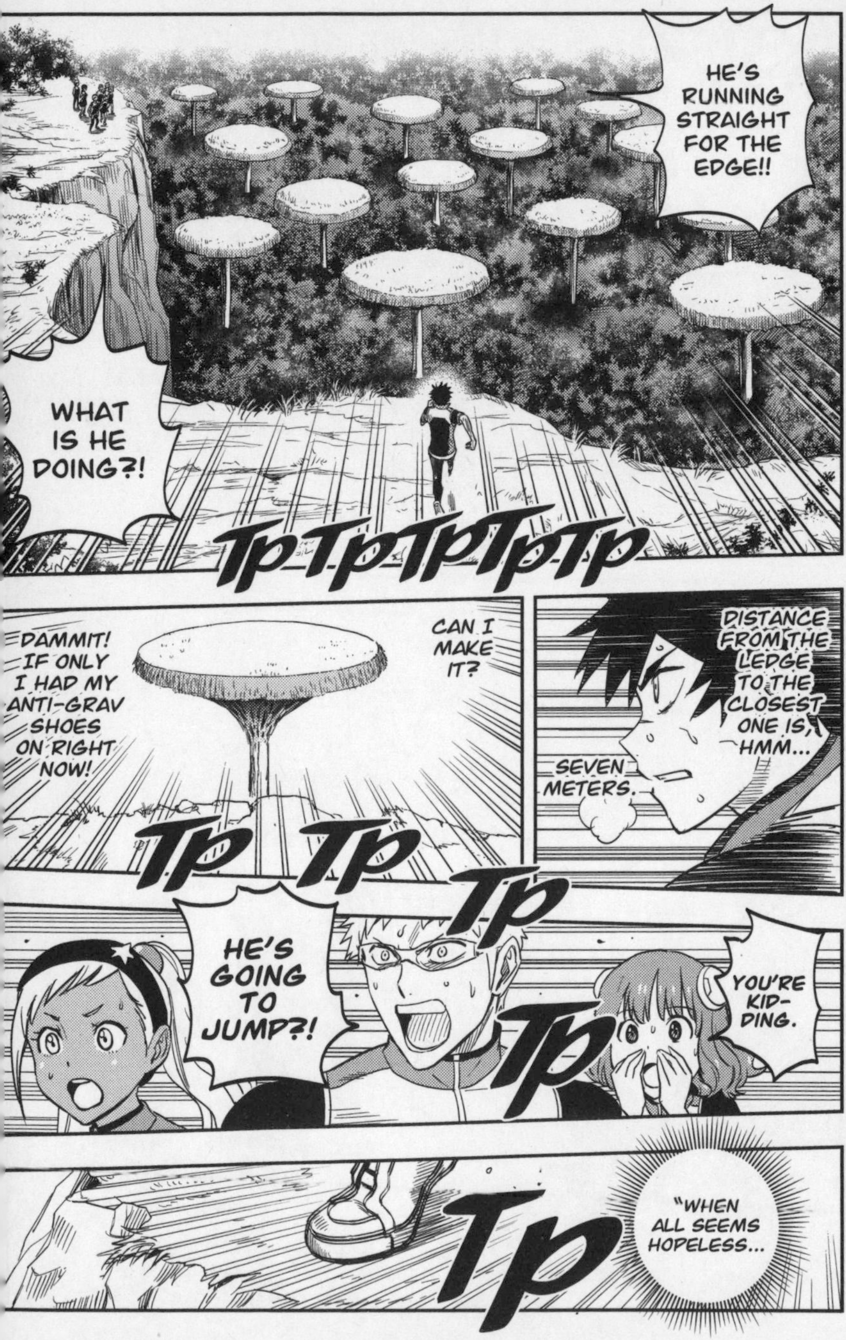
HE'S RUNNING STRAIGHT FOR THE EDGE!!
WHAT IS HE DOING?!
TpTpTpTpTpTp
DISTANCE FROM THE LEDGE TO THE CLOSEST ONE IS, HMM...
SEVEN METERS.
CAN I MAKE IT?
DAMMIT! IF ONLY I HAD MY ANTI-GRAV SHOES ON RIGHT NOW!
Tp Tp
Tp
YOU'RE KID-DING.
Tp
HE'S GOING TO JUMP?!
"WHEN ALL SEEMS HOPELESS...
Tp

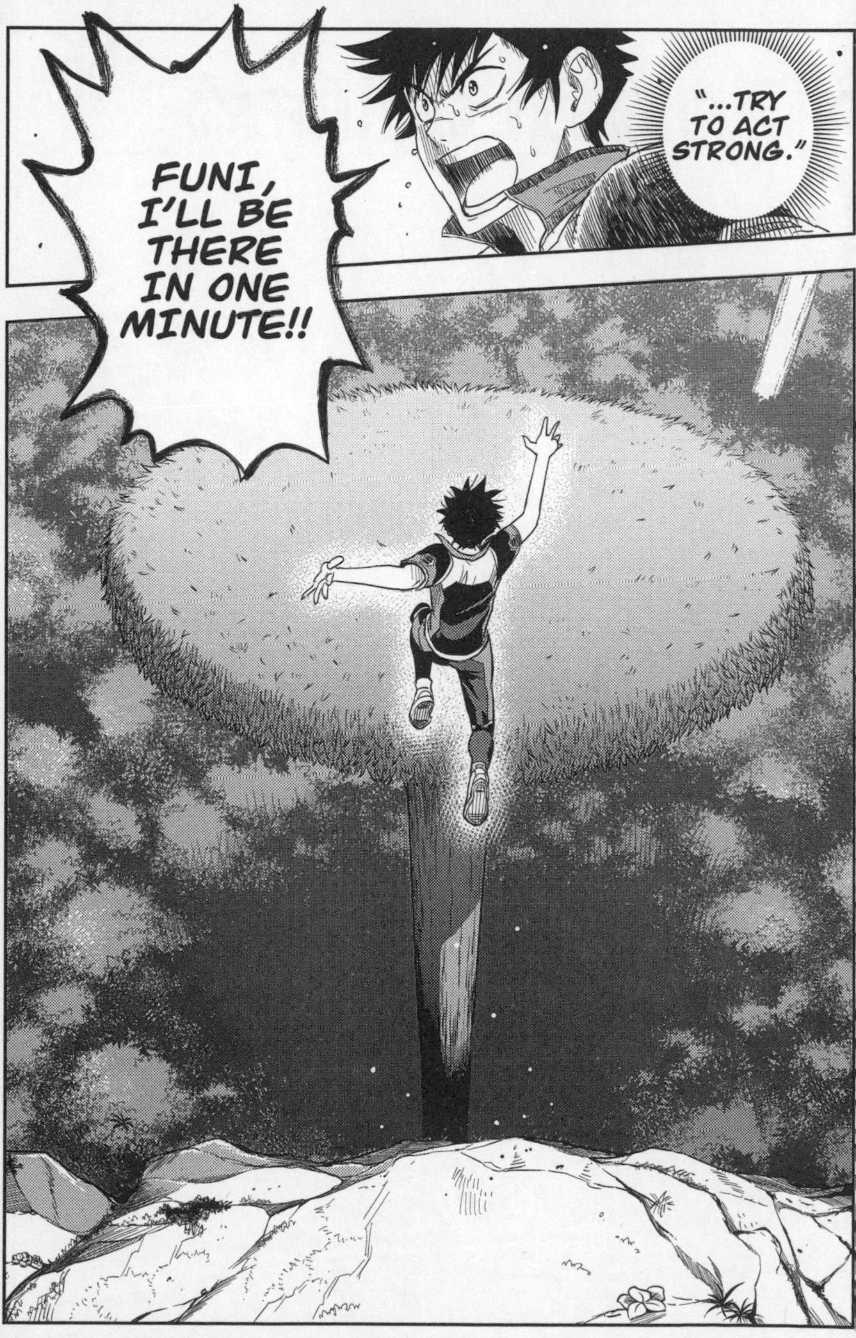
"...TRY TO ACT STRONG."
FUNI, I'LL BE THERE IN ONE MINUTE!!

Material Collection
Costume Design 05

AIRD HIGH SCHOOL GYM UNIFORM

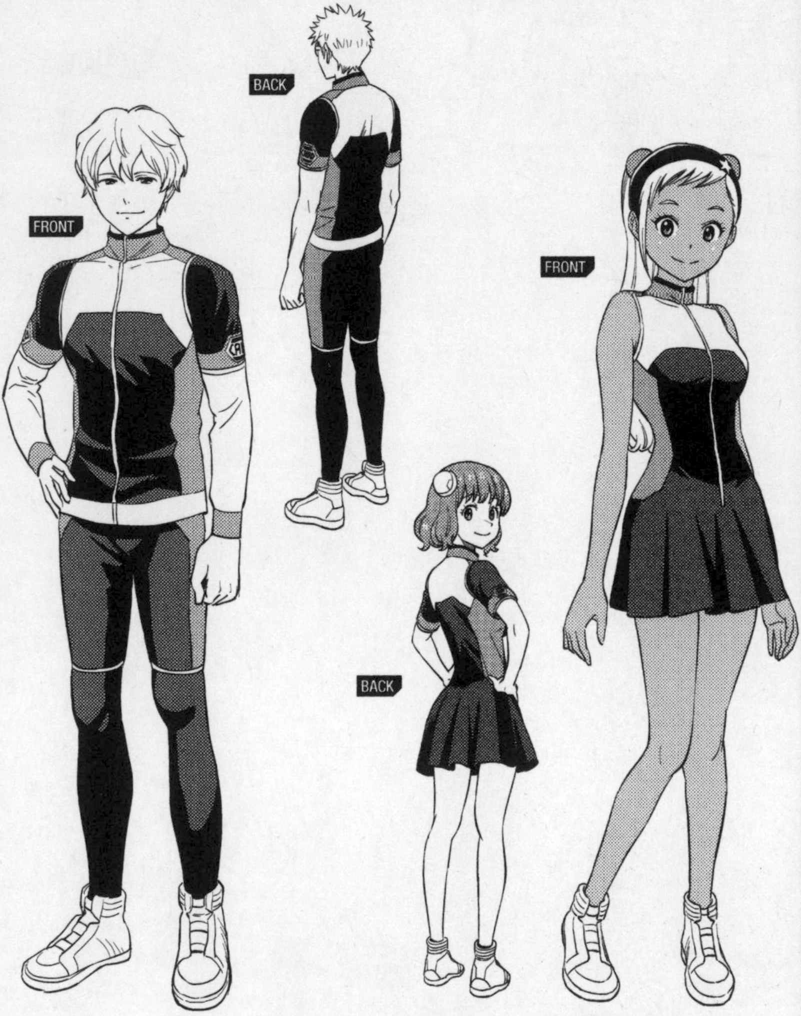
BACK
FRONT
FRONT
BACK

Both the boys' and girls' gym uniforms are made from a sturdy, lightweight and flexible fabric. Strategic placement of rippers allows for the uniform to change from long sleeve to short sleeve to no sleeve, as well as from long pants to shorts. The Caird High School emblem is placed on the upper arm of both sleeves.

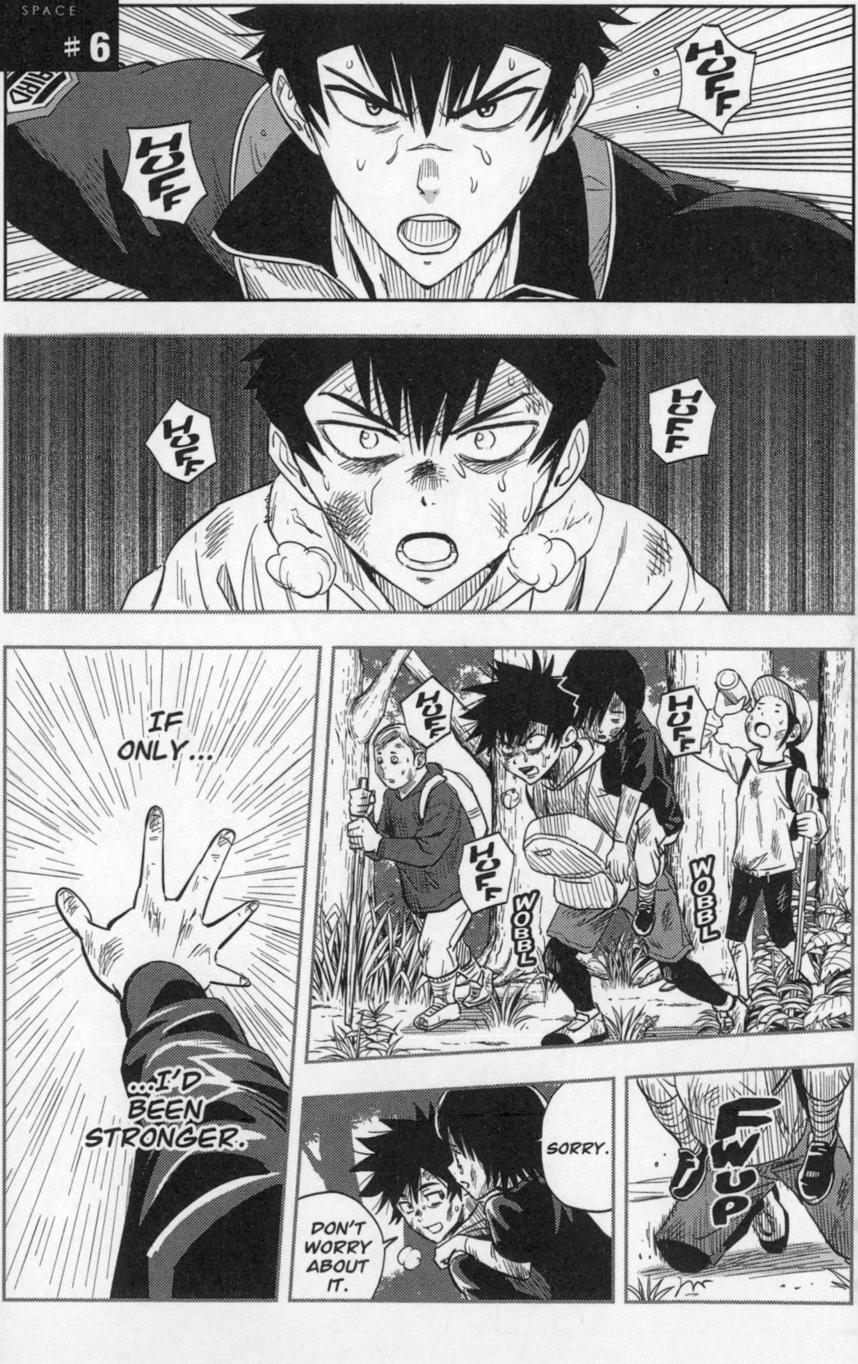
HUFF
HUFF
HUFF
HUFF
HUFF
HUFF
HUFF
WOBBL
WOBBL
FWUP
SORRY.
DON'T WORRY ABOUT IT.
IF ONLY...
...I'D BEEN STRONGER.

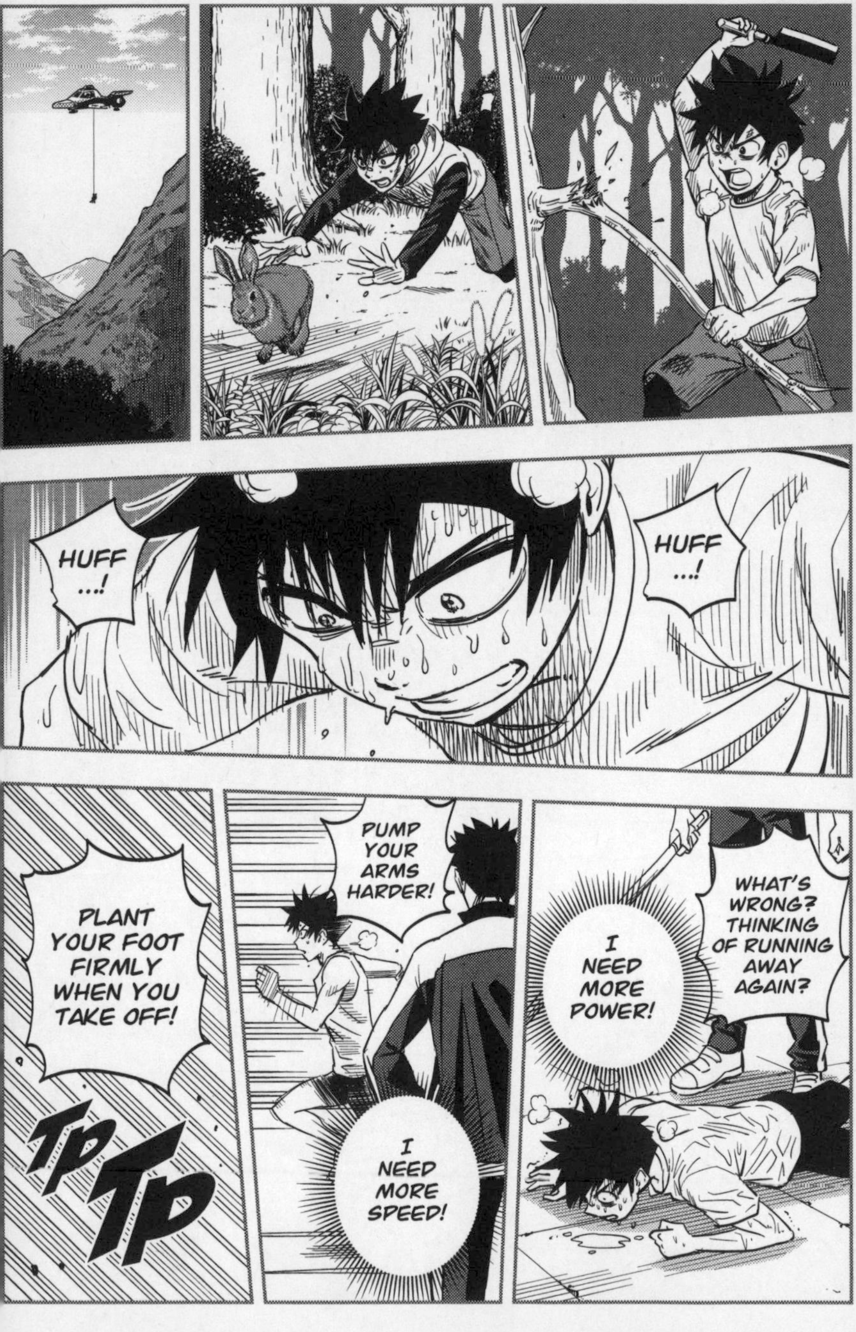
HUFF ...!
HUFF ...!
WHAT'S WRONG? THINKING OF RUNNING AWAY AGAIN?
I NEED MORE POWER!
PUMP YOUR ARMS HARDER!
I NEED MORE SPEED!
PLANT YOUR FOOT FIRMLY WHEN YOU TAKE OFF!
TP TP

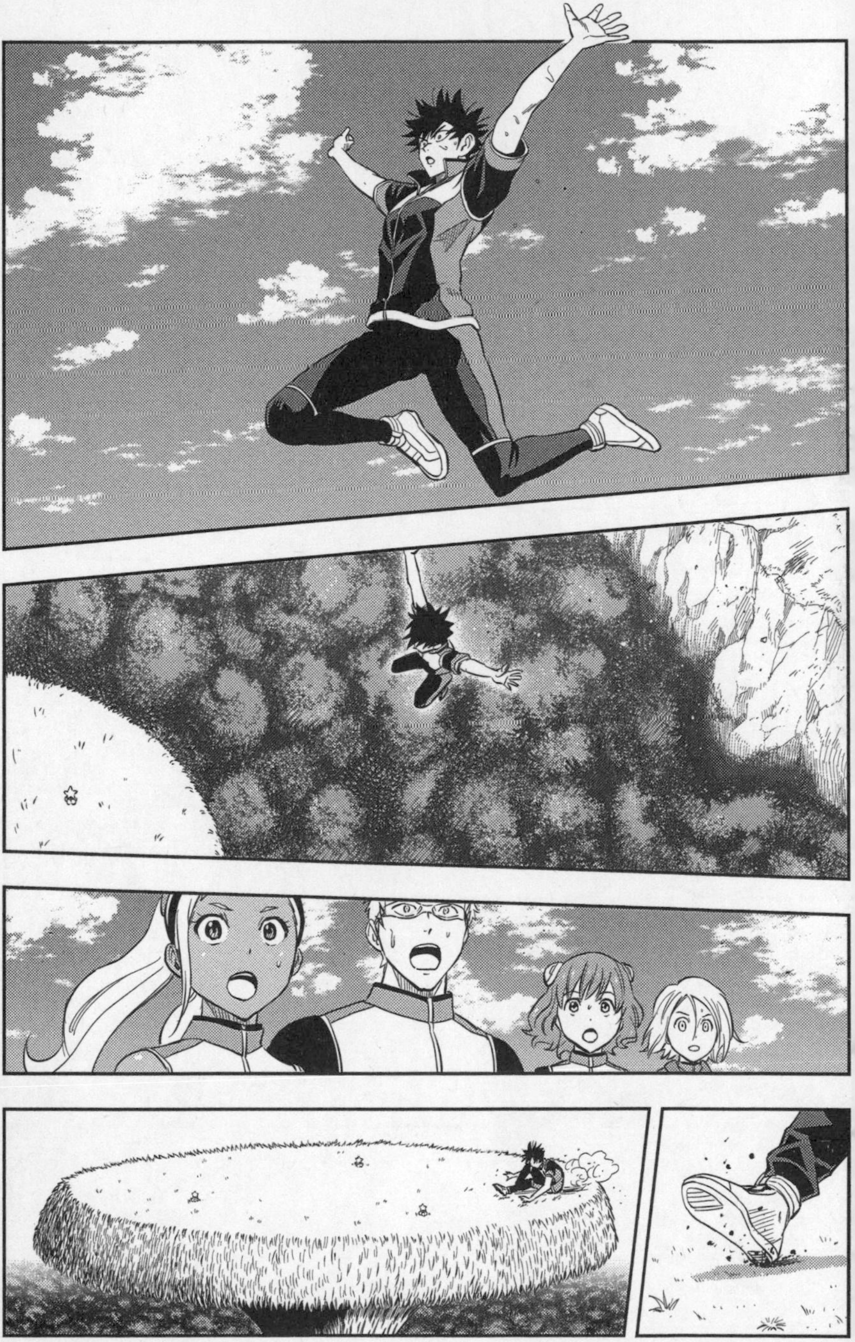

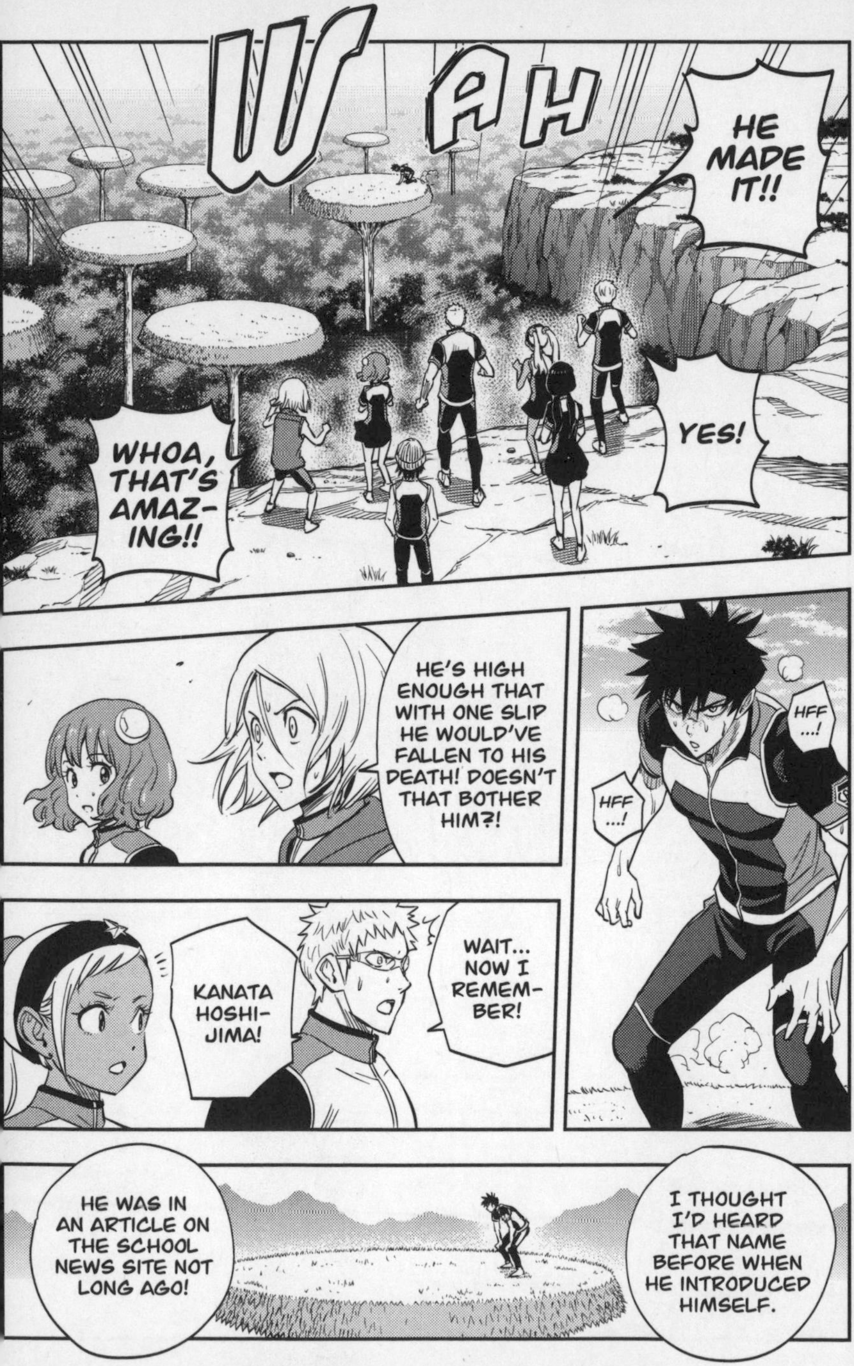
HE MADE IT!!
WAH
YES!
WHOA, THAT'S AMAZ-ING!!
HFF ...!
HFF ...!
HE'S HIGH ENOUGH THAT WITH ONE SLIP HE WOULD'VE FALLEN TO HIS DEATH! DOESN'T THAT BOTHER HIM?!
WAIT... NOW I REMEM-BER!
KANATA HOSHI-JIMA!
I THOUGHT I'D HEARD THAT NAME BEFORE WHEN HE INTRODUCED HIMSELF.
HE WAS IN AN ARTICLE ON THE SCHOOL NEWS SITE NOT LONG AGO!

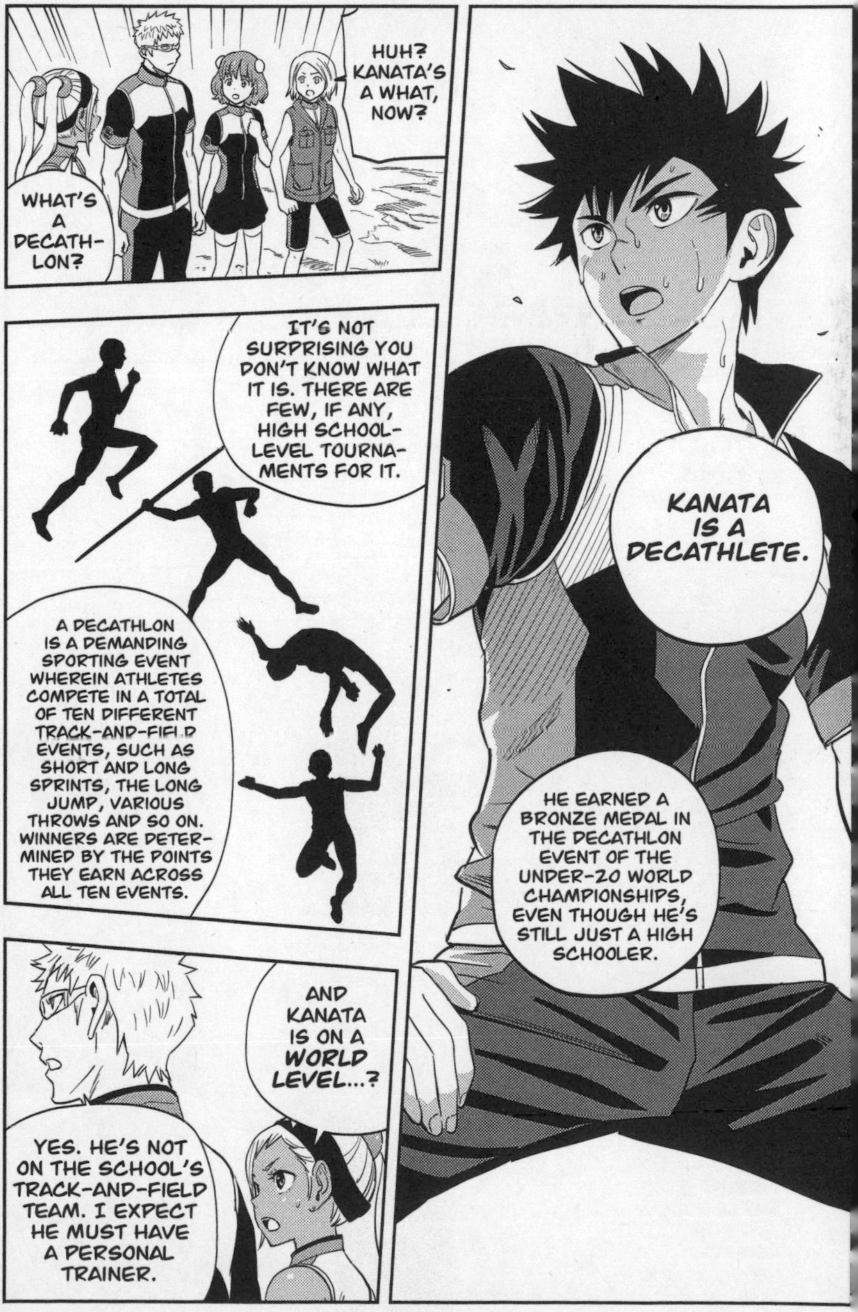
KANATA IS A DECATHLETE.
HE EARNED A BRONZE MEDAL IN THE DECATHLON EVENT OF THE UNDER-20 WORLD CHAMPIONSHIPS, EVEN THOUGH HE'S STILL JUST A HIGH SCHOOLER.
HUH? KANATA'S A WHAT, NOW?
WHAT'S A DECATHLON?
IT'S NOT SURPRISING YOU DON'T KNOW WHAT IT IS. THERE ARE FEW, IF ANY, HIGH SCHOOL-LEVEL TOURNAMENTS FOR IT.
A DECATHLON IS A DEMANDING SPORTING EVENT WHEREIN ATHLETES COMPETE IN A TOTAL OF TEN DIFFERENT TRACK-AND-FIELD EVENTS, SUCH AS SHORT AND LONG SPRINTS, THE LONG JUMP, VARIOUS THROWS AND SO ON. WINNERS ARE DETERMINED BY THE POINTS THEY EARN ACROSS ALL TEN EVENTS.
AND KANATA IS ON A WORLD LEVEL...?
YES. HE'S NOT ON THE SCHOOL'S TRACK-AND-FIELD TEAM. I EXPECT HE MUST HAVE A PERSONAL TRAINER.

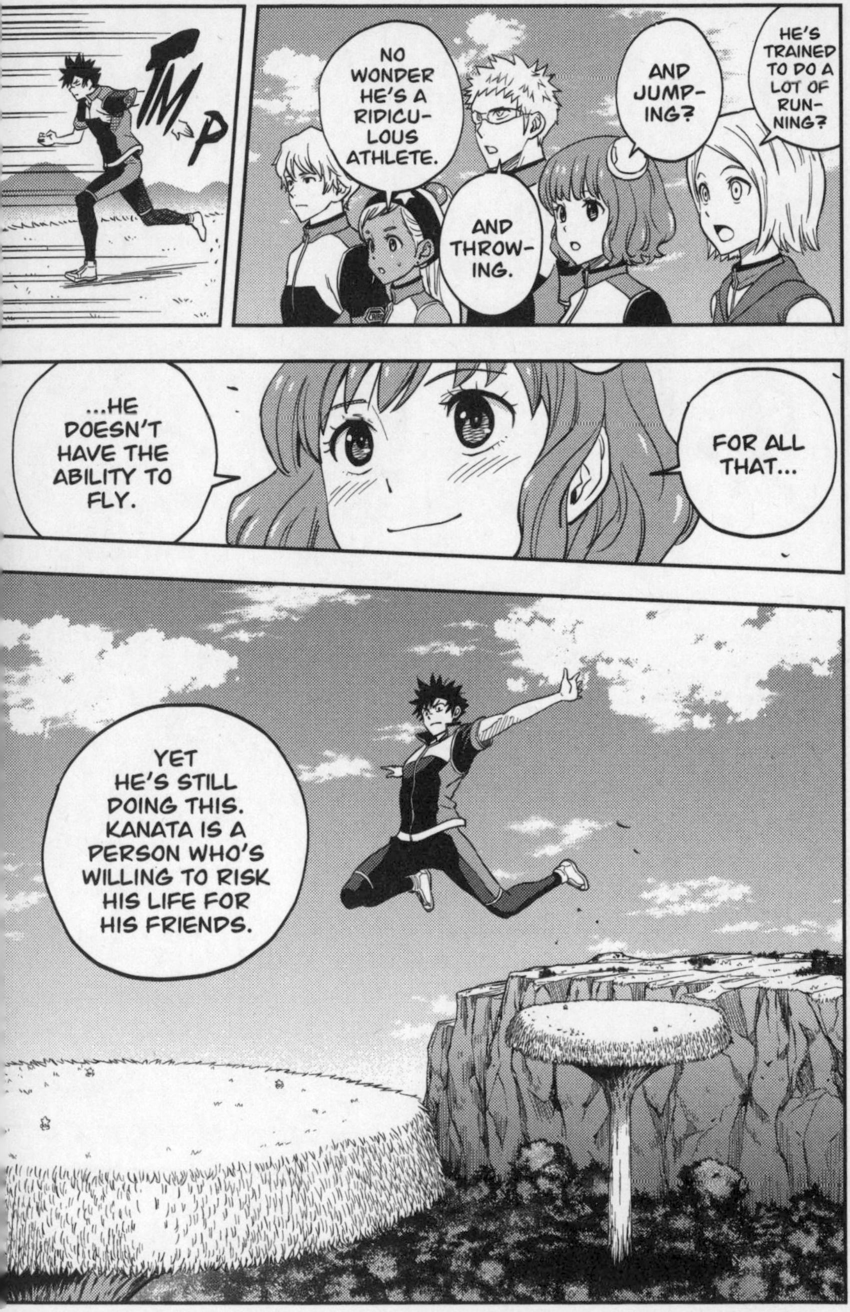
HE'S TRAINED TO DO A LOT OF RUN-NING?
AND JUMP-ING?
AND THROW-ING.
NO WONDER HE'S A RIDICU-LOUS ATHLETE.
TMP
FOR ALL THAT...
...HE DOESN'T HAVE THE ABILITY TO FLY.
YET HE'S STILL DOING THIS. KANATA IS A PERSON WHO'S WILLING TO RISK HIS LIFE FOR HIS FRIENDS.

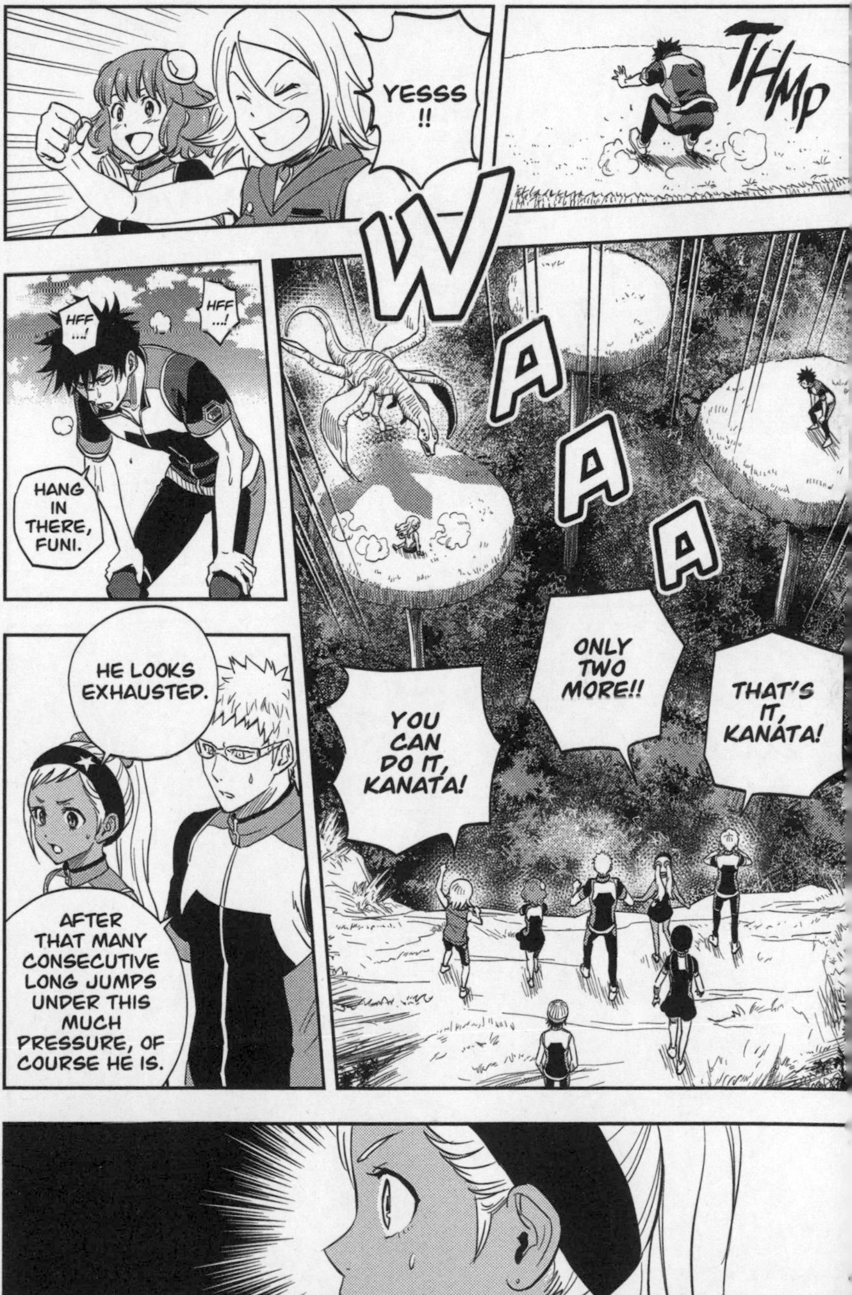
THMP
YESSS!!
WAAAA
THAT'S IT, KANATA!
ONLY TWO MORE!!
YOU CAN DO IT, KANATA!
HFF ...!
HFF ...!
HANG IN THERE, FUNI.
HE LOOKS EXHAUSTED.
AFTER THAT MANY CONSECUTIVE LONG JUMPS UNDER THIS MUCH PRESSURE, OF COURSE HE IS.

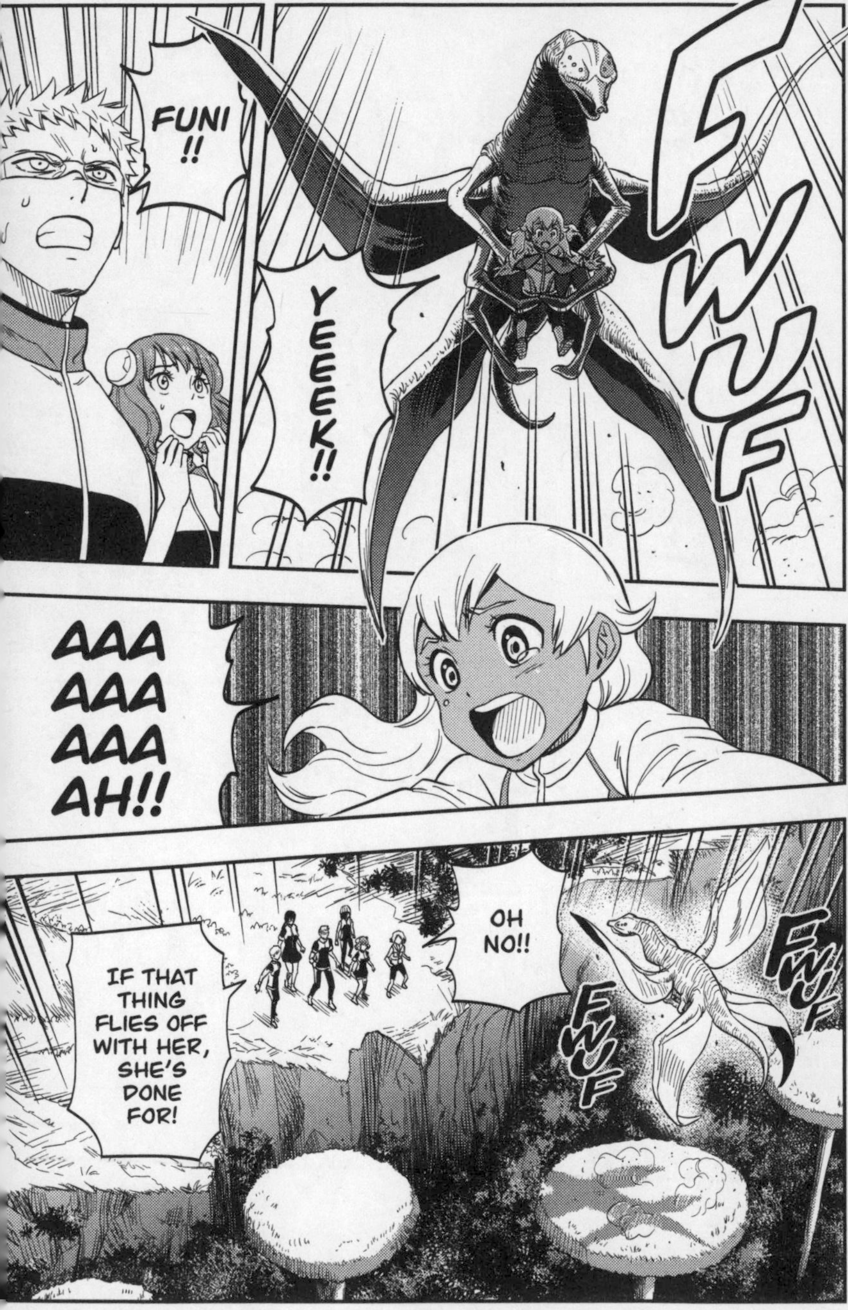
FWUF
YEEEK!!
FUNI!!
AAAAAAAAAAH!!
OH NO!!
FWUF
IF THAT THING FLIES OFF WITH HER, SHE'S DONE FOR!
FWUF

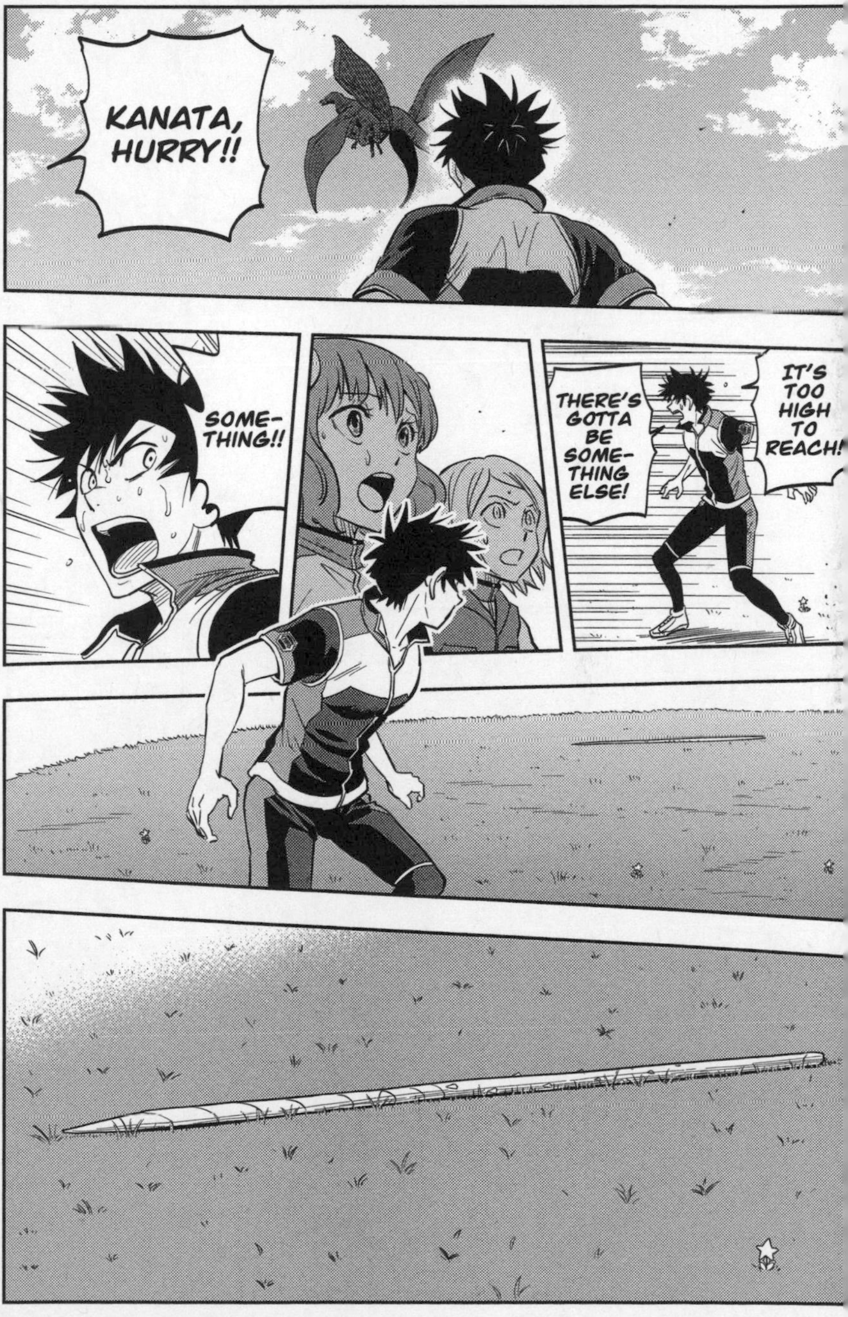
KANATA, HURRY!!
IT'S TOO HIGH TO REACH!
THERE'S GOTTA BE SOME-THING ELSE!
SOME-THING!!

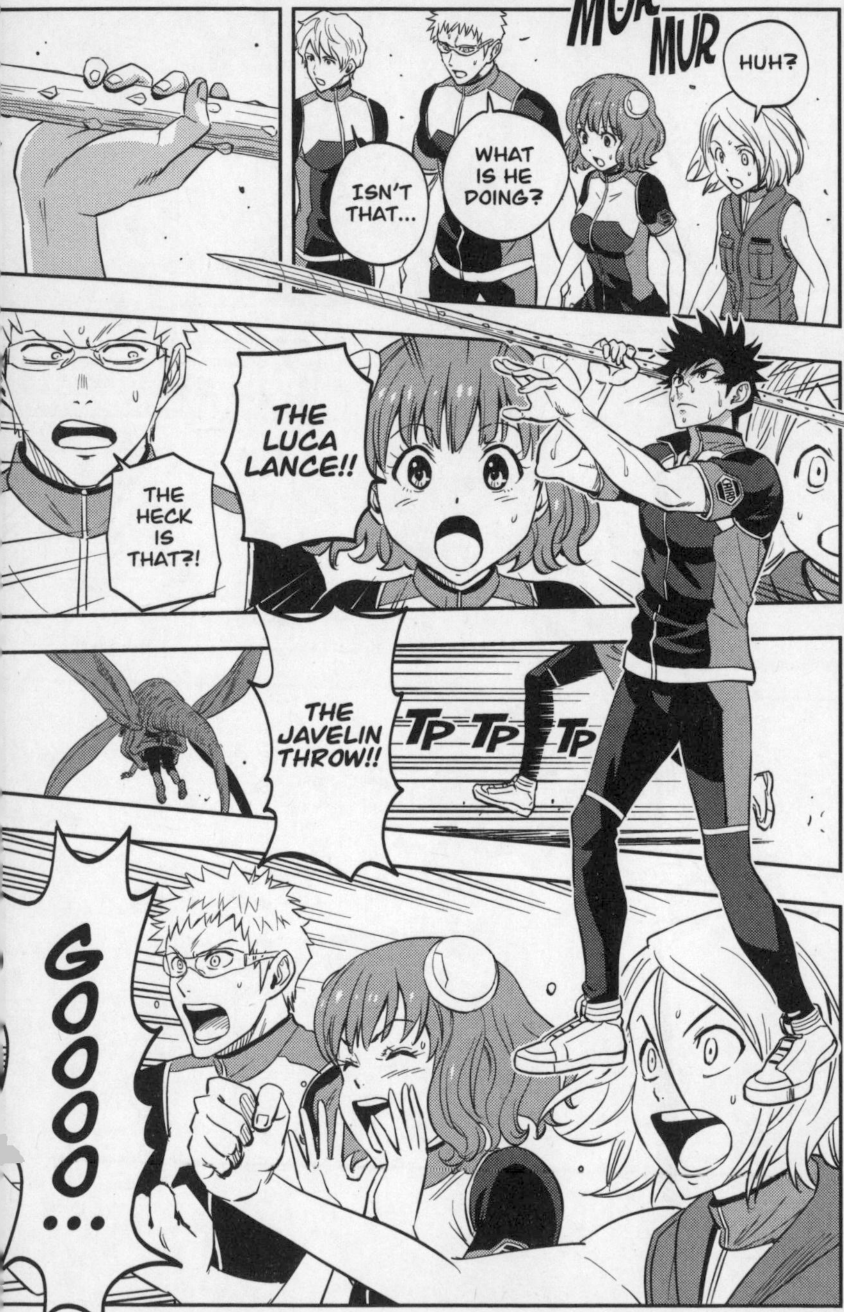
MUR MUR
HUH?
WHAT IS HE DOING?
ISN'T THAT...
THE LUCA LANCE!!
THE HECK IS THAT?!
TP TP TP
THE JAVELIN THROW!!
GOOOO...

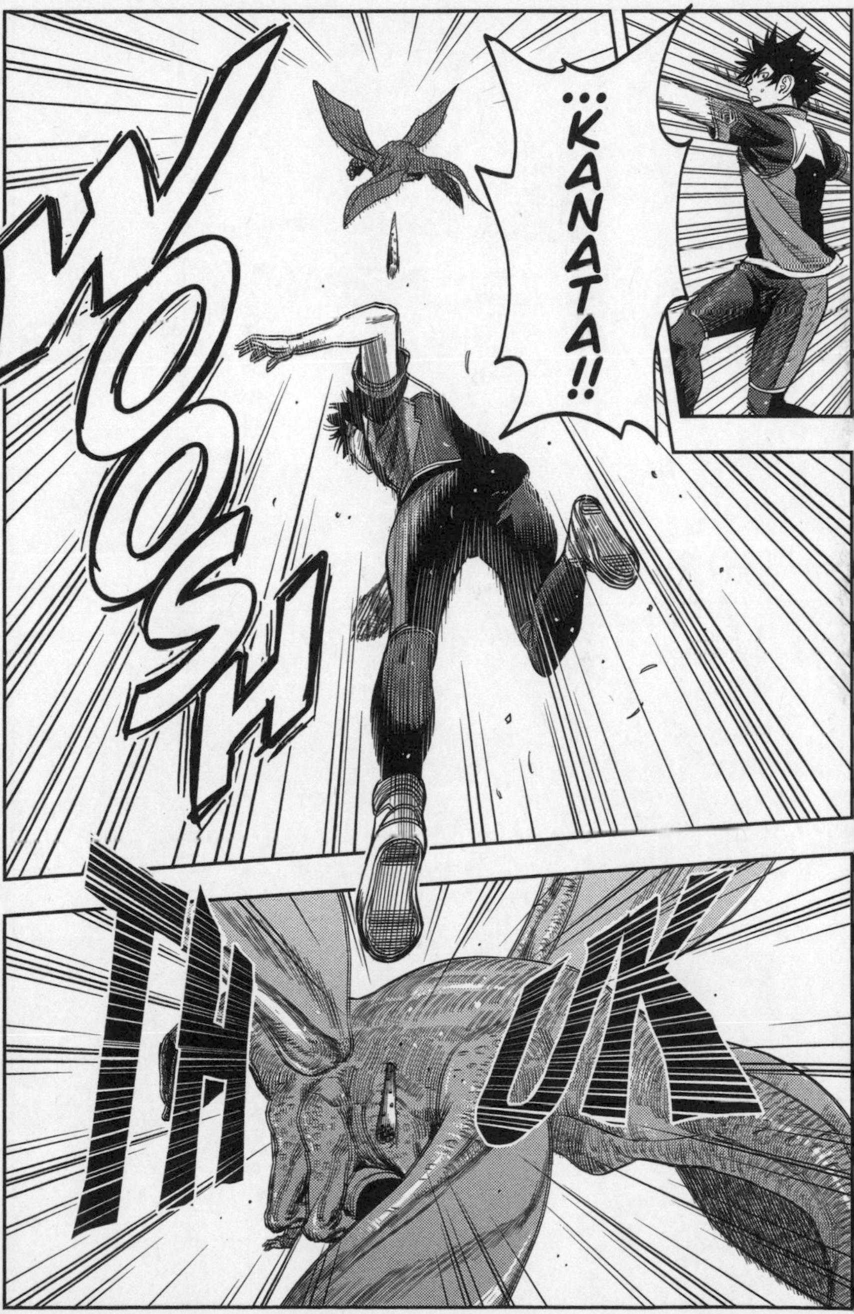
...KANATA!!
WHOOSH
THUK

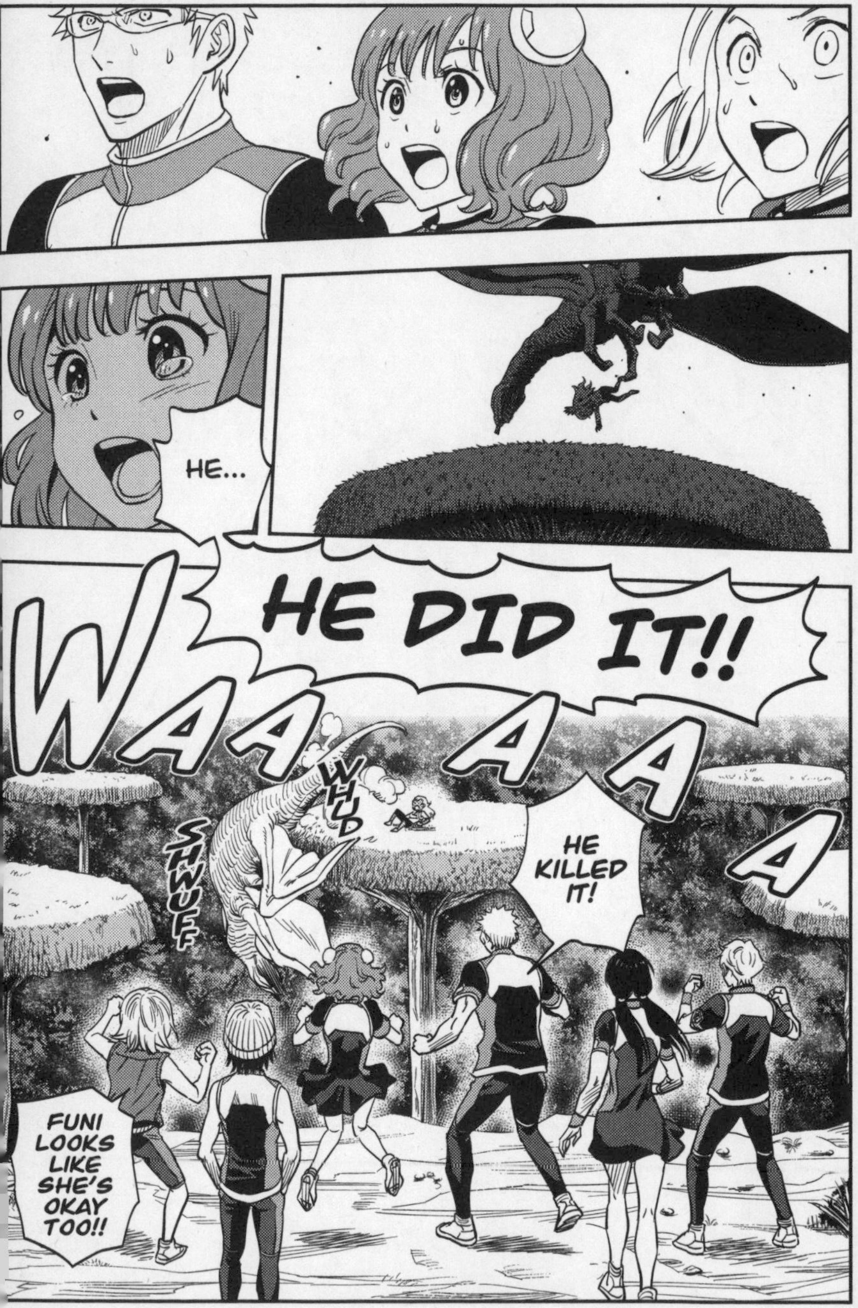
HE...
HE DID IT!!
WAAAAAA
WHUD
SHWUFF
HE KILLED IT!
FUNI LOOKS LIKE SHE'S OKAY TOO!!

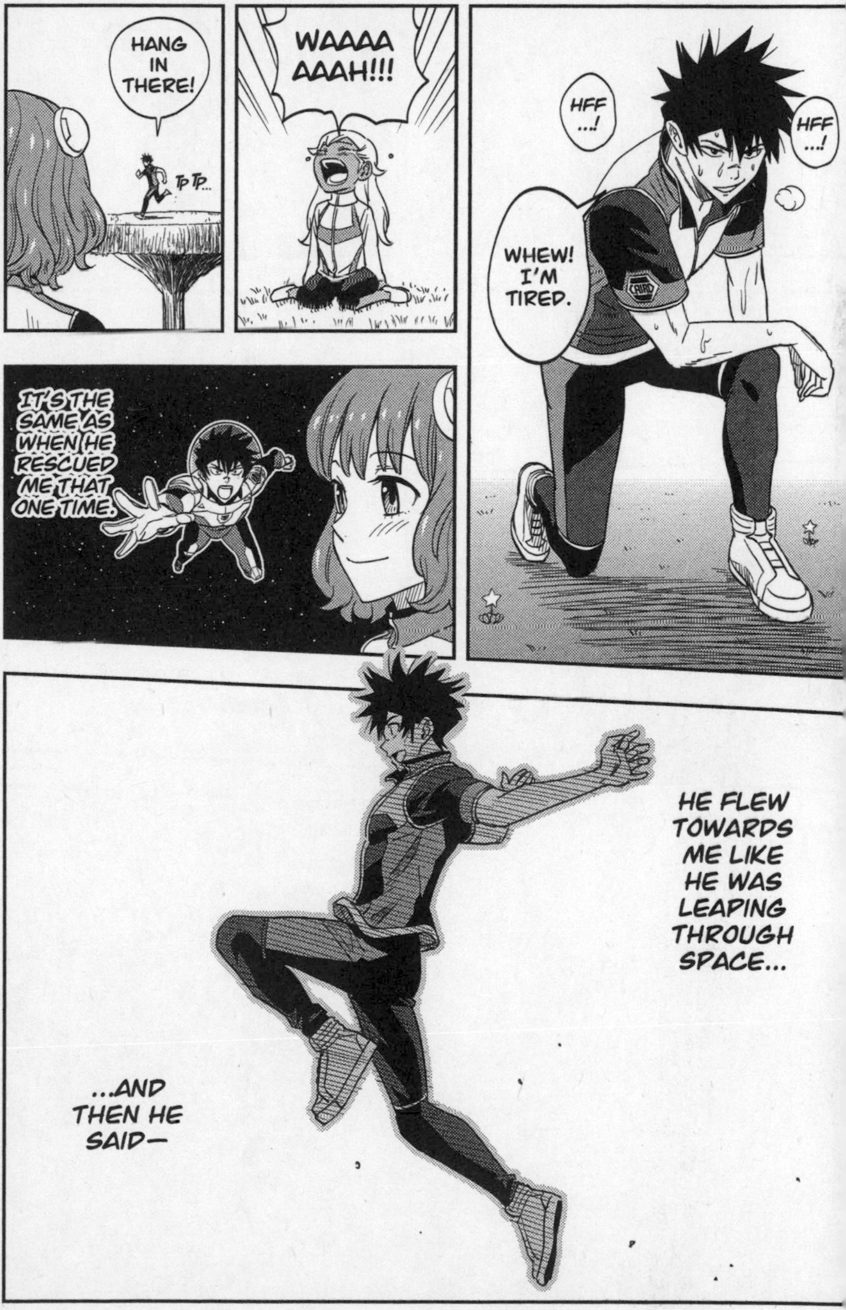

HFF ...!
HFF ...!
WHEW! I'M TIRED.
WAAAA AAAH!!!
HANG IN THERE!
TP TP...
IT'S THE SAME AS WHEN HE RESCUED ME THAT ONE TIME.
HE FLEW TOWARDS ME LIKE HE WAS LEAPING THROUGH SPACE...
...AND THEN HE SAID—

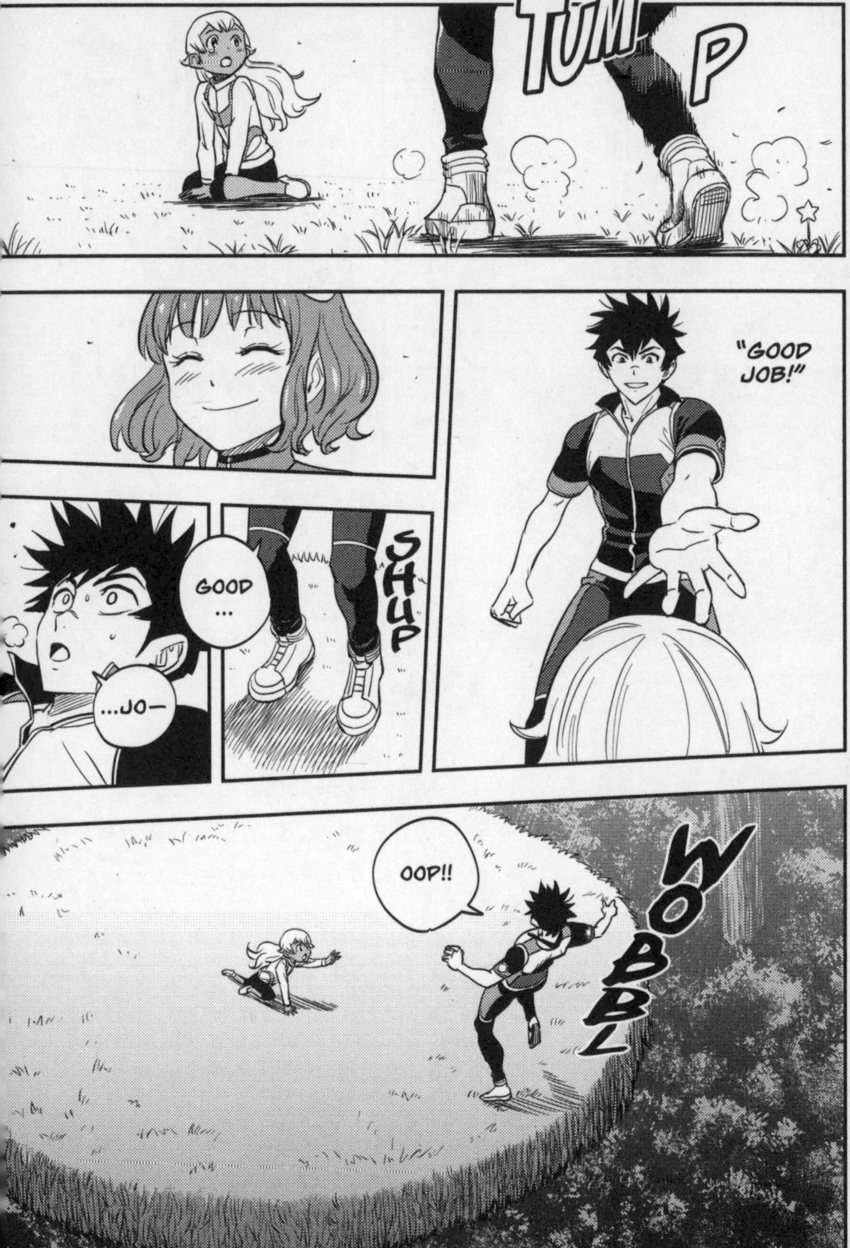
TUMP
"GOOD JOB!"
SHUP
GOOD ...
...JO—
WOBBL
OOP!!

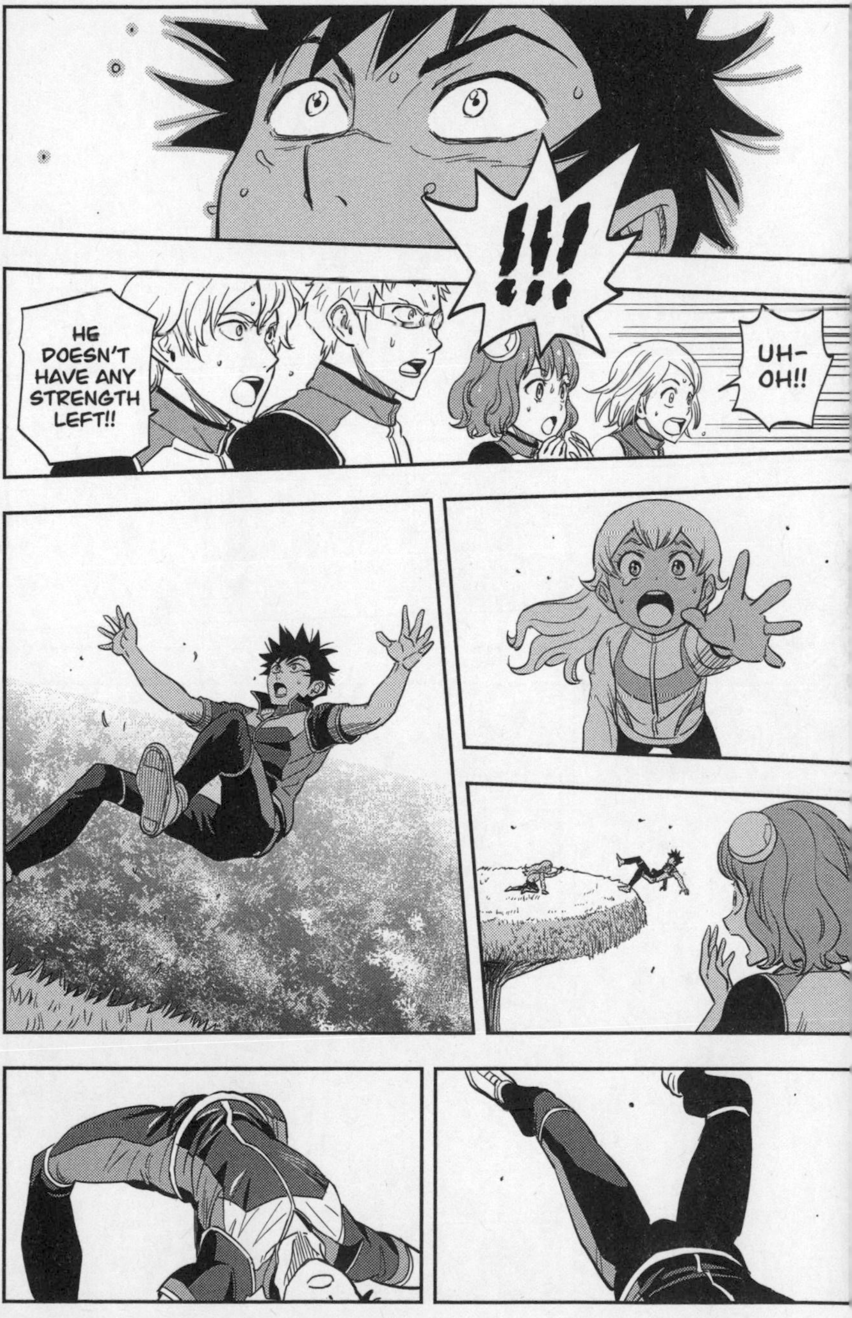
!!!
UH-OH!!
HE DOESN'T HAVE ANY STRENGTH LEFT!!

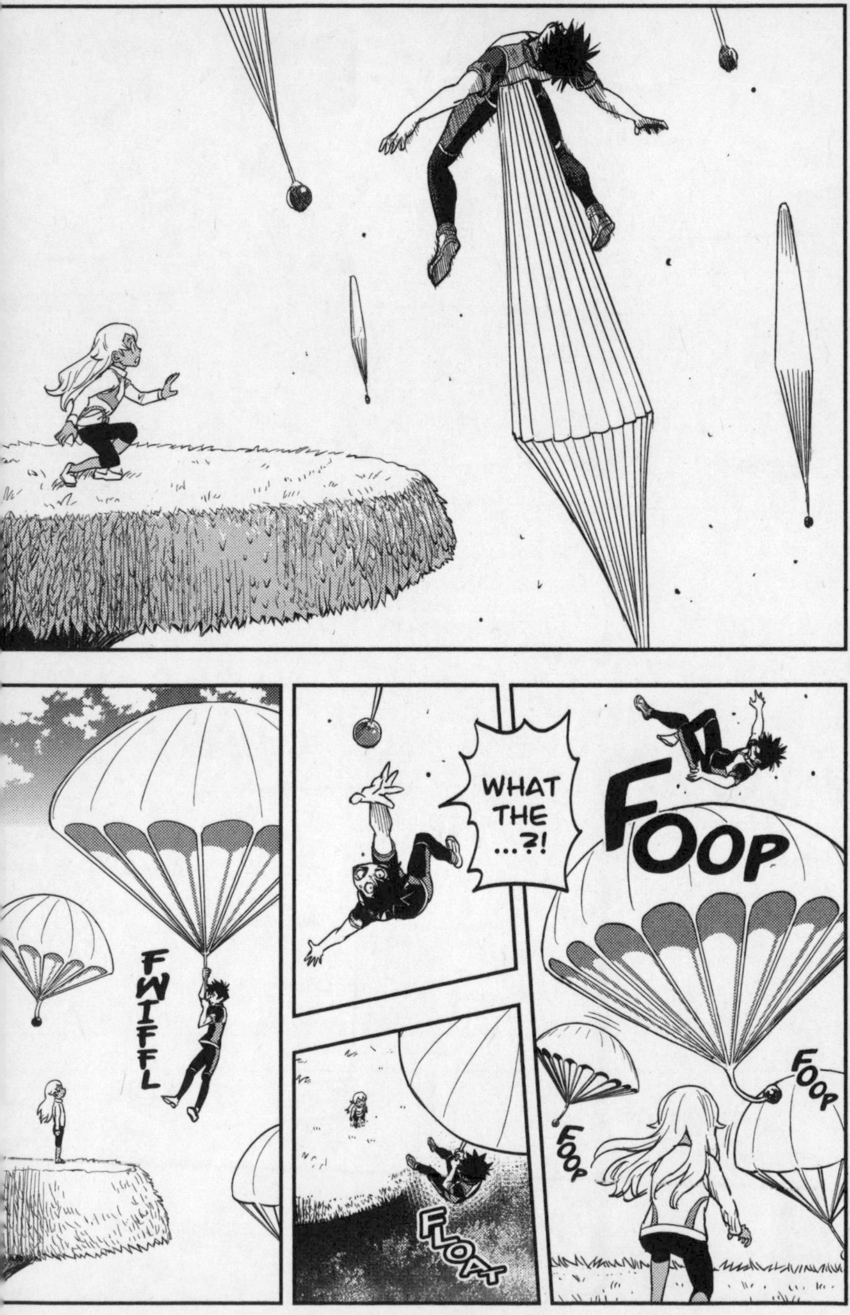
FOOP
FOOP
FOOP
WHAT THE ...?!
FLOAT
FWIFFL

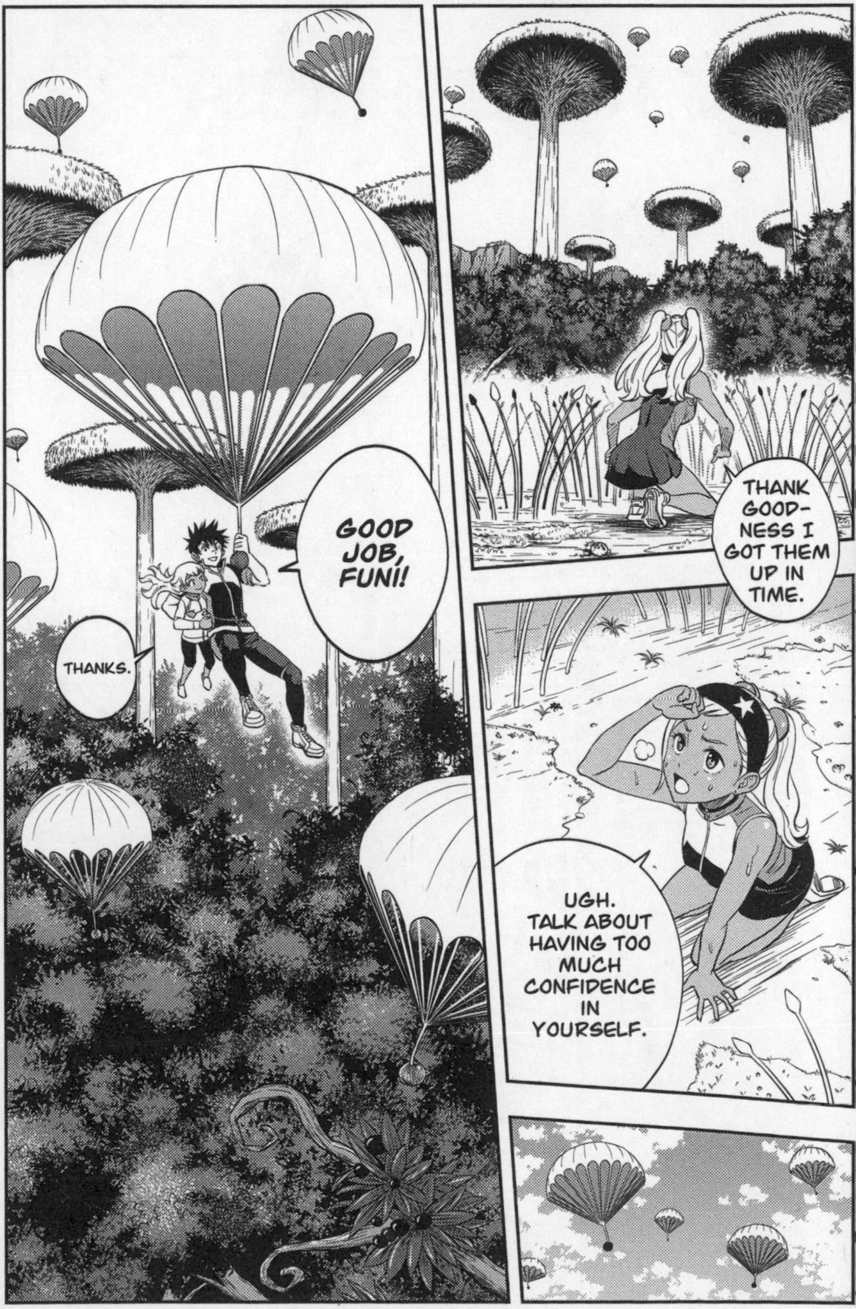
THANK GOODNESS I GOT THEM UP IN TIME.
UGH. TALK ABOUT HAVING TOO MUCH CONFIDENCE IN YOURSELF.
GOOD JOB, FUNI!
THANKS.

Material Collection
Character Profile **06**

KANATA HOSHIJIMA

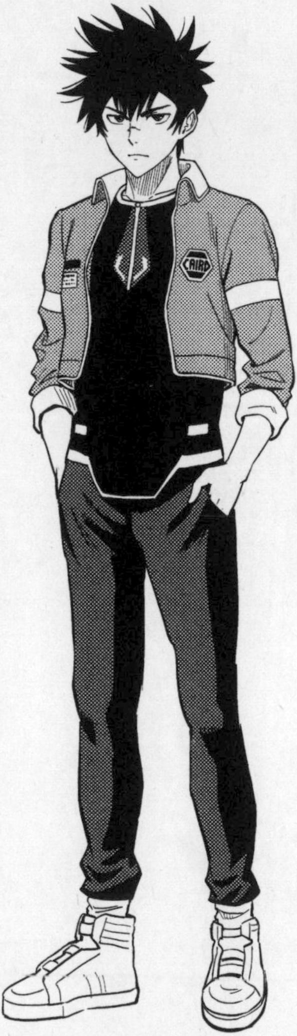

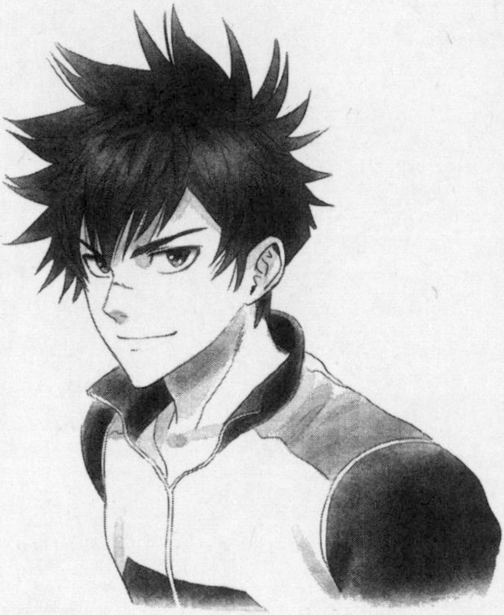

DATA

Name: **Kanata Hoshijima**

Age: **17**

Birthday: **May 5**

Height: **5'11"**

Weight: **157 lbs.**

Blood Type: **AB**

Eye Color: **Brown**

Hometown: **Mousanish District**

Naturally athletic, Kanata is a highly trained decathlete. He competed in the decathlon event in the latest Under-20 World Championships, taking home the overall bronze medal. Influenced by the dreams of his late mentor, he wants to be a space explorer someday.

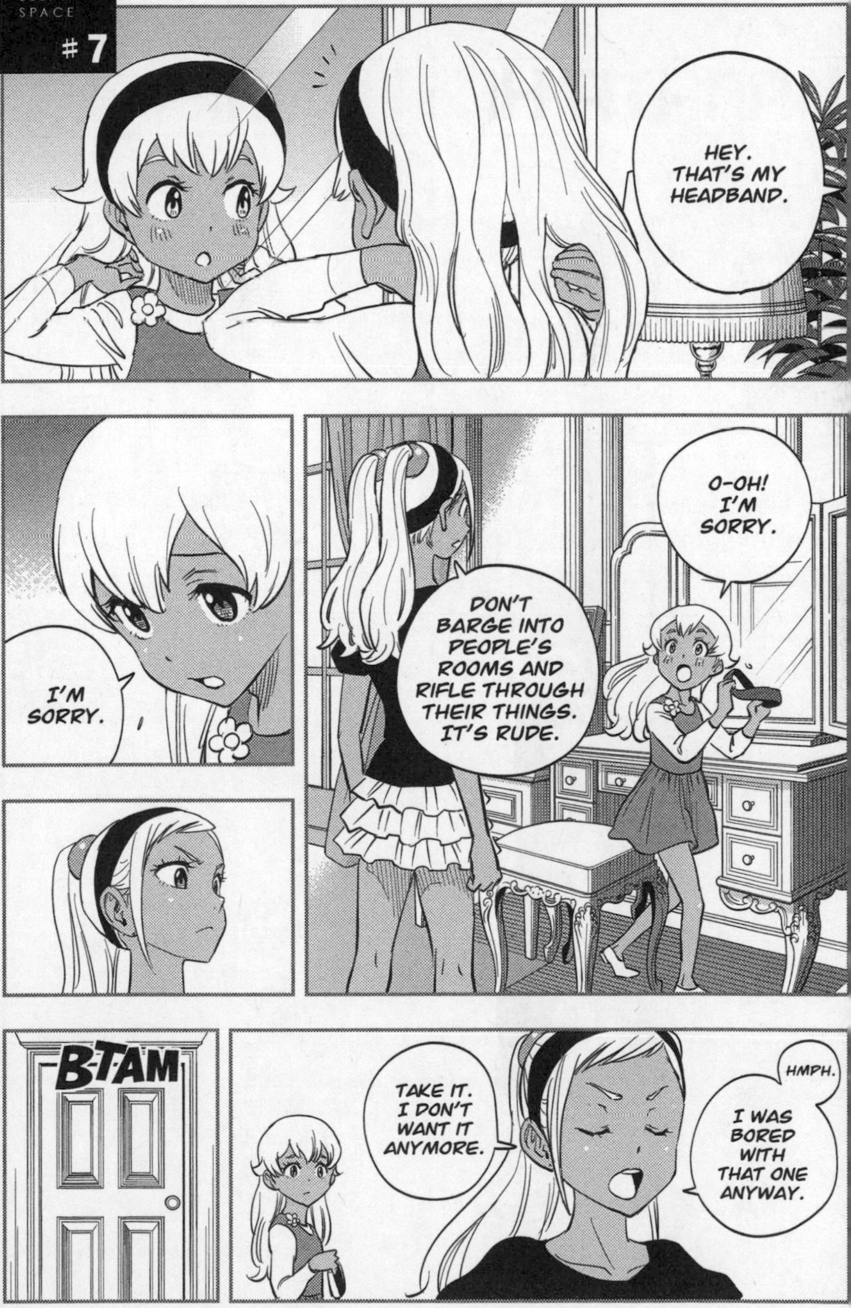
HEY. THAT'S MY HEADBAND.
O-OH! I'M SORRY.
DON'T BARGE INTO PEOPLE'S ROOMS AND RIFLE THROUGH THEIR THINGS. IT'S RUDE.
I'M SORRY.
HMPH.
I WAS BORED WITH THAT ONE ANYWAY.
TAKE IT. I DON'T WANT IT ANYMORE.
BTAM

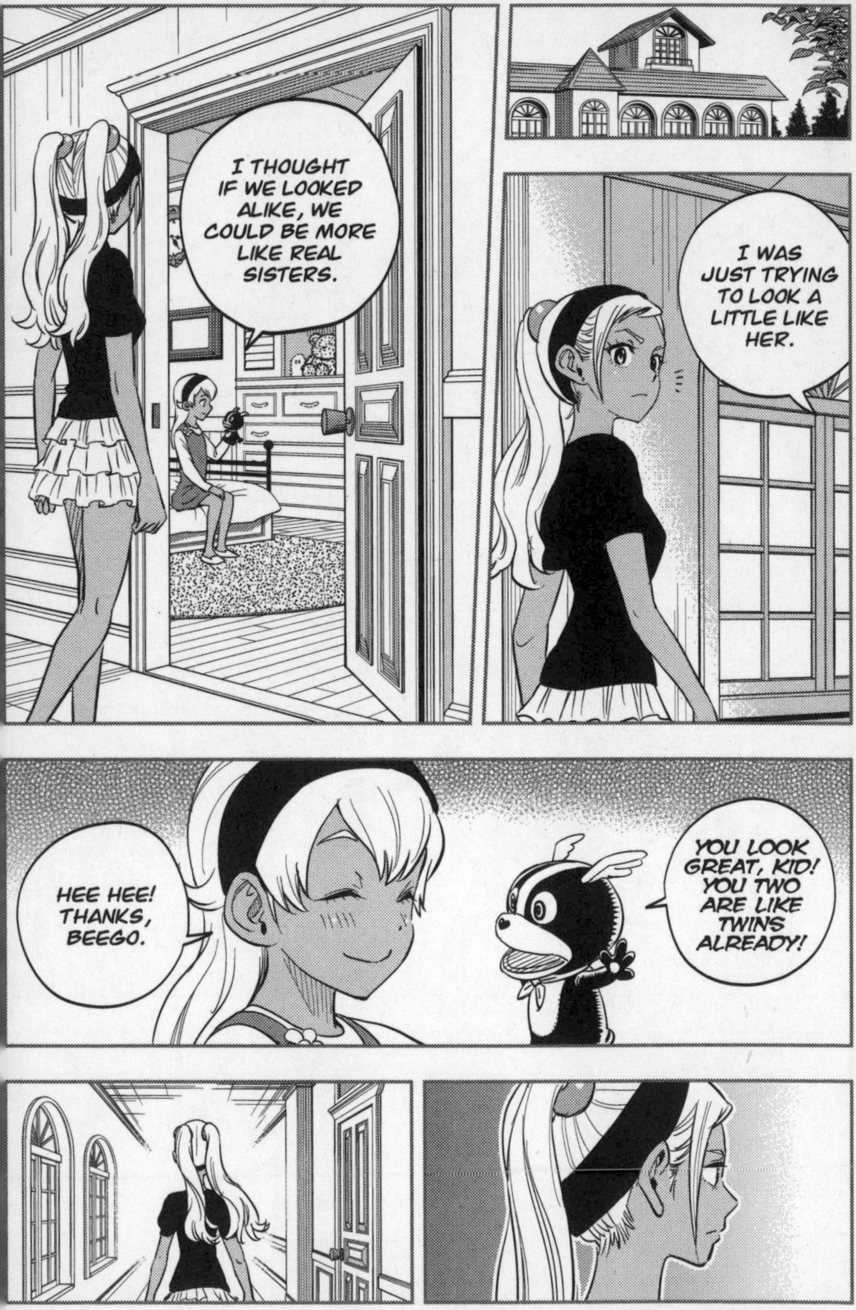
I WAS JUST TRYING TO LOOK A LITTLE LIKE HER.
I THOUGHT IF WE LOOKED ALIKE, WE COULD BE MORE LIKE REAL SISTERS.
YOU LOOK GREAT, KID! YOU TWO ARE LIKE TWINS ALREADY!
HEE HEE! THANKS, BEEGO.

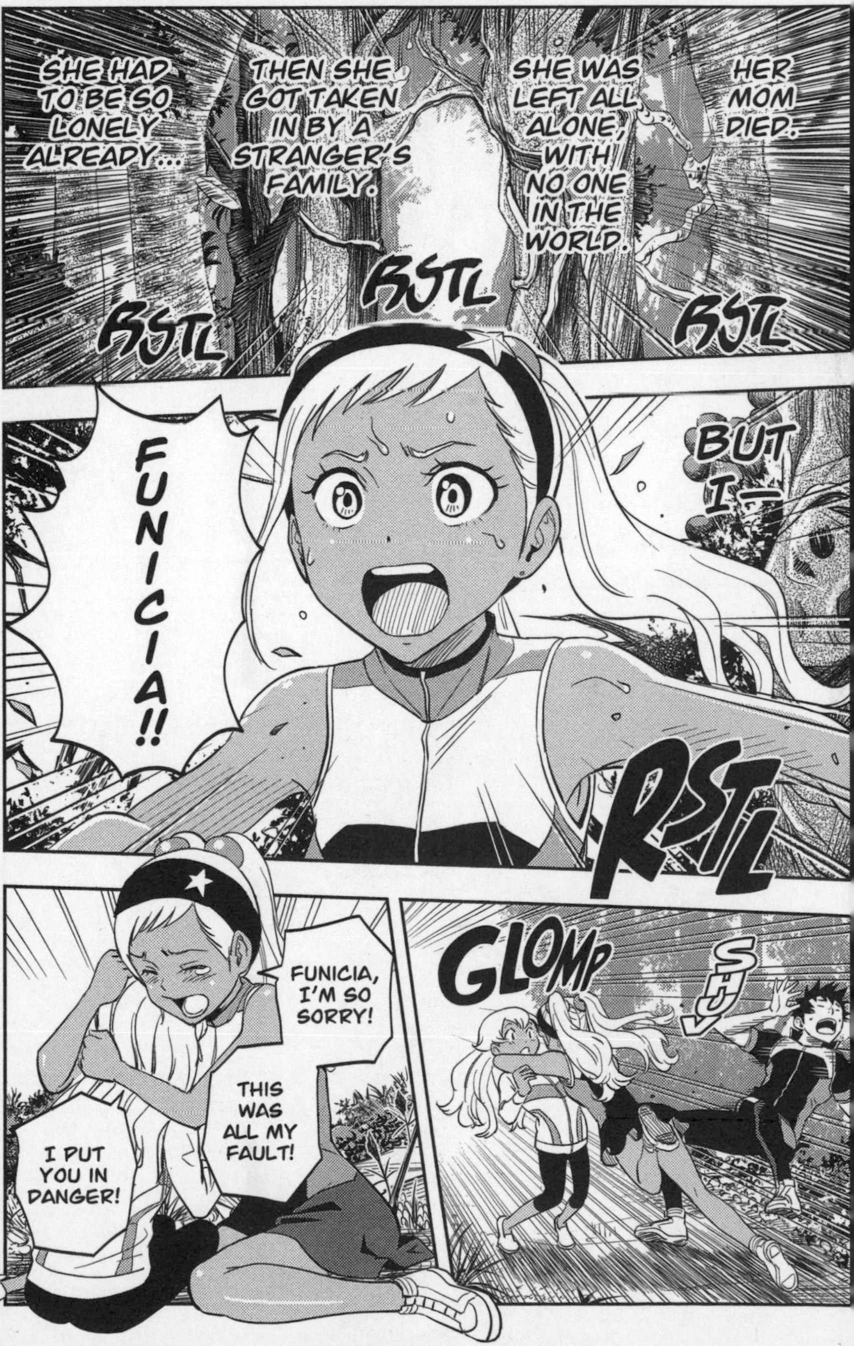
HER MOM DIED.
SHE WAS LEFT ALL ALONE, WITH NO ONE IN THE WORLD.
THEN SHE GOT TAKEN IN BY A STRANGER'S FAMILY.
SHE HAD TO BE SO LONELY ALREADY...
RSTL
RSTL
RSTL
BUT I—
FUNICIA!!
RSTL
GLOMP
SHUV
FUNICIA, I'M SO SORRY!
THIS WAS ALL MY FAULT!
I PUT YOU IN DANGER!

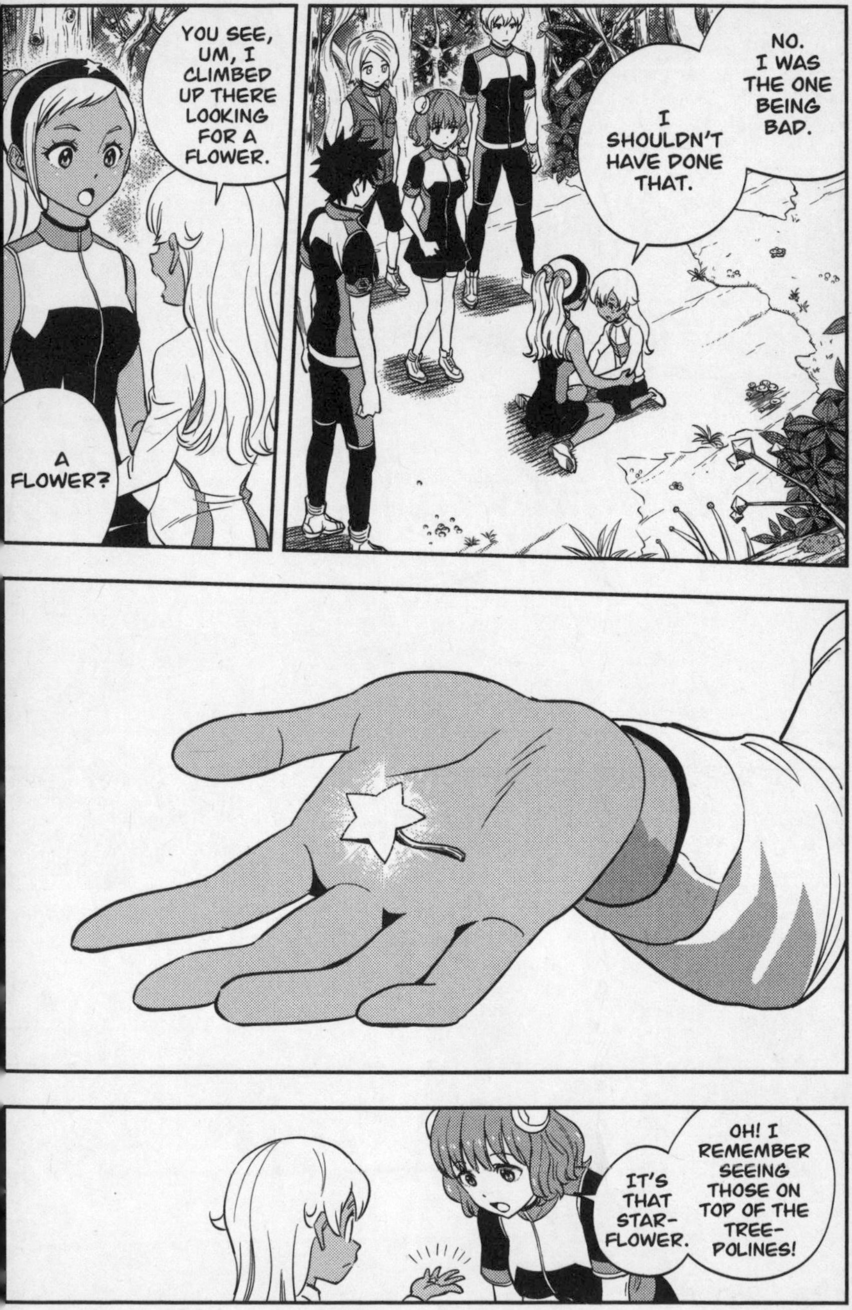
NO. I WAS THE ONE BEING BAD.
I SHOULDN'T HAVE DONE THAT.
YOU SEE, UM, I CLIMBED UP THERE LOOKING FOR A FLOWER.
A FLOWER?
OH! I REMEMBER SEEING THOSE ON TOP OF THE TREE-POLINES!
IT'S THAT STAR-FLOWER.

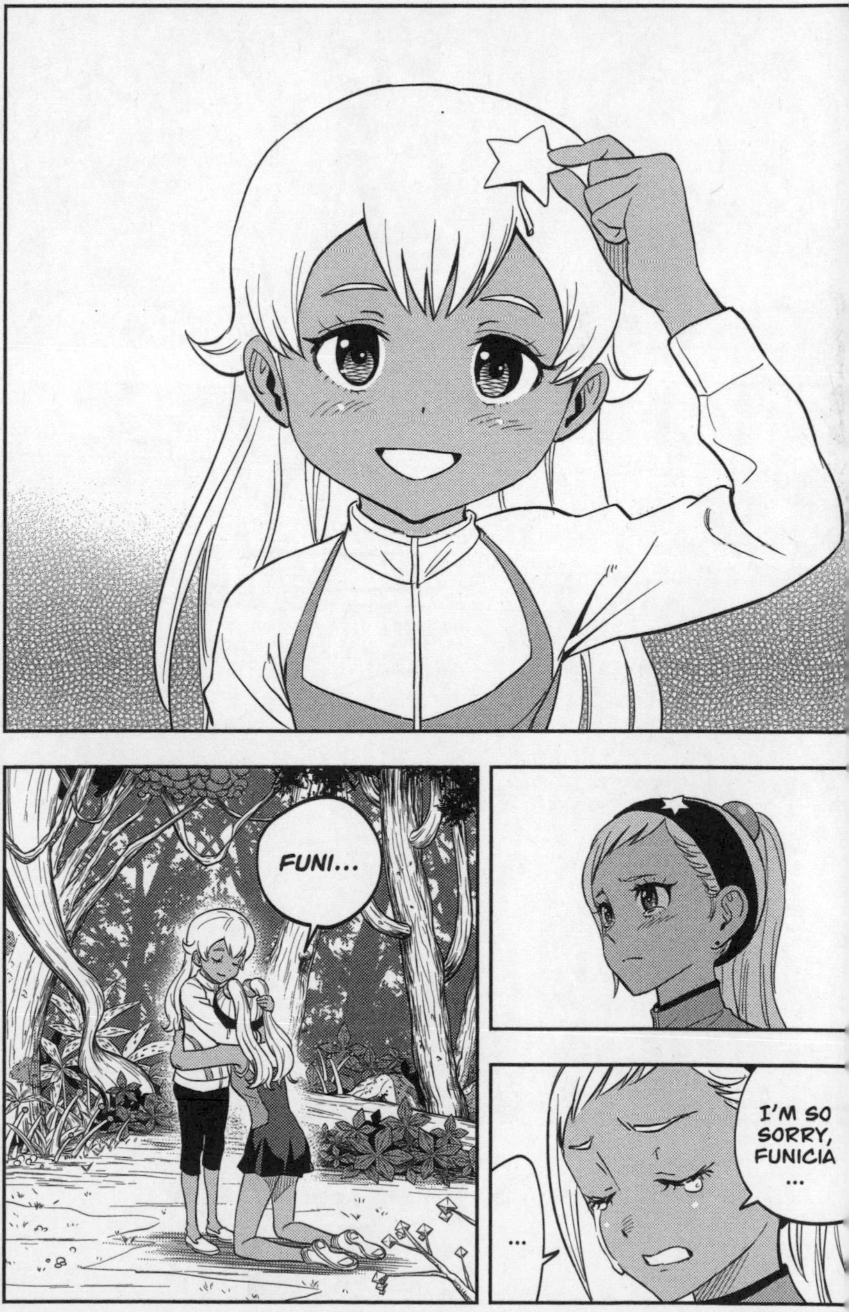
I'M SO SORRY, FUNICIA ...
...
FUNI...

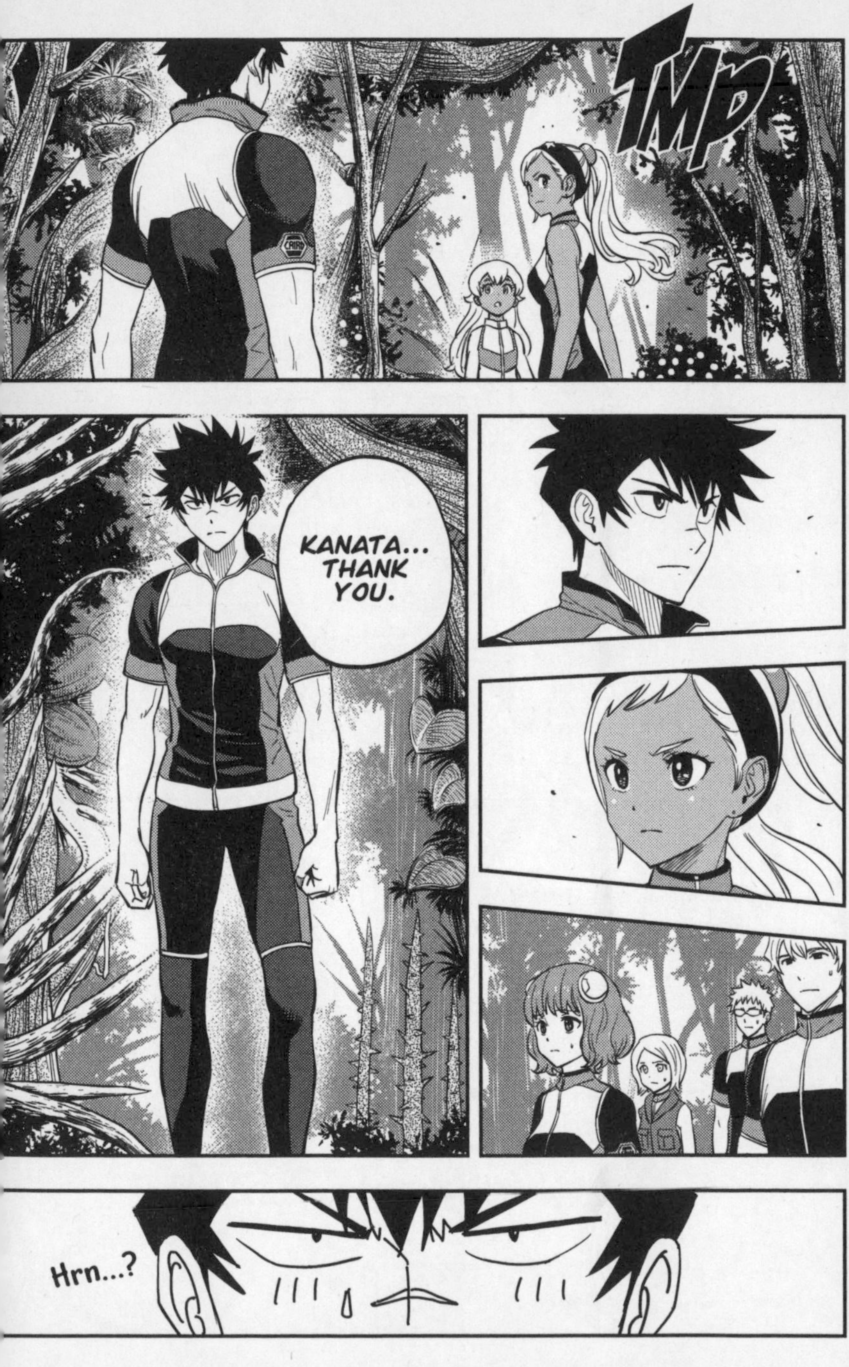
TMP
KANATA... THANK YOU.
Hrn...?

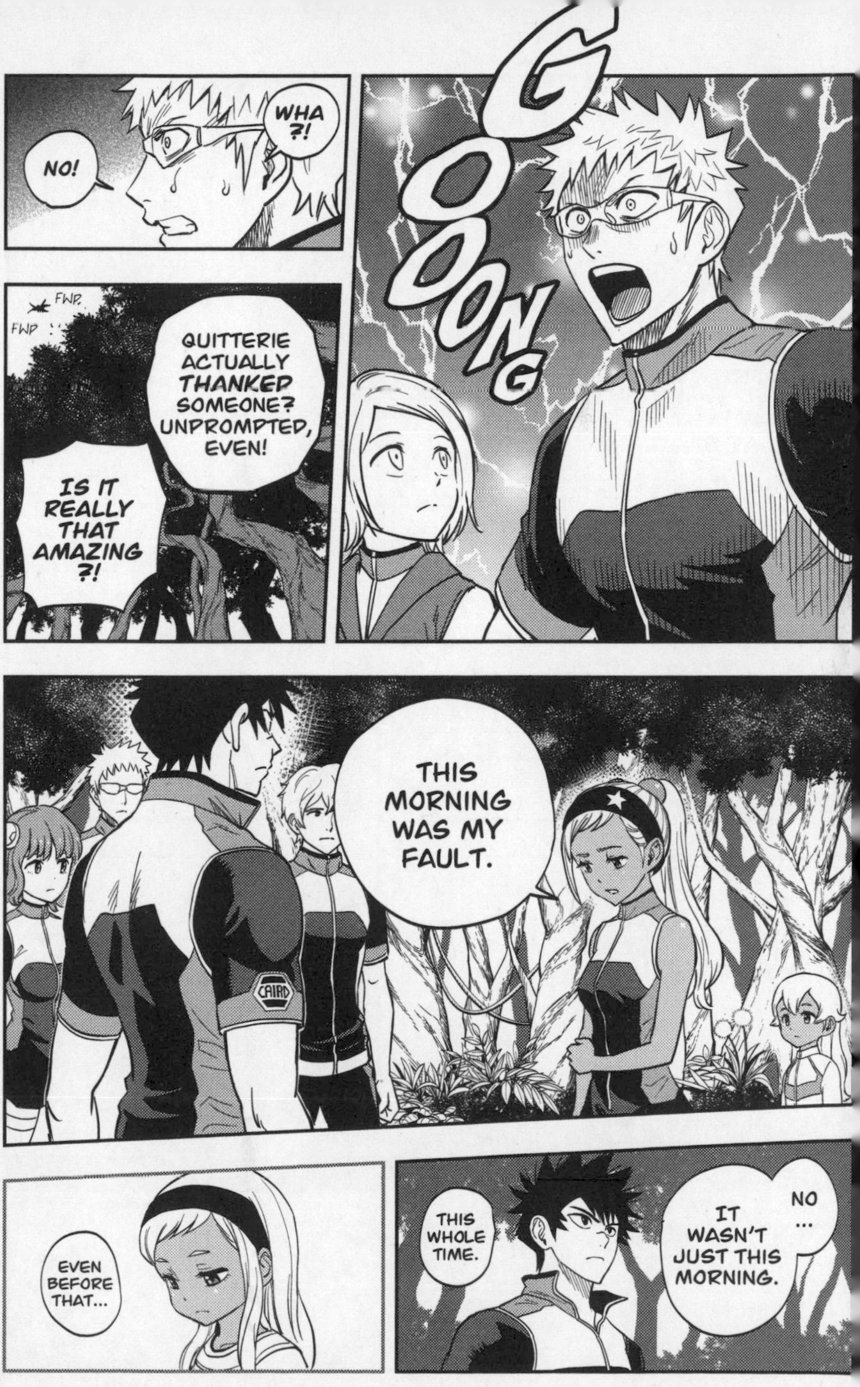
GOOONG
WHA ?!
NO!
FWP.
FWP
QUITTERIE ACTUALLY THANKED SOMEONE? UNPROMPTED, EVEN!
IS IT REALLY THAT AMAZING ?!
THIS MORNING WAS MY FAULT.
CAIRD
NO ...
IT WASN'T JUST THIS MORNING.
THIS WHOLE TIME.
EVEN BEFORE THAT...

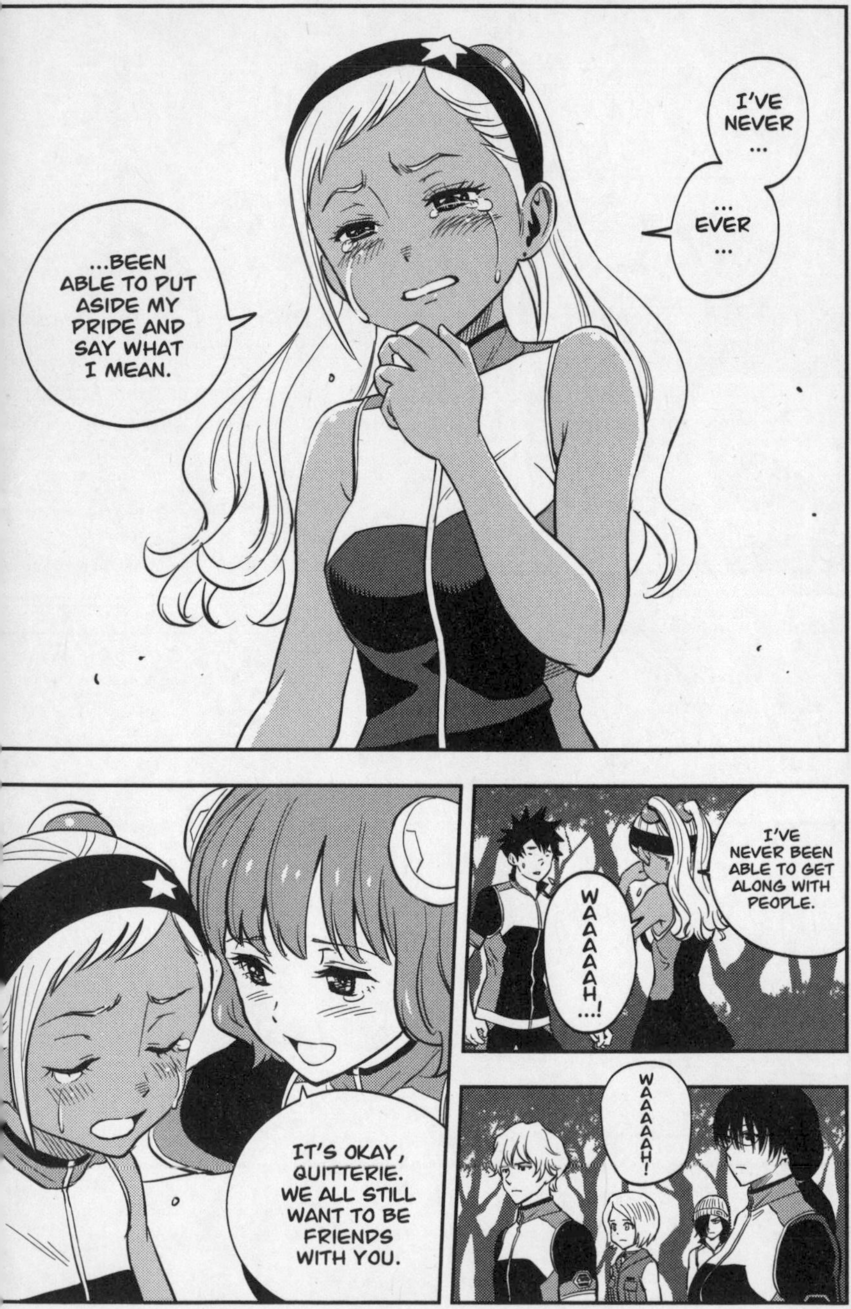
I'VE NEVER ...
... EVER ...
...BEEN ABLE TO PUT ASIDE MY PRIDE AND SAY WHAT I MEAN.
I'VE NEVER BEEN ABLE TO GET ALONG WITH PEOPLE.
WAAAAAH...!
WAAAAAH!
IT'S OKAY, QUITTERIE. WE ALL STILL WANT TO BE FRIENDS WITH YOU.

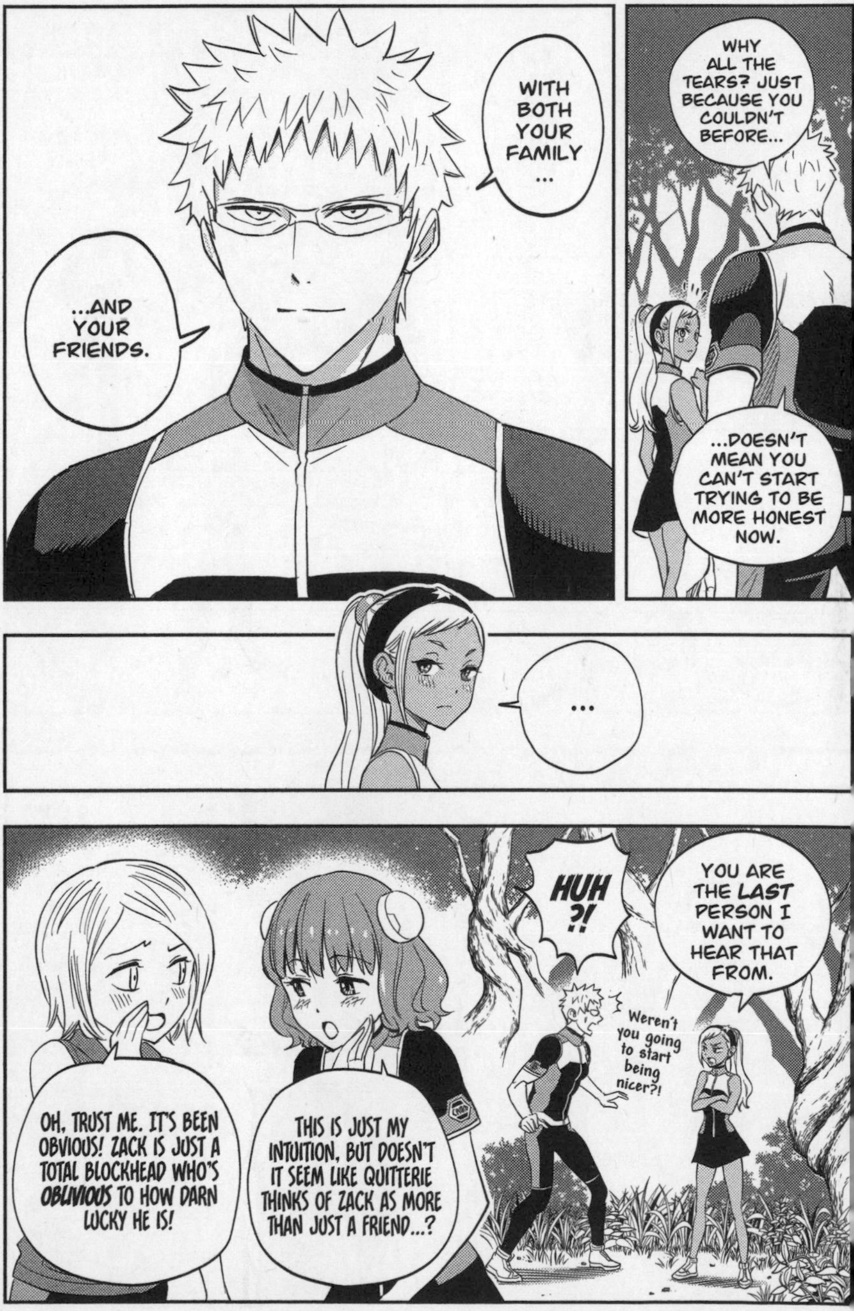
WHY ALL THE TEARS? JUST BECAUSE YOU COULDN'T BEFORE...
...DOESN'T MEAN YOU CAN'T START TRYING TO BE MORE HONEST NOW.
WITH BOTH YOUR FAMILY ...
...AND YOUR FRIENDS.
...
YOU ARE THE LAST PERSON I WANT TO HEAR THAT FROM.
HUH ?!
Weren't you going to start being nicer?!
THIS IS JUST MY INTUITION, BUT DOESN'T IT SEEM LIKE QUITTERIE THINKS OF ZACK AS MORE THAN JUST A FRIEND...?
OH, TRUST ME. IT'S BEEN OBVIOUS! ZACK IS JUST A TOTAL BLOCKHEAD WHO'S OBLIVIOUS TO HOW DARN LUCKY HE IS!

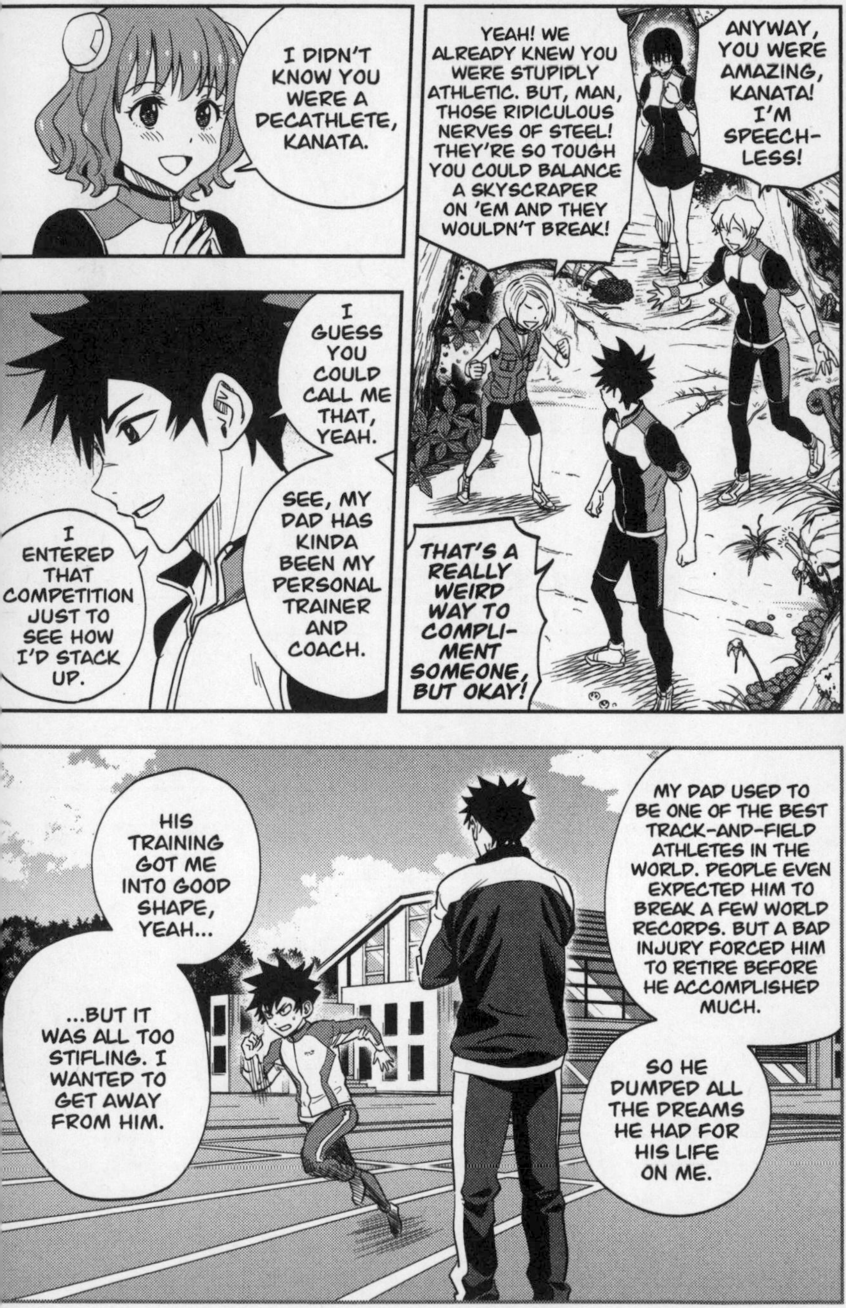
ANYWAY, YOU WERE AMAZING, KANATA! I'M SPEECH-LESS!
YEAH! WE ALREADY KNEW YOU WERE STUPIDLY ATHLETIC. BUT, MAN, THOSE RIDICULOUS NERVES OF STEEL! THEY'RE SO TOUGH YOU COULD BALANCE A SKYSCRAPER ON 'EM AND THEY WOULDN'T BREAK!
THAT'S A REALLY WEIRD WAY TO COMPLI-MENT SOMEONE, BUT OKAY!
I DIDN'T KNOW YOU WERE A DECATHLETE, KANATA.
I GUESS YOU COULD CALL ME THAT, YEAH.
SEE, MY DAD HAS KINDA BEEN MY PERSONAL TRAINER AND COACH.
I ENTERED THAT COMPETITION JUST TO SEE HOW I'D STACK UP.
MY DAD USED TO BE ONE OF THE BEST TRACK-AND-FIELD ATHLETES IN THE WORLD. PEOPLE EVEN EXPECTED HIM TO BREAK A FEW WORLD RECORDS. BUT A BAD INJURY FORCED HIM TO RETIRE BEFORE HE ACCOMPLISHED MUCH.
SO HE DUMPED ALL THE DREAMS HE HAD FOR HIS LIFE ON ME.
HIS TRAINING GOT ME INTO GOOD SHAPE, YEAH...
...BUT IT WAS ALL TOO STIFLING. I WANTED TO GET AWAY FROM HIM.

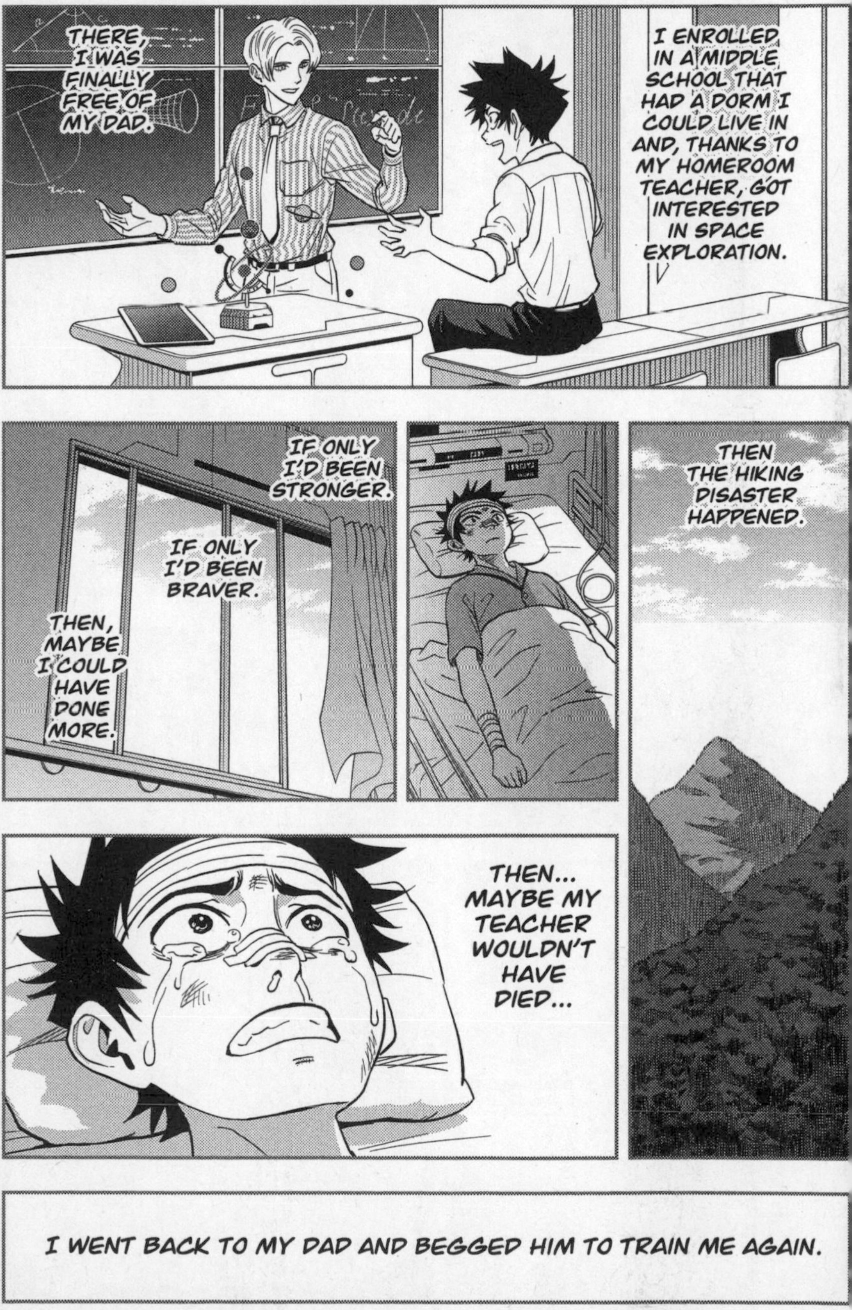
I ENROLLED IN A MIDDLE SCHOOL THAT HAD A DORM I COULD LIVE IN AND, THANKS TO MY HOMEROOM TEACHER, GOT INTERESTED IN SPACE EXPLORATION.
THERE, I WAS FINALLY FREE OF MY DAD.
THEN THE HIKING DISASTER HAPPENED.
IF ONLY I'D BEEN STRONGER.
IF ONLY I'D BEEN BRAVER.
THEN, MAYBE I COULD HAVE DONE MORE.
THEN... MAYBE MY TEACHER WOULDN'T HAVE DIED...
I WENT BACK TO MY DAD AND BEGGED HIM TO TRAIN ME AGAIN.

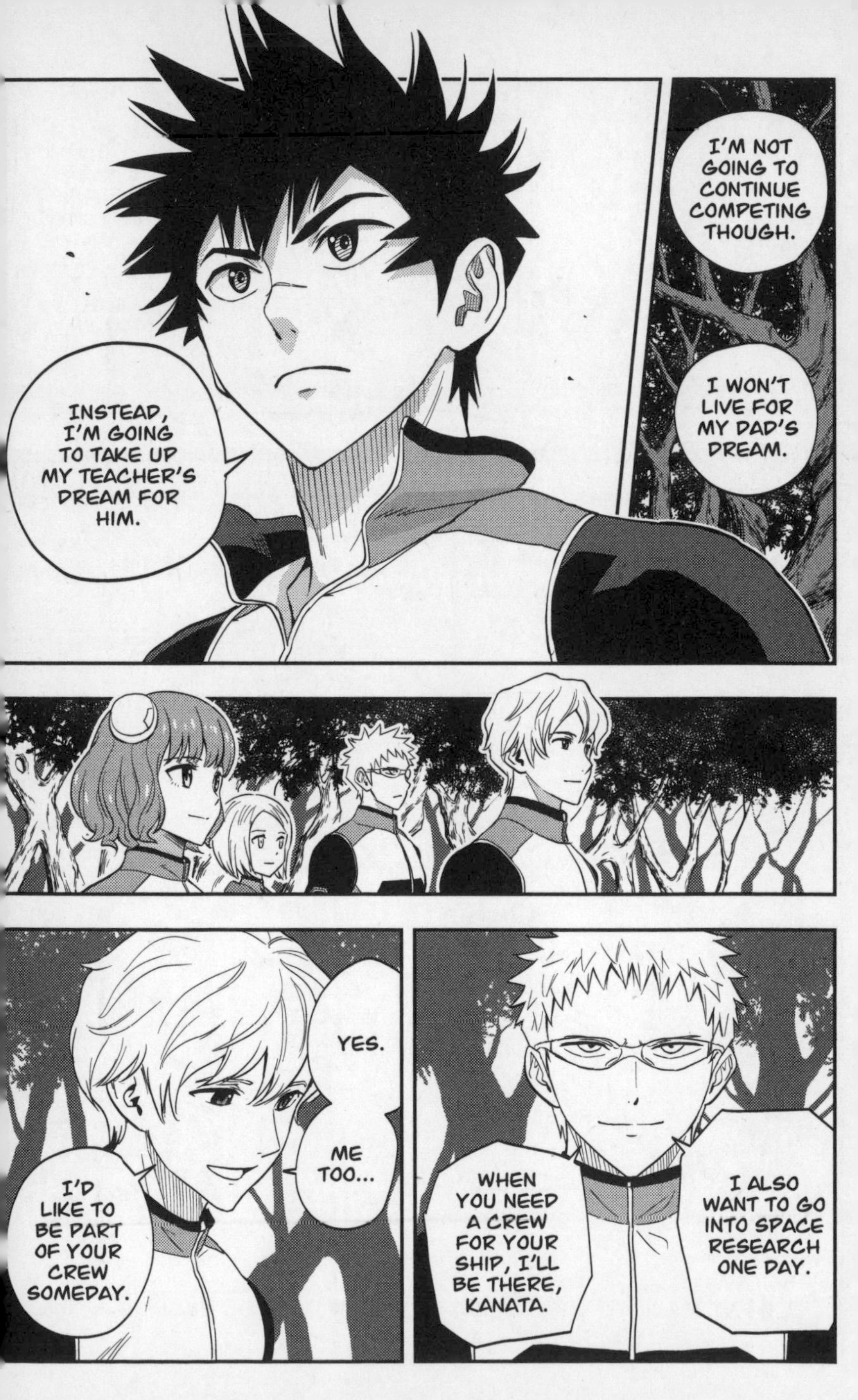
I'M NOT GOING TO CONTINUE COMPETING THOUGH.
I WON'T LIVE FOR MY DAD'S DREAM.
INSTEAD, I'M GOING TO TAKE UP MY TEACHER'S DREAM FOR HIM.
I ALSO WANT TO GO INTO SPACE RESEARCH ONE DAY.
WHEN YOU NEED A CREW FOR YOUR SHIP, I'LL BE THERE, KANATA.
YES.
ME TOO...
I'D LIKE TO BE PART OF YOUR CREW SOMEDAY.

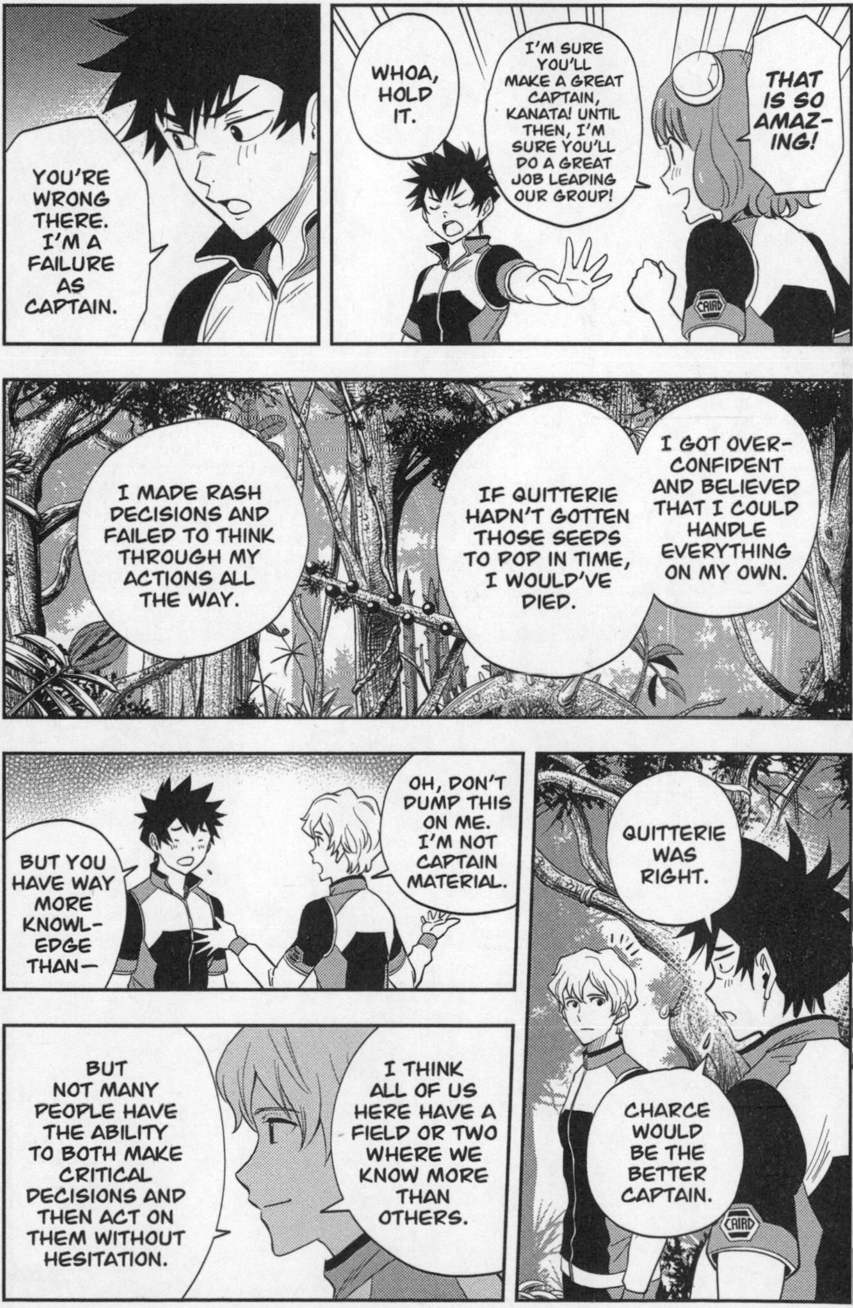
THAT IS SO AMAZING!
I'M SURE YOU'LL MAKE A GREAT CAPTAIN, KANATA! UNTIL THEN, I'M SURE YOU'LL DO A GREAT JOB LEADING OUR GROUP!
WHOA, HOLD IT.
YOU'RE WRONG THERE. I'M A FAILURE AS CAPTAIN.
I GOT OVER-CONFIDENT AND BELIEVED THAT I COULD HANDLE EVERYTHING ON MY OWN.
IF QUITTERIE HADN'T GOTTEN THOSE SEEDS TO POP IN TIME, I WOULD'VE DIED.
I MADE RASH DECISIONS AND FAILED TO THINK THROUGH MY ACTIONS ALL THE WAY.
QUITTERIE WAS RIGHT.
CHARCE WOULD BE THE BETTER CAPTAIN.
OH, DON'T DUMP THIS ON ME. I'M NOT CAPTAIN MATERIAL.
BUT YOU HAVE WAY MORE KNOWL-EDGE THAN—
I THINK ALL OF US HERE HAVE A FIELD OR TWO WHERE WE KNOW MORE THAN OTHERS.
BUT NOT MANY PEOPLE HAVE THE ABILITY TO BOTH MAKE CRITICAL DECISIONS AND THEN ACT ON THEM WITHOUT HESITATION.

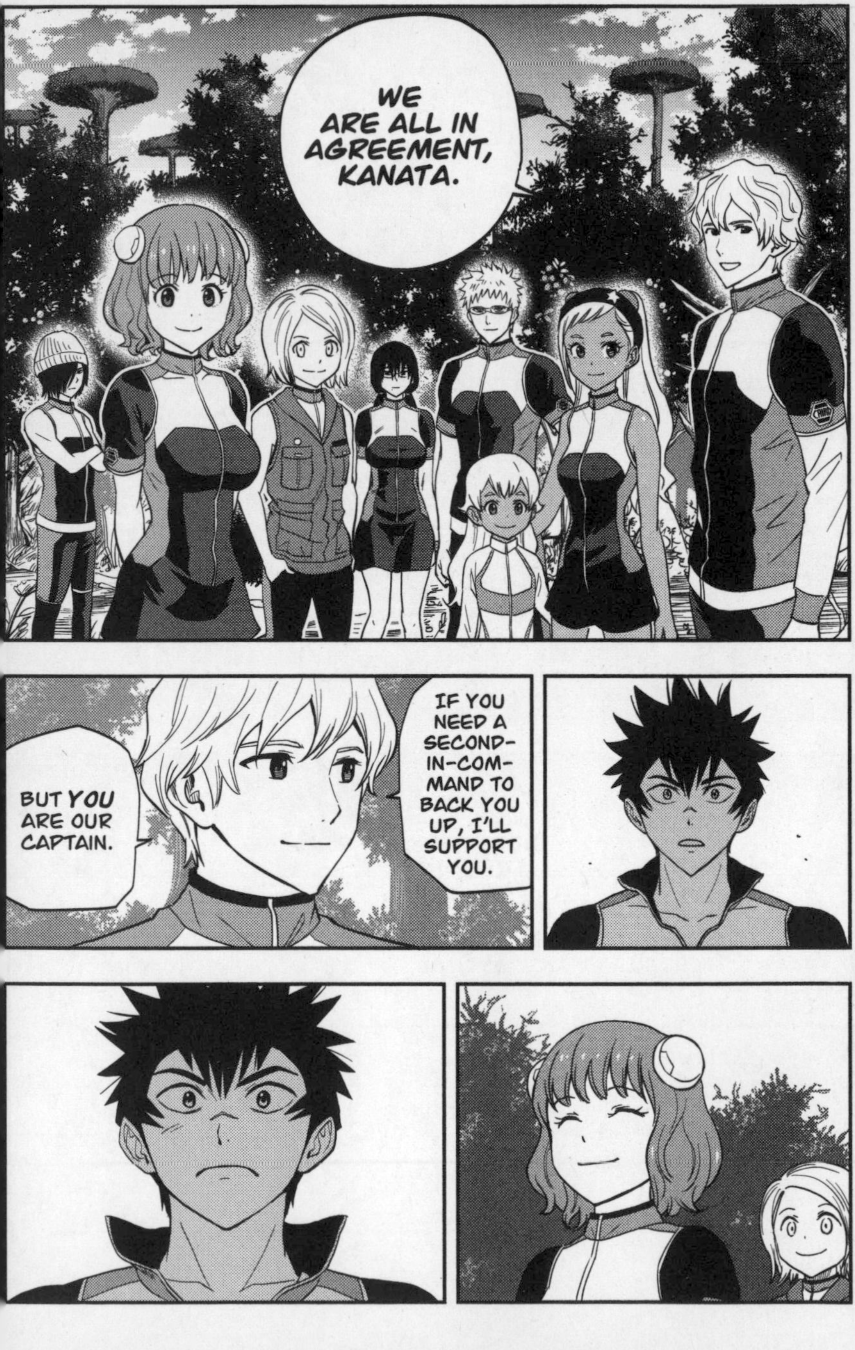
WE ARE ALL IN AGREEMENT, KANATA.
IF YOU NEED A SECOND-IN-COMMAND TO BACK YOU UP, I'LL SUPPORT YOU.
BUT YOU ARE OUR CAPTAIN.

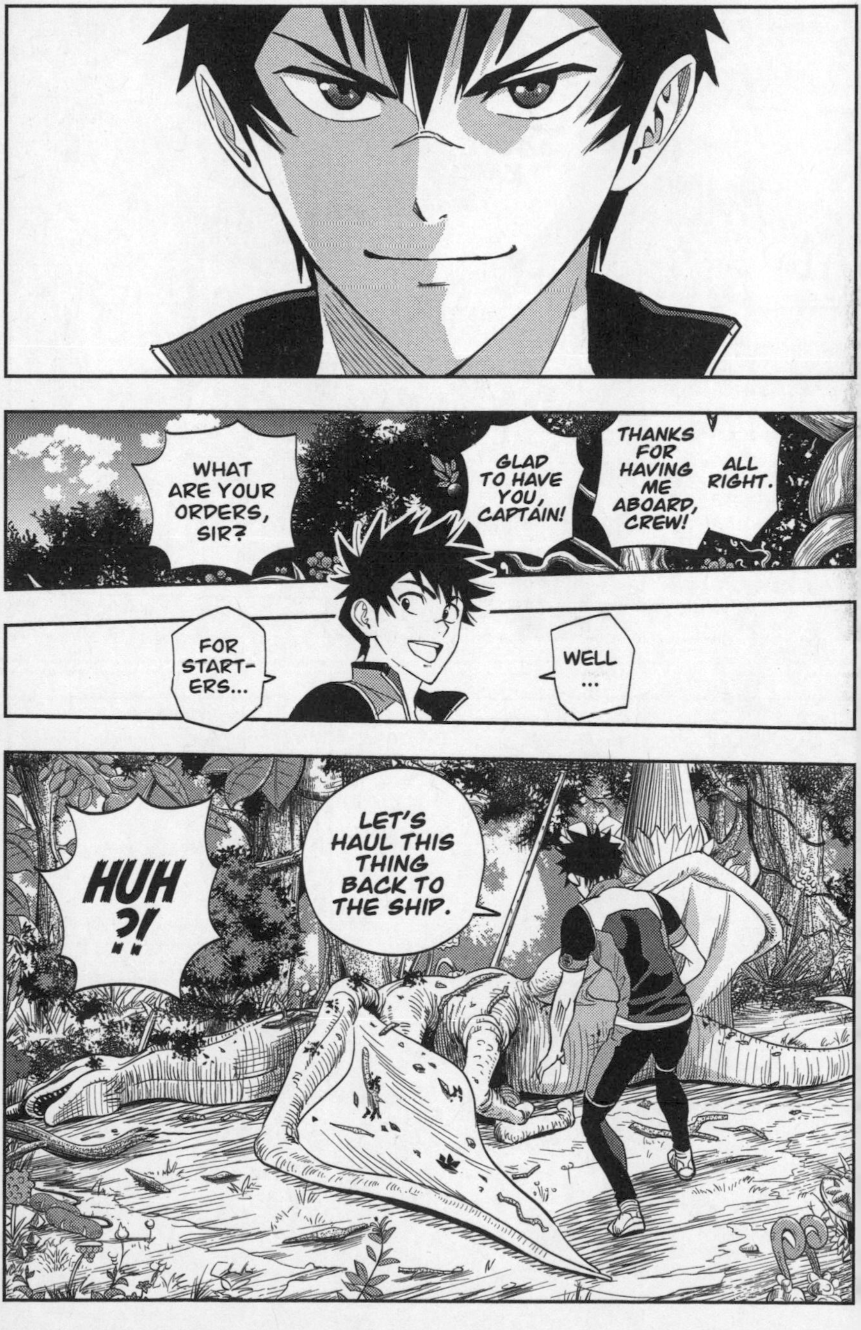
ALL RIGHT.
THANKS FOR HAVING ME ABOARD, CREW!
GLAD TO HAVE YOU, CAPTAIN!
WHAT ARE YOUR ORDERS, SIR?
WELL ...
FOR START-ERS...
LET'S HAUL THIS THING BACK TO THE SHIP.
HUH ?!

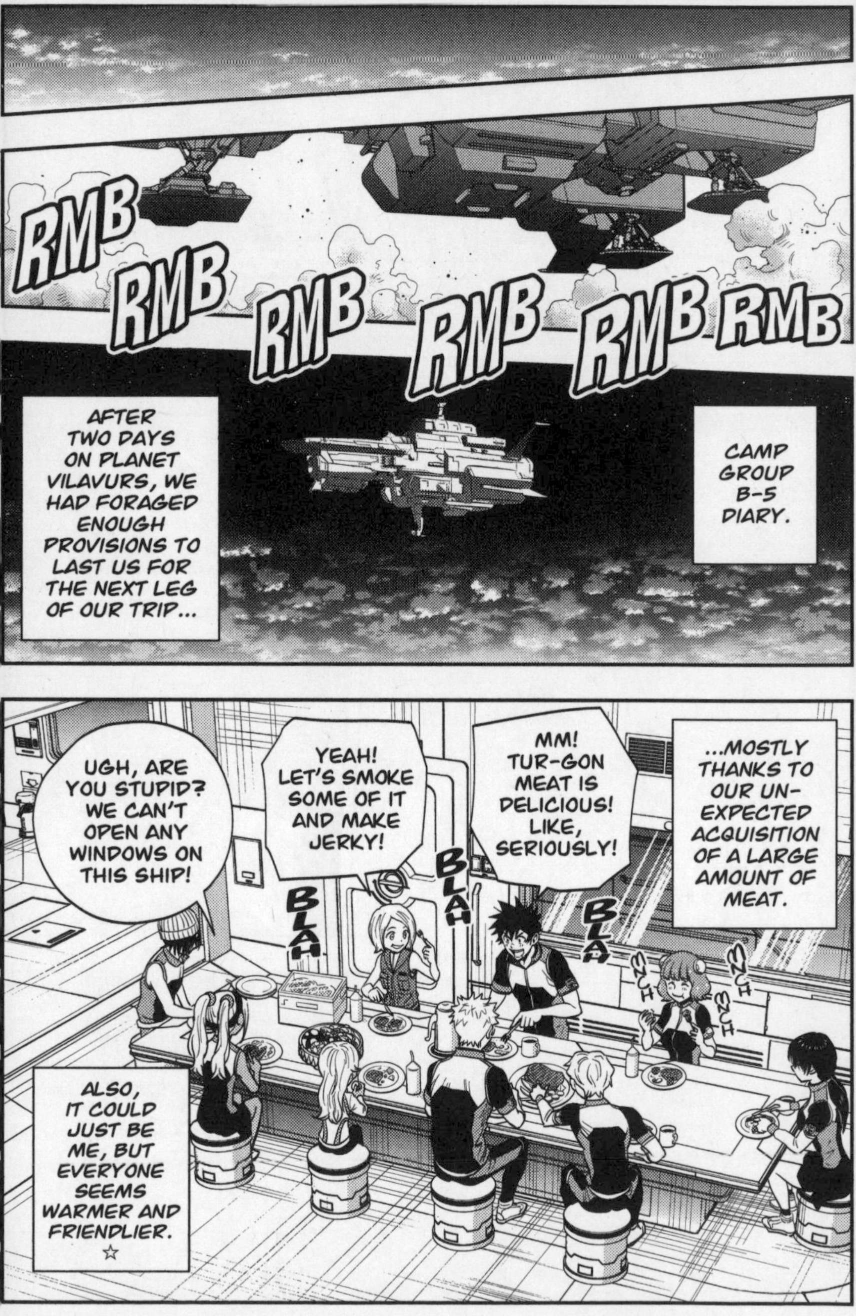
RMB RMB RMB RMB RMB RMB
CAMP GROUP B-5 DIARY.
AFTER TWO DAYS ON PLANET VILAVURS, WE HAD FORAGED ENOUGH PROVISIONS TO LAST US FOR THE NEXT LEG OF OUR TRIP...
...MOSTLY THANKS TO OUR UN-EXPECTED ACQUISITION OF A LARGE AMOUNT OF MEAT.
MUNCH MUNCH MUNCH MUNCH
MM! TUR-GON MEAT IS DELICIOUS! LIKE, SERIOUSLY!
BLAH BLAH
YEAH! LET'S SMOKE SOME OF IT AND MAKE JERKY!
BLAH
UGH, ARE YOU STUPID? WE CAN'T OPEN ANY WINDOWS ON THIS SHIP!
ALSO, IT COULD JUST BE ME, BUT EVERYONE SEEMS WARMER AND FRIENDLIER. ☆

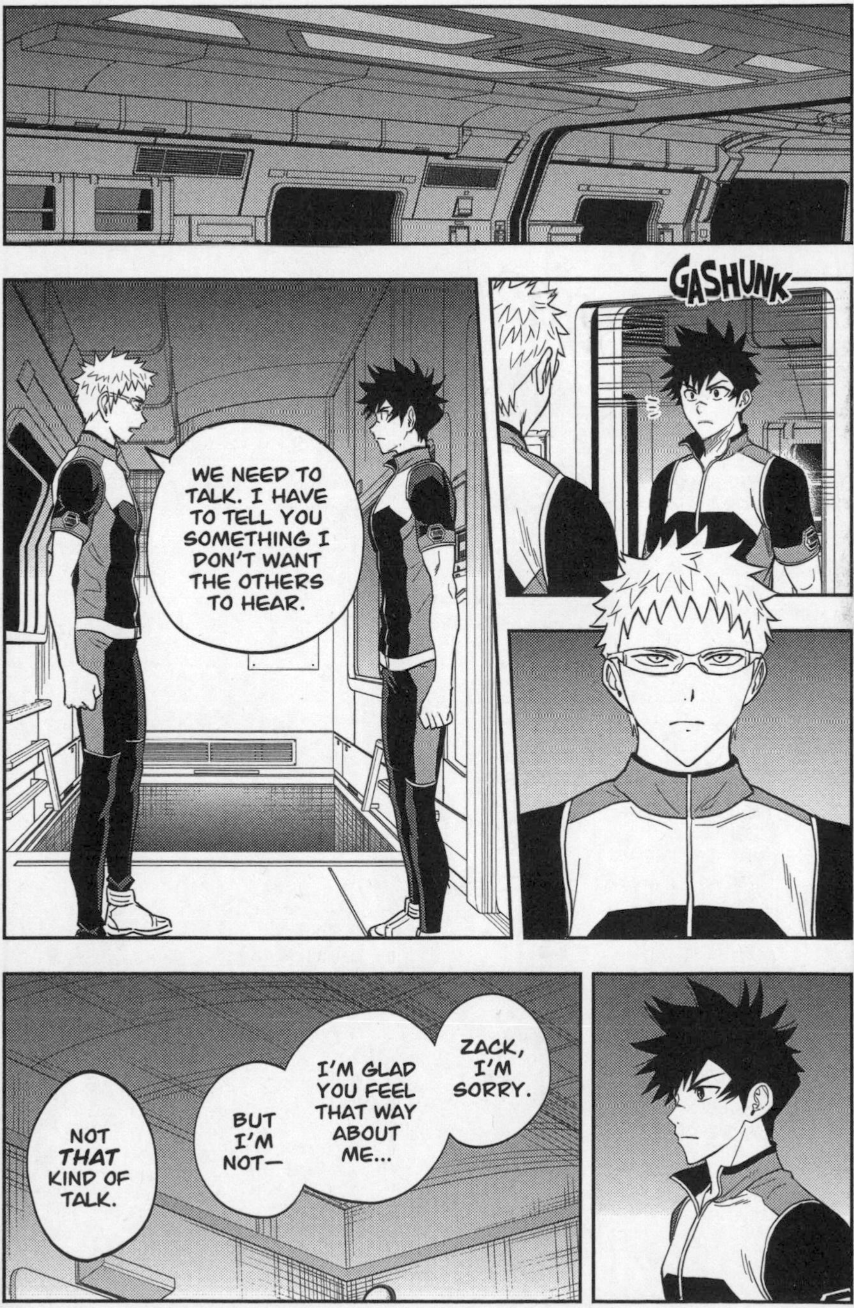
GASHUNK
WE NEED TO TALK. I HAVE TO TELL YOU SOMETHING I DON'T WANT THE OTHERS TO HEAR.
ZACK, I'M SORRY.
I'M GLAD YOU FEEL THAT WAY ABOUT ME...
BUT I'M NOT—
NOT THAT KIND OF TALK.

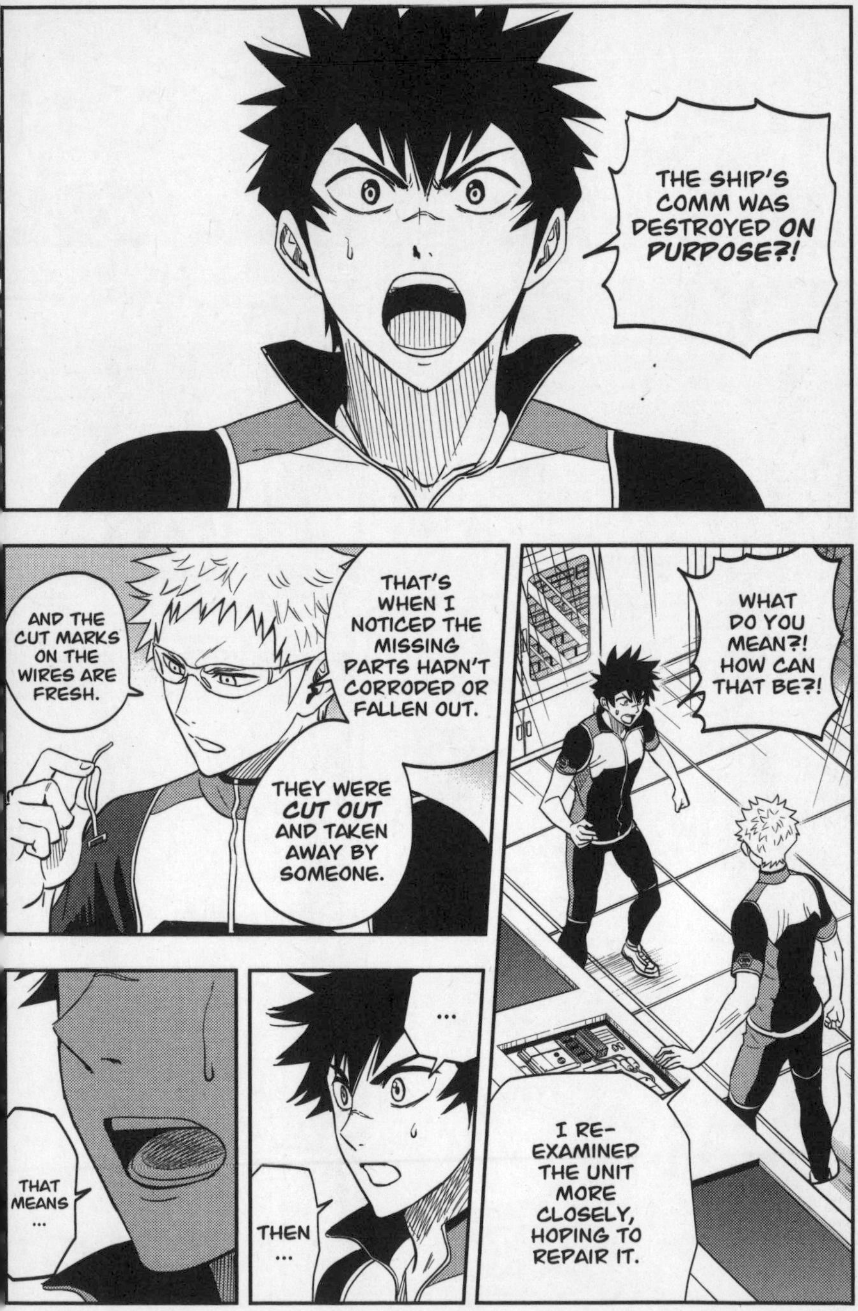
THE SHIP'S COMM WAS DESTROYED ON PURPOSE?!
WHAT DO YOU MEAN?! HOW CAN THAT BE?!
I RE-EXAMINED THE UNIT MORE CLOSELY, HOPING TO REPAIR IT.
THAT'S WHEN I NOTICED THE MISSING PARTS HADN'T CORRODED OR FALLEN OUT.
THEY WERE CUT OUT AND TAKEN AWAY BY SOMEONE.
AND THE CUT MARKS ON THE WIRES ARE FRESH.
...
THEN ...
THAT MEANS ...

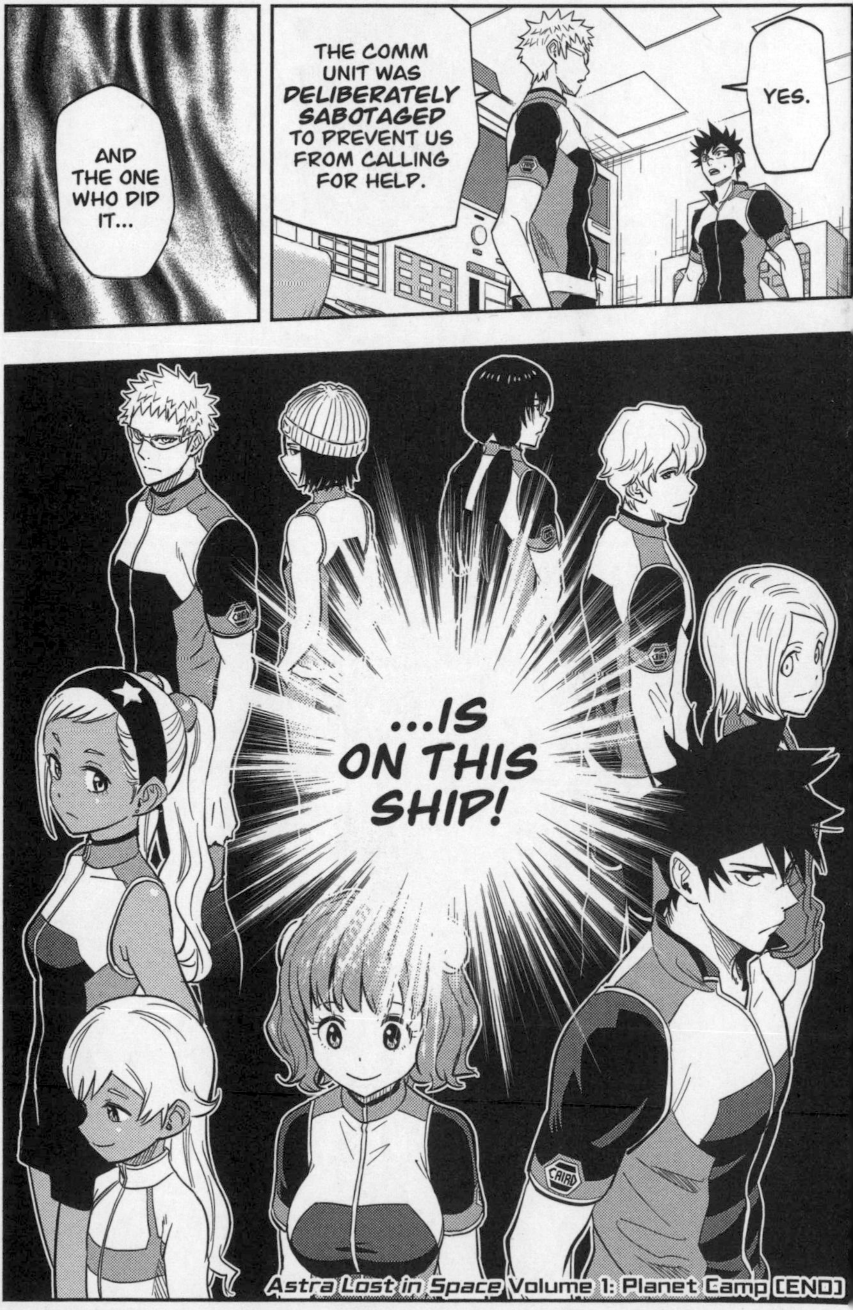
YES.
THE COMM UNIT WAS DELIBERATELY SABOTAGED TO PREVENT US FROM CALLING FOR HELP.
AND THE ONE WHO DID IT...
...IS ON THIS SHIP!
Astra Lost in Space Volume 1: Planet Camp [END]

KENTA SHINOHARA started his manga career as an assistant to the legendary creator Hideaki Sorachi of **Gin Tama**. In 2006, he wrote and published a one-shot, **Sket Dance**, that began serialization in 2007 in **Weekly Shonen Jump** in Japan. **Sket Dance** went on to win the 55th Shogakukan Manga Award in the shonen manga category and inspired an anime in 2011. Shinohara began writing **Astra Lost in Space** in 2016 for **Jump+**.

ASTRA LOST IN SPACE 1

SHONEN JUMP MANGA EDITION

STORY AND ART BY KENTA SHINOHARA

Translation/Adrienne Beck
Touch-Up Art & Lettering/Annaliese Christman
Design/Julian [JR] Robinson
Editor/Marlene First

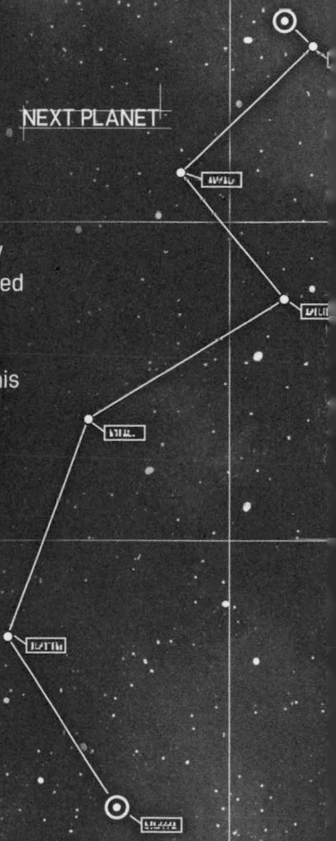

NEXT PLANET

Printed in the U.S.A.

Published by VIZ Media, LLC
P.O. Box 77010
San Francisco, CA 94107

10 9 8 7 6 5 4 3 2 1
First printing, December 2017

viz.com

shonenjump.com

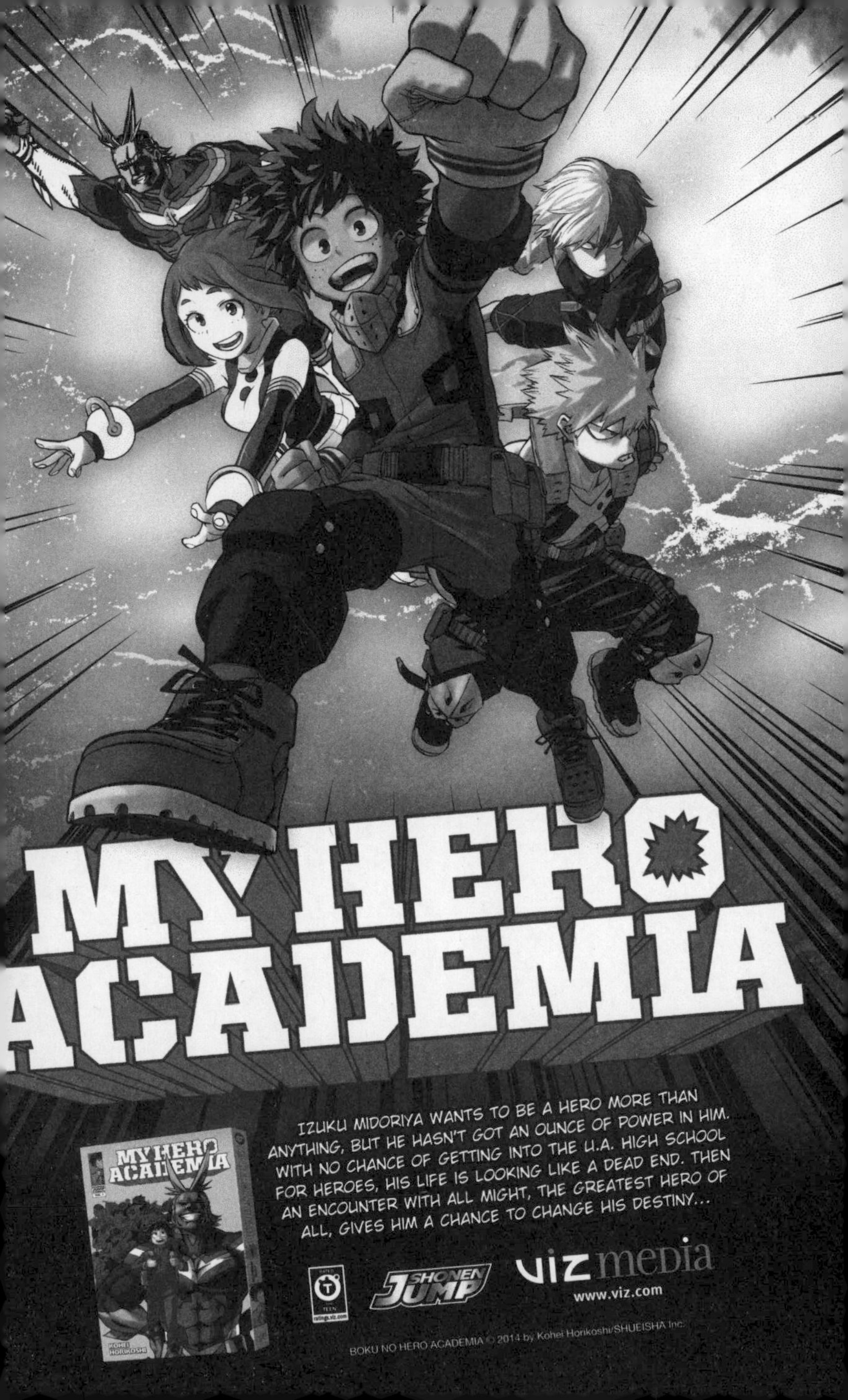
MY HERO ACADEMIA
IZUKU MIDORIYA WANTS TO BE A HERO MORE THAN ANYTHING, BUT HE HASN'T GOT AN OUNCE OF POWER IN HIM. WITH NO CHANCE OF GETTING INTO THE U.A. HIGH SCHOOL FOR HEROES, HIS LIFE IS LOOKING LIKE A DEAD END. THEN AN ENCOUNTER WITH ALL MIGHT, THE GREATEST HERO OF ALL, GIVES HIM A CHANCE TO CHANGE HIS DESTINY...
MY HERO ACADEMIA
KOHEI HORIKOSHI
TEEN
ratings.viz.com
SHONEN JUMP
viz media
www.viz.com
BOKU NO HERO ACADEMIA © 2014 by Kohei Horikoshi/SHUEISHA Inc.

DRAGON BALL SUPER

STORY BY **Akira Toriyama** ART BY **Toyotarou**

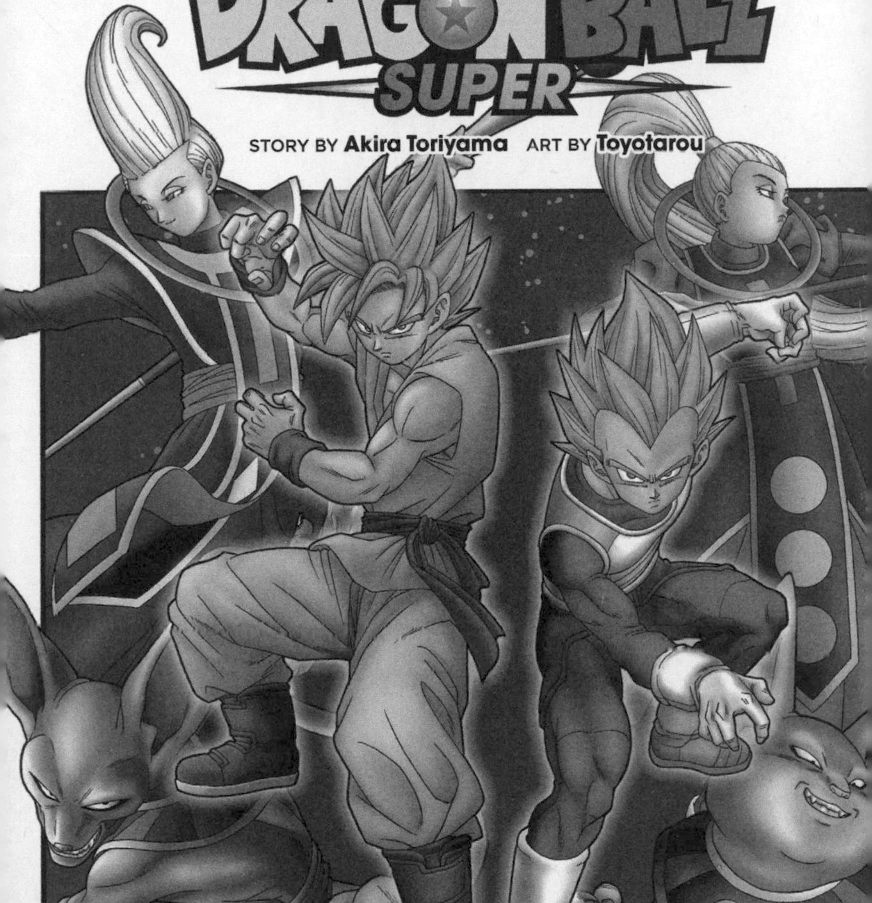

Goku's adventure from the best-selling classic manga *Dragon Ball* continues in this new series written by Akira Toriyama himself!

Ever since Goku became Earth's greatest hero and gathered the seven Dragon Balls to defeat the evil Boo, his life on Earth has grown a little dull. But new threats loom overhead, and Goku and his friends will have to defend the planet once again!

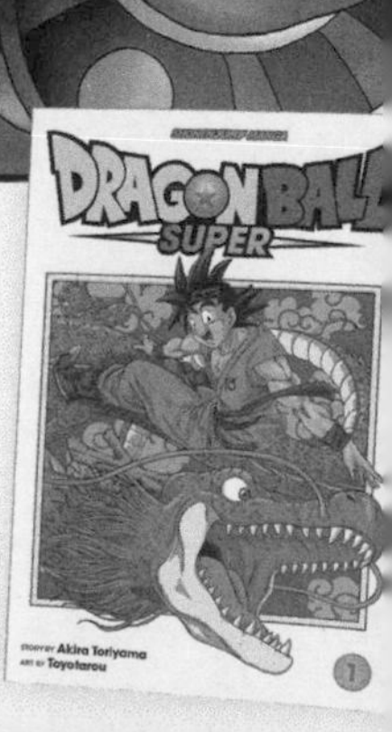
DRAGON BALL SUPER
STORY BY Akira Toriyama
ART BY Toyotarou
1

RATED T FOR TEEN

VIZ media

viz.com

SHONEN JUMP

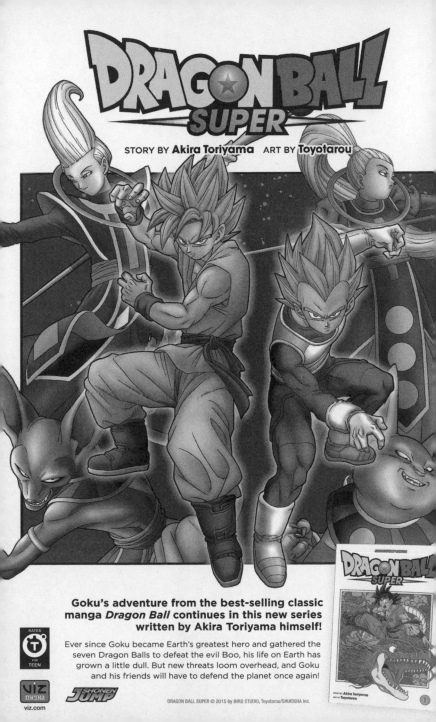

Black ✤ Clover

STORY & ART BY YŪKI TABATA

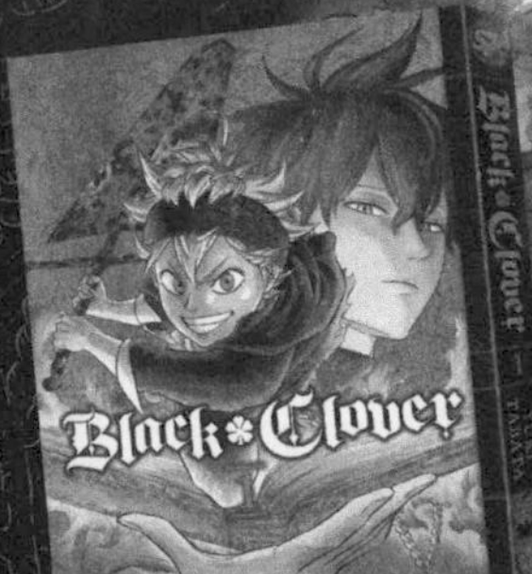

Asta is a young boy who dreams of becoming the greatest mage in the kingdom. Only one problem—he can't use any magic! Luckily for Asta, he receives the incredibly rare five-leaf clover grimoire that gives him the power of anti-magic. Can someone who can't use magic really become the Wizard King? One thing's for sure—Asta will never give up!

SHONEN JUMP   VIZ media
www.viz.com

WORLD TRIGGER

Story and Art by
DAISUKE ASHIHARA

DESTROY THY NEIGHBOR!

A gate to another dimension has burst open, and invincible monsters called Neighbors invade Earth. Osamu Mikumo may not be the best among the elite warriors who co-opt other-dimensional technology to fight back, but along with his Neighbor friend Yuma, he'll do whatever it takes to defend life on Earth as we know it.

YOU'RE READING THE WRONG WAY!

Astra Lost in Space reads from right to left, starting in the upper-right corner. Japanese is read from right to left, meaning that action, sound effects and word-balloon order are completely reversed from English order.

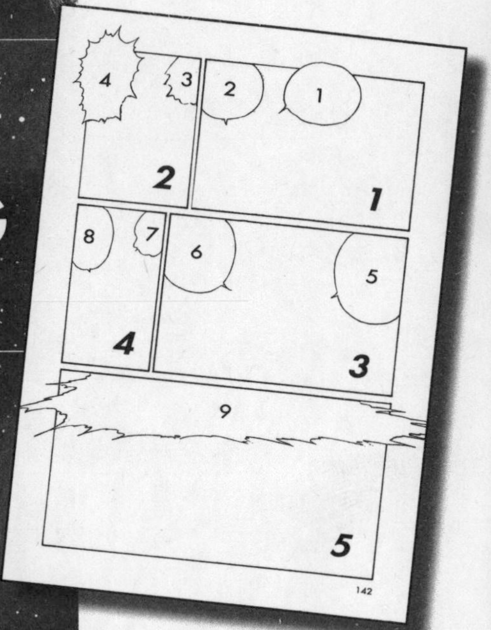
1
1
2
2
3
4
3
5
6
4
7
8
5
9
142

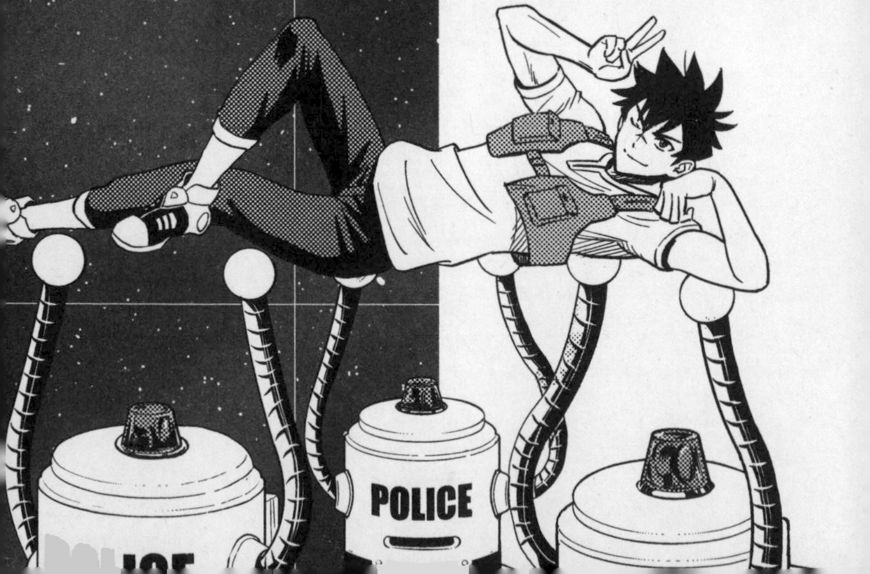
POLICE